Critical Ethr
Language, F
and Education

LANGUAGE, EDUCATION AND DIVERSITY

The Language, Education and Diversity series aims to publish work at the intersections of language policy, language teaching and bilingualism/ multilingualism, with a particular focus on critical, socially-just alternatives for minoritised students and communities. The series is interdisciplinary, drawing on scholarship from language policy, language education, sociolinguistics, applied linguistics, linguistic anthropology and the sociology of language, including work in raciolinguistics and translingualism. We welcome a variety of methodological approaches, although critical ethnographic accounts are of particular interest.

Topics covered by the series include:

- Bilingual and Multilingual Models of Education
- Indigenous Language Education
- Multicultural Education
- Community-based Education

All books in this series are externally peer-reviewed.

Full details of all the books in this series and of all our other publications can be found on http://www.multilingual-matters.com, or by writing to Multilingual Matters, St Nicholas House, 31-34 High Street, Bristol, BS1 2AW, UK.

LANGUAGE, EDUCATION AND DIVERSITY: 2

Critical Ethnography, Language, Race/ism and Education

Edited by
Stephen May and Blanca Caldas

MULTILINGUAL MATTERS
Bristol • Jackson

DOI https://doi.org/10.21832/MAY8700
Library of Congress Cataloging in Publication Data
A catalog record for this book is available from the Library of Congress.
Names: May, Stephen, editor. | Caldas, Blanca, editor.
Title: Critical Ethnography, Language, Race/ism and Education /Edited by Stephen May and Blanca Caldas.
Description: Bristol, UK; Jackson, TN: Multilingual Matters, 2022. | Series: Language, Education and Diversity: 2 | Includes bibliographical references and index. | Summary: "This book provides a contemporary overview of work in critical ethnography that focuses on language and race/ism in education, as well as cutting edge examples of recent critical ethnographic studies addressing these issues. The chapters draw on a range of critical theoretical perspectives and address significant methodological questions"—Provided by publisher.
Identifiers: LCCN 2022030563 (print) | LCCN 2022030564 (ebook) | ISBN 9781788928700 (hardback) | ISBN 9781788928694 (paperback) | ISBN 9781788928717 (pdf) | ISBN 9781788928724 (epub)
Subjects: LCSH: Educational anthropology. | Critical ethnography. | Racism in education. | Language and languages.
Classification: LCC LB45 .C75 2022 (print) | LCC LB45 (ebook) | DDC 306.43—dc23/eng/20220812 LC record available at https://lccn.loc.gov/2022030563
LC ebook record available at https://lccn.loc.gov/2022030564

British Library Cataloguing in Publication Data
A catalogue entry for this book is available from the British Library.

ISBN-13: 978-1-78892-870-0 (hbk)
ISBN-13: 978-1-78892-869-4 (pbk)

Multilingual Matters
UK: St Nicholas House, 31-34 High Street, Bristol, BS1 2AW, UK.
USA: Ingram, Jackson, TN, USA.

Website: www.multilingual-matters.com
Twitter: Multi_Ling_Mat
Facebook: https://www.facebook.com/multilingualmatters
Blog: www.channelviewpublications.wordpress.com

The policy of Multilingual Matters/Channel View Publications is to use papers that are natural, renewable and recyclable products, made from wood grown in sustainable forests. In the manufacturing process of our books, and to further support our policy, preference is given to printers that have FSC and PEFC Chain of Custody certification. The FSC and/or PEFC logos will appear on those books where full certification has been granted to the printer concerned.

Typeset by Deanta Global Publishing Services, Chennai, India.

Contents

Contributors vii
Foreword xi

Introduction: Contextualizing and Reimagining Critical Ethnography in Education 1
Stephen May and Blanca Caldas

Part 1: Theoret/Methodolog/ical Connections

1 Critical Ethnography, Language, Race/ism and In/equity in Education: Charting the Field 19
Stephen May

2 Beyond Silence: Disrupting Antiblackness through BlackCrit Ethnography and Black Youth Voice 42
Justin A. Coles

3 Multilingual Radical Intimate Ethnography 65
Youmna Deiri

Part 2: Rethinking Reflexivity and Positionality

4 Race Reflexivity: Examining the Unconscious for a Critical Race Ethnography 91
Laura C. Chávez-Moreno

5 Interrogating Our Interpretations and Positionalities: Chicanx Researchers as Scholar Activists in Solidarity with Our Communities 108
Idalia Nuñez and Suzanne García-Mateus

6 Toward Reflexive Engagement: Critical Ethnography's Challenge to Linguistic Homogeneity and Binary Relationships 123
Julie S. Byrd Clark

7 Dialogical Relationships and Critical Reflexivity as Emancipatory Praxis in a Community-Based Educational Program 152
Randy Clinton Bell, Manuel Martinez and Brenda Rubio

Part 3: Conflicts, Collaborations and Community

8 Critical Ethnographic Monitoring and Chronic Raciolinguistic Panic: Problems, Possibilities and Dreams 171
Teresa L. McCarty

9 Unequal Language Policy, Deficit Language Ideology and Social Injustice: A Critical Ethnography of Language Education Policies in Nepal 191
Prem Phyak

10 'But This Program is Not For Them!': Challenging the Gentrification of Dual Language Bilingual Education through Critical Ethnography 213
Dan Heiman and Michelle Yanes

11 Becoming an 'Avocado' – Embodied Rescriptings in Bilingual Teacher Education Settings: A Critical Performance Ethnography 240
Blanca Caldas

Index 254

Contributors

Randy Clinton Bell is an assistant professor of bilingual/ESL education at the University of North Texas, Dallas, Texas. A national board-certified, former bilingual elementary school teacher, Randy's research considers bilingualism in education broadly, with specific attention to how teachers' and students' languaging practices intersect within colonizing, racial, class and gender subjectivities. Randy's service and research also focuses on linguistically and culturally sustaining, community-based, educational initiatives and partnerships with public schooling.

Julie S. Byrd Clark is professor of language and Indigenous education at the Faculty of Education of Western University, Ontario, Canada. She is an internationally recognized applied linguist with expertise in the domains of critical sociolinguistics, bi/multilingual education, didactique du français, language planning/policy, discourse analysis, Indigenous epistemologies and postmodern, transdisciplinary and ecopsychological approaches for the study of language, communication, teaching and learning.

Blanca Caldas is a transnational Latina scholar of Quechuan descent and an associate professor at the University of Minnesota, Twin Cities, Minneapolis, Minnesota. Her research focuses on bilingual teacher education, minoritized language practices and critical pedagogy. She presents her work in local, national and international conferences, including ethnographic performances of her work. Her work is published in both English and Spanish.

Laura C. Chávez-Moreno is an assistant professor at the University of California-Los Angeles (UCLA) César E. Chávez Department of Chicana/o and Central American Studies. Her research has won awards from the American Association of Hispanics in Higher Education and from three different special interest groups of the American Educational Research Association. Her research agenda seeks to (a) understand the practices of teachers of underserved populations of students, especially

Latinxs; and (b) demonstrate possibilities and successes in teacher practices that support an education for self-determination. Some of her work has been published in the *Handbook of Latinos & Education* (2nd edn), *American Educational Research Journal* and *Journal of Teacher Education* and is forthcoming in *Educational Researcher* and *Research in the Teaching of English*.

Justin A. Coles is an assistant professor of social justice education in the Department of Student Development at the University of Massachusetts, Amherst College of Education. Within the college, Dr Coles serves as the director of arts, culture and political engagements at the Center of Racial Justice and Youth Engaged Research. His research agenda converges at the intersections of critical race studies, urban education, language and literacy and Black studies. Specifically, he is committed to using critical race frameworks and methodologies to learn from and with the liberatory language and literacy practices that urban youth are engaged in, and how these practices serve as analytics in addressing and countering oppressive sociostructural regimes within US schooling and society. He serves as co-editor-in-chief for *Equity & Excellence in Education*.

Youmna Deiri is an assistant professor at the College of Education at Texas A&M International University, Laredo, Texas. Her scholarship focuses on multilingualism related to K-12 teacher education, and radical intimate inquiry alongside immigrant communities. Dr Deiri earned her PhD in teacher education at Ohio State University in 2018. She teaches and publishes in both English and Arabic and her work has appeared in *The International Journal of Bilingual Education and Bilingualism*, *The Journal of Ethnic and Cultural Studies* and *The International Review of Qualitative Research*.

Suzanne García-Mateus is an assistant professor of bilingual education and the director of the Monterey Institute for English Learners in the College of Education at California State University, Monterey Bay, California. Her research examines the intersection of race, class and language in a two-way immersion bilingual education program. As a professor, she aims at centering the experiences of culturally and linguistically diverse students by including a social justice framework in all her courses. Through her work as a researcher, practitioner and mamá raising multilingual children, she continues to advocate for equitable schooling experiences for all children.

Dan Heiman is an assistant professor of bilingual/biliteracy education in the Department of Teacher Education at the University of Texas at El Paso, Texas. A former bilingual teacher in El Paso, Texas, and teacher educator at the University of Veracruz (Mexico), his critical ethnographic research examines critical pedagogies, activism and acompañamiento in dual-language bilingual education (DLBE) and bilingual teacher preparation contexts. He teaches and publishes in both English and Spanish and his work has appeared in *Anthropology & Education Quarterly*, *The Journal of Language, Identity and Education*, *Language Policy* and *La Revista Bilingüe.*

Manuel Martinez works for the Austin Independent School District (AISD) as a curriculum and instruction designer. He has also worked as a technology design coach, coaching K-12 teachers designing and facilitating blended-personalized learning experiences for students. Additionally, he has worked as a dual-language teacher in elementary where doctoral students conducted research about the pedagogical practices he implemented in the classroom. In addition to AISD, he has worked for Academia Cuauhtli for the last seven years as teacher, mentor and curriculum developer.

Stephen May is professor of education in Te Puna Wānanga (School of Māori and Indigenous Education Education) at the University of Auckland, New Zealand. His research and teaching focus on language rights, language policy, Indigenous language revitalization and education, bilingual education, critical multiculturalism and critical ethnography. His books include *Making Multicultural Education Work* (1994, Multilingual Matters), *Critical Multiculturalism: Theory and Praxis* (2010, Routledge, with Christine Sleeter), *Language and Minority Rights* (2012, Routledge [2nd edn]), *The Multilingual Turn* (Routledge, 2014) and, most recently, *Critical Ethnography and Education: Theory, Methodology and Ethics* (2022, Routledge, with Katie Fitzpatrick). Stephen is editor-in-chief of the 10-volume *Encyclopedia of Language and Education* (2017, Springer, 3rd edn), and founding co-editor of the journal *Ethnicities* (Sage). He is an AERA fellow and a fellow of Te Apārangi, the Royal Society of New Zealand (FRSNZ). With Teresa L. McCarty, Serafín Coronel-Molina and Constant Leung, he co-edits the Language, Education and Diversity book series for Multilingual Matters.

Teresa L. McCarty is distinguished professor and G.F. Kneller chair in education and anthropology, and faculty in American Indian Studies, at the University of California-Los Angeles (UCLA), California. Her research, teaching and community work center on Indigenous education and language reclamation, language planning and policy and the critical ethnography of education. Her books include *Ethnography and Language Policy* (2011, Routledge), *Language Policy and Planning in Native America* (2013, Multilingual Matters), *Indigenous Language Revitalization in the Americas* (2019, Routledge, with Serafín Coronel-Molina) and *A World of Indigenous Languages* (2019, Multilingual Matters, with

Sheilah E. Nicholas and Gillian Wigglesworth). Dr McCarty is principal investigator on a US-wide study of Indigenous language immersion schooling funded by the Spencer Foundation. With Stephen May, Serafín Coronel-Molina and Constant Leung, she co-edits the Language, Education and Diversity book series for Multilingual Matters.

Idalia Nuñez is an assistant professor of language and literacy and bilingual-ESL education at the University of Illinois Urbana-Champaign, Chicago, Illinois. Her research is focused on linguistic equity in bilingual classrooms serving students from culturally and linguistically diverse backgrounds. Her work looks closely at Latinx bilingual students' everyday language practices, experiences in and out of school spaces and agency.

Prem Phyak is an assistant professor at the Chinese University of Hong Kong. His research interest includes language policy, multilingual education, social justice, Indigenous language education and teacher education. He has co-authored the book *Engaged Language Policy and Practices* (Routledge, 2017) and published articles in journals such as *Language Policy*, *Language in Society*, *Critical Inquiry in Language Studies* and *Multilingua*. Dr Phyak previously served as head of the Department of English Education at Tribhuvan University in Nepal (2017–2019).

Brenda Rubio is an assistant professor at the University of North Texas, Denton, Texas. Her research and policy agenda focuses on the development of critically conscious educational leadership and community–district–university partnerships for additive transformational education.

Michelle Yanes obtained her BA at McMaster University, Hamilton, Canada, and her MEd at Concordia University, Austin, Texas, and worked as a classroom teacher for 12 years. Currently, she is a PhD student at OISE in the University of Toronto in the language and literacy program. Her main research interest is promoting outdoor environmental justice education for young students of color.

Foreword

I have done critical ethnography since I began to be a researcher, interrogating race, class and language equity in a two-way, dual language, bilingual program in California in the early 2000s through a combination of discourse analysis and ethnography, and drawing on critical analytic frameworks (Palmer, 2009). But I didn't call it that. In fact, even in 2015 when I was invited by Stephen May (the editor of this volume) to write an encyclopedia piece defining critical ethnography, I didn't fully understand why I had been invited. What did he see in my research identity that I did not? Because I saw her work (more than mine) falling into the category of 'critical ethnography', I invited my doctoral student at the time, Blanca Caldas Chumbes (the other editor of this volume) to co-author that piece with me (Palmer & Caldas, 2017). Working together with Blanca to craft it, I began to define for myself this approach, and to see why Stephen had brought me into the conversation.

Critical ethnography has emerged as a methodology both in opposition to and, at the same time, directly out of, the colonialist roots of anthropology – not all at once, but through the innovation and creativity of myriads of researchers and theorists who developed the tools to do critical transformative work within an ethnographic frame. Critical ethnographers draw from fields such as anthropology, sociology, sociolinguistics, discourse studies and critical race studies; we embrace critical frameworks to explore questions of intersectional identities (race, gender, class, ethnicity, etc.), equality and language, and we are dedicated to building authentic relationships with the individuals and communities with whom we partner. We strive not just to shine light on issues of inequality, racism, injustice – but to endeavor to address them. Centering reflexivity and working to flatten endemic hierarchies, critical ethnography has evolved as a way to leverage research to disrupt White supremacy and colonial narratives, and to more systematically interrogate our own role and position in the researcher/researched relationship.

As a field, we have learned over time – primarily by listening deeply to our community partners – to approach this work with heart and creativity, with big ears and small egos. Humility and innovation are central to the work of critical ethnography. But, of course, we struggle still. We struggle with hierarchies of power and privilege, which continue to exist in spite of our doing our best to make the world aware of them, and which persist even as we actively work to mitigate or disrupt or confront them. We struggle with our own intersectional identities as researchers and as humans, as current or former or partial members of the communities we partner with, or as members of dominant or subaltern communities. We struggle with the relationship (which sometimes feels tenuous) between the work we are doing to systematically document, analyze and understand, and the work that will actually make change where change needs to be made... even as we acknowledge (or perhaps wish) this to be the primary outcome and purpose of our work.

In all these struggles, this volume will move our efforts forward.

First, the volume frames and pushes the field. The authors in Part 1 offer methodological innovation, explicitly elaborating new frameworks, new methods, new approaches. There is so much space to explore, to co-construct new knowledge and imagine our way into new worlds; to build upon the work of our predecessors; to draw on the arts, on history, on literature. These chapters will inspire.

Next, this book pushes us more deeply into self-reflection. What does it mean to be a researcher, in relationship with a community or collaborator? The chapters in Part 2 focus explicitly upon reflexivity, digging into the nature, purpose and process of thoughtful reflexivity. How can critical ethnographers embrace this process to move beyond merely considering our positionalities' influences upon our research, to explore the contradictions inherent in embracing, for example, decolonial frameworks to do work that inevitably falls within the troubled paradigms we reject?

Finally, the book provides exquisite examples. Part 3 offers explicit examples of research partnerships but, truthfully, all the chapters share findings from critical ethnographies, carried out across a wide range of contexts around the world in which researchers engaged with communities and individuals in shared production of knowledge and in a shared commitment to justice, interrogating inequalities and exploring social relations between communities, languages and larger societies – and building better worlds.

I encourage you to take, from these rich examples of critical ethnography, the inspiration to innovate with your methodologies, to move yourselves ever closer to authentic engagement, toward transformation. I encourage you to read these words, and like the authors who wrote them, to theorize into the future and begin to transform the world.

Deborah Palmer
University of Colorado, Boulder, USA

References

Palmer, D.K. (2009) Middle-class English speakers in a two-way immersion bilingual classroom: 'Everybody should be listening to Jonathan right now…'. *TESOL Quarterly* 43 (2), 177–202. https://doi:10.1002/j.1545-7249.2009.tb00164.x

Palmer, D. and Caldas, B. (2017) Critical ethnography. In K. King, Y-J. Lai and S. May (eds) *Research Methods in Language and Education. Encyclopedia of Language and Education* (3rd edn, pp. 1–12). New York: Springer. https://doi.org/10.1007/978-3-319-02329-8_28-1

Introduction: Contextualizing and Reimagining Critical Ethnography in Education

Stephen May and Blanca Caldas

Critical ethnography in education is a methodology that has been with us for 50 years. And yet, it is (still) most often associated with its earliest exemplars – exemplars that adopted a neo-Marxist theoretical framework in order to focus primarily on social class dis/advantage within schools. Paul Willis's (1977) *Learning to Labor* remains, perhaps, the most visible and influential of these early contributions with its examination of the interstices of British working-class culture and (toxic)[1] masculinity in relation to a group of 'lads' and their educational trajectories. Prominent early examples in the United States included Lois Weis's (1985) exploration of student cultures among Black and other minority students in a local US community college. In another important contribution, Michelle Fine (1991) examined the racism directed at African-American students as a key contributing factor to their disproportionate dropout rates from school. And then there are Peter McLaren's two significant critical ethnographic accounts: *Schooling as Ritual Performance* (1999), first published in 1986, and *Life in Schools* (2015), first published in 1989. In both accounts, McLaren analyzes the often oppressive rituals of schooling and the various forms of resistance to them, particularly with respect to often marginalized students of color. Meanwhile, Phil Carspecken provided important empirical (1991) and theoretical (1996) contributions on critical ethnography within education, albeit still primarily neo-Marxist in orientation.

These early neo-Marxist associations perhaps explain, as Deborah Palmer alludes to in her foreword, why many contemporary critical scholars/educators, undertaking long-term and immersive educational fieldwork and focused on questions of power in/justice and in/equity, nonetheless, do not necessarily associate their work now with critical ethnography. And yet, while neo-Marxist accounts of schooling still have an important place historically in the critical ethnographic tradition, critical ethnography within education has clearly moved and engaged with ongoing theoretical developments since those times, even if this has not always been recognized as such. Indeed, as Fitzpatrick and May (2022) argue, in a reimagined account of critical ethnography in education, a wide range of critically oriented theoretical approaches can be allied within and to ethnography in still highly productive ways – including, crucially, developments in postmodernism, posthumanism and postcolonialism, as well as post-qualitative methodologies. Reimagined in this way, critical ethnography can thus be viewed as an expansive, eclectic and inclusive methodology.

It is in this light, that this current volume can be viewed. The volume charts both the long history of critical ethnographic work with a particular focus on language, race/ism and education, as well as providing the latest exemplars of such work in the contemporary moment, primarily in relation to the US. But for those who may not be as familiar with the critical ethnographic tradition, what follows is a brief overview of its development and influence in relation to the field of education.

Critical Ethnography and Education: Origins and Developments

Ethnographic fieldwork, with its origins in anthropology and sociology, and its application in a wide range of contexts, has a strong interdisciplinary history (May & Fitzpatrick, 2019). But ethnographic fieldwork is also deeply imbued with colonial and often overtly racist presumptions and practices. Traditionally, this saw anthropologists select a setting – often involving Indigenous or other marginalized groups – and then 'research' their participants and ways of life, inevitably exoticizing/othering them in the process (Villenas & Foley, 2011). Traditional anthropological ethnographies also adopted an interpretivist approach, casting the researcher as a disinterested observer who by 'deep hanging out' (Geertz, 1998) and through participant observation, field notes, etc. ended up providing 'thick descriptions' (Geertz, 1973) of the culture and practices under examination.

While critical ethnographies retained the use of participant observation and related ethnographic methods, they specifically eschewed the supposedly disinterested interpretive approach, replacing it with an overtly critical theoretical framework. This was in keeping with their aim of providing in-depth analyses that focused unapologetically on issues of in/justice, in/equity and dis/advantage within (and beyond) education. As Jim Thomas (1993: vii) usefully summarized it:

> Critical ethnography is a way of applying a subversive worldview to the conventional logic of cultural inquiry. It does not stand in opposition to conventional ethnography. Rather, it offers a more direct style of thinking about the relationships among knowledge, society and political action.

As noted above, early examples of critical ethnography in education most often adopted a neo-Marxist (often, Bourdieusian or Freirian) framework – a theoretical framing that has continued to be used productively in subsequent critical ethnographies in education (see e.g. Fahey *et al.*, 2015; Fitzpatrick, 2013; Fitzpatrick & May, 2015; May, 1994; Thomson, 2002; Weis *et al.*, 2014). But the adoption of other critical theory orientations is also clearly evident. These include (but are not limited to) cultural studies and postcolonialist readings (e.g. Murillo, 1999; Noblit *et al.*, 2004; Yon, 2000; cf. Deiri, Bell, Martinez & Rubio, this volume), critical race theory (CRT) (e.g. Alim, 2004; Paris, 2011; Reyes, 2007; cf. Chávez-Moreno, Coles, this volume) and ethnographies grounded in critical feminist theories (e.g. Epstein *et al.*, 2001; Pascoe, 2007; Youdell, 2005; cf. Nuñez & García-Mateus, this volume). Many of these subsequent analyses are also overtly intersectional – moving away from the early focus on social class to actively explore the interstices of ethnicity, race, nationality, class, gender and sexuality (e.g. Fitzpatrick, 2013; Kustatscher, 2017; Qin & Li, 2020; cf. Byrd Clark, Chávez-Moreno, Deiri, this volume).

These developments have also occurred in parallel with what have since come to be known as feminist and poststructuralist ethnographies of education. Drawing on the likes of Foucault, Butler, Sedgwick, Deleuze and Guattari, among others, this 'new ethnography', as Patti Lather (2001) termed it, also focused specifically on methodological issues – subsequently expanded upon by post-qualitative methodologies – including positionality and critical reflexivity, textuality and a related dissatisfaction with realist forms of writing. As Lather (2001: 201) describes it, this was a move toward 'partial and fluid epistemological and cultural assumptions, fragmented writing styles, and troubled notions of ethnographic legitimacy'. Underpinning feminist poststructuralist critical ethnographic accounts, as Britzman (2003: 34) elaborates, 'are the assumptions that meaning is historically contingent, contextually bound, socially constructed, and always problematic'; that ethnography is both a set of practices and a set of discourses. For Britzman (2003: 244), poststructuralist ethnographers 'read the absent against the present' so that the 'promise of a holistic account is betrayed by the slippage born from the partiality of language—of what cannot be said precisely because of what is said, and of the impossible difference within what is said, what is intended, what is signified, what is repressed, what is taken, and what remains'. As Lather (2001: 205) suggests, developments in feminist poststructuralism thus allow a move from the realist writing that initially dominated ethnographic work to a more 'interrogative' text, reflecting 'the epistemological paradox of knowing through not knowing'.

These developments were further complemented by the concurrent emergence of 'postcritical ethnographies', including those grounded in CRT and/or postcolonial theory. Postcritical ethnographers focused on acknowledging the sometimes overly deterministic use of theory in earlier critical ethnographic work. They emphasized instead the contingencies of context, situatedness and, in particular, the construction of knowledge, along with the inevitably partial, positional and personal representations of (and in) their own critical accounts (Anders, 2019; Lather, 2007; Noblit, 2003). As Anders (2019: 7) usefully summarizes, '[t]here were no conclusions in post-critical work; understandings were always contingent on context, one's biography and community.... Power and history worked through ethnography... and always present was incommensurability between experience and representation'. Anders (2019: 6) notes that, in postcritical ethnography, the 'post' rejects stable positions and unified accounts. However, she also points out that this recognition of 'the importance of reflexivity, positionality, or the contingencies of context, situatedness... and the particular... in knowledge production' has long been recognized by African-American, Chicanx, feminist, post/neocolonial, critical race and critical race feminist scholars. The likes of Donna Haraway, W.E.B. Du Bois, Gloria Anzaldúa, Derrick Bell, Franz Fanon and Kimberlé Crenshaw 'had [all] understood their significance' and in so doing 'confronted, resisted, and delegitimated white, Anglo, settler-colonial and colonial, cis-heteronormative, patriarchal, positivist Western histories and discourses' (Anders, 2019: 6). The important legacy of this work, and its ongoing challenge to these power-laden normativities, can be seen, for example, in more recent developments in CRT, BlackCrit, LatCrit and raciolinguistics (see Alim *et al.*, 2020, for a useful recent overview).

Key Tenets of Critical Ethnography

The various related developments mentioned previously in this Introduction, we argue, can be (re)situated within a more expansive, inclusive and eclectic understanding of critical ethnography in education as modeled in each of the chapters of this volume. Fitzpatrick and May (2022; also May & Fitzpatrick, 2019) provide a framework or benchmarks of critical ethnographic work with the following nine key tenets that foreground this book: (1) orienting to power, in/justice and in/equity; (2) (social) theory and ontology; (3) troubling the questions (meaningful question setting); (4) relationalities, relationships and reciprocity; (5) positionality, reflection and reflexivity; (6) time, 'deep hanging out'; (7) understanding and communicating cultures; (8) fieldwork; and (9) addressing change. Here, we provide a brief summary of each of these tenets as a further useful orientation for the reader as to what constitutes critical ethnographic work in education.

(1) Orienting to power, in/justice and in/equity

Historically, critical ethnographers have undertaken social critiques that focus on both privilege and disadvantage – and, crucially, their dialectic – in the hope of promoting a more open, egalitarian and inclusive society – or, at the very least, exploring and drawing attention to in/justice. Underpinning this approach is what Michelle Fine (2006: 86) calls 'the political urgency of critical research'. In more recent work, critical ethnographic accounts have expanded their focus to include issues of space, place and materiality. Indeed, contemporary critical ethnographies – drawing on, for example, new materialism – are increasingly mapping spatial, materialist and social concerns (e.g. Ball, 2016; Youdell & Armstrong, 2011). As points of ethnographic focus continue to diversify, so too does critical ethnography's relationship with social and political activism, sometimes overtly (e.g. Foley & Valenzuela, 2005; Villenas & Foley, 2011). Poststructuralist and postcritical ethnographers are considerably more cautious about invoking or enacting change, lest they fall into the trap of what Berlant (2001) describes as 'cruel optimism' that diverts our 'attention from important ethical, social and political questions' (Rasmussen, 2015: 193; see also Tenet 9).

That said, critical ethnographers should remain committed at the very least to the ethical responsibility of attending to, highlighting, disrupting and troubling the status quo, where possible (Madison, 2019). Understanding and interrogating what counts as un/fairness or in/justice – when, under what conditions and for whom – are also a precondition for any meaningful change that might ensue – even if the latter is to be approached cautiously. That is why critical ethnographers also need to begin, and engage deeply, with (critical) social theory.

(2) (Social) theory and ontology

We argue that whatever social theory(ies) one engages with, the theory should/must underscore the research framing, analyses and arguments. For example, in her arguments for poststructuralist and postcritical ethnographic research, Patti Lather (2007: 157) reflects that 'My central argument has been that the turn that matters in this moment of the post is away from abstract philosophizing and toward concrete efforts to put the theory to work'. Taking this further, St Pierre (2018), from a post-qualitative perspective, argues that theory cannot be 'put to work' as such (after the fact) but must be the starting point, that then works its way into the study, into the researcher's body and into the project – becoming an agent that makes itself known in the work. However, some ethnographers also insist that the theory cannot (should not) blind us to context (Atkinson, 2019). We cannot ignore context when we are immersed in it, in the theory and the context and in the knowledge production.

This is where Barad's (2007) notion of 'ethico-onto-epistemology' is useful (see also Tenet 7). This conception acknowledges that we are, as critical researchers, inextricably entangled in the contexts we inhabit and in the processes of knowledge production. In this sense, '[e]thics, knowing, and being… [are] productively entwined' (Geerts & Carstens, 2019:

920). The theory is already in the context and in the knowledge production as we engage ethnographically; it is in the body and the research ethics. Theory and context thus work dynamically and relationally in and through the ethnographer, in and through and in between the researcher, people, places and non-human objects and animals. These relationalities are not static but responsive (cf. Deiri, this volume). The intersection of theory and experience and context will thus give rise to research questions which are in turn dynamic and evolving.

(3) Troubling the questions (meaningful question setting)

Many researchers enter a site with a clear and certain framework and particular research foci that they think are important. And yet, because of this, it is too easy for presumptive research foci to misunderstand the issues of the context and/or to be irrelevant (or even at cross purposes) to those at the center of the research and the site/s of research (see also below). If this is to be avoided, Palmer and Caldas (2017: 384) argue that knowledge must be 'constructed and interpreted from the vantage point of the people whose voices are marginalized'.

The key questions to begin any inquiry, then, as Fine (2006: 90) argues, are 'do I have a right to do this research? Are these my stories to tell?'. In effect, critical ethnographers must continually ask 'who-am-I-to do-this-work?' (Fine, 2006: 90) and to be ready to change the questions they are asking in response to the places and people they encounter and the contexts with(in) which we interact. While this critically reflective theoretical process can be disconcerting and challenging, it keeps open the possibility that the research undertaken ends up connecting – most importantly, not only to the research participants, their communities and the challenges they face, but also to the fields into which the researcher hopes to write. This ongoing, often iterative, process requires critical ethnographers to (continuously) explore how their own positionality impacts on, in and through the research (see Tenet 5).

(4) Relationalities, relationships and reciprocity

Asking the most appropriate and useful questions for the research community and its context is an initial step to doing critical ethnography but it is not enough. As Indigenous scholars have consistently highlighted over recent years, ethnographic fieldwork in Indigenous contexts has most often contributed to the further re/colonizing of Indigenous peoples and the reinforcement of longstanding deficit conceptions of the Indigenous participants, their languages and cultures (Smith, 2012). Linda Tuhiwai Smith (2012; see also Smith *et al.*, 2016), for one, has questioned whether White academics should be allowed to continue researching in Indigenous communities at all. Similar arguments have been made by

BlackCrit and LatCrit scholars (see e.g. Dumas & ross, 2016; Villenas & Foley, 2011) with respect to their own communities.

This position remains moot, however, among Indigenous and other critical scholars of color (cf. McCarty, Phyak, this volume). This is because the preferential status that it necessarily accords insider versus outsider, or insider/outsider, in ethnographic accounts is not necessarily so straightforward (cf. Nuñez & García-Mateus, this volume). As Paechter (2012) observes, an insider's account can come to be read in a certain way that may limit, rather than extend, their access, while insider research may also compromise, or be affected by, the social relationships within which they are enmeshed (see also Pillow, 2003; Delgado-Gaitan, 1993). Issues of exclusion and inclusion occur at the intersection of social norms and power relations, which both researchers and participants are implicated in and engaged in reproducing. Critical ethnographers then need to be less concerned with insider/outsider designations and more concerned with the quality and reciprocity of their ongoing and dynamic research (inter)relationships. This means attending closely to the research context and viewing research as a collaborative endeavor – researching with and for people (or places), rather than 'on' them. Such a dialogic and relational approach, in turn, requires the critical ethnographic researcher to be connected with, accepted and trusted by the research participants.

(5) Positionality, reflection and reflexivity

Attending directly to these issues of power relations, reciprocity and relationalities in the research context also highlights the need to acknowledge and address one's own subjectivity and positionality. As Madison (2019: 8) observes, as critical ethnographers, we need 'to understand that we bring our belongings into the field with us'. Positionality takes this one step further, however, by requiring 'that we direct our attention beyond our individual or subjective selves. Instead, we attend to how our subjectivity *in relation to others* informs and is informed by our engagement and representation of others' (Madison, 2019: 9; emphasis in original).

This requires taking specific account of one's positionality – e.g. background, experiences and theoretical influences – as well as how this positionality frames the ethnographic research and related interpretative schema employed within it. This is also a dialogic process – requiring simultaneous attention to the wider spatial, social and political contexts that shape both who we are and those with whom we interact. Bourdieu has argued that researchers must remain reflexive, not only with regard to gender, social class, ethnicity and the like (particularly as this relates to the study context and participants therein), but also in relation to the field of academia: their academic habitus which enables them to 'see' certain things and not others (Bourdieu & Wacquant, 1992; May, 2014a, 2014b).

As researchers then, we are all implicated in our studies in ways that require critical reflexivity and an orientation to the wider contexts of the research, as well as the relations between our own and other contexts. By fully contextualizing our positionality in these ways, we make 'it accessible, transparent, and vulnerable to judgment and evaluation' (Madison, 2019: 8). Such a critically reflexive focus also extends to the research methods we use, and how positionality makes possible certain analytical directions or may privilege some arguments over others.

(6) Time, 'deep hanging out'

Calling a study ethnographic does not make it necessarily so because, above all, ethnography *takes time*. Critical ethnographers need sufficient time to become part of and fully immersed in the context, relationally, reciprocally and reflexively, in the ways described above. Jeffrey and Troman (2004), for example, usefully identify three different time modes for ethnography. The first, *compressed time mode*, is when the researcher immerses themselves in a research setting (usually day and night) for a compressed period of time, ranging from a few days to a few weeks. This approach requires 'a proliferation of observations and perspectives, which need organising in situ' (Jeffrey & Troman, 2004: 539). The second approach, *selective intermittent time mode*, allows the researcher to respond flexibly to possible areas of investigation, and revisit the site to gain experience of, and observe particular events or moments. The third variation is a *recurrent time mode*, where the researcher visits the site to coincide with particular events (the end or beginning of certain phases or time periods), or at regular intervals regardless of what is happening, to ascertain the significance of certain time periods and to gain a view of what happens over those time periods.

There is thus more than one way to achieve the necessary time in a research context for it to constitute being an ethnographic study. Geertz's (1998) notion of 'deep hanging out' – a term he borrowed and reimagined from anthropologist James Clifford – is useful in this regard. The key consideration is that time spent needs to be sufficient in the end for critical ethnographers to understand the nuances of cultural expression or the varied interactions and contradictions that emerge over time in the research site. What is enough time is a question for each project to answer.

(7) Understanding and communicating cultures

While time spent in research settings is one of the key things that sets ethnography apart from other methodologies, what is done with the time is also important. It is not possible to undertake ethnography successfully without seeking to understand cultural contexts in depth (and over time). In other words, to do critical ethnography, the researcher must be fundamentally interested in understanding, exploring, interrogating and challenging cultures within context.

To achieve this successfully, the critical ethnographer must simultaneously acknowledge, attend to and evaluate critically and contextually, what Barad (2007) refers to as our 'ethico-onto-epistemologies'. This combination of ethics, knowing and being situates us as the researcher(s) in relation to the study and wider flows of power, knowledge and relationalities – highlighting how our world views, knowledge, ethics and understandings inform, and are informed by, our research experiences and interactions. Barad describes this process as 'intra-action' – highlighting that we are not only of/in the world, but also co-constituted by it. As she argues: '"We" are not outside observers of the world. Nor are we simply located at places in the world; rather, we are part of the world in its ongoing intra-activity' (Barad, 2007: 828). Being emplaced and enmeshed, and reflexively engaging with these positionings throughout the research project, is what makes critical ethnography so exciting but also, simultaneously, challenging research – research that will extend, unsettle and change us, as it should.

(8) Fieldwork

Ethnographic fieldwork is a broad term, although it is perhaps best encapsulated by Geertz's (1998) notion of deep hanging out (see Tenet 6). Like all ethnography, critical ethnography requires the researcher to develop deep, lived understandings of a context and to reflect on the meanings of cultures within that context. This requires significant time in the field, but it can also engage with materiality in the form of places, spaces, objects, landscapes and architectures. In the process, a wide variety of ethnographic methods can be employed, depending on the research focus and the site. Contemporary ethnographers are increasingly using participant-generated research methods and engaging participants as co-researchers, videographers, diarists and interviewers (Cammarota & Fine, 2008; Delamont & Atkinson, 2018; Pink, 2021; Pink *et al.*, 2016). As Delamont (2016) observes, ethnographic methods can thus also extend to

> [R]esearch on documents such as Tweets or blogs, interviewing with open-ended questions, oral history, life history, collecting informants' drawings, photographs or 'films', exploring personal constructions and mental maps as well as observation, whether the observer is participating or trying to be unobtrusive. (Delamont, 2016: 8)

In short, ethnographic work is not bound by any rigid methodological rules. Rather, it draws on a range of methods and is flexible, dependent on practicality, the research foci and relationships between participants and researchers. This is possible in ethnography as a range of methodological tools can be used within a broad framework and, crucially, wider social and political contexts can be analyzed alongside, and in relation to, specific contextual incidences.

(9) Addressing change

As with critical educational research more broadly, social and political activism – the desire for and advocacy of change – is often a key feature of critical ethnographic research. Critical ethnographers often seek to create change and challenge inequities in research sites, in themselves, in the academy and in the communities in which they live. However, this drive for change is not without its own pitfalls. As discussed above (see Tenet 1), poststructuralist and postcritical ethnographers are considerably more cautious about invoking or enacting change. Indeed, critical approaches to education have a problematic history with notions of emancipation that too often assume external intervention and tend toward paternalistic relationships that reinscribe power relations even while attempting to work against them (Biesta, 2015).

Given this, we need to be cautious in seeking change and continue to ask questions reflectively and reflexively in this regard. Who gets to choose what change is needed? Whose ethico-onto-epistemological position is privileged and how do we know the change we propose or try to enact won't create other kinds of inequity? Returning to Fine's (2006: 90; see Tenet 3) question 'who-am-I-to do-this-work?', we must also then ask, 'who am I to make this change?' And what of the stories we tell; the voices we highlight? We noted earlier Palmer and Caldas's (2017: 384) observation that knowledge must be 'constructed and interpreted from the vantage point of the people whose voices are marginalized', but, as Fine (1994) cautions, giving voice to participants is also a power move that can all too easily slip into ventriloquy (see also Biesta, 2015). And so, while not resiling from the need for change – after all, this is what often galvanizes critical ethnographic work in the first place – seeking change must be approached slowly, seriously, selectively and collaboratively. This tension clearly highlights both the challenges and possibilities of critical ethnographic work – the complexities of in/equity and in/justice, how we as researchers might negotiate these and how our work might contribute to (rather than undermine) changing them for the better.

Book Outline

This edited book brings together current cutting-edge critical ethnographic research in education, predominantly from the US, and with a particular focus on the interstices of language and race/ism. Each chapter also illustrates the various tenets outlined above from different vantage points and from diverse communities, each with its own urgencies, tensions and hopes. The collective work presented here stems from an initial colloquium at the American Association of Applied Linguistics (AAAL) Annual Conference in 2017, convened by Stephen and focusing on current critical ethnographic work in North America – hence, the predominance of US-oriented work in this current volume. Over the last five years, our transnational, transcontinental collaborations have expanded somewhat and since endured births, deaths, diseases, political unrest, natural disasters and various uprootings to finally reach readers. These chapters show the authors' ethico-onto-epistemological stances grounded in critical and anti/decolonial schools of thought, along with their related advocacy for the (bi/multilingual) communities they serve. They thus model what critical ethnography in language education can look like and its future possibilities for both seasoned and emergent ethnographers who plan to work at similar intersections as the authors herein. The current volume can also be viewed as a complementary publication to Fitzpatrick and May (2022), which provides a broad overview of critical ethnography in relation to the field of education and draws on a wide range of critical ethnographic work across various national contexts.

This volume is divided into three sections. Part 1 highlights the theoretical and methodological eclecticism that is encompassed by a broader understanding of critical ethnography, as highlighted in this Introduction. In Chapter 1, Stephen May reviews the developments of critical ethnography in language education and highlights the need for interdisciplinary and multilinguistic approaches to critical ethnography in language education, centering on diverse contexts and critical theoretical frameworks. Also in this chapter, May creates a genealogy of critical ethnography in language and education, along with its key contributions. These contributions focus, on the one hand, on denouncing the harm that racial, linguistic and educational inequalities inflict on linguistic minoritized and racialized populations. On the other hand, they also often examine the possibilities of counter-insurgent spaces where bi/multilingualism can exist/persist, despite the tensions of homogenization and stigmatization associated with the ongoing neoliberal globalization of language and education.

In Chapter 2, Justin Coles pairs CRT and BlackCrit ethnography as praxis and focuses on the lived experiences of Black youth to examine anti-blackness and explore how they experience Blackness, resistance and justice in education. Closing Part 1, Youmna Deiri in Chapter 3 outlines her conceptualization of multilingual radical intimate ethnography (MRIE) as a more relational ethnography that involves the unlearning of colonial and monolingual mindsets acquired in academic spaces, even when engaged in multilingual research. Deiri argues that we need to 'trouble our own monolingual and colonial gaze as researchers' in a dynamic process of unlearning and relearning. Such a process responds to the urgency of debunking fossilized and colonial notions of language research, devoid of sociocultural, geographical and historical context, along with its deficit views of multilingual populations. Instead, she argues, we need to reconnect with language learning, as a relationship, a way to foster kinship for the well-being and healing of multilingual communities from racial and linguistic violence.

Part 2 foregrounds issues of positionality and critical reflexivity in ethnographic work. In Chapter 4, Laura Chávez-Moreno applies a race-reflexivity approach to her critical race ethnography. She used this approach in her journey toward a robust theory of race for examining how the CRT tenets (e.g. Whiteness as property) work in educational contexts. She models what race reflexivity looks like at three different levels of the unconscious (social, discipline and scholastic) for scholars who want to engage in rigorous CRT ethnographic work concerning racial ideologies. Through discussion of two separate critical ethnographies, Idalia Nuñez and Suzanne García-Mateus in Chapter 5 re-examine and challenge their own positionalities in this research through a Chicanx feminist epistemology. In so doing, they also challenge other researchers with privileged identities to engage in similar interrogations as part of their responsibility toward the communities they partner, the data collected and conclusions drawn.

In Chapter 6, Julie Byrd Clark creates a transdisciplinary approach to reflexive engagement for critical ethnography, which moves away from the 'this or that' Cartesian binaries and explores the rich multidimensional and plurilinguistic experiences of bi/multilingual teacher education students in Canada, and how these influence their linguistic ideologies and pedagogy. Closing Part 2, Randy Bell, Manuel Martinez and Brenda Rubio in Chapter 7 discuss their ethnographic engagements with a grassroots community language initiative that speaks back to dominant discourses of (English) monolingualism. Drawing on a postcolonial theoretical framework, they argue that critical reflexivity is central to engaging in critical ethnography because it requires a serious examination of colonial grammars acquired through the embeddedness of White supremacy and capitalism in social institutions, and especially in academic spaces. In examining their own positionalities with/in this research, the authors caution other researchers about the pitfalls of conducting research without considering the sociohistorical and geopolitical context, and also highlight the careful navigation of tensions required when working for and with subalternized communities.

Part 3 foregrounds the collaborative, reciprocal and relational engagements required of critical ethnographers in relation to the communities within which and with whom they research. Such engagements are crucial to the critical examination of existing social, political, ethnic/racial and linguistic inequities and, as discussed above, the challenges and possibilities of highlighting, addressing and, where possible, changing them. In Chapter 8, Teresa McCarty focuses on 'raciolinguistic panics' and their deleterious consequences, particularly for Indigenous and other minoritized students. She also draws on the notion of ethnographic monitoring, derived from the sociolinguistic work of Dell Hymes (see May, this volume), as a 'way of being a researcher'. For McCarty this is enacted through her longstanding collaborative work with Native American and other Indigenous communities, locating her as 'witness, co-inquirer, and allied other'. McCarty draws from three ethnographic studies to illustrate raciolinguistic violence and raciolinguistic possibilities, as well as highlighting Indigenous communities-led projects as blueprints for emerging Indigenous de/anticolonization work.

Following an exploration of the deficit-oriented educational language policies amidst the ongoing privatization of Nepali schools, Prem Phyak in Chapter 9 examines the exclusion and erasure of Nepali Indigenous languages and the promotion of a *de facto* English-only curriculum. Through a critical and engaged approach, Phyak also problematizes the forces behind the linguistic homogenization of Nepali education due to the neoliberalization of schooling and public discourses that both normalize English as a medium of instruction and stigmatize ethnic and multilingual practices. Daniel Heiman and Michelle Yanes in Chapter 10 focus on a local curricular intervention in a dual-language bilingual education (DLBE) program in the middle of its ongoing gentrification. Their work exemplifies both the critical edge of the fourth principle for DLBE programs (Cervantes-Soon *et al.*, 2017) in action, the role of advocacy in critical ethnography and the process of reflexivity as praxical endeavor. Blanca Caldas in Chapter 11 closes Part 3 with a chapter/script of her one-person performance based on her critical performance ethnographic work on the linguistic, personal and professional identity development of a group of Mexican-American/Latinx pre-service bilingual teachers. It also charts their evolution as advocates in the making through the pedagogical use of Theater of the Oppressed. Inspired by the work of Soyini Madison and Omi Jones, Caldas's performance ethnography is grounded on co-performance witnessing, which, apart from self-reflexivity, requires community accountability, open advocacy and audience engagement.

We would like to close this Introduction by underlining that becoming and being a critical ethnographer at the crossroads of language and race/ism, as we outline in this volume, is the 'option' (Mignolo, 2008) that we have all collectively taken. It aligns with who we are as researchers and our (socio)political stances toward and commitments to fostering bi/multilingualism and, relatedly, challenging the often highly racialized normative ascendency of monolingualism. In our varied ethnographic discussions, outlined here, we also highlight the challenges and rewards that this work brings, which extend, trouble and enrich us personally, professionally and collectively. We invite the readers to examine these pages, engage with (and critique) our stories and consider this important critical ethnographic option for their own bi/multilingual research.

Note

(1) Willis did not necessarily acknowledge this toxic masculinity fully; indeed, he sometimes appeared to glamorize it – a key critique that feminist scholars subsequently leveled at his account (e.g. McRobbie, 1990).

References

Alim, H.S. (2004) *You Know My Steez: An Ethnographic and Sociolinguistic Study of Style-shifting in a Black American Speech Community*. Durham, NC: Duke University Press.

Alim, H.S., Reyes, A. and Kroskrity, P. (eds) (2020) *The Oxford Handbook of Language and Race*. New York: Oxford University Press.

Anders, A. (2019) *Post-Critical Ethnography*. Oxford Research Encyclopedia. Oxford: Oxford University Press. https://doi.org/10.1093/acrefore/9780190264093.013.342

Atkinson, P. (2019) *Writing Ethnographically*. Los Angeles, CA: Sage.

Ball, S. (2016) Following policy: Networks, network ethnography and education policy mobilities. *Journal of Education Policy* 31 (5), 549–566.

Barad, K. (2007) *Meeting the Universe Halfway: Quantum Physics and the Entanglement of Matter and Meaning*. Durham, NC: Duke University Press.

Berlant, L. (2011) *Cruel Optimism*. Durham, NC: Duke University Press.

Biesta, G.J. (2015) *Beautiful Risk of Education*. London: Routledge.

Bourdieu, P. and Wacquant, L. (1992) *An Invitation to Reflexive Sociology*. Chicago, IL: Polity Press.

Britzman, D.P. (2003) *Practice Makes Practice: A Critical Study of Learning to Teach* (rev. edn). Albany, NY: State University of New York Press.

Cammarota, J. and Fine, M. (eds) (2008) *Revolutionizing Education: Youth Participatory Action Research in Motion*. Abingdon: Routledge.

Carspecken, P. (1991) *Community Schooling and the Nature of Power: The Battle for Croxteth Comprehensive*. London: Routledge.

Carspecken, P. (1996) *Critical Ethnography in Educational Research: A Theoretical and Practical Guide*. New York: Routledge.

Cervantes-Soon, C., Dorner, L., Palmer, D., Heiman, D., Schwerdtfeger, R. and Choi, J. (2017) Combating inequalities in two-way language immersion programs: Toward critical consciousness in bilingual education spaces. *Review of Research in Education* 41 (1), 403–427.

Delamont, S. (2016) *Fieldwork in Educational Settings: Methods, Pitfalls and Perspectives* (3rd edn). London: Routledge. https://doi.org/10.4324/9781315758831

Delamont, S. and Atkinson, P. (2018) The ethics of ethnography. In R. Iphofen and M. Tolich (eds) *The Sage Handbook of Qualitative Research Ethics* (pp. 119–132). London: Sage.

Delgado-Gaitan, C. (1993) Researching change and changing the researcher. *Harvard Education Review* 64 (4), 389–411.

Dumas, M.J. and ross, K.M. (2016) 'Be real black for me': Imaging BlackCrit in education. *Urban Education* 51 (4), 415–442.

Epstein, D., Kehily, M., Mac An Ghaill, M. and Redman, P. (2001) Boys and girls come out to play: Making masculinities and femininities in school playgrounds. *Men and Masculinities* 4 (2), 158–172.

Fahey, J., Prosser, H. and Shaw, M. (eds) (2015) *In the Realm of the Senses: Social Aesthetics and the Sensory Dynamics of Privilege*. Dordrecht: Springer.

Fine, M. (1991) *Framing Dropouts: Notes on the Politics of an Urban Public High School*. Albany, NY: SUNY Press.

Fine, M. (1994) Dis-tance and other stances: Negotiations of power inside feminist research. In A. Gitlin (ed.) *Power and Methods* (pp. 13–55). London: Routledge.

Fine, M. (2006) Bearing witness: Methods for researching oppression and resistance: A textbook for critical research. *Social Justice Research* 19 (2), 83–108. https://doi.org/10.1007/s11211-006-0001-0

Fitzpatrick, K. (2013) *Critical Pedagogy, Physical Education and Urban Schooling*. New York: Peter Lang.

Fitzpatrick, K. and May, S. (2015) Doing critical educational ethnography with Bourdieu. In M. Murphy and C. Costa (eds) *Theory as Method in Research: On Bourdieu, Education and Society* (pp. 101–114). Abingdon: Routledge.

Fitzpatrick, K. and May, S. (2022) *Critical Ethnography and Education*. New York: Routledge.

Foley, D. and Valenzuela, A. (2005) Critical ethnography: The politics of collaboration. In N. Denzin and Y. Lincoln (eds) *Handbook of Qualitative Research* (2nd edn, pp. 217–234). London: Sage.

Geertz, C. (1973) Thick description: Toward an interpretive theory of culture. In C. Geertz (ed.) *The Interpretation of Cultures* (pp. 3–30). New York: Basic Books.

Geertz, C. (1998) Deep hanging out. *The New York Review of Books* 45 (16), 69.

Geerts, E. and Carstens, D. (2019) Ethico-onto-epistemology. *Philosophy Today* 63 (4), 915–925.

Jeffrey, B. and Troman, G. (2004) Time for ethnography. *British Educational Research Journal* 30 (4), 535–548. https://doi.org/10.1080/0141192042000237220

Kustatscher, M. (2017) The emotional geographies of belonging: Children's intersectional identities in primary school. *Children's Geographies* 15 (1), 65–79.

Lather, P. (2001) Postbook: Working the ruins of feminist ethnography. *Signs: Journal of Women in Culture and Society* 27 (1), 199–227.

Lather, P. (2007) *Getting Lost: Feminist Efforts toward a Double(d) Science*. Albany, NY: SUNY Press.

Madison, D.S. (2019) *Critical Ethnography: Method, Ethics, and Performance* (3rd edn). New York: Sage.

May, S. (1994) *Making Multicultural Education Work*. Clevedon: Multilingual Matters.

May, S. (2014a) Disciplinary divides, knowledge construction and the multilingual turn. In S. May (ed.) *The Multilingual Turn: Implications for SLA, TESOL and Bilingual Education* (pp. 7–31). New York: Routledge.

May, S. (2014b) Overcoming disciplinary boundaries: Connecting language, education and (anti)racism. In R. Race and V. Lander (eds) *Advancing Race and Ethnicity in Education* (pp. 128–144). London: Palgrave Macmillan.

May, S. and Fitzpatrick, K. (2019) Critical ethnography. In P. Atkinson, S. Delamont, A. Cernat, J.W. Sakshaug and R.A. Williams (eds) *Sage Research Methods Foundations*. London: Sage. https://doi.org/10.4135/9781526421036831954

McLaren, P. (1999 [1986]) *Schooling as a Ritual Performance* (3rd edn). Lanham, MD: Rowman & Littlefield.

McLaren, P. (2015 [1989]) *Life in Schools* (6th edn). London: Routledge. https://doi.org/10.4324/9781315633640

McRobbie, A. (1990) *Feminism and Youth Culture: From 'Jackie' to 'Just Seventeen'*. London: Macmillan International Higher Education.

Mignolo, W. (2008) La opción decolonial: Desprendimiento y apertura. Un manifiesto y un caso. *Tabula Rasa* 8, 243–281.

Murillo, E.G. (1999) Mojado crossings along neoliberal borderlands. *Educational Foundations* 13, 7–30.

Noblit, G.W. (2003) Reinscribing critique in educational ethnography: Critical and postcritical ethnography. In K.B. deMarrais and S.D. Lapan (eds) *Foundations for*

Research: Methods of Inquiry in Education and Social Sciences (pp. 197–218). London: Routledge.

Noblit, G.W., Flores, S.Y. and Murillo, E. Jr (eds) (2004) *Postcritical Ethnography: Reinscribing Critique*. New York: Hampton Press.

Paechter, C. (2012) Researching sensitive issues online: Implications of a hybrid insider/outsider position in a retrospective ethnographic study. *Qualitative Research* 13 (1), 71–86.

Palmer, D. and Caldas, B. (2017) Critical ethnography. In K. King, Y. Lai and S. May (eds) Research methods in language and education. *Encyclopedia of Language and Education* (3rd edn, pp. 381–392). London: Springer.

Paris, D. (2011) *Language across Difference: Ethnicity, Communication, and Youth Identities in Changing Urban Schools*. Cambridge: Cambridge University Press.

Pascoe, C.J. (2007) *Dude, You're a Fag: Masculinity and Sexuality in High School*. Berkeley, CA: University of California Press.

Pillow, W.S. (2003) Confession, catharsis or cure? Rethinking the uses of reflexivity as methodological power in qualitative research. *International Journal of Qualitative Studies in Education* 16 (2), 175–196.

Pink, S. (2021) *Doing Visual Ethnography* (4th edn). Thousand Oaks, CA: Sage.

Pink, S., Horst, H., Postill, J., Hjorth, L., Lewis, T. and Tacchi, J. (2016) *Digital Ethnography: Principles and Practice*. London: Sage.

Qin, K. and Li, G. (2020) Understanding immigrant youths' negotiation of racialized masculinities in one US high school: An intersectionality lens on race, gender, and language. *Sexuality & Culture* 24, 1046–1063.

Rasmussen, M.L. (2015) 'Cruel optimism' and contemporary Australian critical theory in educational research. *Educational Philosophy and Theory* 47 (2), 192–206.

Reyes, A. (2007) *Language, Identity and Stereotype among Southeast Asian American Youth: The Other Asian*. Mahwah, NJ: Lawrence Erlbaum Associates.

Smith, L.T. (2012) *Decolonising Methodologies: Research and Indigenous Peoples* (2nd edn). London: Zed Books.

Smith, L.T., Maxwell, T.K., Puke, H. and Temara, P. (2016) Indigenous knowledge, methodology and mayhem. What is the role of methodology in producing Indigenous insights? A discussion from mātauranga Māori. *Knowledge Cultures* 4 (3), 131–156.

St Pierre, E. (2018) Writing post qualitative inquiry. *Qualitative Inquiry* 24 (9), 603–608.

Thomas, J. (1993) *Doing Critical Ethnography*. London: Sage.

Thomson, P. (2002) *Schooling the Rustbelt Kids: Making the Difference in Changing Times*. Crow's Nest: Allen & Unwin.

Villenas, S. and Foley, D. (2011) Critical ethnographies of education in the Latino/a diaspora. In R.R. Valencia (ed.) *Chicano School Failure and Success: Past, Present and Future* (3rd edn, pp. 175–196). London: Routledge.

Weis, L. (1985) *Between Two Worlds: Black Students in an Urban Community College*. Boston, MA: Routledge.

Weis, L., Cipollone, K. and Jenkins, H. (2014) *Class Warfare: Class, Race, and College Admissions in Top-Tier Secondary Schools*. Chicago, IL: University of Chicago Press.

Willis, P. (1977) *Learning to Labor: How Working Class Kids Get Working Class Jobs*. Farnborough: Saxon House.

Yon, D. (2000) *Elusive Culture: Schooling, Race and Identity in Global Times*. Albany, NY: SUNY Press.

Youdell, D. (2005) Sex-gender-sexuality: How sex, gender and sexuality constellations are constituted in secondary schools. *Gender and Education* 17 (3), 249–270. https://doi.org/10.1080/09540250500145148

Youdell, D. and Armstrong, F. (2011) A politics beyond subjects: The affective choreographies and smooth spaces of schooling. *Emotion, Space and Society* 4 (3), 144–150. https://doi.org/10.1016/j.emospa.2011.01.002

Part 1

Theoret/Methodolog/ical Connections

1 Critical Ethnography, Language, Race/ism and In/equity in Education: Charting the Field

Stephen May

In this chapter, I explore the pivotal role that critical ethnography can play in understanding, critiquing and contesting the often malignant confluence of language, race/ism and in/equity in education. This combination of factors disproportionately and negatively affects linguistically minoritized students' experiences of, and success in, education. As a precursor to, and an illustration of just what is at stake here, I begin with a personal vignette, followed by a brief personal narrative about the two schools that have most influenced my own views on language, race/ism and in/equity in education. First, the vignette:

> It is 10 September 2018, and I find myself sitting in and observing in Te Whānau Whāriki (WW), the Indigenous Māori language immersion program at Te Kura o Ritimana, Richmond Road Primary School, in Auckland, New Zealand. The classroom day begins, as always, with two students from the program being responsible for leading *whaikōrero* (formal speech), *karakia* (blessing) and *waiata* (song) for all. The first classroom session to follow focuses on *pānui* (reading). The three *kaiako* (teachers) work collectively, rather than individually – in this instance, each leading/facilitating a particular reading group. Students from across the program are divided into three groups based on current reading levels in Māori, rather than strictly based on age/level. The pedagogies used include group work and scaffolded learning (by both teachers and students), with emphasis placed throughout on the multimodal interconnections between reading and exploratory talk in Māori. It is just one of the many innovative pedagogical practices evident in Te Whānau Whāriki and the wider school, with its long and successful history of critical bilingual and multicultural approaches to bilingual teaching and learning. This history now stretches to some 30-odd years – much of which I have also had the pleasure and privilege of being involved in as a researcher

and friend/critical ally of the school. It is also strikingly different from the usual pedagogies adopted in mainstream (English-medium) schools in New Zealand, where Indigenous Māori, Pacific and other linguistically minoritized students tend to fare much less well...

School 1: Diverse Students, Institutional Homogeneity (The Usual)

The predominantly negative experiences of schooling for Māori and Pacific students in mainstream New Zealand schools were clearly apparent in the first school I taught in. It was the mid-1980s, and I had chosen to begin my teaching career at this school in Petone, a then still predominantly working-class suburb of Wellington, because it was a low socioeconomic, ethnically and linguistically diverse high school. It was, both figuratively and literally, on the wrong side of the railway line – in fact, the school grounds abutted the Petone railway line, separating it physically from the (slightly) more salubrious suburbs on the other side. I was young, idealistic, committed to social justice and diversity and, above all, wanted to make a difference in education, and for my students. If I'm honest, this specifically chosen school context was also the antithesis of my own resolutely and relentlessly White monocultural and monolingual background, which I was increasingly desperate to both repudiate and renounce.

Most of the students at the school were ethnically and linguistically minoritized students – predominantly Māori students and Pacific students. They were challenging, at times, but also wonderfully engaging, talented, smart and so obviously (and often proudly) culturally located. Many of them were bilingual or multilingual. I had high hopes and aspirations for them – aspirations which, over time, I found increasingly difficult to fulfill. Many of these students continued to leave school as soon as they could; very few of those who remained went on to higher education; and, while the school's student population continued to reflect a vibrant ethnic and linguistic diversity at the individual level, the only space in which such diversity was institutionally recognized and valued was in *te reo Māori* (Māori language) classes and in the Māori and Pacific students' *kapa haka* (cultural performance) group. Even here though, there were issues: for example, te reo Māori was still viewed as a low-status (even remedial) language subject option by the school's administrators and some teachers, in sharp contradistinction to other language subjects, such as French and German. And while Māori and Pacific cultures were acknowledged elsewhere in the school, these were limited largely to ceremonial and/or celebratory occasions.

As a result of these, often dispiriting, early experiences of teaching, I began to think that perhaps schools – and all those within them – couldn't make any (significant) difference to the educational and life trajectories of ethnically and linguistically minoritized students, after all. It was a sobering, even crushing, reassessment of my initially naïve assumptions about the (supposedly) transformative power of education.

School 2: Recognizing Diversity Systemically (The Unusual)

It was upon returning to postgraduate study some years later that I first became aware of Richmond Road Primary School. Through a number of unexpected serendipities (see May, 1998), I ended up undertaking a three-year critical ethnography of the school from 1990 to 1992. This was to be the focus of my dissertation and, subsequently, my first book (May, 1994). Richmond Road was the first urban elementary school in New Zealand, and perhaps also one of the first of its kind internationally (Cazden, 1989; Corson, 1990), to focus extensively on bilingual/immersion education as an avenue for furthering educational and wider social justice aims for linguistically minoritized students. In the 1980s, Richmond Road implemented a radically reconceptualized educational program to better serve the educational needs of its predominantly Māori and Pacific students.

Richmond Road's broader philosophy centered on critical multiculturalism (see May, 1999a; May & Sleeter, 2010), developing and institutionalizing a whole-school recognition of cultural and linguistic diversity, with bilingual provision at its core. It was the first urban school in New Zealand to establish multiyear-level, bilingual classrooms (in Māori, Samoan and, subsequently, in the 1990s, French). The bilingual programs provided a partial immersion approach (at least 50% medium of instruction in the target language) – broadly equivalent pedagogically to the subsequent development of dual-language programs in the United States. They were explicitly predicated on an additive approach to bilingualism – viewing the achievement and/or maintenance of student bilingualism, via the use of minoritized languages as mediums of instruction, as a core educational and wider societal value. As the late Jim Laughton, the visionary principal who established these programs at Richmond Road, observed in a position paper on their development:

> There are many children at Richmond Road School whose mother tongue is not English. Submerged unavoidably in a strange language from school entry these children are particularly vulnerable. It is the school's task to ameliorate that condition—to show them respect, to encourage pride in their identity by including their languages and cultures to a significant degree… In short, to facilitate educational advancement from a solid platform of self-knowledge, self-assurance and an acknowledged first language competence. (Cited in May, 1994: 114)

Richmond Road's bilingual programs were also predicated on a student-centered approach, and the related reciprocity of teaching and learning, exemplified by the principle 'everyone who has knowledge teaches' (May, 1995). Both developments were underpinned by the school's extensive engagement with critical educational theory and practice – including regular staff interaction at the time with my own Bourdieusian analysis over the course of the three-year critical ethnographic study (Fitzpatrick & May, 2015; May, 1998; cf. Coles, this volume).

I titled my 1994 book on Richmond Road, *Making Multicultural Education Work*, to highlight how it can do so, structurally, epistemically and pedagogically within a critical multicultural and additive bilingual framework. However, the title also alluded ironically to the fact that multicultural education seldom actually works – highlighting the rarity of such school examples. Nonetheless, Richmond Road restored, for me, a belief in the *possibilities* of radical, transformative change via schooling – particularly with respect to the institutionalized recognition of ethnic and linguistic diversity. The school has continued to reinforce this belief for me ever since and I have remained actively engaged, albeit episodically, with the school's ongoing efforts to this end. In 2006, I was involved in an action research project, led by teachers in the school, that reflected critically and developmentally on the school's long history of bilingual teaching and learning. And in 2018, as foregrounded in the vignette, I was once again involved in researching the school. This time it was to review its three bilingual programs – including Te Whānau Whāriki, the Māori immersion program where it all began – in terms of the latest identified best practices in bilingual/immersion teaching and learning.

Critical Ethnography: Making the Connections; Examining the Disjunctures

I begin with these two juxtaposed school examples because they have fundamentally shaped, and continue to shape, my own ongoing engagement with issues of language, race/ism and education, along with the inequities that still so often attend them. However, the two schools also highlight, for me, the possibilities that critical ethnography affords in exploring, critiquing and contesting these issues. If I could have applied the theoretical and methodological knowledge of critical ethnography that I later acquired to the first school I taught in, I might have been able to better understand, and contest, the systemic inequities that still constructed the school's ethnically and linguistically diverse students in predominantly deficit terms. This was most obvious, retrospectively, in the ongoing disconnect between students' own individual ethnicities and bi/multilingual repertoires, and the institutionalized (non)recognition of these within the school.

Critical ethnography would also have been useful here in highlighting how these school processes are inevitably underpinned by wider educational and related public policies that promote monolingualism in the dominant societal language as a principal aim (Gramling, 2016; May, 2016), and which are often situated in conjunction with highly racialized views of linguistically minoritized individuals and groups, as explored throughout this current volume. The latter is most often seen in the nomenclature regularly adopted to describe such students, and almost always referenced in deficit terms with respect to the dominant language – most often, English. This includes students in so-called 'mainstream' (dominant, most often national, language) compulsory education contexts, as well as so-called limited English proficient (LEP) students, English language learners (ELLs), English second language (ESL) and English foreign language (EFL) students in both compulsory education and tertiary contexts. All these terms highlight the normative ascendancy of English, either nationally and/or in relation to English as the current world language.

Foregrounding these wider historical, social and cultural inequities through critical ethnography might also have led me to apply a far greater degree of critical reflexivity to my own well-meaning, but often naïve, misguided and misdirected, 'missionary' intentions as a beginning teacher. These were grounded in a commitment to social justice but were still inevitably shaped (and occluded) by my personal positionality – coming from a monolingual, relatively privileged background (May, 1998), being cisgender and being sociohistorically and socioculturally *situated* as a member of the White ethnic majority in a postcolonial state 'historically embedded in colonial flows of power' (see Bell, Martinez & Rubio, this volume).

Meanwhile, via my critical ethnography of Richmond Road, I began to see how schools *can* potentially make a difference, and just what that entails, by critically exploring the often complex – and, at times, contradictory and competing – interstices between ethnicity, language, education, racism and related in/equities. While not wanting to overstate the possibilities of change here (cf. Berlant, 2011), given just what we are up against, critical ethnography can nonetheless provide the (potential) basis for exploring resistances and alternatives to existing discriminatory educational processes and practices toward linguistically minoritized students. These include (re)centering students' dynamic bi/multilingualism within the school, along with employing these as a direct counter to, and subversion of, monolingual conceptions of language use. It also includes highlighting the institutional responses that overtly – and in Richmond Road's case, *systemically* – (re)value the languages and cultures of minoritized students.

Such critical ethnographic work is necessarily interdisciplinary (see Fitzpatrick & May, 2022; May & Fitzpatrick, 2019), while also traversing a wide range of different language education contexts within (and across) different national domains. The former includes, among others, the fields of education, applied linguistics, sociolinguistics, anthropology, cultural studies and sociology. The latter includes a range of related language education contexts and associated points of research focus, such as bilingual language development and use, bilingual and multilingual education programs and pedagogy, biliteracy, language revitalization, Indigenous language education and critical multicultural and antiracist education approaches that focus centrally on bi/multilingualism.

Specific theoretical sources and influences in this critical ethnographic work on language and education are also wide ranging. They include the use of interactional sociolinguistics, which explores how students communicate in face-to-face contexts to highlight bi/multilingual students' often transgressive linguistic practices within education (Alim, 2004; Paris, 2011; Rampton, 2006). This focus on students' dynamic bilingual language use has also been more recently examined with respect to the related notion of 'translanguaging' (García, 2009; García & Li, 2014). Bourdieusian ethnographic analyses of linguistic habitus, capital and fields in education (see Grenfell *et al.*, 2012; Grenfell & Pahl, 2018) foreground both the reproduction/reinforcement of monolingual language education for bi/multilingual students, as well as the potential for critical bilingual alternatives (May, 1994; Palmer, 2011). Latinx cultural and educational studies focus on students' existing 'funds of knowledge' (González *et al.*, 2005), alongside postmodernist and postcolonial critiques of education highlighting the linguistic and wider marginalization of Latinx students within US education, in particular (Villenas & Foley, 2002, 2011). Latinx studies, as well as key critical ethnographies of African-American students, also draw directly on critical race theory (CRT), Black critical theory (BlackCrit), Latino critical race theory (LatCrit) and raciolinguistics (see Alim *et al.*, 2020; Bernal, 2002; Dumas & ross, 2016; Flores & Rosa, 2015; Rosa & Flores, 2017) to explore the racialized construction of bilingual students and the impact of linguistically discriminatory processes toward them in US education (Baker-Bell, 2020; Malsbary, 2014; Paris, 2011). Tribal critical race theory (Brayboy, 2005; McCarty, this volume; see also below) likewise explores these issues specifically in relation to Native American (and other Indigenous) students.

Likewise, there is a long history of engagement with Indigenous epistemologies, language practices and language education policies as a basis for educational and wider social change (Fitzpatrick & May, 2022; Hermes *et al.*, 2012; Smith, 2012). These Indigenous epistemologies, language policies and practices underpin advocacy for, and the implementation of, Indigenous education initiatives worldwide. Such initiatives aim to contest the ongoing cultural and linguistic assimilation of Indigenous peoples in dominant language educational contexts, along with the related entrenchment of wider educational and social inequities for Indigenous peoples (Hill & May, 2011; McCarty, 2014, this volume).

With this background in mind, I now turn to a more detailed examination of *what* and *how* critical ethnography can contribute usefully to explicating the links between language, ethnicity, race/ism and in/equity.

What does (Critical) Ethnography do for Work in Language, Race/ism and Education?

Critical ethnography provides a materials-rich and theory-driven approach to questions of language representation and practices within education. As Monica Heller (2008: 250) observes of this:

> Ethnographies… allow us to see how language practices are connected to the very real conditions of people's lives, to discover how and why language matters to people in their own terms, and to watch processes unfold over time. They allow us to see complexities and connections, to understand the history and geography of language. They allow us to tell a story…

These ethnographic stories have often focused in depth on the discriminatory representation, exclusion and/or repudiation of the language varieties of linguistically minoritized students within schools, alongside the often unquestioned valorization of dominant national languages and/or international languages (such as English), which are also invariably the dominant language(s) of school instruction. In this sense, critical ethnographies of language and education provide a macro critique of the quest for linguistic homogeneity and the normalization of institutionalized monolingualism within modern nation-states – the product of the 'the desirous and quixotic dream' (Gramling, 2016: 9) of the nationalism of the last few centuries (see also Bauman & Briggs, 2003; May, 2012, 2021). This analysis sits alongside a related critique of the commodification and depoliticization of the globalization of English (May, 2015; Pennycook, 1994), exemplified in the ongoing rapid expansion of the ESL/EFL teaching industries worldwide (Phillipson, 2010), exploring the implications of both via micro analyses of their often exclusionary consequences within classrooms.

Or, more accurately perhaps, critical ethnographies of language and education provide a *multiscalar* approach to these issues. They recursively link language ideologies with respect to the relative value of languages – what Liddicoat (2013) describes as linguistic 'hierarchies of prestige' – with actual language use, curriculum policy and related pedagogical practices. In turn, these issues relate to broader processes of globalization and racialization that, more often than not, position the often bi/multilingual linguistic repertoires of linguistically minoritized students as having little or no value. In so doing, dichotomizations between macro and micro language and education policies, monolingualism and bi/

multilingualism, localization and globalization and the related normalized uses (and perceived usefulness) of so-called local and global language varieties are both usefully challenged and deconstructed. In this sense, critical ethnographic work makes overt the links between wider historical and contemporary patterns of linguistic inequity in specific relation to individual, family, classroom and educational language practices – charting the often discriminatory pressures evident within these various language domains for students.

Voice and repertoire

The origins of this kind of research can be traced back to the 1960s and the emergence of the related fields of linguistic ethnography and educational linguistics. Championed by the noted sociolinguist Dell Hymes (1980: 20) (see also McCarty, this volume), ethnographic approaches to language and education within these traditions focused on the illumination of 'diverse ways of speaking' and their *validation* within a wider humanizing, democratizing and anti-hegemonic research stance. What this Hymesian approach foregrounded was the notion of 'voice', in conjunction with its inherent pluralization via the related notion of linguistic 'repertoires'. Voice can be described as 'the capacity to make oneself understood in one's own terms, to produce meanings under conditions of empowerment' (Blommaert, 2013: 22) – something which still regularly eludes linguistically minoritized students in education. Linguistic repertoires 'are an organized complex of specific resources, such as [language] varieties, modes, genres, registers, and styles' (Blommaert, 2013: 13). All of us have access to these complex linguistic repertoires. However, such repertoires often differ markedly both within and across social, racial/ethnic and linguistic groups, depending on wider socialization processes and related opportunities for, or constraints on, language use in specific contexts. For linguistically minoritized students, they also often include bi/multilingual competencies – although, again, the opportunities for such competencies to be recognized and used invariably depend on the wider social and educational contexts in which students find themselves.

Linguistic diversity as deficit or resource?

Critical ethnography is thus particularly apposite for exploring the diversity, complexity, contradictions, contest and (dis)continuities inherent within the actual language practices of students, along with the varied – often discriminatory, sometimes emancipatory – institutionalized educational responses to them. A key point of focus in this work has been the construction of the linguistic diversity of students as (more often) a deficit or (far less often) a resource. The best of this ethnographic work concurrently explores the dynamic, complex dialectic between these two conceptions, as they are situated within educational settings, and related professional (teacher/student) engagement and institutionalized policies and practices. The work is necessarily theoretically eclectic, drawing on a range of critical traditions, as highlighted earlier, while their points of focus inevitably tend to fall on a continuum. At one end is a primary focus on the linguistic discrimination and related marginalization of linguistically minoritized students in educational settings. At the other end is a focus on the processes of dynamic bi/multilingualism – or, more accurately, the use of students' complex bi/multilingual repertoires – as a *counter-insurgent* means of language identity, celebration and reclamation. For heuristic purposes, and to the degree that I can, I will chart these different emphases separately in what follows.

Linguistic discrimination and exclusion in education

Don't act dumb, like ESL students.

(Quoted in Talmy, 2009: 243)

ESL programs, in both compulsory schooling and in tertiary contexts worldwide, have been a particular point of focus for exploring and critiquing the deficit positioning of linguistic minority students in critical ethnographic work. Drawing on his two-and-a-half-year long critical ethnography of ESL students in a Hawaiian public high school, Talmy (2009), for example, traces how ESL students were encouraged by teachers to participate 'respectfully' in the classroom. Such respect was, however, intrinsically linked to monolingual English language teaching and learning norms, in apparent contradistinction to the students' own emergent English abilities and language backgrounds. In the process, the students' bi/multilingualism and their communicative and pragmatic competence as emergent bilinguals were either ignored or, as encapsulated by the teacher's comment above, specifically derided. The result, not surprisingly, was that the ESL students in these classes – a diverse group of students, comprising a fifth of the school's overall population – often felt they 'learned nothing' in their ESL classes. However, as Talmy concludes:

> [T]hey and their classmates [actually] learnt plenty, or at least, there was plenty made available for them to learn: the assimilationist aims of ESL, the deficit-oriented (language) ideologies constituting the stigma of ESL, the valorization of the mainstream [English-medium classrooms], the power of the L2 [second language] teacher to mediate classroom participation through local definitions of respect, the acceptability of so grossly and openly disrespecting ESL. (Talmy, 2009: 250)

Ibrahim's (1999) critical ethnography of the experiences of migrant African students in an urban, French immersion high school in Ontario,

Canada, similarly highlights how teachers regularly construct students' language backgrounds in deficit terms. In Ibrahim's study, there is an added irony, since the focus of teachers often remained on English language ability – widely used by students outside the classroom – despite it being a French-medium schooling context. As one of Ibrahim's participating students, Asma, observes:

> If you don't speak English, like... my Grade 7 [teacher said], 'Oh, so she doesn't speak! Oh, we are sorry, you can explain to her, she doesn't understand English, *la petite*. Can you [help]?' They think we are really stupid, that we are retarded, that we don't understand the language. Now I know English, I speak it all the time. I show them that I understand English [laughs], I show them that I do English. Oh, I got it, it gives me great pleasure. (Ibrahim, 1999: 359)

The emphasis on linguistic performativity (*doing* English), highlighted in Asma's comment, is a key feature of Ibrahim's (1999: 350) study – what he terms more broadly the 'ethnography of performance', drawing on, among others, the work of Butler (1990). This is because his ethnography was one of the first to explore how students identified with Black (African-American) English, primarily via their active engagement with rap and hip-hop, as a result of, and a counter-response to, their highly racialized experiences at this school – of which more later. Meanwhile, both Ibrahim's and Talmy's critical ethnographic studies illustratively foreground the racialized experiences, and the related dismissal of students' linguistic repertoires, as an all too regular discriminatory feature of schooling (see also, e.g. Malsbary, 2014; Zentella, 1997).

This focus on linguistic discrimination, and the repudiation of the language backgrounds of students, builds on earlier, important work in linguistic ethnography. Most notable here, perhaps, are Shirley Brice Heath and Susan Philips's pivotal studies. Heath's (1983) still influential book, *Ways with Words*, was a decade-long ethnographic exploration of the language practices of children among three communities in the Piedmont Carolinas in the United States: Roadville (a working-class White community), Trackton (a working-class Black community) and Maintown (a middle-class Black and White community). Heath's title is significant here for two reasons. The pluralization of 'ways' highlights the multiple language practices evident across the three communities, differentiated by both race and class. Meanwhile, the 'ways with words' metaphor itself extends the Hymesian notion of 'ways of speaking', discussed earlier, to encompass and directly explore its relationship to the acquisition of literacy and related academic success.

Heath found that Trackton and Roadville children were less academically successful, primarily because of their familial language and literacy practices being viewed by teachers as 'divergent' from those expected at school – Trackton because of the predominant use of 'Black English vernacular' and Roadville because of differing, class-based communicative practices. Maintown students were more successful because their middle-class language practices were most closely aligned with those of the school, although middle-class African-American students still did not accrue the same level of educational benefit as their White peers, highlighting the ongoing intersectionality of race, class and language in relation to academic achievement.

Susan Philips (1983) combined macro analysis and microethnography with long-term, in-depth participant observation and interviewing to explore the language practices of Native American children in the Warm Springs Reservation in the US state of Oregon. As with Heath, she found that these children's 'styles of learning' and communicative 'participation structures' in the home differed, at times markedly, from those of the school. Warm Springs Indian children were socialized at home into communicative practices that emphasized listening and observing rather than talking and speaking up, and in voluntary, rather than involuntary, group participation. This contrasted with the emphasis their teachers placed on regular and public verbalization in class as a required demonstration of (successful) learning – a key language practice identified with White, middle-class language practices. Consequently, the reluctance of Warms Springs children to speak in class resulted in subsequent low levels of achievement in verbal competency tests, and a related deficit construction by (White) teachers of their language practices.

The confluence of critical ethnographic studies, such as Talmy's and Ibrahim's, and linguistic ethnographies such as those of Heath and Philips, highlights the regular mismatch between the communicative practices of students from different class and/or racial/ethnic groups and those of the school, where the latter, in fact, represent (and occlude) White middle-class language practices as the norm. As Reyes (2010: 413) observes, these studies effectively 'reveal how ethnic majority groups establish and maintain power by having their speech norms legitimized in institutional settings, such as classrooms. Mainstream practices become accepted as "normal", "proper", and "standard"'.

In contrast, Indigenous and other linguistic minority language practices, and their communicative participation structures, are pathologized and/or dismissed. However, a related development in critical ethnographic work on language and education has been a shift in focus from the disjunctures among these home and school language practices, and their discriminatory consequences for linguistic minority students, toward what schools (and teachers, in particular) can do to (more effectively) bridge them. In so doing, these studies highlight how validating and using home language practices can become a key pedagogical resource for more successful teaching and learning in the classroom for linguistic minority students.

Funds of knowledge

One key framework that has emerged in this regard, and which has since been widely used in critical ethnographic work, focuses on students' and their families' 'funds of knowledge'. Originally developed by Moll *et al.* (1992: 133), funds of knowledge describe 'the historically accumulated and culturally developed bodies of knowledge and skills essential for households and individual functioning and well-being'. Its initial conceptualization arose from Moll *et al.*'s exploration of the family resources of Mexican-American families in Tucson, Arizona, and how these could be used as a basis for local curricular reform.

The researchers elicited everyday household knowledge and practices from local Mexican-American families, and then engaged teachers in the ethnographic study of these family practices. Following from this, teachers developed a more relevant and contextualized curriculum for students from those families. A key dimension of funds of knowledge in Moll *et al.* (1992) and subsequent studies (Gonzáles *et al.*, 2005; Moreno, 2002; Vasquez *et al.*, 1994) are the often fluid and blurred bi/multilingual language practices, and related transnational cultural practices within these linguistic minority Latinx families and communities – what Gutierrez and Rogoff (2003) describe as 'cultural repertoires of practice'. Such cultural repertoires of practice for Latinx families, for example, include *consejos* (advice-giving narratives) and *historias* (stories), both of which differ from normative school-based language practices (Vasquez *et al.*, 1994; Villenas & Foley, 2011; see Nuñez & García-Mateus, this volume).

Funds of knowledge have since been used in conjunction with the development of what have come to be known as asset or resource pedagogies, which specifically acknowledge and value the practices of linguistic minority students, seeing these 'as resources and assets to honor, explore, and extend' (Paris & Alim, 2014: 87). Such asset pedagogies include culturally relevant, culturally responsive and, most recently, culturally sustaining pedagogies. It is beyond the scope of this chapter to engage with the development of these pedagogies over time in any further detail (see Missingham, 2017, for a useful overview), except to say that each development is increasingly informed by CRT, to which I will return. However, by way of a brief example, Alim and Paris (2017: 3) assert that culturally sustaining pedagogy 'asks us to reimagine schools as sites where diverse, heterogeneous [student] practices are not only valued but sustained', and that, in so doing, it seeks 'to perpetuate and foster—to sustain—linguistic, literate, and cultural pluralism as part of schooling for positive social transformation' (Alim & Paris, 2017: 2).

Bilingual education

Another key means by which such educational (and wider social) transformation can perhaps be achieved is via the successful development and implementation of bilingual education. Bilingual education has the potential not only to (re)value students' bi/multilingualism as a basis for teaching and learning, but also to act as a broader counternarrative to the ideology of monolingualism that still underpins much educational delivery worldwide (May, 2014). Critical ethnographies that focus on bilingual education programs thus provide important, rich and much needed pedagogical alternatives to the still regular linguistic marginalization and discrimination of bi/multilingual students discussed in the preceding sections. These ethnographies encompass a focus on both individual school programs and system-wide educational and language policy developments promoting additive forms of bilingual education.

I discussed earlier my three-year ethnographic study of Richmond Road School (May, 1994), informed by Bourdieusian theory, and so will not revisit it again. Other ethnographic studies of progressive bilingual school contexts include Freeman's (1998) account of Oyster Bilingual School in Washington DC, which drew upon a theoretical combination of ethnography and critical discourse analysis to explore the school's trailblazing Spanish–English dual-language program. Teresa McCarty's (2002) 20 year ethnographic engagement with Rough Rock Demonstration School in the Navajo reservation in Arizona is another key exemplar – charting the school's efforts to maintain, and where necessary, revitalize Navajo via the establishment of a Navajo language immersion program within the school. McCarty situates her ethnographic account within the wider context of community-led Indigenous language revitalization efforts which, in the case of Rough Rock, included establishing a publishing center for Navajo curricula, offering initial literacy instruction in Navajo and providing additional summer camps for students, teachers and elders to share in research, storytelling, dramas and art projects on local themes (see also McCarty & Nicholas, 2012; McCarty, this volume).

Indigenous language education has provided a rich locus for critical ethnographic work – although, interestingly, to date much of this work has been situated primarily within the field of language policy rather than education per se. With my colleague, Richard Hill, for example, I have ethnographically explored the role of Māori language immersion pedagogies in relation to both Indigenous language revitalization and their educational effectiveness in improving academic outcomes for Indigenous Māori students in Aotearoa New Zealand (Hill & May, 2011, 2013a, 2013b). Drawing on an ethnography of *Rakaumangamanga*, a combined Māori-medium elementary and high school, we highlight how a high-level additive immersion program in Māori (81%–100% of the school day), alongside a structured approach to the acquisition of academic English, results in the successful achievement of bilingualism and biliteracy for students (the vast majority of whom are first language English speakers or have Māori as their heritage language). Achieving biliteracy is also a key indicator for the wider academic achievement that these students also experience over time (May, 2017).

The effectiveness of additive Indigenous language education programs has also been explored at the macro level of language policy development and via multi-site ethnographic analyses. One of the earliest and most influential of these was Nancy Hornberger's (1988) ethnographic study of bilingual education policy and practice in Puno, Peru, examining the critical role of local schools in Quechua language revitalization. Hornberger's (2006) study was one of the first to highlight how official language policies can open what she later described as 'ideological and implementational spaces' for the development of bi/multilingual education at the local level. However, whether or not these policies are enacted effectively inevitably rests with the decisions of local actors, the degree of local support and the related development and implementation of effective pedagogies and practices in those local contexts. Subsequent studies have continued to explore the interstices of ethnography and language policy development with respect to these macro–micro dialectics in a range of Indigenous language education initiatives internationally, albeit again primarily in relation to the field of language policy (see Hornberger, 2008; May, 1999b, 2013; May & Aikman, 2003; McCarty, 2011).

Dynamic Bilingualism and Everyday Language Practices

These studies consistently highlight the crucial role of bilingual education in the maintenance and/or revitalization of Indigenous and other minoritized languages (May, 2017). However, additive bilingual programs, as their description suggests, still tend to compartmentalize languages – treating them as accretive and discrete. This reflects, in turn, an ongoing monolingual perspective of language learning, even in bilingual education contexts. Monica Heller (1999, 2006) was one of the first to explore this conundrum directly. Heller examined the broader language policy imperatives underpinning French immersion schooling in Canada via a critical ethnography of a French immersion high school in Toronto. She highlighted how the school's strict emphasis on separating languages of instruction, along with its wider aim of achieving an elite, 'balanced' bilingualism in the formal language varieties of French and English, created tensions for students in relation to their own individual language use. Indeed, she found that students' everyday bi/multilingual language practices were far more fluid, dynamic, informal and transgressive than the formal bilingual education context the school accounted for or allowed. Ibrahim (1999), whom I discussed earlier, also highlights these differences in his focus on the everyday use of Black (African-American) English among migrant African students in another French immersion high school in Toronto.

Ibrahim drew specifically (although Heller did not) on Ben Rampton's (1995) notion of 'language crossing' – a key concept that has since informed much sociolinguistic work on bi/multilingual language use. Rampton explored this concept in his ethnographic study of London youth – charting how the young people in his study would regularly cross into a new ethnicity via the use of language practices associated with another ethnic group. Drawing on interactional linguistics (how communication occurs in everyday face-to-face contexts), and methodologically via the use of omnidirectional microphones, he explored 'the ways that [London] youngsters of Asian and Anglo descent used Caribbean-based Creole, the ways Anglos and Caribbeans used Punjabi, and "the way… stylised Asian English"… was used by all three' (Rampton, 1995: 489).

Rampton's (1995) study was neighborhood based, but it has provided an important conceptual and methodological benchmark for subsequent school-based ethnographies focused on language crossing, including in his own later work. Rampton (2006), for example, adopts the same broad conceptual and methodological parameters to explore language practices ethnographically among students in classrooms in Central High, a multiethnic and multilingual London secondary school. By this, he argues:

> [C]lassrooms emerge as sites where day-in-day-out, participants struggle to reconcile themselves to each other, to their futures, to political edicts and to the movements of history, where vernacular aesthetics often provide as much of the momentum as the transmission of knowledge, where the curriculum cohabits with popular music and media culture, where students make hay with the most unrewarding subjects, and where participants wrestle with the meaning of class stratification, their efforts inflected with social ambivalence (and sexual desire). (Rampton, 2006: 3–4)

Rampton examines the students' use of stylization – drawing on Bakhtin's (1981: 362) description of this practice as the production of 'an artistic image of another's language'. As Rampton (2006: 27) observes, 'these accent shifts represent moments of critical reflection on aspects of educational domination and constraint that become interactionally salient on… particular occasion[s]'. These are most clearly demonstrated in Rampton's study on students' regular movement between exaggerated posh (received pronunciation/British standard English) and Cockney (working-class London) accents, both with teachers and each other. In so doing, the students address (and critique) issues of social class, class subjectivities and related social positioning and power relations, within their classroom and in wider educational contexts.

Language crossing has also been explored in the United States via the work of, among others, Mary Bucholtz, Angela Reyes and H. Samy Alim. Bucholtz (1999, 2001) focuses on the language use of 'White kids' in a San Francisco Bay Area school. She explores how some students used Black English to identify with Black cultural practices and associated conceptions of coolness, while others used 'super-standard' English and a related 'nerd' identity, to specifically distance themselves from these same cultural practices. Reyes (2007) combines ethnography and critical discourse analysis to examine how Southeast Asian-American students in the United States form their identities in relation to circulating stereotypes (both positive and negative) of Asian-American pan ethnicity. Via the use of an after-school video project in an alternative education setting, she investigates how these students critique yet also internalize constructions of Asian Americans as 'foreign'. On the one hand, the students criticize how 'mainstream' media films depict Asian newcomers with mock Asian accents and martial arts stereotypes. On the other hand, the students utilize similar Asian stereotypes and 'mock Asian English' in their own videos, particularly in order to differentiate themselves from those they describe as FOB ('fresh off the boat'). As Reyes (2007: 60) observes, while they resented the stereotype of all Asian Americans as foreigners, 'the teens tended to authenticate depictions of recently arrived Asian immigrants as familial reality, allowing them to justify the recirculation of Asian newcomer portrayals in their own teen-created videos'.

Alim's (2004) ethnographic study of the linguistic practices of African-American students at an alternative Northern California high school, Sunnyside High, explores the students' varied uses of African-American English, which Alim termed Black language (BL), influenced by hip-hop and related language style shifting. Alim found that BL was a prominent feature of student language use, but that style shifting was also clearly apparent, particularly when these high school students interacted with students from a prestigious local university. The high school students' varied language practices thus provide a counternarrative to those teachers in the study who continued to view BL in homogeneous and racialized terms vis-à-vis American standard English. The analysis is further informed by Alim's own personal knowledge and command and use of these student language registers, which allows him to interact authentically with the students throughout the course of the study.

Recent Theoretical Orientations: CRT, Translanguaging and Superdiversity

Alim, along with Django Paris (Alim & Paris, 2017; Paris & Alim, 2014), has also been at the forefront of exploring the bi/multilingual language practices of students via CRT and ethnography. Paris's ethnographic study in South Vista, a small charter high school in the California Bay Area, is a key exemplar in this regard. He focused on a small group of African-American, Latinx and Pacific youth, exploring 'their ways with language and text and their forging of ethnic and linguistic identities in the face of continued segregation and racism, in the face of poverty, in the face of a changing community, and in the midst of their high school years' (Paris, 2011: 2). Paris (2011: 16) pays particular attention to these students' 'multiethnic youth space—a social and cultural space centered on youth communication within and across communities'. He explores a continuum of language and textual practices associated with this youth space, ranging from those that maintain ethnic and linguistic exclusion to those that inhabit 'common ground' (Paris, 2011: 18), thus establishing ethnic and linguistic solidarity among students.

Regarding the latter, Paris extends Rampton's notion of language crossing to examine students' language *sharing*. Language sharing focuses on the ratification across ethnic boundaries of momentary and sustained uses of language normally associated with particular ethnic groups (e.g. the use of BL by African-American students or Spanish among Latinx students). A key exemplar of language sharing includes what Paris (2011: 127) describes as 'flowed texts': rap performance texts shared among students that blur and reconstitute the boundaries between students' everyday oral and literate practices. Paris observes that these flowed texts could potentially have been drawn upon as a resource for, and/or a bridge to, the teaching of school-based academic literacies but, as with most such bi/multilingual language practices, were not recognized or mobilized by teachers in any way. As he concludes, 'by silencing the linguistic and textual economy of multiethnic youth space, we are silencing knowledge about language, literacy and plurality' (Paris, 2011: 159), both in classrooms and in wider society (see also Chávez-Moreno, Coles, this volume).

The consistent overlooking of everyday bi/multilingual language practices has also been highlighted in recent related ethnographic work framed by understandings of superdiversity (Blommaert, 2013; Vertovec, 2007), raciolinguistics (Flores & Rosa, 2015; Rosa & Flores, 2017; Caldas, McCarty, this volume) and translanguaging (García, 2009; García & Li, 2014). Superdiversity explores the complex and fluid language practices evident among multiethnic and multilingual populations in major cities worldwide, resulting from increasing migration and transmigration, along with the increasing use of technology to traverse transnational spaces. Raciolinguistics foregrounds the normative influence of Whiteness in the ongoing racialized construction of linguistic minority language practices. Translanguaging explores the pedagogical consequences of drawing on students' dynamic and fluid language practices as a basis for teaching and learning (for recent debates on the merits of translanguaging as a theoretical framework, see MacSwan, 2022; May, 2022).

Methodological innovations

Along with new developments in critical theory, ethnographic work in language and education has also demonstrated a number of key methodological innovations. Paris's (2011: 9) ethnography, for example, was specifically framed within what he terms a humanizing research stance, which 'involve[s] dialogic consciousness-raising and the building of relationships of dignity and care for both researchers and participants'. This emphasis on reciprocity and positionality is a key feature of other critical ethnographic work in this area – see, for example, Hill and May's (2013a) discussion of these issues in relation to ethnographic work in Indigenous language contexts. Paris's study also drew on a combination of methodological approaches, including discourse analysis, the ethnography of communication, linguistic anthropology and quantitative sociolinguistics. Again, this builds on earlier critical ethnographic work in the language and education field that specifically combines qualitative and quantitative analyses (see e.g. Alim, 2004; May, 1994; Zentella, 1997).

Innovative methods have also featured in critical ethnographic work in this field. These include Rampton's (1995, 2006) use of omnidirectional microphones to capture everyday language use in real time, and in both formal classroom and informal youth spaces, as well as his use of retrospective participant commentaries where he asked participants to comment on recorded interactions. Alim (2004: 27) extended the traditional sociolinguistic interview method via his use of the 'semi-structured conversation' (SSC), where he asked his participants to engage in a conversation among themselves about preselected topics, based on his own ethnographic insights. Alim argued that SSCs were methodological advancements that allowed for more free-flowing 'natural' interactions to occur. The use of counter-stories has been a prominent feature of recent critical ethnographies on language and education that draw on a CRT/BlackCrit framework (see e.g. Caldas, 2018; Kinloch *et al.*, 2017; Malsbary, 2014; see also Coles, this volume), as has the use of *historias* and *testimonios* (Villenas & Foley, 2011; also Nuñez & García-Mateus, this volume) in LatCrit.

Caldas (2018, this volume) also foregrounds the use of drama and performance ethnography in her explorations of bilingual student teachers' identity and advocacy development. Finally, the role and use of photo methods, social media and digital ethnography, while still relatively underutilized, are gaining traction in critical ethnographies focused on language and education (see Boucher, 2017; Gallagher *et al.*, 2013; James & Busher, 2013; Reyes, 2007; Thorne & May, 2017).

All these developments highlight both the ongoing saliency and the significance of critical ethnography as a key methodological contribution in exploring questions of language, race/ism, in/equity and education. This is especially so in light of the ongoing dominance of the ideologies of public and educational monolingualism, which continue to shape and constrain the education that linguistically minoritized students experience – foisting the dominant language on these students, while concomitantly ignoring and/or disavowing their individual bi/multilingual language repertoires (May, 2014). These monolingual ideologies within education are further exacerbated by the increasingly pervasive influence of English as the currently ascendant world language. The hegemony of English acts here to sediment existing linguistic hierarchies at all levels: from the macro (via globalization and nation-state language policies), the meso (local education policies; school boards) to the micro (tertiary and compulsory education classrooms). Critical ethnographies that focus on the racialized experiences of linguistically minoritized students in education aim to address, and contest, the silencing of bi/multilingual students at all three levels – not only by supporting their 'diverse ways of speaking' but also in their 'speaking back to power'.

References

Alim, H.S. (2004) *You Know my Steez: An Ethnographic and Sociolinguistic Study of Styleshifting in a Black American Speech Community*. Durham, NC: Duke University Press.

Alim, H.S. and Paris, D. (2017) What is culturally sustaining pedagogy and why does it matter? In D. Paris and H.S. Alim (eds) *Culturally Sustaining Pedagogies: Teaching and Learning for Justice in a Changing World* (pp. 1–21). New York: Teachers College Press.

Alim, H.S., Reyes, A. and Kroskrity, P. (eds) (2020) *The Oxford Handbook of Language and Race*. New York: Oxford University Press.

Baker-Bell, A. (2020) Dismantling anti-Black linguistic racism in English language arts classrooms: Toward an anti-racist Black language pedagogy. *Theory into Practice* 59 (1), 8–21.

Bakhtin, M. (1981) *The Dialogic Imagination: Four Essays* (trans. M. Holquist). Austin, TX: University of Texas Press.

Bauman, R. and Briggs, C. (2003) *Voices of Modernity: Language Ideologies and the Politics of Inequality*. Cambridge: Cambridge University Press.

Berlant, L. (2011) *Cruel Optimism*. Durham, NC: Duke University Press.

Bernal, D. (2002) Critical race theory, Latino critical theory, and critical raced-gendered epistemologies: Recognizing students of color as holders and creators of knowledge. *Qualitative Inquiry* 8 (1), 105–126.

Blommaert, J. (2013) *Ethnography, Superdiversity and Linguistic Landscapes: Chronicles of Complexity*. Bristol: Multilingual Matters.

Boucher, M. (2017) The art of observation: Issues and potential of using photo-methods in critical ethnography with adolescents. *International Journal of Adult Vocational Education and Technology* 8 (2), 1–15.

Brayboy, B.M.J. (2005) Toward a tribal critical race theory in education. *The Urban Review* 37 (5), 425–446. https://doi.org/10.1007/s11256-005-0018-y

Bucholtz, M. (1999) You da man: Narrating the racial other in the production of white masculinity. *Journal of Sociolinguistics* 3 (4), 443–460.

Bucholtz, M. (2001) The whiteness of nerds: Superstandard English and racial markedness. *Journal of Linguistic Anthropology* 11 (1), 84–100.

Butler, J. (1990) *Gender Trouble: Feminism and the Subversion of Identity*. New York: Routledge.

Caldas, B. (2018) 'More meaningful to do it than just reading it': Rehearsing praxis among Mexican-American/Latinx pre-service teachers. *Teaching Education* 29 (4), 370–382.

Cazden, C. (1989) Richmond Road: A multilingual/multicultural primary school in Auckland, New Zealand. *Language and Education, An International Journal* 3, 143–166.

Corson, D. (1990) *Language Policy Across the Curriculum*. Clevedon: Multilingual Matters.
Dumas, M. and ross, K.M. (2016) 'Be real Black for me': Imagining BlackCrit in education. *Urban Education* 51 (4), 415–442.
Fitzpatrick, K. and May. S. (2015) Doing critical educational ethnography with Bourdieu. In M. Murphy and C. Costa (eds) *Theory as Method in Research: On Bourdieu, Social Theory and Education* (pp. 101–114). Oxford: Routledge.
Fitzpatrick, K. and May, S. (2022) *Critical Ethnography and Education*. New York: Routledge.
Flores, N. and Rosa, J. (2015) Undoing appropriateness: Raciolinguistic ideologies and language diversity in education. *Harvard Educational Review* 85, 149–171.
Freeman, R. (1998) *Bilingual Education and Social Change*. Clevedon: Multilingual Matters.
Gallagher, K., Wessels, A. and Ntelioglou, B. (2013) Becoming a networked public: Digital ethnography, youth and global research collectives. *Ethnography and Education* 8 (2), 177–193.
García, O. (2009) *Bilingual Education in the 21st Century: A Global Perspective*. New York: Blackwell/Wiley.
García, O. and Li, W. (2014) *Translanguaging: Language, Bilingualism and Education*. Basingstoke: Palgrave Macmillan.
González, N., Moll, L. and Amanti, C. (eds) (2005) *Funds of Knowledge: Theorizing Practices in Households and Classrooms*. Mahwah, NJ: Lawrence Erlbaum.
Gramling, D. (2016) *The Invention of Monolingualism*. New York: Bloomsbury Academic.
Grenfell, M. and Pahl, K. (2018) *Bourdieu, Language-Based Ethnographies and Reflexivity: Putting Theory into Practice*. New York: Routledge.
Grenfell, M., Bloom, D., Hardy, C., Pahl, K., Rosswell, J. and Street, B. (2012) *Language, Ethnography and Education: Bridging New Literacy Studies and Bourdieu*. New York: Routledge.
Gutierrez, K. and Rogoff, B. (2003) Cultural ways of learning: Cultural traits or repertoires of practice. *Educational Research* 32, 19–35.
Heath, S. (1983) *Ways with Words: Language, Life, and Work in Communities and Classrooms*. Cambridge: Cambridge University Press.
Heller, M. (1999) Heated language in a cold climate. In J. Blommaert (ed.) *Language Ideological Debates* (pp. 143–170). Berlin: Mouton de Gruyter.
Heller, M. (2006) *Linguistic Minorities and Modernity* (2nd edn). London: Longman.
Heller, M. (2008) Doing ethnography. In W. Li and M.G. Moyer (eds) *The Blackwell Guide to Research Methods in Bilingualism and Multilingualism* (pp. 249–262). Oxford: Blackwell.
Hermes, M., Bang, M. and Marin, A. (2012) Designing indigenous language revitalization. *Harvard Educational Review* 82 (3), 381–402.
Hill, R. and May, S. (2011) Exploring biliteracy in Māori-medium education: An ethnographic perspective. In T. McCarty (ed.) *Ethnography in Language Policy* (pp. 161–184). New York: Routledge.
Hill, R. and May, S. (2013a) Non-indigenous researchers in indigenous language education: Ethical implications. *International Journal of the Sociology of Language* 219 (1), 47–65.
Hill, R. and May, S. (2013b) Balancing the languages in Māori-medium education in Aotearoa/New Zealand. In V. Zenotz, D. Gorter and J. Cenoz (eds) *Minority Languages and Multilingual Education* (pp. 171–189). Berlin: Springer.
Hornberger, N. (1988) *Bilingual Education and Language Maintenance: A Southern Peruvian Quechua Case*. Dordrecht: Foris.
Hornberger, N.H. (2006) Nichols to NCLB: Local and global perspectives on US language education policy. In O. García, T. Skutnabb-Kangas and M.E. Torres-Guzmán (eds)

Imagining Multilingual Schools: Languages in Education and Glocalization (pp. 223–237). Clevedon: Multilingual Matters.
Hornberger, N.H. (ed.) (2008) *Can Schools Save Indigenous Languages?* London: Palgrave Macmillan.
Hymes, D. (1980) *Language in Education: Ethnolinguistic Essays*. Washington, DC: Center for Applied Linguistics.
Ibrahim, A. (1999) Becoming Black: Rap and hip-hop, race, gender, identity, and the politics of ESL learning. *TESOL Quarterly* 33 (3), 349–369.
James, N. and Busher, H. (2013) Researching hybrid learning communities in the digital age through educational ethnography. *Ethnography and Education* 8 (2), 194–209.
Kinloch, V., Burkhard, T. and Penn, C. (2017) When school is not enough: Understanding the lives and literacies of Black youth. *Research in the Teaching of English* 52 (1), 34–54.
Liddicoat, A.J. (2013) *Language-in-Education Policies: The Discursive Construction of Intercultural Relations*. Bristol: Multilingual Matters.
MacSwan, J. (ed.) (2022) *Multilingual Perspectives on Translanguaging*. Bristol: Multilingual Matters.
Malsbary, C. (2014) 'Will this hell never end?': Substantiating and resisting race-language policies in a multilingual high school. *Anthropology & Education Quarterly* 45 (4), 373–390.
May, S. (1994) *Making Multicultural Education Work*. Clevedon: Multilingual Matters.
May, S. (1995) Deconstructing traditional discourses of schooling. *Language and Education* 5, 1–29.
May, S. (1998) On what might have been: Some reflections on critical multiculturalism. In G. Shacklock and J. Smyth (eds) *Being Reflexive in Critical Educational and Social Research* (pp. 159–170). London: Falmer Press.
May, S. (ed.) (1999a) *Critical Multiculturalism: Rethinking Multicultural and Antiracist Education*. London: Falmer Press.
May, S. (ed.) (1999b) *Indigenous Community-Based Education*. Clevedon: Multilingual Matters.
May, S. (2012) *Language and Minority Rights: Ethnicity, Nationalism and the Politics of Language* (2nd edn). New York: Routledge.
May, S. (2013) Indigenous immersion education: International developments. *Journal of Immersion and Content-Based Education* 1 (1) 34–69.
May, S. (2014) *The Multilingual Turn: Implications for SLA, TESOL and Bilingual Education*. New York: Routledge.
May, S. (2015) The problem with English(es) and linguistic (in)justice. *Critical Review of International Social and Political Philosophy* 18 (2), 131–148.
May, S. (2016) Language, imperialism and the modern nation-state system: Implications for language rights. In O. García and N. Flores (eds) *Oxford Handbook on Language and Society* (pp. 35–53). Oxford: Oxford University Press.
May, S. (2017) Bilingual education: What the research tells us. In O. García, A. Lin and S. May (eds) *Bilingual/Multilingual Education. Encyclopedia of Language and Education* (3rd edn, pp. 81–100). New York: Springer.
May, S. (2021) Rethinking the principle of linguistic homogeneity in the age of superdiversity. In Y-Y. Tan and P. Mishra (eds) *Language, Nations, and Multilingualism: Questioning the Herderian Ideal* (pp. 37–53). New York: Routledge.
May, S. (2022) Afterword: The multilingual turn, superdiversity and translanguaging: The rush from heterodoxy to orthodoxy. In J. MacSwan (ed.) *Multilingual Perspectives on Translanguaging* (pp. 343–355). Bristol: Multilingual Matters.
May, S. and Aikman, S. (2003) Indigenous education: Addressing current issues and developments. *Comparative Education* 39 (2), 139–145.

May, S. and Sleeter, C. (eds) (2010) *Critical Multiculturalism: Theory and Praxis*. New York: Routledge.
May, S. and Fitzpatrick, K. (2019) Critical ethnography. In P. Atkinson, S. Delamont, A. Cernat, J. Sakshaug and R. Williams (eds) *Sage Research Methods Foundations*. London: Sage Publications.
McCarty, T. (2002) *A Place to be Navajo: Rough Rock and the Struggle for Self-determination in Indigenous Schooling*. Mahwah, NJ: Routledge.
McCarty, T. (ed.) (2011) *Ethnography and Language Policy*. New York: Routledge.
McCarty, T. (2014) Ethnography in educational linguistics. In M. Bigelow and J. Ennser-Kananen (eds) *The Routledge Handbook of Educational Linguistics* (pp. 23–37). New York: Routledge.
McCarty, T. and Nicholas, S. (2012) Indigenous education: Local and global perspectives. In M. Martin-Jones, A. Blackledge and A. Creese (eds) *The Routledge Handbook of Multilingualism* (pp. 145–166). New York: Routledge.
Missingham, B. (2017) Asset-based learning and the pedagogy of community development. *Community Development* 48 (3), 339–350.
Moll, L.C., Amanti, C., Neff, D. and Gonzáles, N. (1992) Funds of knowledge for teaching: Using a qualitative approach to connect homes and classrooms. *Theory into Practice* 31, 132–141.
Moreno, J. (2002) The long-term outcomes of Puente. *Educational Policy* 16 (4), 572–587.
Palmer, D. (2011) The discourse of transition: Teachers' language ideologies within transitional bilingual education programs. *International Multilingual Research Journal* 5 (2), 103–122.
Paris, D. (2011) *Language across Difference: Ethnicity, Communication, and Youth Identities in Changing Urban Schools*. Cambridge: Cambridge University Press.
Paris, D. and Alim, H.S. (2014) What are we seeking to sustain through culturally sustaining pedagogy? A loving critique forward. *Harvard Educational Review* 84 (1), 85–100.
Pennycook, A. (1994) *The Cultural Politics of English as an International Language*. Harlow: Longman.
Philips, S. (1983) *The Invisible Culture: Communication in Classroom and Community on the Warm Springs Indian Reservation*. Prospect Heights, IL: Waveland.
Phillipson, R. (2010) *Linguistic Imperialism Continued*. London: Routledge.
Rampton, B. (1995) *Crossing: Language and Ethnicity among Adolescents*. Harlow: Longman.
Rampton, B. (2006) *Language in Late Modernity: Interaction in an Urban School*. Cambridge: Cambridge University Press.
Reyes, A. (2007) *Language, Identity and Stereotype among Southeast Asian American Youth: The Other Asian*. Mahwah, NJ: Lawrence Erlbaum Associates.
Reyes, A. (2010) Language and ethnicity. In N.H. Hornberger and S.L. McKay (eds) *Sociolinguistics and Language Education* (pp. 398–426). Bristol: Multilingual Matters.
Rosa, J. and Flores, N. (2017) Unsettling race and language: Toward a raciolinguistic perspective. *Language in Society* 46, 621–647.
Smith, L.T. (2012) *Decolonizing Methodologies: Research and Indigenous Peoples* (2nd edn). London: Zed Books.
Talmy, S. (2009) A very important lesson: Respect and the socialization of order(s) in high school ESL. *Linguistics and Education* 20 (3), 235–253.
Thorne, S. and May, S. (eds) (2017) *Language and Technology. Encyclopedia of Language and Education* (3rd edn). New York: Springer.
Vasquez, O., Pease-Alvarez, L. and Shannon, S. (1994) *Pushing Boundaries: Language and Culture in a Mexicano Community*. Cambridge: Cambridge University Press.

Vertovec, S. (2007) Super-diversity and its implications. *Ethnic and Racial Studies* 30, 1024–1054.

Villenas, S. and Foley, D. (2002) Chicano/Latino critical ethnography of education: Borderlands cultural productions from *la Fonterra*. In R. Valencia (ed.) *Chicano School Failure and Success: Past, Present and Future* (2nd edn, pp. 195–226). London: RoutledgeFalmer.

Villenas, S. and Foley, D. (2011) Critical ethnographies of education in the Latino/a diaspora. In R. Valencia (ed.) *Chicano School Failure and Success: Past, Present and Future* (3rd edn, pp. 175–196). London: RoutledgeFalmer.

Zentella, A.C. (1997) *Growing Up Bilingual: Puerto Rican Children in New York*. Oxford: Blackwell.

2 Beyond Silence: Disrupting Antiblackness through BlackCrit Ethnography and Black Youth Voice

Justin A. Coles

'We Killed Our Children': Reflections on Antiblackness and Implications for Education Research

During the spring of 2017, I had the opportunity to visit the National Museum of African American History and Culture (NMAAHC) in Washington, DC. Level C3, 'Defending Freedom, Defining Freedom: The Era of Segregation 1876–1968', houses the Emmett Till Memorial. At the center of the curation lies the original casket in which Emmett Till was buried. In the summer of 1955, Emmett Till, a Black boy, left his home in Chicago, Illinois, for Money, Michigan, for a two-week vacation visiting his relatives (Harold & DeLuca, 2005). While visiting Bryant's Grocer and Meat Market in Money with several teenaged relatives, Emmett uttered words such as 'goodbye baby' and whistled to Carolyn Bryant, a White woman staffing the store. That evening, two White men, Roy Bryant (husband to Carolyn) and John William (JW) Milan (Roy's half-brother) kidnapped Emmett from his Uncle Mose Wright's home. Three days after the kidnapping, a boy named Rodger Hodges saw Emmett's knees and feet surfacing in the Tallahatchie river (Tyson, 2017). When officials retrieved Emmett's body, which was in the river for approximately two days, resulting in bloating and decomposition, it was clear that he had been tortured. His body was found naked and badly beaten; with a cotton gin tied around his neck, his eyes out of their sockets and a bullet hole in his head (Anderson, 2015). Bryant and Milan were found not guilty at the trial for Emmett's murder, making Till's death a huge miscarriage of justice, serving as a major impetus for the civil rights movement of the 1950s and 1960s (Hudson-Weems, 1994).

During my visit, the line to see Emmett's casket extended well beyond the memorial entryway, wrapping around the showroom floor. A quick observation revealed to me that a majority of the people in line at the time were Black, like myself. Entering the memorial was also different from other parts of the museum, as there was a docent at the entryway who periodically repeated the rules of entry, which included things such as no photography and keeping hands off the casket. I remember thinking to myself, 'why would anyone want to touch the casket?'. There was a stillness, a calmness throughout the entire time I was waiting to enter the room where the casket was on display. It almost felt that we had all been transported to 1955 to Roberts Temple Church of God in Chicago, and were actually preparing to view Emmett's body in real time. I suddenly found myself emotional.

I learned about the story of Emmett throughout my childhood and countless other horrors Black youth, adults and communities experienced at the hands of antiblackness. In this moment, however, I was on the precipice of directly confronting a highly visible example of anti-Black violence in US history, which facilitated a wave of shock through my body. Such a gross and definitive moment of overt antiblackness was about to become tangible. I began to think that maybe the rule prohibiting people from touching the casket was not a silly one after all, because as the emotional shock rolled through my body I had an intense desire to touch the casket, as if there was some inexplicable gravitational pull. Whether I imagined the pull or not, I did find myself leaning in, desiring the casket to speak, or rather thinking that I might actually hear Emmett's incorporeal being speak out to me. In the midst of this moment and these feelings, I wondered why no other particular part of the museum caused such a gathering or required a designated docent, for all of the museum is truly marvelous. I also wondered why I felt no other part of the museum pulling me toward it, as Emmett's casket. However, as I drew closer to the casket, the popular image of Emmett taken at his open-casket funeral at the request of his mother, began to resolve my wonderings. It dawned on me that Emmett was a Black *child* whose future was brutally robbed by antiblackness, characterized, especially in this case, as the complete lack of regard for Black humanity, Black life. Perhaps, all of the museum-goers, waiting up to an hour in line, needed to see the vessel which held Emmett's destroyed body. Perhaps, I waited in line to be reminded, or rather to remind myself, that at the center of this complex tapestry of Black history and culture on display was the fact that in the United States, Black children *still* exist in a social context dictated by antiblackness that can result in the destruction of their being, which can play out in a myriad of ways.

Although it may sound rather strange, my exact viewing of the casket, once it was finally my turn, is actually quite hazy. Perhaps I was so caught up in the emotion of it all that I somehow transcended briefly to such an intense period of reflection on what it meant to be Black in the US, the world, that I was somehow present, but not present at all. Maybe I was blinded by the illusory likeness of Emmett once I finally leaned toward the casket and imagined what this Black child must have felt, must have looked like in the moments before his death. Or perhaps,

I was under the spell of a sort of Black, ancestral magic trick that can only be facilitated by one directly confronting the Black past, while very much living in the present: It felt as if I was in an in-between space that would allow me to engage in true reflection by briefly detaching from the continuum of antiblackness that existed well before Emmett's death and that will exist into the foreseeable future. When I emerged from the viewing, I felt as if I could breathe again and that I was back in the real world. Although the Black past can be painful and, in this case, suffocating, confronting it was a necessity that I would not know I needed until I emerged from that space. Marable (2006: 4) detailed that for Black people, 'the past is not simply prologue; it is indelibly part of the fabric of our collective destiny'. After leaving this space, I immediately felt the importance of understanding antiblackness, which 'operates on visceral and affective registers' (Myers, 2017), as a sociostructural regime that has worked to dictate social life in the US for Black and non-Black peoples (Hart, 2018; Sharpe, 2016; Vargas, 2018; Yancy, 2016). Furthermore, this experience prompted me to consider how I might better leverage critiques of antiblackness in conducting research with Black children and communities. When speaking of the museum's choice to include Emmett's casket, the museum's deputy director, Kinshasha Holman Conwill, explained, 'What this museum is going to do is make sure that America remembers that, at one point—and unfortunately some of that still goes on—we killed our children' (Thompson, 2016). The casket was an attack on the historical amnesia of the US. Kinshasha was right in that, after Emmett, Black children have continued to be on the receiving end of deathly anti-Black violence across the decades. For example, I have previously connected the deaths of Emmett Till (1955), Latasha Harlins (1991) and Trayvon Martin (2012) to expose the ways antiblackness operationalizes across time and space to cause disproportionate hurt and harm to Black youth (Coles, 2018). Herein lies a point of major importance for centering critiques of antiblackness when conducting research with Black children in the US: Antiblackness is not a metaphorical phenomenon that is meant merely to refer to unfair treatment against Black people, but rather a literal racial regime that 'dislodges brains, blocks airways, rips muscle, extracts organs, cracks bones, breaks teeth' (Coates, 2015: 10).

In conjunction with the physical violence that antiblackness enacts against Black children, there also exists a more diffuse and symbolic violence (Bourdieu, 2001), which is particularly helpful here as I consider the presence of antiblackness, which does not always result in physical death, in the social and educational experiences of Black youth. As I have written elsewhere:

> Pedagogic actions in schools serve as one of the main extensions of symbolic violence... Schools and the teachers housed there impose meaning

> on students, rarely stopping to consider how various student populations may make sense of the knowledge being imposed upon them differently. In some cases, the difference of meanings constructed due to the varying epistemologies of students that may not directly align with the schools can be so drastic that harm is done to students who cannot understand or connect with the meaning imposed by the cultural arbitrary. (Coles, 2016: 24–25)

When considering physical and symbolic forms of antiblackness, it can be deduced that those working with Black youth in research and/or in practice have a responsibility not to simply acknowledge antiblackness, but also to provide the time and environs necessary for counter-structures to antiblackness to be constructed and sustained. What might it mean for researchers and educators of Black youth to not only be concerned with what happens with Black youth in schools and classrooms, but to also be attentive to how the social context of the US directly organizes the ways Black youth are dis/engaged and mis/educated in their school settings? In other words, how do we commit ourselves to become researchers of both school and society, always seeing the two as inextricably linked and bi-directional? In this chapter, I respond to these questions by sharing my use of a Black critical theory (BlackCrit) (Dumas & ross, 2016) guided critical race ethnography with nine Black urban high school youth as one potential way forward. In sharing my enactments of BlackCrit ethnography, my goal is to reveal how it provides the necessary theoretical and practical methodological space/s to fully immerse myself in the lifeworlds of youth in ways that center their Black-specific languages and literacies. It is my assertion that ethnographies of Black specificity allow Black youths' individual and collective voices to inform how researchers and educators can reorient the ways we think about race and urban schooling.

Moving Beyond Silence to Hear Our Children in Research

As I further reflected on my visit to the NMAAHC and my viewing of Emmett's casket, which is now five years ago, I was propelled to think about what research looks like with Black youth in the US that is precisely attentive to the myriad ways antiblackness is enacted against Black youth in their social and educational lives. Moreover, I began to think about what it means to engage in such research, intentionally centering the voices – the rich languages and literacies – of Black youth, given that these voices have been historically marginalized and invisibilized through the oppression of antiblackness (Kirkland, 2013). For example, earlier I mentioned that I may have been leaning into Emmett's casket due to some underlying desire to *hear* him, whatever that might have meant in that moment. The silencing of Emmett's voice, and more so, the silencing of his life challenged me to engage in research with more political intentions (Quantz, 1992), particularly understanding the urgency in research that sees Black youth lived experience, as explicated from their voice, as essential to educational scholarship that truly seeks to fight toward justice and equity for Black children and communities. With this urgency in mind, I build alongside Black scholars and youth workers such as Lyiscott (2020: 259), who explains, 'For educators committed to racial equity with an understanding of the enduring systemic violences that continue to threaten Black lives, sustaining fugitive literacy practices—where youth develop the tools to liberate themselves from Whiteness and anti-Blackness—is crucial'. My desire and belief in the necessity to hear Black youth drive my research.

To engage in such liberatory research, during the 2016–2017 academic school year, I engaged in what I refer to as an urban BlackCrit ethnography, with nine Black boys and girls at an urban high school in Philadelphia, Pennsylvania (see Coles, 2019, 2020). My primary intention behind the larger ethnographic study was to better understand the organizing role of antiblackness in the societal and educational lives of the nine Black youth, as gathered from their dynamic language and literacy practices in order to (1) put forth a youth-informed understanding of antiblackness in P-12 US urban educational scholarship; and (2) develop pedagogical, curricular and school environmental counter-structures to antiblackness in urban education based on these youth's lived experiences and retellings of antiblackness. The research questions from the larger ethnography that guided my explorations included: 'What understandings of antiblackness emerge through Black youth's critical engagements with literacy?' and 'How do Black youth's understandings of antiblackness through critical engagements with literacy function as resistance to antiblackness?' In this chapter, I reserve space to detail the utility of pairing BlackCrit ethnography with the study of Black youth languages and literacies as a means toward critical race educational praxis (Knaus, 2009). My goal here is to speak about the utility of BlackCrit ethnography when conducting critical ethnographic work with Black youth and their languages and literacies, specifically.

On Silencing and Antiblackness: Unpacking Critical Race Praxis with Black Youth

The US is a country that has historically engaged Black youth through the logics of antiblackness, which Dumas (2016: 8) has described as the 'disgust and disdain for Black bodies, a refusal to acknowledge Black peoples as Human, and worthy of regard, recognition, and resources'. And its schools, in particular, have long perpetuated and sustained the silencing of Black youth voices (Coles & Powell, 2020; Feierman & Sawyer, 2019; Fine, 1987; Ginwright, 2007; Sosa, 2019).

Here, I position Black youth's literacies or how Black youth communicate through various uses of words, images, their bodies and countless other texts in the world (Coles, 2019), modes of communicating voice, as a prime tool to disrupt anti-Black silencing. I do this because 'the study of literacy quite literally means to search past silences, to listen to the behaviors of words as they perform meaning in people's lives' (Kirkland, 2013: 9). As detailed by Montoya (2000: 265), concerns with 'silence and silencing have been among other linguistic concepts that have already appeared in the writings of Race Crits', especially those that have explored 'the relationship between language and subordination'. Scholars of race crits, stemming from the broad terrain of critical race theory (CRT), have leveraged the languages and literacies of vulnerable racial populations through methods of narrative and storytelling to convey 'personal racialized experiences but also as a way of countering the metanarratives—the images, preconceptions, and myths—that have been propagated by the dominant culture of hegemonic Whiteness as a way of maintaining racial inequality' (Trevino *et al.*, 2008: 8). Through the leveraging of voices, critical theories of race help 'provide us with a better understanding of the multi-dimensionality of racism in America' (Trevino *et al.*, 2008: 8). CRT directly 'enables scholars to ask the important question of what racism has to do with inequities in education in unique ways', through the enactment of methods that scrutinize 'the insights, concerns, and questions students of color have about their educational experiences, whether they are in elementary school or graduate programs' (Howard & Navarro, 2016: 258).

Understanding the varying dimensions of racism in the US becomes a necessity when analyzing education in that social institutions bent toward Whiteness mean that 'the voices of White youth are more likely to be supported in schools, while the voices of minority youth are more likely to be suppressed' (Curtis, 2019: 415). Specifically relevant to the focus of Black youth voices, a 'focus on expression of voice and narrative by students who are intentionally silenced by the everyday practices of schooling in the US' is what makes CRT praxis (Knaus, 2009: 142). According to Yamamoto (1997: 829–830), the central organizing ideal of critical race praxis 'is that racial justice requires antisubordination practice... justice is something experienced through practice'. In my work with the languages and literacies of Black youth to explicate critiques of antiblackness, critical race praxis then is about how the youth actually *experience*, not just imagine, justice through the process of centering their lived realities in order to understand and resist antiblackness. To arrive at justice, Yamamoto (1997) detailed that critical race praxis can be understood, more specifically as an

> [E]nhanced attention to theory translation and deeper engagement with frontline action... increased attention to a critical rethinking of what

> race is, how civil rights are conceived, and why law sometimes operates discursively as a power strategy… it may encompass a critical reframing of and engagement with racialized practices. (Yamamoto, 1997: 874)

Through utilizing BlackCrit in researching with the languages and literacies of Black youth, I demonstrate how we can reframe the ways we all come to know and understand antiblackness by directly centering the voices of the youth who exist on the frontline of the regime every day. Thus, my pairing of BlackCrit (a Black-specific race crit) to disrupt the silences of Black youth voice, via their languages and literacies, proves to be a theoretically and methodologically sound pairing for continuing the work of youth voice in critical race scholarship.

Citing the work of Patricia Williams (1995), Montoya (2000: 265) notes that, while the complete 'silence of African Americans has been broken and their story of being spoken for is over, the struggle now is to give their stories "a hearing of [their] own" so they are not merely the ironic sound of "silent voice[s]"'. However, despite the ways Black communities have fought against anti-Black systems to speak for themselves and to have a *hearing of their own*, the oppressive nature of schooling can still work to marginalize the voices of Black children (Johnson *et al.*, 2017) while maintaining Black abjection and dispossession (Givens, 2016). In other words, although Black people do have agency to assert their voice in ways that 'are inherently antithetical to the social suffering perpetuated by antiblackness' (Coles, 2019: 5), the ability for antiblackness to facilitate silencing still remains. For example, when discussing mainstream media's bent toward White supremacy and antiblackness, Baker-Bell *et al.* (2017: 136) detail the ways the media's construction of 'images that promote racial inferiority contributes to a lack of empathy for Black life. Through this lack of empathy, society becomes desensitized to Black suffering and Black humanity'. While the silencing of Black youth voice may not immediately come to mind when we think of media dissemination, such anti-Black distortions of our reality that seek to warp our sense of empathy toward Black people are wholly a matter of silencing. If you cannot empathize with someone, you cannot see them or hear them. Through the ways the mainstream media distorts Black *and* non-Black people's perceptions of Black people, we render Black lived experiences, and simultaneously Black voices, as not worthy of being heard. In particular, the ways we all become desensitized to the anti-Black violence experienced by Black people, and Black youth, fuses into what we expect from US social practice, becoming 'part of the normal order of business' (Baker-Bell *et al.*, 2017: 136). I suggest BlackCrit ethnography as one way to disrupt how antiblackness becomes accepted as business as usual in the lives of Black youth in school and society.

Black Youth Literacies as Anti-Black Interceptive and Facilitator of Change

In her work with adolescent-aged Black girls, Richardson (2007: 806) came to the conclusion that Black youth possess the knowledge that makes them aware of dominating forces that seek to oppress them and that such knowledge 'acknowledges marginalized lives in certain lifeworld domains that are overlooked or devalued by the dominant society'. While Black youth possess such knowledge of oppressive forces, such as antiblackness, they may not always be given the space to unpack and think through this knowledge in safe and affirming ways, which can often lead to them internalizing their oppression or seeing it as a result of their own doing. Despite not always having spaces to detail the ways oppression operationalizes in their lives, this knowledge is still present in Black youth as it is informed by their body epistemologies or the production of knowledge in the body that arises from lived experiences (Butler, 2018; Cruz, 2001; Moraga & Anzaldúa, 1983). For example, policies and practices that traditionally benefit White students and victimize Black students, such as 'biased curriculum; standardized testing, ability grouping, disproportionate rates of suspension, detention, and expulsion; and inadequate school funding', are positioned as race neutral, leaving Black youth to believe that their Blackness is a problem, not the actual racism of schooling (Donaldson, 1996). To counter this, Richardson (2007: 807) explains that 'our critical pedagogies must guide them beyond challenging to *changing* [emphasis added] systems that tolerate inequality, sexism, and racism'. As Freire (2000: 47) explained, 'to surmount the situation of oppression, people must first critically recognize its causes, so that through transforming action they can create a new situation, one which makes possible the pursuit of a fuller humanity'. Moreover, Richardson (2007: 807) suggests that we create new situations for fuller humanity by looking 'deeply into the everyday lives and language of our youth', because 'doing so may be a first step in facilitating societal change'. In line with Richardson (2007), I argue that tapping into the power of one's own languages and literacies leads to the direct change of one's situation, such change that is directly representative of critical race praxis – achieving true justice via practical changes.

Given the importance of youth voice to acting as a pathway to change, any attempt to suppress the languages and literacies of Black youth is an act of aggression intended to sustain, rather than mitigate, racial inequity. For example, social science researchers have extensively documented the ways enslaved Blacks were denied access to the tools that would develop and advance their literacy (Anderson, 2004; Cornelius, 1983; Gundaker, 2007; Mitchell, 2008; Muhammad, 2019; Williams, 2009); the institution of slavery benefitted from the suppression of Black voices and bodies. According to Fine (1987: 157), 'silencing signifies a terror of words, a fear of talk'. Whites had a terror for the words of the enslaved because 'the very act of learning to read and write subverted the master–slave relationship' (Williams, 2009: 7). There is power to be maintained in silencing. Within a social context dictated by antiblackness, if Black people are not silenced, there is a fear that racist societal conditions will change and disrupt the racial hierarchy of the US. With this knowledge, in the face of this suppression, Blacks understood that the development of their literacy was essential 'to the individual and collective elevation of their people', and would lead to 'solid citizenship and socioeconomic ability' (Martin, 1998: 42). Current social science researchers have continued to document the ways language and literacy have served as a site of anti-Black suppression. Namely, Baker-Bell (2020: 9) explains that even when Black people engage in the richness of their own Black-centric language practices (e.g. African-American vernacular English), they are routinely silenced by *anti-Black linguistic racism*, which she defines as 'the linguistic violence, persecution, dehumanization, and marginalization that Black Language (BL) speakers endure when using their language in schools and in everyday life'. Baker-Bell (2020) further details anti-Black linguistic racism as

> [T]eachers' silencing, correcting, and policing students when they communicate in BL. It is the belief that there is something inherently wrong with BL; therefore, it should be eradicated. It is denying Black students the right to use their native language as a linguistic resource during their language and literacy learning. It is requiring that Black students reject their language and culture to acquire White Mainstream English (WME), and it is also insisting that Black students code-switch to avoid discrimination. (Baker-Bell, 2020: 9)

Through the historical ways Black language and literacy have served as a site of racial oppression, centering these languages and literacies should be understood as a stance against systemic aggression. Despite the linguistic terrorism (Anzaldúa, 1987) experienced by speakers of Black language, Black youth continue to preserve their language and literacies within and beyond school walls; these practices are rooted and sustained over time within community spaces (e.g. Anyiwo *et al.*, 2021; Ellison & Kirkland, 2014; Haddix, 2018; Kelly, 2018; Kinloch, 2015; Kirkland, 2013; Kirkland & Jackson, 2009; Kynard, 2010; Lyiscott, 2017; Muhammad, 2015; Richardson & Ragland, 2018). Moreover, language and literacy for Black people can be understood as an inherent site of survivance (Vizenor, 1998) that moves one from challenging oppressive racial systems to changing these conditions. In his work documenting the ways autoethnography could foster community across minoritized student populations, Camangian (2010: 197) outlined that the sharing of stories unpacking struggle led to the students articulating and affirming their 'collective sense of survival' rather than 'wallowing in group self-pity'. Camangian (2010: 197) further stated, 'more than a misery-loves-company gratification, their connectedness was rooted in overcoming'.

As Khaleeq and Rendell, two Black adolescent males demonstrated in the work of Kinloch *et al.* (2017: 36), Black youth engagements with literacy can lead to an interrogation of 'racialized experiences inside and outside school' and 'produce counternarratives to popular assumptions about Black youth from low-income urban communities'. In other words, Black youth's critical enactments with literacy to make sense of the social context around them can facilitate a change catalyzed by the ways Black youth come to be wholly aware of their marginalization and create the conditions for their own stories to be told regarding this social context. In reference to adolescent Black girls, Price-Dennis *et al.* (2017: 4) explained that 'their racialized-gendered experiences necessitate spaces, places, and an understanding about literacies that foreground and honor their lives'. What I gather from this is that researchers and educators of adolescent Black girls and boys must engage in work that facilitates the creation of such space, which can lead to change. In the vein of Enciso (2019: 47), I suggest we engage in such space-making by constructing 'spaces with youth that enable us to create worlds, imaginatively enter into one another's worlds and interpret our worlds together'. As Kinloch *et al.* (2017: 39) explain, counter-stories from Black adolescents 'in education emphasize their agency in negotiating structural forms of racism and inequity'. The goal then must be first to develop the ideologies and dispositions that truly value the narratives of Black youth. And second, to be intentional about the cultivation of these narratives to be used as a tool to disrupt the logics of racial oppression, specifically antiblackness, that come to encroach on Black youth's dynamic lives. As I have outlined previously in my work with Black youth languages and literacies:

> Given their unique social positioning and identities, Black urban youth experience antiblackness and thus it is not necessarily something that they find difficult to talk about or strive to imagine as out of sight. Through the uniqueness of their experiences, Black youth have the power to lead the charge in critically examining their conditions. (Coles, 2019: 5–6)

I argue that the key to this change is collective action. Soja (2004: x) explained, 'If our spaces and places, our human geographies, are socially constructed... this means that they can be socially changed, made into something better than they were through collective action' (as cited in Watson & Beymer, 2019: 300). In fact, in struggles to search past the silences imposed by systems of dominance, 'it is essential for students of color to have a collective understanding of themselves and one another' (Camangian, 2010: 179). Through my use of BlackCrit ethnography, my participants and I co-created a Black-centric space, rooted in critiques of antiblackness guided by their collective Black languages and literacies, to imagine how we might catalyze change, together.

BlackCrit and Lit: Unpacking BlackCrit Ethnography and Black Literacies

As I embarked on engaging in critical research methods that would best allow me to capture and center Black urban youth languages and literacies, as representative of their voice in efforts to make sense of antiblackness, I immediately looked to CRT. CRT proved useful as an entry point to my research desires in that, fundamentally, CRT rests in the idea that 'race continues to be a significant factor in determining inequity in the United States' (Ladson-Billings & Tate, 1995: 48). Specifically, CRT holds that the social contexts of Black youth are 'a manifestation of the racial politics that are intrinsic, even vital, to the day-to-day functions of U.S. society and social institutions such as schools' (Duncan, 2002: 131). Given the history of race and racism in the US, it was clear to me that my work with Black youth would be best conceptualized through a theoretical and methodological frame that held the realities of racism as both real and central to the ways that we all make sense of our social existences. There was no way that I could engage in research that attempted to position race as neutral after my experience with Emmett's casket and his life. Even prior to my visit to the NMAAHC and encounter with Emmett's casket, I had been wading through a myriad of anti-Black assaults against Black youth, both in schools and society, that propelled me to center race and racism in my research. In fact, four years prior to my visit to the NMAAHC, a new civil rights era was being introduced to our nation via the #BlackLivesMatter movement, which was erected in direct response to the murder of Trayvon Martin, a Black boy, in 2012. At the time of Trayvon's death, I wondered if, at Miami Carol City High, where Trayvon attended, he learned about the breakability of his body (Coates, 2015) brought on by antiblackness that would eventually result in his death? So, within the span of these four years between Trayvon and Emmett, I was consumed with engaging with youth in ways that would provide the space for their lived experiences in an anti-Black nation. These experiences also serve as data for how educators might better construct schools and classrooms that are both attentive to antiblackness and seek to lessen antiblackness.

From Race to Blackness: Specifying Blackness in Research with Black Youth

While the work of critical race scholars in education has set a foundation to research with Black youth, in order to unearth the specificity of antiblackness, BlackCrit is necessary. CRT is not positioned to address how antiblackness 'informs and facilitates racist ideology and institutional practice' (Dumas & ross, 2016: 417). I thus extend the work that education scholars using CRT have put forth, by moving from broad conceptions of race and racism to specifically examining Blackness and antiblackness (Dumas & ross, 2016). For example, by revisiting my reflections on Trayvon and Emmett via my ethnographic research, I wanted to examine Blackness through a lens that would help make sense as to why and how the death of these two Black boys could happen. I was looking for a method that would locate itself within Black racial histories and the Black racial experience. Thus, BlackCrit became desirable, as it speaks to a specific wrestling with the unique ways Black people experience the US, in inhumane and violent ways. Nakagawa (2012: np) explained:

> Our Constitution was written by slave owners. They managed to muster some pretty nice language about equality, justice, and freedom for 'men' because they considered Africans less than human. Our federal system is based on a compromise intended to accommodate slavery. Our concept of ownership rights, the structure of our federal elections system, the segregated state of our society, the glut of money in politics, our conservative political culture, our criminal codes and federal penitentiaries all evolved around or were/are facilitated by anti-black racism.

Given how the basis of US society has been formed around an ideological opposition to Black people, a theoretical orientation centering such opposition paired best with the aims of my research. BlackCrit is not meant to reject the larger project of CRT – as it is located within the broader critical race project – but rather as a framing that provides space for further development and imagination as the field thinks more deeply about Blackness in the social construction of White supremacy (Dumas & ross, 2016). Thus, I do not see my use of BlackCrit as replacing CRT, but rather always in partnership with it. In other words, I see both CRT and BlackCrit as needing to be employed to make sense of the experiences of Blackness in America, and that only using CRT would be incomplete. CRT, as a theory of racism, focuses on addressing the ways Whiteness is regarded as superior, a structure that negatively impacts all non-White people. BlackCrit, as a theory of antiblackness, focuses on addressing the ways Black people are regarded as inferior, a structure that negatively impacts Black people.

Duncan (2005: 95) proposed a critical race ethnography – specifically, 'the analysis of the various ontological categories that inform the way race functions as a stratifying force in school and society, as one measure to build around and advance the rich corpus of CRT studies in education' (see also Chávez-Moreno, this volume). In essence, my extension of critical race ethnography to a BlackCrit ethnography allowed me to analyze education in the US for Black youth, through a specific Black lens. In other words, moving from CRT to BlackCrit takes into account particular Black cultural ways of being and moving through the world, with an understanding that moving through the world is a different experience for non-Blacks. This then allowed me to challenge the assumptions in school and (US) society that uphold White cultural norms that ignore the ways of being and norms of Black communities. In my use of BlackCrit and the explication of antiblackness in conceptualizing urban Black youth's schooling and societal experiences, I must note that it is not a theory 'best served by the kind of fixedness implied by the notion of tenets, a term most commonly associated with religious statements of faith, or rigid ideological schools of thought' (Dumas & ross, 2016: 429). As Dumas and ross (2016: 429) explained, in their initial article on BlackCrit in education, they wanted to resist the desire to develop tenets, but rather leave space for 'further scholarship and collective deliberation'. However, while Dumas and ross (2016) did not provide tenets *per se*, they did provide broad framings that were directly connected to the framings of CRT, which specified Blackness. The framings of BlackCrit put forth by Dumas and ross (2016) that guide my use of BlackCrit ethnography include:

- Antiblackness is endemic to, and is central to, how all of us make sense of the social, economic, historical and cultural dimensions of human life (Dumas & ross, 2016: 429).
- Blackness exists in tension with the neoliberal-multicultural imagination (Dumas & ross, 2016: 430).
- BlackCrit should create space for Black liberatory fantasy, and resist a revisionist history that supports dangerous majoritarian stories that disappear Whites from a history of racial dominance (Leonardo, 2004), rape, mutilation, brutality and murder (Bell, 1987: 431).

Working from these framings of BlackCrit can help us understand 'how antiblackness serves to reinforce the ideological and material "infrastructure" of educational inequity—the misrecognition of students and communities of color, and the (racialized) maldistribution of educational resources' (Dumas & ross, 2016: 432).

Considerations for BlackCrit Method/ologies

When noting their resistance to put forth a very strict set of tenets for BlackCrit in education, Dumas and ross (2016: 429) explained that they wanted 'to leave space for further scholarship and collective deliberation'. Their goal here was to invite other researchers to take up their initial framings in ways that would expand how the theory might be used to guide research, and more so, how the concept might be used to inform the development of expansive methods and methodologies that would best capture Black-specific knowledges. I do not mean here that there are research techniques that are cure-alls for Black people, but rather that we must engage in research techniques (whether old or new) that are intentionally attentive to explicating Blackness and antiblackness as they relate to education. Thus, for me, BlackCrit methods and methodologies are more about the researcher's possession of a standpoint epistemology that allows them to use critical race methods in ways that are attentive to Black knowledge/s and lived experiences. In order for BlackCrit methods and methodologies to be sound and meaningful, the researcher must see the importance and value in Black lived experiences. Researchers of BlackCrit must value Black life. Considering BlackCrit is a narrowing of the ways scholars have taken up CRT, much of the research using critical race methodologies directly informed my methodologies and can inform how other BlackCrit scholars engage in everything from research design, data collection to data analysis. In terms of data collection within my BlackCrit ethnography, learning from critical race ethnography proved to be extremely valuable and appropriate. According to Duncan:

> Critical race ethnography seeks to engage the multiple ontological categories that give meaning to lived experience. Engaging multiple ontological categories entails bringing to bear on our work data from different sources, for example, sociolinguistic, interview, observational, statistical, documentary and so forth, to provide stronger warrants for or even more plausible alternatives to the claims that result from our inquiries. In my view, the experiences of oppression that people of color in the US encounter are at times so outrageous and unimaginable to outsiders that it makes it difficult for even the most open-minded and reasonable person to grasp the enormity of some of our claims. (Duncan, 2005: 106)

Antiblackness, I posit, is one of those 'outrageous and unimaginable' phenomena that will be difficult for non-Blacks to grasp. Since antiblackness frames so much of Black existence, there is so much to be documented, which is why the influence of broader race crits was informative, as 'critical ethnography should be data rich' (Vaught, 2011: 24). Given this leaning to data richness, I, too, included multiple data sources (semi-structured interviews, life history interviews, participant and non-participant observations including field notes), audiovisual recorded after-school sessions, digital dialogic journaling (group multimodal text messages), student academic and disciplinary data, researcher reflection journal memos and literacy artifacts (e.g. photographs, school mapping, body maps, visual concepts of racism, autobiographies and clothing) in my BlackCrit ethnography to document the students' recognitions of antiblackness, and their subsequent resistances to it. Antiblackness is such a specific mental, emotional and embodied assaultive system, that is layered with centuries of nuance, that for many who are not Black themselves, it will be very difficult for them to understand what it is like to exist in the world as a Black body. Thus, it is crucial when studying Black youth to use methodological approaches that take this into consideration, both by exploring the history and roots of anti-Black racism and also centering antiblackness in research designs, data collection and methods. Given my earlier discussion about the ways antiblackness silences Black youth and communities, I see that providing space for Black youth to move beyond such silence is a crucial and necessary component to BlackCrit methods, particularly through seeing Black youth languages and literacies as a prime form of data. Literacy is a part of who we are – as people we are literate beings. Therefore, in my use of BlackCrit ethnography with the nine Black youth, I knew it would be important to engage these students in various literacy encounters, in conjunction with traditional ethnographic techniques such as interviews and observations, because antiblackness does not often present itself in traditional or readily identifiable ways.

A BlackCrit Research Note on Black Storywork as a Literacy Encounter

A prime literacy encounter that I have used in my BlackCrit ethnographic research has been what I refer to as Black storywork. Specifically,

> I define Black storywork as the individual or collective stories, which emerge from the lived experiences of Black people and communities that uses Black knowledge/s as a tool to extend and author oneself beyond the conditions of anti-Blackness. Here, Black storywork captures the youth's critical collective storying rooted in their own words to bridge the contradictions between their lived experiences and distorted anti-Black narratives. (Coles, 2020: 4)

Black storywork emerged from my intentionality in carving out a co-created community with Black youth to be what Winn and Ubiles (2011) call a worthy witness. In this co-created community, which was the ethnographic social location, we spent a year meeting once weekly (often twice weekly) after school, to engage in multimodal discourse on the ways the students understood antiblackness and how they leveraged those understandings to resist antiblackness.

The multimodal discourse that came to be the Black storywork was characterized by a combination of collective storying layered with dialogue, freestyle rapping, writing, reading, drawing images, sharing photos, clothing (e.g. #BlackLivesMatter shirts), social media posts and dancing. Each time we met, our after-school space was centered around food and the collectivity that comes with breaking bread, music and endless laughter. Over the food and sounds, we would sit in a circle around a table and engage in collective conversations.

Prompts for the Black storywork were either brought forth by me or the students in response to things heard or discussed during my non-participant observations (i.e. classrooms, hallways, cafeterias and after-school extra-curricular activities), our after-school sessions, interviews, group text messaging threads or responses that emerged from our shared readings (e.g. excerpts from literary texts, spoken word videos and social media posts). Black storywork should not be confused with focus group data: Black storywork does not emerge from a group interview. There is no predetermined list of questions and the researcher is not the primary driver of dialogue. In my research, the students would share their stories and organically build off one another, in an improvisational manner as if they were simply having conversations with their friends. The significance of this talk is that the students repeatedly shared that they are not given space inside their school to discuss the realities of their Blackness and antiblackness. Another significant component was my presence as a Black critical educator in this space to help (not dictate) their processing and sense-making of their collective storying. Any onlookers passing by could have easily mistaken our community as having nothing to do with racial suffering because of the ways the students' Black literacies were oriented toward a radical love of Blackness (Johnson *et al.*, 2017), even in the face of precarious existences. My BlackCrit ethnography was not a project on hopelessness at all, rather it was about the cultivation of a liberatory space with and for Black urban youth to document their Black human experiences in relation to US urban schooling and society. BlackCrit methods and methodologies need not be characterized by the absence of joy.

Critical Race Theory Counter-Stories and Black Storywork

Directly inspired by the centrality of storytelling in critical race scholarship (Bell, 1993; Delgado, 1995), Black storywork is an embodiment of CRT's key tenet, the voice-of-color thesis or the idea that people of color have a 'presumed competence to speak about race and racism' (Delgado & Stefancic, 2001: 9) given their direct racialized lived experiences. This thesis on the value of voice in documenting the experiences of people of color in CRT has been largely conceptualized as counter-storytelling, which many Black scholars have used in their research on Black education across the P-20 pipeline (Baszile, 2015; Cook & Dixson, 2013; DeCuir & Dixson, 2004; Ellison, 2019; Ellison & Solomon, 2019; Grey & Williams-Farrier, 2017; Griffin *et al.*, 2014; Howard, 2008; Jenkins *et al.*, 2020; Kynard, 2010; Love, 2014; Tafari, 2018; Terry, 2011; Warren, 2017). Counter-storytelling in CRT can be defined by the capturing of 'stories that run counter to prevailing stock stories that advance ideas of racial neutrality, merit-based systems and equal opportunity' (Rolón-Dow, 2011: 160). I understand counter-storytelling as a foundation for Black storywork as wholly about subversion; working to call out, contradict, reverse and become fugitives of the structural regime of antiblackness in a conscious effort to transform or create completely new ways of being and living that are not swallowed by Black suffering.

Particularly relevant to the use of counter-storytelling for Black storywork as a BlackCrit method, Baszile (2015) linked contemporary counter-stories to the ways Black abolitionists used storytelling to subvert the structure of slavery. According to Baszile (2015: 242), 'the critical race counterstorytelling of Black abolitionists gave rise to an active counterstory culture, which allowed them to develop the common set of beliefs, behaviors, and strategies to establish the sense of group identity necessary for turning their antislavery politics into the abolitionist *movement*' (emphasis in original). In the legacy of Black abolitionists, I have cultivated Black storywork as a BlackCrit method with Black youth for it 'embodies the students' extrapolations of U.S. power relations perpetuated by anti-Black racism that structure their social realities, which serve as a foundation for how they authored new ways to re/imagine the responsibility of urban schools to understanding their unique social context' (Coles, 2020: 4).

Black Youth Voice and Space

The core theoretical underpinning of BlackCrit that informs the ways I employ Black storywork is the acknowledgment that 'we must center the Black voice specifically in research that aims to address and dismantle the violence of antiblackness' (Coles & Powell, 2020: 118). Thus, I center Black youth's languages and literacies in my applications of BlackCrit ethnography through the critical race method of the counter-story, which tell 'the stories of those people whose experiences are not often told' as a way to expose, analyze and challenge 'the majoritarian stories of racial privilege' (Solórzano & Yosso, 2002: 32). To specifically hear these stories, central to my construction of BlackCrit ethnography with youth was the co-creation of an after-school space (within their school site), mentioned previously, that functioned to provide the students with space to speak to their lived experience in an anti-Black nation that privileged and centered their voices. This after-school space:

> [P]rovided a space for the youth and me to think about how things could be—how education for Black youth could exist when Black youth intentionally develop the capacity to name and challenge antiblackness. At the core of this collaboration was the participants engaging in literacy to search past the silences Black voices are often shrouded in… My research provided a platform for students to begin to alter their experiences with their school site through literacy in ways that will be productive for their

> future engagement in urban schooling and the world. The students had the opportunity to document their developing understanding of antiblackness within the context of their lives in order to move forward in addressing the issue collectively. (Coles, 2019: 16)

The creation of a Black-centric space guided by Black youth voices was an intentional part of the research design, as it served as the space where Black knowledge/s of, and experience with, antiblackness would become known. Particularly, given the history of silencing in research and academic spaces of Black youth, I argue that central to BlackCrit ethnography and research designs at large should be the intentional co-creation of space with Black participants that allows them to share and critique their lived experiences in the world as related to antiblackness.

Acknowledging the Tensions of Non-Black Researchers and BlackCrit Method/ology

In the methodological sense, non-Black scholars should proceed with caution in seeking to employ BlackCrit, particularly in research that is rooted in the voices and perspectives of Black people and gathered through the creation of Black-centric spaces. It is important to understand that Black research participants may not feel as compelled to share their most authentic selves (and they should not have to) with those whom they deem as outside of the broader Black community, characterized here as someone who does not move through the world daily in a Black body. Also, while proximity to Blackness is valuable, proximity to Blackness is not Blackness. In the case of Black storywork as a BlackCrit method in my research, a significant aspect was my presence in the space as a Black critical educator. Students routinely told me that our space of storying would not be the same if a White person was leading it and that they would most likely have not agreed to participate. Moreover, since the students did not have any Black male teachers at the time of the research (there were two Black female teachers), the students expressed their want and need to have a non-traditional curricular space that allowed them to engage with a Black adult figure in ways they are not given the space to do so during their traditional engagements with curriculum in school. For non-Black scholars interested in BlackCrit, several scholars have engaged in earlier conversations as to who can and should engage in CRT research and how (Bergerson, 2003; Nebeker, 1998; Rogers & Mosley, 2006; Ullucci, 2011; cf. May, this volume), which can be helpful for the ways we think about the use of BlackCrit across racial lines.

Conclusion

Through my use of BlackCrit ethnography, I challenged the mainstream narratives that shape our educational institutions and rejected any research where the 'problem statement' places the blame on Blackness. Keeping the centrality of experiential knowledge, a key focal point to race crit methodologies, in mind, I focused directly on the words and experiences of Black youth that critiqued the ways antiblackness showed up in their lives. Indeed, one of the major underlying aims of BlackCrit ethnographies with Black youth should be the emphasis on their experiences, as directly told by them. This approach is important to me as a scholar in that, as we think about reimagining schools that better serve Black youth, we get to redesign these spaces having the experiences of Black youth – who experience the brunt of anti-Black violence – as the foundation of this reimagining.

References

Anderson, D.S. (2015) *Emmett Till: The Murder that Shocked the World and Propelled the Civil Rights Movement*. Jackson, MS: University Press of Mississippi.

Anderson, J.D. (2004) The historical context for understanding the test score gap. *National Journal of Urban Education and Practice* 1 (1), 1–21.

Anyiwo, N., Richards-Schuster, K. and Jerald, M.C. (2021) Using critical media literacy and youth-led research to promote the sociopolitical development of Black youth: Strategies from 'Our Voices'. *Applied Developmental Science* 25 (3), 201–216.

Anzaldúa, G. (1987) *Borderlands/la frontera: The New Mestiza*. San Francisco, CA: Aunt Lute Books.

Baker-Bell, A. (2020) Dismantling anti-black linguistic racism in English language arts classrooms: Toward an anti-racist black language pedagogy. *Theory into Practice* 59 (1), 8–21.

Baker-Bell, A., Stanbrough, R.J. and Everett, S. (2017) The stories they tell: Mainstream media, pedagogies of healing, and critical media literacy. *English Education* 49 (2), 130–152.

Baszile, D.T. (2015) Rhetorical revolution: Critical race counterstorytelling and the abolition of white democracy. *Qualitative Inquiry* 21 (3), 239–249.

Bell, D. (1987) *And We are Not Saved: The Elusive Quest for Racial Justice*. New York: Basic Books.

Bell, D. (1993) *Faces at the Bottom of the Well*. New York: Basic Books.

Bergerson, A.A. (2003) Critical race theory and white racism: Is there room for white scholars in fighting racism in education? *International Journal of Qualitative Studies in Education* 16 (1), 51–63.

Bourdieu, P. (2001) *Masculine Domination*. Stanford, CA: Stanford University Press.

Butler, T.T. (2018) Black girl cartography: Black girlhood and place-making in education research. *Review of Research in Education* 42 (1), 28–45.

Camangian, P. (2010) Starting with self: Teaching autoethnography to foster critically caring literacies. *Research in the Teaching of English* 45 (2), 179–204.

Coates, T.N. (2015) *Between the World and Me*. New York: Spiegel & Grau.

Coles, J.A. (2016) Black lives, too, matter in schools: An exploration of symbolic violence against Black youth in America's schools. *Urban Education Research and Policy Annuals* 4 (2), 17–33.

Coles, J.A. (2018) The cost of whistling, orange juice, and skittles: An anti-Black examination of the extrajudicial killings of Black youth. In K. Fasching-Varner, K. Tobin and S. Lentz (eds) *#Broken Promises, Black Deaths, & Blue Ribbons: Understanding,*

Complicating, and Transcending Police-Community Violence (pp. 5–8). Boston, MA: Brill Publishing.

Coles, J.A. (2019) The Black literacies of urban high school youth countering antiblackness in the context of neoliberal multiculturalism. *Journal of Language & Literacy Education* 15 (2), 1–35.

Coles, J.A. (2020) A BlackCrit re/imagining of urban schooling social education through Black youth enactments of Black storywork. *Urban Education* 1–30.

Coles, J.A. and Powell, T. (2020) A BlackCrit analysis on Black urban youth and suspension disproportionality as anti-Black symbolic violence. *Race Ethnicity and Education* 23 (1), 113–133.

Cook, D.A. and Dixson, A.D. (2013) Writing critical race theory and method: A composite counterstory on the experiences of Black teachers in New Orleans post-Katrina. *International Journal of Qualitative Studies in Education* 26 (10), 1238–1258.

Cornelius, J. (1983) 'We slipped and learned to read': Slave accounts of the literacy process, 1830–1865. *Phylon* 44 (3), 171–186.

Cruz, C. (2001) Toward an epistemology of a brown body. *International Journal of Qualitative Studies in Education* 14 (5), 657–669.

Curtis, C.A. (2019) Observing Black youth sociopolitical group participation and high school democratic climate through the lens of critical race theory. *Race Ethnicity and Education* 22 (3), 410–427.

DeCuir, J.T. and Dixson, A.D. (2004) 'So when it comes out, they aren't that surprised that it is there': Using critical race theory as a tool of analysis of race and racism in education. *Educational Researcher* 33 (5), 26–31.

Delgado, R. (1995) *The Rodrigo Chronicles: Conversations about America and Race*. New York: New York University Press.

Delgado, R. and Stefancic, J. (2001) *Critical Race Theory: An Introduction*. New York: New York University Press.

Donaldson, K.B.M. (1996) *Through Students' Eyes: Combating Racism in United States Schools*. Westport, CT: Praeger Publishers.

Dumas, M.J. (2016) Shutting ish down: Black lives matter as a challenge to the field of education. *Division B Newsletter: Black Lives Matter* (pp. 7–10). Washington, DC: AERA.

Dumas, M.J. and ross, K.M. (2016) 'Be real black for me': Imagining BlackCrit in education. *Urban Education* 51 (4), 415–442.

Duncan, G.A. (2002) Beyond love: A critical race ethnography of the schooling of adolescent Black males. *Equity & Excellence in Education* 35 (2), 131–143.

Duncan, G.A. (2005) Critical race ethnography in education: Narrative, inequality and the problem of epistemology. *Race Ethnicity and Education* 8 (1), 93–114.

Ellison, T.L. (2019) The matter of parents' stories: Urban African American mothers' counter-stories about the common core state standards and quality teaching. *Urban Education* 54 (10), 1431–1461.

Ellison, T.L. and Kirkland, D.E. (2014) Motherboards, microphones and metaphors: Re-examining new literacies and Black feminist thought through technologies of self. *E-Learning and Digital Media* 11 (4), 390–405.

Ellison, T.L. and Solomon, M. (2019) Counter-storytelling vs. deficit thinking around African American children and families, digital literacies, race, and the digital divide. *Research in the Teaching of English* 53 (3), 223–244.

Enciso, P. (2019) Stories of becoming: implications of future-oriented theories for a vital literacy education. *Literacy* 53 (1), 46–55.

Feierman, J. and Sawyer, A.C. (2019) The U.S. has been silencing Black girls' voices for decades. *Teen Vogue*. See https://www.teenvogue.com/story/juvenile-justice-black-girls-leesburg-stockade (accessed 25 July 2022).

Fine, M. (1987) Silencing in public schools. *Language Arts* 64 (2), 157–174.
Freire, P. (2000) *Pedagogy of the Oppressed*. New York: Continuum.
Ginwright, S.A. (2007) Black youth activism and the role of critical social capital in Black community organizations. *American Behavioral Scientist* 51 (3), 403–418.
Givens, J.R. (2016) A grammar for Black education beyond borders: Exploring technologies of schooling in the African diaspora. *Race Ethnicity and Education* 19 (6), 1288–1302.
Grey, T.G. and Williams-Farrier, B.J. (2017) #Sippingtea: Two black female literacy scholars sharing counter-stories to redefine our roles in the academy. *Journal of Literacy Research* 49 (4), 503–525.
Griffin, R.A., Ward, L. and Phillips, A.R. (2014) Still flies in buttermilk: Black male faculty, critical race theory, and composite counterstorytelling. *International Journal of Qualitative Studies in Education* 27 (10), 1354–1375.
Gundaker, G. (2007) Hidden education among African Americans during slavery. *Teachers College Record* 109 (7), 1591–1612.
Haddix, M.M. (2018) What's radical about youth writing?: Seeing and honoring youth writers and their literacies. *Voices from the Middle* 25 (3), 8–12.
Harold, C. and DeLuca, K.M. (2005) Behold the corpse: Violent images and the case of Emmett Till. *Rhetoric & Public Affairs* 8 (2), 263–286.
Hart, W.D. (2018) Constellations: Capitalism, antiblackness, Afro-pessimism, and Black optimism. *American Journal of Theology & Philosophy* 39 (1), 5–33.
Howard, T.C. (2008) Who really cares? The disenfranchisement of African American males in preK-12 schools: A critical race theory perspective. *Teachers College Record* 110 (5), 954–985.
Howard, T.C. and Navarro, O. (2016) Critical race theory 20 years later: Where do we go from here? *Urban Education* 51 (3), 253–273.
Hudson-Weems, C. (1994) *Emmett Till: The Sacrificial Lamb of the Civil Rights Movement*. Bedford, NY: Bedford Publishers.
Jenkins, D.A., Tichavakunda, A.A. and Coles, J.A. (2020) The second ID: Critical race counterstories of campus police interactions with black men at historically white institutions. *Race Ethnicity and Education* 24 (2), 149–166.
Johnson, L.L., Jackson, J., Stovall, D.O. and Baszile, D.T. (2017) 'Loving Blackness to death': (Re)Imagining ELA classrooms in a time of racial chaos. *English Journal* 106 (4), 60–66.
Kelly, L.L. (2018) A snapchat story: How black girls develop strategies for critical resistance in school. *Learning, Media and Technology* 43 (4), 374–389.
Kinloch, V. (2015) *Harlem on Our Minds: Place, Race, and the Literacies of Urban Youth*. New York: Teachers College Press.
Kinloch, V., Burkhard, T. and Penn, C. (2017) When school is not enough: Understanding the lives and literacies of Black youth. *Research in the Teaching of English* 52 (1), 34–54.
Kirkland, D.E. (2013) *A Search Past Silence: The Literacy of Young Black Men*. New York: Teachers College Press.
Kirkland, D.E. and Jackson, A. (2009) 'We real cool': Toward a theory of Black masculine literacies. *Reading Research Quarterly* 44 (3), 278–297.
Knaus, C.B. (2009) Shut up and listen: Applied critical race theory in the classroom. *Race Ethnicity and Education* 12 (2), 133–154.
Kynard, C. (2010) From candy girls to cyber sista-cipher: Narrating Black females' color-consciousness and counterstories in and out of school. *Harvard Educational Review* 80 (1), 30–53.
Ladson-Billings, G. and Tate, W. (1995) Toward a critical race theory of education. *Teachers College Record* 97 (1), 47–68.

Leonardo, Z. (2004) The color of supremacy: Beyond the discourse of 'White privilege'. *Educational Philosophy and Theory* 36 (2), 137–152.
Love, B.L. (2014) Urban storytelling: How storyboarding, moviemaking, and hip-hop-based education can promote students' critical voice. *English Journal* 103 (5), 53–58.
Lyiscott, J. (2017) Racial identity and liberation literacies in the classroom. *English Journal* 106 (4), 47–53.
Lyiscott, J. (2020) Fugitive literacies as inscriptions of freedom. *English Education* 52 (3), 256–263.
Marable, M. (2006) *Living Black History: How Reimagining the African-American Past can Remake America's Racial Future*. Cambridge: Civitas Books.
Martin, W.E. (1998) Roberts v. City of Boston (1849). In W.E. Martin (ed.) *Brown v. Board of Education: A Brief History with Documents* (pp. 42–60). New York: Palgrave Macmillan.
Mitchell, A.B. (2008) Self-emancipation and slavery: An examination of the African American's quest for literacy and freedom. *The Journal of Pan African Studies* 2 (5), 78–98.
Montoya, M.E. (2000) Silence and silencing: Their centripetal and centrifugal forces in legal communication, pedagogy and discourse. *University of Michigan Journal of Law Reform* 33 (3), 263–327.
Moraga, C. and Anzaldúa, G. (1983) Entering the lives of others: Theory in the flesh. In C. Moraga and G. Anzaldúa (eds) *This Bridge Called My Back: Writings by Radical Women of Color* (2nd edn, pp. 23–57). New York: Kitchen Table/Women of Color Press.
Muhammad, G. (2019) *Cultivating Genius: An Equity Framework for Culturally and Historically Responsive Literacy*. Jefferson, MO: Scholastic Teaching Resources.
Muhammad, G.E. (2015) 'Inducing colored sisters of other places to imitate their example': Connecting historic literary societies to a contemporary writing group. *English Education* 47 (3), 276–299.
Myers, E. (2017) Beyond the wages of whiteness: Du Bois on the irrationality of antiblack racism. Social Science Research Council. See https://items.ssrc.org/reading-racial-conflict/beyond-the-wages-of-whiteness-du-bois-on-the-irrationality-of-antiblack-racism/ (accessed 25 July 2022).
Nakagawa, S. (2012) Blackness is the fulcrum. *Race Files*, 4 May. See https://www.racefiles.com/2012/05/04/blackness-is-the-fulcrum/ (accessed 25 July 2022).
Nebeker, K.C. (1998) Critical race theory: A white graduate student's struggle with this growing area of scholarship. *International Journal of Qualitative Studies in Education* 11 (1), 25–41.
Price-Dennis, D., Muhammad, G.E., Womack, E., McArthur, S.A. and Haddix, M. (2017) The multiple identities and literacies of black girlhood: A conversation about creating spaces for Black girl voices. *Journal of Language and Literacy Education* 13 (2), 1–18.
Quantz, R.A. (1992) On critical ethnography (with some postmodern considerations). In M.D. Lecompte, W.L. Millroy and J. Preissle (eds) *The Handbook of Qualitative Research in Education* (pp. 447–505). San Diego, CA: Academic Press.
Richardson, E. (2007) 'She was workin like foreal': Critical literacy and discourse practices of African American females in the age of hip hop. *Discourse & Society* 18 (6), 789–809.
Richardson, E. and Ragland, A. (2018) #StayWoke: The language and literacies of the #BlackLivesMatter movement. *Community Literacy Journal* 12 (2), 27–56.
Rogers, R. and Mosley, M. (2006) Racial literacy in a second-grade classroom: Critical race theory, whiteness studies, and literacy research. *Reading Research Quarterly* 41 (4), 462–495.
Rolón-Dow, R. (2011) Race(ing) stories: Digital storytelling as a tool for critical race scholarship. *Race Ethnicity and Education* 14 (2), 159–173.
Sharpe, C. (2016) *In the Wake: On Blackness and Being*. Durham, NC: Duke University Press.

Soja, E.W. (2004) Preface. In K.M. Leander and M. Sheehy (eds) *Spatializing Literary Research and Practice* (pp. ix–xvi). New York: Peter Lang.

Solórzano, D.G. and Yosso, T.J. (2002) Critical race methodology: Counter-storytelling as an analytical framework for education research. *Qualitative Inquiry* 8 (1), 23–44.

Sosa, T. (2019) 'That sure is racist': Classroom race talk as resistance. *Education and Urban Society* 52 (7), 1039–1065.

Tafari, D.N.H. (2018) 'Whose world is this?': A composite counterstory of Black male elementary school teachers as hip-hop otherfathers. *The Urban Review* 50 (5), 795–817.

Terry, C.L. (2011) Mathematical counterstory and African American male students: Urban mathematics education from a critical race theory perspective. *Journal of Urban Mathematics Education* 4 (1), 23–49.

Thompson, K. (2016) Painful but crucial: Why you'll see Emmett Till's casket at the African American museum. *The Washington Post*, 18 August. See https://www.washingtonpost.com/lifestyle/style/painful-but-crucial-why-youll-see-emmett-tills-casket-at-the-african-american-museum/2016/08/18/66d1dc2e-484b-11e6-acbc-4d4870a079da_story.html (accessed 25 July 2022).

Trevino, A.J., Harris, M.A. and Wallace, D. (2008) What's so critical about critical race theory? *Contemporary Justice Review* 11 (1), 7–10.

Tyson, T.B. (2017) *The Blood of Emmett Till*. New York: Simon & Schuster.

Ullucci, K. (2011) Learning to see: The development of race and class consciousness in White teachers. *Race Ethnicity and Education* 14 (4), 561–577.

Vargas, J.H.C. (2018) *The Denial of Antiblackness: Multiracial Redemption and Black Suffering*. Minneapolis, MN: University of Minnesota Press.

Vaught, S.E. (2011) *Racism, Public Schooling, and the Entrenchment of White Supremacy: A Critical Race Ethnography*. Albany, NY: SUNY Press.

Vizenor, G. (1998) *Fugitive Poses: Native American Indian Scenes of Absence and Presence*. Lincoln, NE: University of Nebraska Press.

Warren, C.A. (2017) *Urban Preparation: Young Black Men Moving from Chicago's South Side to Success in Higher Education*. Cambridge, MA: Harvard Education Press.

Watson, V.W. and Beymer, A. (2019) Praisesongs of place: Youth envisioning space and place in a literacy and songwriting initiative. *Research in the Teaching of English* 53 (4), 297–319.

Williams, H.A. (2009) *Self-Taught: African American Education in Slavery and Freedom*. Chapel Hill, NC: University of North Carolina Press.

Williams, P. (1995) *The Rooster's Egg: On the Persistence of Prejudice*. Cambridge, MA: Harvard University Press.

Winn, M.T. and Ubiles, J.R. (2011) Worthy witnessing: Collaborative research in urban classrooms. In A. Ball and C. Tyson (eds) *Studying Diversity in Teacher Education* (pp. 295–308). Lanham, MD: Rowman & Littlefield.

Yamamoto, E.K. (1997) Critical race praxis: Race theory and political lawyering practice in post-civil rights America. *Michigan Law Review* 95 (4), 821–900.

Yancy, G. (2016) *Black Bodies, White Gazes: The Continuing Significance of Race in America*. Lanham, MD: Rowman & Littlefield.

3 Multilingual Radical Intimate Ethnography

Youmna Deiri

In this chapter, I weave internal monologues, poetry, theoretical frameworks, vignettes and questions to invite you on a journey of understanding multilingual radical intimate ethnography (MRIE) and multilingualism as a radically intimate relationship. Our first stop along the journey of understanding MRIE is an invitation to do research from the heart by describing the context from which this chapter was born. Then, I set the stage with questions as reading guidelines. Following this, I describe my own relationship with writing as a multilingual researcher. Then, I delve deeper into the importance of questioning our linguistic positionality (see also Nuñez & García-Mateus, this volume). In the second major stop on this journey, I lay out the tenets of MRIE and the overall challenges of doing research multilingually. As you are journeying through this chapter, I invite you to stop, to breathe, to write down your own reflections and, finally, to respond to some of the questions as they relate to you.

Invitation to Intuition

The writing of this chapter comes at a time that demands the visible, invisible and imagined collective pausing and witnessing of the #BlackLivesMatter uprising, COVID-19, mass local and global displacements, dispossession of lands by proxy wars, exacerbated incarceration of children and youth, unprecedented xenophobia and anti-Asian racism. Through this collective pausing and witnessing, we see events that manifest the injustice that exists in our world. These events ask us to radically question our contemporary ways of doing, being and knowing.

Most of all, the current recycled events of the present and the past warn us that our ways of capturing non-colonial centric knowledges as hostages of modernity and the empire, no longer work. At the core of this chapter is an invitation to trust our intuitions about the intimacies that exist among us when we move away from understanding language as a commodity to understanding language as a relationship. Retrospectively, the relationship we have with our languages as researchers impacts many facets of how we understand multilingualism and the relationships imposed on participants, students and researchers with respect to their languages.

The concept of intimacy and the relationship we build with language came to me from working with Saudi families and Arabic bilingual teachers, and later on, attending a talk by the author and essayist, Sayed Kashua, in autumn 2018, where he described his educational experiences learning both Hebrew and Arabic. He asked us as listeners to think through what it means to be writers who do not trust the languages in which we write. His question about trust, or lack thereof, helped me think about the intimacy and the interconnectedness of multilingualism and coloniality, and the view of language as an intimate relationship. The intimacy of language is highly manifest through relationships as well. Thinking about the intimacies of languages asks us to think about the types of relationships we desire our students, participants and ourselves to have with the languages we love, speak and write. The types of relationships we hope students and participants have should remain within the realm of desire rather than present themselves as weapons of intervention as is commonly the case, today. Understanding the type of intimate relationship we have as researchers with our languages requires a radical stance of transgression and honesty (Macedo, 2000) based on the context we find ourselves in.

In many ways, this chapter is an invitation to my own journey as a multilingual being and as a researcher delving into the radical intimacy of multilingualism. I call this journey a *multilingual radical intimate ethnography*, as I am motivated by a deep desire to free my heart, mind and soul from the restraints and constraints of being held hostage to modernity, as well as knowledges of colonial empires that have harmed and sought to erase the intimacy of languages we love, write and speak and with which we build relationships. In other words, I invite you to let go of the knowledges of the empire and to trust that the fluidity of Indigenous and postcolonial knowledges extends to us a radically less harmful imagination.

As you dive into this methodological chapter, I will explain what I mean by *intimate* and *radical* within the framework of multilingualism. Throughout this journey, I will present you with inner dialogues resulting from my educational experiences in academia as well as a vignette from a participant/friend that may help unpack what I mean by MRIE.

Reading with an Invited Lens

At this point, as you continue reading about this journey, I ask you to keep the following questions in mind:

(1) What sort of relationships have your ontological, epistemological, axiological and methodological inheritances from your educational

experience left you with in terms of how you understand your relationship to language? Drawing on Wilson's (2008) understandings of these terms, these sub-questions are born:

(a) Ontology: What sort of 'relationships' do you have with your 'truths' and 'realities' around language? (Wilson, 2008: 73).
(b) Epistemology: What sort of 'systems of knowledge' have you inherited from your educational and lived contexts and relationships? (Wilson, 2008: 74).
(c) Axiology: What sort of value systems have you inherited that shape how you view your relationship with your own research, participants and language? And what is your 'responsibility' toward these relationships in your research? (Wilson, 2008: 77).
(d) Methodology: How have these aforementioned inheritances shaped how you do your multilingual research and your own relationship with methodology?

(2) Based on the above set of questions: What sort of relationships have you developed with the languages you speak, write, learn and use for doing research? What are the systemic forces that shaped your relationship with language?
(3) How does your relationship with language impact the sort of relationships you hope and desire that your students will build with their own languages, and the languages of their families, their communities, their friends, teachers and coworkers?

I also ask you, as a reader, to notice how your heart, mind and spirit are interacting with this chapter and with the questions laid out above. Keep notes of how you are feeling and the questions that you are asking along the way. These noticings and questions might be useful in understanding your own practice and your linguistic positionality, and how these are imbued with issues of power (Cormier, 2018), as you enter and engage with your own multilingual ethnographic work. Lastly, think about answering these questions with intentional avoidance of tropes of 'helping' and 'saving' and seeking justice for 'othered' people. These questions are about us as researchers and what we have inherited from our Western-centric educational experiences and not about 'others' who may very well not need any of our help (cf. May & Caldas, this volume). In other words, these questions are about our hearts as researchers and where our hearts are at in shaping our relationship to multilingual research and multilingualism.

Writing as an Intimately Dreadful Relationship

Let me begin with how monolingual education has influenced the relationship I have with my languages that are specifically linked to academia and research. Without a doubt, I have a terrible relationship with 'academic' writing. I resist such writing. Writing for academic books and journal publications rarely comes easily, and I seldom write without considerable drama, crying, anxiety and fear. The feelings I experience are not inherent, yet they are surely internalized. As a multilingual/multiliterate person, educated in Aleppo, Syria, and who was one of the top five students at the University of Aleppo before moving to the US, I was rarely if ever asked to prove my academic worth. However, after immigrating and pursuing my graduate education in the US, I was left with the feeling that my writing would never be good enough for a reader steeped in monolingual ideologies.

Let us unpack such anxiety together. My writing has always been subject to layers of coercive surveillance of grammar, spelling and punctuation, before any consideration of its content. I internalized that writing with the heart is often dissuaded, discouraged and unwelcomed in academia. I learned that I have to think one way and render myself in another. In such a rendering, one language – in this case, English – is always considered superior to any other. In short, my future of having an academic career in the field of education, or not, rests on the form of my knowledge in written English rather than the content of the knowledges that are very much tied to my ways of being and knowing in the world. As a multilingual person, I have had a dreadful relationship with writing in English in academic contexts. While I do not believe in the separation of language into academic and non-academic, as such categorizations only serve empires, my intimate thoughts and experiences of education are silenced through the relationships built in my monolingual academic surroundings.

Tension and Relearning

When I was invited to write this chapter, I was awarded the opportunity to write from the heart. However, with such an invitation lies a great deal of tension. There lies a problem between my heart and my imagination, and the space in between is something I hope this chapter will help us reconcile. I repeatedly ask myself about the restrictions postcolonial experiences have imprinted on the ways we imagine ourselves as multilingual beings operating in academia. One certainty I have about my research is that the conversations I have with participants in any research project I am part of will not privilege English. As you establish your research, think deeply about the sort of relationships with languages that emerge from your project. What kinds of relationships emerge in the light of knowledges of modernity and the empire? Is it a relationship of being hostage to language and the commodification of language to serve monolingual ways of understanding the world? Your commitment to that relationship is the guide to your methodological choices such as methods of data collection and research design. For me, the decision to avoid privileging English for research came from the disconnect between what I learned in academia and what I was desperately missing, grieving and desiring: the ability to feel at home. And, in these instances, my languages became my home.

Listening to the Heart, Reconciling the Self and Claiming Self-Sovereignty

While I took a doctoral-level qualitative methodology course, held once a week late in the evenings, I also lived 35 miles away from my university campus. Furthermore, the proxy war between Russia and the US occurring in Syria, where I grew up, learned English and worked, was at its height. Also, I had many family commitments at the time. Having lived in a few big cities, outside the US, with innovative and robust public transportation networks, I could not make peace with the minimal public transportation that exists in the US. Driving a car, often considered a privilege, felt like a burden to me and I resented the drive because it provided me ample alone time to ruminate on my current realities and doctoral studies. To avoid driving in the snow at an odd hour, sometimes, I would spend the night with a Saudi family, who were both friends and research participants. Beyond loving this family as friends and their genuine hospitality, spending time with them meant I could speak Arabic. I lived in a small town in Ohio with no noticeable Arabic-speaking population at the time. I needed the intimacy of speaking a language that reminded me of home. However, a conventional ethnographic standpoint, often taught at prominent universities, warns researchers against having participants/friends. Beyond the physically imposed dislocation of immigration and the impossibility of visiting Aleppo, I also felt that such a conventional ethnographic standpoint asked me to dislocate myself from my community. So, the commute back and forth was yet another reminder of being neither fully here nor there and gave me ample time to think of the ironic contrasts of safety and unsafety in my life. At times, I spent the journey driving home reflecting on my doctoral studies in privileged, guilt-ridden ways. Overall, I looked forward to classes as a form of escape from more bitter realities, hence a privilege. However, these same courses created a source of yet another level of non-tangible trauma that I could not name. I could not make sense of how I could feel this way while my world 'here' is ideally 'safe' in the US, and my soul, left 'there' in Aleppo, Syria, is crumbling into pieces because of imperial politics and powers beyond any population's control.

On one particular festering session after a class, I ruminated over the fact that, yet again, I could not see what everyone else was seeing. The majority of the class was spent discussing the insider–outsider position and the legitimacy, or lack thereof, in the discussed work. In conventional ethnographic terms, or colonial ways of doing ethnography in order to maintain 'objectivity', the researcher must be an outsider (Aiello & Nero, 2019; Collins, 1986; Corbin Dwyer & Buckle, 2009). Simply because the ethnographer was an inbetweener (Anzaldúa, 1987), her legitimacy was questioned, instead of discussing the power, tension, richness and ways of knowing the world her inbetweener position brings (Aiello & Nero, 2019; Cormier, 2018). It had not occurred to me that there was a problem at all with being an inbetweener because, I assumed, we are past the conventional rigid dichotomies of an insider–outsider! I asked: 'How is an outsider's legitimacy to conduct ethnography valid, while the languages, cultural repertoires, and understandings of the world of an inbetweener are a problem?'. More interestingly, I was more amazed that, during the entire class discussion, only one of my doctoral colleagues brought up the issue of colonialism and ethnography. The classroom discussion did not include the history of the ethnographic researcher's role to explain and justify the odd behavior of the colonial subject who is assumed to be emotional and less human than the researcher and colonizers overall (Said, 1979). And to be a superior researcher you must be an outsider in order to have less emotion than your subjects toward the practices you are studying. This is not to assume that an inbetweener is magically prepared and, hence, academia should not offer support for developing inbetweener acumen. The problem of ethnography is not one that can be remedied by the open-mindedness of one professor when so many academic spaces rely on colonial ethnographic conventions.

From discussions like these, I came to understand that, in many ways, I am still a hostage to colonial modernity and the ways of creating knowledges together continue to make us hostages to the empire and colonial thinking. Eventually, I started asking the following questions: What if perfectly 'safe' is violent? What if it is unsafe to ask you to split your heart, body and mind? What if I find a methodology that fits my postcolonial, multilingual and displaced realities instead of fitting myself into dominant Whitestream (Urrieta, 2010) ethnographic conventions? What if all the ethnographies that fit me are already out there, but they are intentionally, or unintentionally, kept hidden away from me? What would learning be when it is like a river that is not confined to hierarchies of compartmentalization? What if research is the researcher's homeland (Deiri, 2018) shaped by a desire to speak our languages freely without the added disgust of colonial knowledge or surveillance of our language practices and memories?

In the Ways We Are Skinned Lies All the Difference
The reflection of the colonizer appears to me
So vividly
in my thoughts
I reflect it onto me

As I leaned back in the love seat my therapist
had in her office, in silence, I pondered
Could those who have experienced or are continuously
colonized ever redeem themselves?
Were my hopes and desires of being in the academy my own?
I doubt myself and think again.
Was it all the mirage of an image projected by a colonizer onto me?
Did I become a reflection of a colonizer that
dictates who and how I should be?
I do not share these thoughts with my therapist
She asked me what I have been doing to cope
I told her
I have been watching stand-up comedies.
In being on the continuum of the colonizer and
colonized I have no answers to redeem me

I see myself reflected in all colonial logics.

This lingering thought disturbs me;
The only thing I can afford is courageous hope.

Moments of frustration propelled me to 'pause' (Carini, 2001; Tuck, 2010; Tuck & Yang, 2018), to think and to understand the fact that as a postcolonial person, a way to find healing is to reconcile the fact that parts of my thinking are a reflection of colonial thinking. Later, I learned that these pauses and moments of frustration were invitations to follow one's own methodological path by claiming self-sovereignty, as much as one can, in order to escape the conditioning of how knowledge is produced when living in the belly of the empire. There is no denying that I felt the deep pressure to follow particular White, colonial canons of knowledge, yet the greater pressure came from the incongruence between where my heart was, the wisdom I had learned from growing up elsewhere and how I was reading myself, my thinking and the people I was learning with in someone else's format or structure. I learned that methodological pathways and research questions for me are about questions of the heart and mind and that everything else flows, reconciling the idea that, in coming to academia, there is a colonial part in my thinking. Claiming self-sovereignty lies in knowing what I do not want my methodological pathways to look like (Wilson, 2008). The journey started for me with finding an already existing knowledge of people who have been touched by colonization and the White and European gaze (empire-centric gaze). Such empire-centric gazes are not innocent and, using Yancy's (2008: xviii) definition, empire-centric is a type of gaze that is a 'performance of distortional "seeing" that evolves out of, and is inextricably linked to, various raced and racist myths, white discursive practices, and centripetal processes of white systemic power and white solipsism... processes of dehumanizing interpellation'. As such, '[t]he white colonialist gaze was invested in a racist regime of classificatory "truth"' (Yancy, 2008: 2).

I found that my journey has been interspersed with moments of clarity of the heart of knowing, despite the prospect that I would rather fail in my methodological journey if it is from a dominant standpoint than appease it. There are no right or wrong answers to what a methodological journey should be, yet it is profoundly essential to know where your heart lies prior to doing your study and the implications of the pathways we take on people like me. People have toiled in the misery of colonization and postcolonial realities for centuries. Such coloniality does not allow for potential or brilliance to flourish.

Educational weapons

A Capitalist Research Luscious Gap of Greed
Screaming
Convince me
Tell me
Why should I read your so insignificant knowledge?
And I wonder why I have to cater to and appease your esteemed majesty of madness
And your endless consumption of our souls, minds and bodies
Producing our bodies into a lens
Contorting us into a form of knowledge shaped in differently sized evenly sharpened symmetrical bullets and bombs
Research journals giving meanings to our lives in ways that scream irrelevant
To me, they sometimes read as pointless!
Generational Syrian ways of knowing telling me
You don't have to follow white supremacist leads
Just enjoy knowledge for knowledge.
Enticed by research sins
I hone my educational weapons again
I shape my methodologies
Family, friends, food, and fun and vanity fair of colonizing imperialist affair
I breathe
And with a smile
In a settler colonial style
I settle in my own skin
And my educational weapons start to indulge in research sin.

Language as an Intimate Relationship

Language is intimate in the ways we express love, ourselves, our thoughts, desires, fears, delusions and nostalgias. When we sever or demonize or mark one language for the purpose of supporting English-only movements and policies (Macedo, 2000), for example, one must ask what sort of severing is happening with who we are as researchers and our conversations with our own communities as multilinguals. Multilingualism can be transgressive, depending on the context, the perspective of the person receiving it, the time period and in the sociohistorical political moment we find ourselves. Language can instill fears and persecution depending on who is in power; simultaneously, language is a way of loving and desire. The intimate relationships we have with our languages impact our connectedness with our thoughts, stories of our parents, grandparents and communities. For example, in their Indigenous conversation and research group, Lessard *et al.* (2020) included Indigenous elders to urge us to think about how language becomes visible within and through relationships:

> I'm reading in-between the lines. I teach children about Kitsi, the Cree word for belly button or umbilicus. I ask them: who are you attached to? Who is your mother, grandmother, clan mother? It is in these relationships that you see the connections and the relationships… It is in our life path that we choose to connect our spirit, body, mind, and emotion. (Elder Francis, cited in Lessard *et al.*, 2020: 5)

Through Elder Francis' emphasis on how language emerges in the intimacy of conversations, histories and communities, the intimate and political nature of language as a radical stance emerges. The connectedness with our lives, bodies, spirit and emotions all come together in language.

Elder Francis (cited in Lessard *et al.*, 2020: 6) elaborated on the importance of language as a relationship and in connecting relationships:

> The language is important, as it links the world around us and the people we meet. The Cree words *waskawewin* and *miyo waskawewin* call us to attend to a sense of movement, movement marked by moving in a beautiful way. These words signify the importance of moving in a good way in our relationships … language has a way of connecting relationships.

The methodological, non-linear path that we pursue, and the way we move along that path through the relationships we hold on to, let go of, be with, are very much part of multilingual radical intimate ways of understanding. The conversations that Elder Francis and Elder Isabelle (who engaged in the research collaborative mentioned earlier) bring, while particular to Indigenous knowledges, are the spirit of understanding the importance of language in relationships. Following the path of this conversation, I think about the relationships in which I understood language, and how it impacted my relationship with language. Part of multilingual, radical, intimate methodology is to move through our paths by asking questions and answering ourselves with deep, personal honesty about the relationships of trust, and care, fear and intervention that we have built, and that are sometimes forcibly imposed upon us, in order to infiltrate the intimacy of languages we experience as multilingual researchers.

The intimately political nature of language and how it impacts our relationships with our intimate communities, languages and thoughts, and how they are surveilled, monitored and treated, need to be considered. As racialized bilingual researchers (Flores, 2016), and the racialized people we connect with, there is always the possibility of indictment for using languages other than English, such as Arabic (Deiri, 2021). How can an ethnography with a centrality on language come to fruition without a discussion of relationships with participants and the type of intimacies we have developed as researchers who use language with the people with whom we connect? Retrospectively, it was an act of existence and playing within an academic space that deemed the relationships I have with the languages I speak and write with colonially that made them invisible, based on racial, ethnic and xenophobic dimensions among others (Bonfiglio, 2007). Examining issues of power within our own linguistic positionality as multilingual researchers is an iterative and critical process throughout all phases of research (Cormier, 2018; Court & Abbas, 2013; cf. May & Caldas, this volume; see also Part 2 of this book). A few helpful questions to interrogate our linguistic positionality are:

(1) How do we view and position people from our own communities who speak various varieties of languages we share with them?
(2) What sort of surrogacy to colonial hierarchies have we internalized into categories such as race, language, gender, classism in relation to learning and education?
(3) How are our language ideologies shaped by the type of education we received about what counts as exceptional language and the relationships our teachers have built with us?
(4) How did we come to create particular judgments and ideologies of purity and perfection about language and education that occur in English?
(5) How have our life experiences, histories and the ways we have been socialized impact our linguistic or multilingual positionality?
(6) How might these internalizations (i.e. life experiences, educational experiences, socializations and ideologies about language, race, gender, educational status and whose bodies are considered multilingual) impact how we view and interact with friends, participants or people we consider intimates?

We need to interrogate our own internalization of linguistic supremacy – in particular, the assumption that one language, in this case standard English (but which can apply to Arabic and all other major languages as well) is inherently better, more intelligible and more civilized in ways that are also tied to race, ethnicity and colonialism. How we understand our linguistic positionality as multilingual researchers will affect the axiology, the value system, by which we approach our research questions and engagements with participants: friends, intimates and community members.

Intimacy is not always about love but rather is about renditions of relationships we have been socialized with and learned to establish, and that is what we need to be critical of. For example, the hostile orientation of viewing language as a resource (Ruíz, 1984) rather than a relationship affects the type of intimacy we establish with our languages. Intimacy can be about anxiety and fear and severing relationships as much as it is about love and visibility within relationships, depending on the context and how language ideologies are deployed to hurt multilingual researchers, peoples and communities (Anzaldúa, 1987).

As I describe in the introduction to this chapter, while I do think of myself as a writer, when I write, I realize I have internalized how my English is perceived by English users. I wonder if the reader will dismiss the content of anything I write when my punctuation is not up to par, or if my sentences are too long, a practice common and fully accepted in so many languages except American English. Such assumptions that a reader might make are loaded with ideologies of ignorance, level of education, backwardness, progressiveness, level or quality of knowledge; in other words, orientalism (Said, 1979). Many of these assumptions work in service to, and prop up, the monolingual researcher or the researcher whose first language is colonial English. The reality is that I believe punctuation is about the rhythm of the writer, as do other researchers and writers. In my view, rhythm is often co-opted to serve those who insist on language standardization. Retrospectively, when I am analyzing conversations with participants, I am mindful and watchful, to the best of my ability, of how I may have internalized such fears; how I dilute my lens with such internalizations; how I project them onto participants and myself; and how I view their education or language learning.

Language Education as Radical and Intimate

A couple of years ago, I was heading to campus to give a talk about something to do with Ramadan and Eid El-Fiter festivities. I was neither an expert on the topic, nor did I understand why I said yes. Driving my car on this day allowed me to deepen my thoughts and made me less connected with my reality. I wondered if it was the insular frame of the car or my philosophical desperation to get out of it that instigated the situation.

I noticed the sun rays and the beautiful green trees on the roadside, and I dove back into a subliminal state of mind. A recent conversation about my thoughts on methodology with a friend of mine popped into my head. I told him I was thinking of calling the methodology I was working on multilingual radical intimate ethnography. My friend chuckled and said: 'With you being Syrian and raised Muslim, good luck using the word "radical"!'. The radical contradiction of who I am and how the word is misused in today's media discourses made the use of *radical* even more appealing to me. Specifically, because of the paradox of following your heart, being who you are feels radical in academia even though it is not radical at all!

I often use the word radical for its historical capacity to remind us of struggle, self-sovereignty and violence, and yet also the comedic effects of how the word is co-opted, distorted and violated to coerce violence into peace, and smother peace at times of violence. To be radical for me is to be self-sovereign; to be aware; to be connected; connected to inner peace; to be in harmony with one's mind, heart and body and ancestral journey; and to follow our hearts. To be radical is to trust our hearts when something does not sit well with our bodies and our minds as fully interconnected. For example, the feeling of being shamed through the languages we speak and love in order to support the empire. To reject such empire-based impositions of hateful intimacy on who we are as postcolonial multilinguals is a radical stance that can ensure self-sovereignty within empire-centric research institutions that at least question the 'track marks of colonization' (Fine *et al.*, 2008: 160) placed on our own minds as multilingual scholars of color.

To be radical is to speak your truth, to connect and open up your mind, heart and body. Most of all, to be radical is to be radically intimate and to know ourselves and how the impositions of the empire are imprinted on how we understand our languages and our bodies. To be radical is to be intimately aware of who we are, where we came from, the languages we love, write and speak, and the powers and circumstances that shape us and shape the relationships we have developed with our languages. To be radical is to radically learn from the historical and political violence of the past in order to open up a space for critical peace in the present.

My understandings of *radical* in many ways draw on certain womanist scholars who opened up my heart and mind. bell hooks' (1989: 15) understandings of radical highlighted a 'defiant political gesture' aimed at transgressing the 'boundaries of race, sex, and class domination' and the location of how we 'position ourselves on the side of colonial mentality'. In this colonial mentality, hooks (1989) asserts that language is a site of struggle. As an extension of that struggle, the ways we expose, call out and promote the violence of monolingual ideologies is very much carved out in our methodological pathways, and the realities of what we are allowed to pursue in our bilingual methodologies within the constraints of a world marked by English-only movements and policies (Macedo, 2000). In such a world, to be radical – to *transgress* – is merely a mode of survival more than anything else – at least that is how I viewed it at the time when I read hooks' words. I needed a homeland and the intimacy of the languages of my mother, aunts, sisters, father and friends. I was determined to follow a methodology that honors languages intimate to my thinking and yet to also learn how I radically internalized colonial ideologies in how I viewed language. From this space of tension, honesty and longing, MRIE emerged in the intimacy of ways to research that helped me establish and create research as a homeland through language. Accepting ourselves as postcolonial multilingual researchers is as powerfully radical as anything we do in the research process. Most of all, to be radical is about intimacy and holding joy and pain side by side and the ways they shape our lives without letting one wash over the other. To remember that as populations touched by colonization, we also share intimacies with one another, despite the violence imposed on us, and that is what keeps us connected.

Venturing into the world of the intimate, and scholars who have done similar work, I learned that intimate ethnography calls for honesty in presenting the intimate details of researchers' emotions (Banerji & Distante, 2009; Lerum, 2001; Pope & deMarrais, 2017; Waterston, 2019; Waterston & Rylko-Bauer, 2006). However, intimacy here does not mean that I am necessarily very close to participants; while it might be true for some participants, it is also indicative of the intimacy that participants establish with one another, and the intimacy through language visible in relationships. I am not, and have never been, a Western-centric, English-speaking researcher writing about Black and Brown racialized bi/multilinguals. I am a postcolonial multilingual who has been impacted by neocolonial projects. Therefore, my view of ethnography is always going to be contextualized within strands of understanding that language research, from the point of view of the empire, is very much about acquiring populations to serve the empire. Therefore, language acquisition and research are also about the acquisition of the empire. I write from the location of academia that writes onto me in ways that are both similar to, and different from, the communities I learn from and with whom I live. And what is more intimate than education? What is more intimate than the ways we learn and teach? What is more intimate than the connections we build, the joys, traumas and healings from what we learn and teach and the relationships we build with and through language? Answering these questions is radically intimate and unique to each one of us as multilingual researchers. So, at this juncture of the chapter, I would invite you to take a deep breath, and circulate and write your responses to these questions.

Recapping and Moving Forward with Multilingual Radical Intimate Ethnography

Intimate, as discussed earlier, focuses on the relationship we have developed with language and the people we learned with and the intimacies of our shared experiences. The languages we write and speak are at the core of who we are and the relationships we form. Other scholars, of course, have conceptualized intimate ethnography as a methodological approach that straddles the fields of ethnography, personal histories and autoethnography, and involves contextualizing the personal lives and stories of the researcher and participants within the larger social, historical, political and structural issues that shape their lives (Pope & deMarrais, 2017; Waterston & Rylko-Bauer, 2006). Adding the understandings of language as intimate and radical, I define MRIE as an ethnography that seeks to understand the power structures that shape the lives of multilingual participants and researchers intimately. In such an ethnographic approach, it is necessary for the researcher to know the power structures that shape the participants' lives intimately through the lived experiences of the heart, body and mind of being subjugated to similar experiences. MRIE seeks to understand how these power structures impact the most intimate aspects of our lives and who we are intimately. Importantly, MRIE takes into account the shapeshifting nature of violence that comes from dominant language ideologies and how these ideologies impact our relationships with ourselves, and intimate family and community members. An essential question to interrogate in MRIE is how the influence of dominant language ideologies seeps into our relationships with our communities, friends, parents, spouses, children and so on. This question is relevant within Western-centric academic contexts that both dismiss the postcolonial multilingual as being equally qualified to monolingual or English-dominant researchers, and yet assume that, by default of multilingualism and ethnic matching, the postcolonial researcher is prepared to work with other multilingual postcolonial communities, regardless of their language uses and internalized ideologies.

The way I have envisioned MRIE builds to some extent on intimate ethnography. For example, I agree with Waterston and Rylko-Bauer (2006), who argue that intimate ethnography helps a researcher capture the transmogrifying nature of violence that comes with migration, such as the impact of borders, language, economic hardship and religion, among other challenges. Intimate ethnography is necessarily portrayed from an insider's perspective, or that of a community with which the researcher identifies, as straddling both the personal and the political domains of the researcher's life. Likewise, Morris (2016) asserts that intimate ethnography enables a researcher to gain a close understanding, as well as a window into analyzing the larger political structures, that shape the lives of the participants involved in such research. Realizing, analyzing, synthesizing and representing (i.e. rendering) intimate ethnographic projects entail straddling multiple creative expressions such as poetry and photography (Banerji & Distante, 2009) and mixing diverse strands of reflexive ethnographic methods.

One of the aspects I most appreciate is that MRIE addresses the intricate politics of representation and, therefore, can be used as a strategy to undermine the ways in which the dominant gaze essentializes views of culture and the body (Banerji & Distante, 2009: 40) by providing points of 'concord' and 'divergence' of 'perspectives' among participants. I also appreciate that it seeks to capture moments of solidarity between researcher and participants as well as between participants and one another. One of the most important goals with MRIE is that it can enable us to capture moments in how Whitestream current educational paradigms betray us as researchers and, likewise, betray our participants. In other words, MRIE captures the intimacy of locating and reclaiming the knowledges that are already there in the languages of the people.

> To avoid driving and to carve out a space of solid writing without the women's burden of additional childcare duties because somehow, we are equipped with 'maternal instinct' that a male partner in a heterosexual relationship apparently does not have, I stayed over at a participant's home. Sitting on a couch, working on an academic paper, I attempted to find definitions and theoretical understanding of learning and literacies. I was desperately annoyed with the hierarchies and compartmentalization of learning and literacies— Academic, non-academic, formal, non-formal, community-based, school-based. I was interested in ways to capture learning and literacies that are taking place in everyday lives. All of a sudden, I found myself thinking about and becoming comfortable with the metaphor of learning like water, learning like a river. Here came the question of what if learning was like a river started to become clearer? This is when and how I found my way to the work of Margret Kovach (2017) which, for me, became a way of research to nourish my soul. While I have always gravitated towards Indigenous methodologies, finding and learning from reading Kovach's work (without actually meeting her) brought me to my homeland in a way that no other work had done. I was also reminded of how my mother, at my own personal moments of frustration about my futurity in academia or lack thereof, would tell me to be less critical of myself and to understand that life is as 'ميات' waters: ebbs, flows, stops, proceeds, and changes direction based on the moment and the obstacle. To control the waters of life it is to lose so much of what life is meant to be and what we are supposed to learn.
>
> On another occasion, I was reading a book on bilingualism and postcolonialism. The author went into an explanation of the importance of ethnography and the refrain of generalizability that is a common practice

> in ethnography. I found myself saying, 'and who would read an ethnography for generalizability!!' And that was that. I did not continue reading the book; I put it away forever. My heart wants to find ethnographies that are written without the shame of lacking the purposefulness of generalizability. Then, outside of my doctoral studies, I stumbled upon ethnographies of the particular and in particular, by Lila Abu-Lughod. That's how ethnographies of the particular from her work on Writing against Culture (Abu-Lughod, 1991) and Writing Women's Worlds (Abu-Lughod, 2008) became part of my spiritual methodological guide to developing MRIE.

In this manner, for me, the main questions at the heart of *multilingual radical intimate ethnography* became: How do I account for the particularities of my life and people's lives and their relationships with their languages without losing sight of the whole? How do I carry a bifocal vision of the intimate realities of researchers and participants without losing the interconnectedness with our communities, knowledges, languages and lives that are intimately shaped by political ideologies and circumstances? Part of the answer to these questions is that MRIE must be rooted in Indigenous ways of knowing and ethnographies of the particular (Abu-Lughod, 1991, 2008; Smith, 2011; see also McCarty, this volume) in which the purpose is to reject engaging in homogenizing narratives of language and culture, as is done in traditional ethnography. The purpose of ethnography that is multilingual, radical and intimate is to particularize rather than generalize. Abu-Lughod (2008: 16) argues that a story is 'always situated; it has both a teller and an audience. Its perspective is partial'. Particularizing the purpose of ethnography means holding onto the intimacy of language for each one of us and in relation to our communities. Rather than merely constructing generalizations and identifying trends, writing against culture or particularizing means we must focus on the *incoherence* among and within the participants' stories, as well as the incoherence that exists within ourselves as researchers living postcolonial realities. Holism, fluidity and interconnectedness create a form of ethnographic methodology that positions the particular and the whole as always interconnected to one another (Kovach, 2017). The goal is to account for the particular while maintaining the interconnectedness of who we are and who we are with, and how all of that is held in relationships with people and our relationship with language. We need to avoid asking questions about generalizations or making judgments about languages and cultural practices – whatever that might mean – in meaningless ways. MRIE, in this sense, embraces an explicitly radical perspective – with a simple caveat that it is only radical because, in the current context of the United States, we live in a context that privileges English monolingualism (cf. May, this volume). In other words, there might be nothing radical or transgressive about this methodology if we were to live in a world that honors racialized multilingual knowledges.

The Tenets of Multilingual Radical Intimate Ethnography

The tenets of MRIE require us to:

(1) Trouble our own gaze as researchers and ask readers to trouble their gazes explicitly (Kovach, 2017).
(2) Understand language as political and intimate and understood in and within relationships.
(3) Disrupt the boundaries of ethnography and autoethnography and weave creative expression as a legitimate part of the research process.
(4) Ensure the researcher's linguistic and post-positional linguistic positionality is woven creatively throughout the methodological process.
(5) Emphasize the importance of an insider's perspective or inbetweener's perspective (Anzaldúa, 2017; Diversi & Moreira, 2018; Sarroub, 2002, 2013) without having to dilute bilingual knowledge for monolingual gains or reductionist understandings of matching races and ethnicities of languages and participants (Cabral & Smith, 2011).
(6) Conduct research with people the researcher considers intimates, such as close friends, family members or close colleagues, and/or entails engaging in the intimate spaces, which destabilizes the normalized power structures and dynamics between the researcher and participant-friends.
(7) Call out the politics and power relations in transcription and language representation, editing the surveillance of bilingual scholarship; explicitly seek ways to redefine traditional ethnographic conventions to honor multilingual/bilingual researchers, communities and participants.
(8) Understand and experience the power structures that imprint and shape the participants' lives intimately.
(9) Focus on the interconnectedness between the particular and the whole throughout the research process, specifically during the data collection process and the data analysis. For my purposes here, I am only going to focus on the first tenet of troubling the gaze, as an initial step toward understanding MRIE within the realm and space of a written chapter.

Troubling the Monolingual Gaze

In order to explain the first tenet of MRIE, I will first speak to the importance of writing from the heart in relation to troubling the gaze. Then, I will provide a vignette as an example of troubling the gaze, as a process, rather than an accomplishable goal. Then, I speak of how 'troubling the gaze' (Kovach, 2017) has aided my research. Without following my heart and the knowledges that my postcolonial experiences imparted onto me, as written previously, and the influences of Indigenous and postcolonial scholars, I doubt that I would be able to trouble my gaze. In order to trouble the gaze, I learned to trust what that incongruence between my heart, mind and body, or between my axiology, epistemology and ontology, is telling me about the methodological pathway that I want to follow. I will share with you, as a reader, a vignette that comes from my dissertation work with Saudi women living in the United States. I had clarity about the following: (a) the conversations will not privilege English; and (b) the locus of the study will not be confined by the boundaries of academic/schooling intuitions, such as the university or schools. The vignette contributes to understanding the body as a site of literacy practices and considers the ways transnational Saudi women read and write themselves creatively, carving out a space of belonging within a context that reads and writes their bodies through an orientalist gaze (Said, 1979).

As you read the vignette as researchers, I would like you to note the type of interpretations you are casting about the written form of this conversation. I would like you to ask yourself: 'What is it about my world understandings and experiences that makes me cast these interpretations onto the story'? 'How might my education have taught me to read and see the world as I do'? These questions are at the core of troubling our gazes. The way we see the world – and the imagination we construct and have learned to construct violently about people – has more to do with our own experiences and socializations in the world than it has to do with the people we converse with, especially for those who come from the world of Western-centric academic spaces. Furthermore, I would like you to reflect on your patience, or lack thereof, while reading the vignette. I ask you to focus on the meaning of the entire story rather than every single word that as academics we are trained to do.

Bahyaa and I had our last face-to-face audio-recorded interview on a sunny end of April day at a coffee shop and our conversation lasted for three hours. We argued, we joked, we asked each other questions. And as it often goes with Bahyaa, it was mostly her interviewing me. On one occasion, I asked Bahyaa about my positionality from her point of view and she responded jokingly 'أنت الباحث' ('you are the researcher') – and that it was on me to figure it out. This encounter pretty much sums up the type of relationship we have developed through friendship and research – one where we often grew closer to one another.

For the reader, be patient with the story. Patience is a requirement of troubling our gazes.

> The night before meeting at the coffee shop, Bahyaa sent me a video about a Saudi man who had a car accident and his appreciation of his older sister. She texted me multiple times to see if I had the chance to see

> the video before we met. I was busy and when I tried to watch the video, I lost interest within the first minute. Mainly, I lost interest because I do not like religious talk. I make judgments about such talk and conversation. Once I sat down at the table after ordering my drink, Bahyaa asked me one more time if I had the chance to watch the video. In a slightly impatient manner, and disregarding all the questions I prepared prior, I asked 'what makes this video so important to you?' She talked about the man's accent, and his sister's clothing, and the way he used words and the judgments or preconceived notions that one might have about him and his sisters' education and social status from these markers in Saudi Arabia. Bahyaa would give me examples, explain, weave in and out of so many other topics. Listening to the audio-recorded conversation afterward was fascinating, complex and exhausting. Most importantly, I felt that my academic journey has not prepared me to honor it well. The lack of focus on the multiplicity of transnational contexts and the layeredness of their politics, history, colonization and so much more, does not allow me to dive deep in understandings. In other words, I felt failed by my academic journey. I did not have access to the heart and to the knowledges that would allow me to honor the stories in my research.

This conversation was like a magnet. Every time I decided to quit its analysis, I would find myself coming back to it the next day. I did not know where I was going with it. I did not know how to make sense of the stories and the vulnerability that she shared. Bahyaa was completely unreserved. She told me about the many tragedies that shaped her life. She talked about her parents, her social status and her need to be perfect. She talked about her struggles in wanting to be seen on her own terms by society and that she does not want to be shamed by others for all the tragedies that she had faced. She reasoned that this was why she always felt that she needed to try to be as close to 'perfect' as possible, including in English. Around the third or fourth time of listening to the audio, I started to listen more vividly. There were times where Bahyaa was telling me that I was not understanding her. Yet, at the same time, I would confirm to her in the conversation that I was listening.

The more I listened to our recorded conversation, and the stories Bahyaa shared, the more I recognized that I was only hearing the conversation. Finally, at the fifth round of listening to this audio-recording, I decided to enter the listening session with attentiveness and respect rather than entering it with my own ways of understanding and judging the world. Or at least before judging it that I judge myself and my understandings first. So, one of these lenses was that I am purely a spiritual person who does not believe in any religious doctrine. I claim that I do not judge people's religions, but all the while I do.

I realized that I was listening with my own gaze rather than listening to Bahyaa. I also recognized that my gaze was violent. This is where ethnography can fall short of the lives of people that gift us their knowledge, their time and their understandings. This vital moment and the relationship established between Bahyaa and me through the recorded conversation even after it ended helped me grow as a researcher. For me, this realization became the locus for starting to trouble my gaze, to put my researcher ego in check and to realize that I am only a learner from the experts – that is friends and participants. Here, I wove my poetic dilemmas about the methodological paths I was trying to make.

By default, the conversations and the stories in the recording shaped how I heard and understood my failure in listening due to my own gaze. In her discussion of Indigenous research, Kovach (2017: 385) highlights the dangers in qualitative research at large when the research is done with 'a non-interrogated western gaze cast upon [I]ndigeneity… the Western gaze sees what it wants'. In the case with Bahyaa, I came to realize that the knowledges a postcolonial researcher like me have are steeped in a Western gaze that I learned through methodological research conventions and practices. Furthermore, I became more aware of the possibility of the extraction of value (Gaudry, 2015) in my work. While Gaudry (2015) speaks to the experience of how academia extracts indigenous knowledges, Chávez-Moreno (2020; see also this volume) explores the same issue of extraction of value of bilingual and multilingual learners in bilingual education and scholarship. Similarly, while many higher academic institutions espouse doing research 'on' bi/multilingual students, they refuse to acknowledge the ways of being and understanding the world that racialized multilingual scholars bring, and so often our scholarship has to contort and dilute itself to fit into the monolingual imaginary.

Interrogating and troubling the Western gaze is one way to combat the systematic extraction of knowledge and value of racialized bilingual students, participants and researchers for the benefit of monolingual ideologies that are ever present in academia. Troubling the Western gaze is important because the epistemology by which we understand language has deep ramifications for the type of meanings a researcher imbues into their bilingual research. For example, Charlo (2015) highlights the dangers of forcing concepts onto languages, in this case, Indigenous languages, because it changes the essence of a language. For example, 'my' she argued, cannot be used to own the natural world as she was informed by other Indigenous elders and community members. She encourages moments of awakening of how we understand the relationships that we establish with language. Similarly, what would racialized bilingual knowledge seeking and understanding look like if it did not have to continuously and consistently contort and dilute itself to fit monolingual possession of the English-only ideologies of research and publications? How much of bilingual research guided by language acquisition and language learning is actually more an acquisition of the knowledges for the gains of the empire than an invested interest in bilingual children, communities or populations? How much of it is about surveilling and controlling populations for the benefit of racial purity (Bonfiglio, 2010). The question for me is about my internal conflicting dilemma of existing as a scholar to navigate these tightropes of violence toward ourselves, our friends, families and bilingual and multilingual communities.

Challenges of Doing Bilingual Research

Taking the soul out of your writing

The problem with monolingual editors is that they take the soul out of your writing. I sometimes spend 30 minutes determining if a word expresses the emotion and the meaning that I would like to convey in my writing. Why did I need an editor in the first place? I needed an editor because the way I write and express myself in academia apparently is not suitable to be submitted just the way it is. For example, in my first version of dissertation writing, listening to stories in the audio-recorded conversations was viewed as listening to data. I am not sure how one can listen to 'data'. Wouldn't listening to data strip the people out of the conversation and turn them into objects?

Editorial censorship and surveillance

The way I write and express my ideas as a bilingual person apparently is in need of hiding and surveillance in institutions and in journal publications. My writing will be rejected, unless the way I write is confined and contorted to the meaning and the ways of writing and speaking of Eurocentric English monolinguals. Multi/bilingual scholarship is apparently better hidden rather than supported. More ironically, while monolingual ways of being and understanding the world are demanding that I contort myself to it, this contortion should happen on my own time and my own dime. Furthermore, in the process of trying to make myself legible to a monolingual world, I become unintelligible to myself. I no longer recognize myself in my words. Often, the sentences become duller, and they lose the meaning I intended. And in the process of diluting my words, my ways of knowing, the relationships that taught me to think of the world in the way I do are now diluted. The stories of my mother, my grandmother and my ancestors are also diluted. The act of diluting one's complexity of life to fit the frames of racial purity of monolingualism under the guise of making bilingual ways of understanding more 'legible' is a very violent act that cannot simply be shrugged off as making one's writing easier to understand.

In closing, I have attempted to argue for the need to use MRIE as a way to represent languages and to give importance to these languages for research purposes that connect with the heart. This chapter presented

Arabic as an object of visibility. Hence, in many ways, it reproduced the dominant monolingual perspective that subscribes to English-only practices that are pervasive in the academy. Multilingualism seems to be considered a subtraction from the quality of research for no obvious or apparent reason other than the functions of White supremacy, among other oppressive ideologies. Bilingual or multilingual research-based methodologies can open spaces for students to engage in various ways of data representation that seek to disrupt dominant gaze understandings and change the representation of languages other than English to something other than a mere visual object. Furthermore, multilingual research, such as MRIE, encourages transnational researchers, specifically within the context of the United States, to be able to understand how to analyze and make sense of what they learn from participants and present their findings in ways that are more representative of their multilingual linguistic affiliations.

Acknowledgments

I would like to thank all the friends/research participants who supported me personally, in every way possible, to make this work happen. I would also like to thank Dr Timothy San Pedro for his guidance on methodology in the early years of my doctoral studies. Special thanks to Dr Tanja Burkard and Dr Elizabeth Mendoza for their diligent reading of the early drafts of this manuscript. Thanks to Dr Theodore Chao and Dr Michiko Hikida for their guidance, mentorship and friendship, and Mollie Blackburn and Binaya Subedi for trusting my need for exploration from which radical intimate ethnography (RIE) came to be.

Multilingual radical intimate ethnography came from my original dissertation work and general framework of radical intimate ethnography and the term *intimate*, and intimacy was born from the participants and all the beautiful lessons they taught me.

Lastly, thanks to my mother Hasnaa Shammaa for teaching to trust my heart.

References

Abu-Lughod, L. (1991) Writing against culture. *Recapturing Anthropology: Working in the Present* 8, 137–162. https://doi.org/10.318220120913-4-IT-4027.00010

Abu-Lughod, L. (2008) *Writing Women's Worlds: Bedouin Stories*. Berkeley, CA: University of California Press.

Aiello, J. and Nero, S.J. (2019) Discursive dances: Narratives of insider/outsider researcher tensions. *Journal of Language, Identity & Education* 18 (4), 251–265. https://doi.org/10.1080/15348458.2019.1623035

Anzaldúa, G. (1987) *Borderlands/La frontera: The New Mestiza*. San Francisco, CA: Aunt Lute Books.

Anzaldúa, G. (2017) How to tame a wild tongue [1987]. In J. Ritchie and K. Ronald (eds) *Available Means* (pp. 357–365). Philadelphia, PA: University of Pittsburgh Press. https://doi.org/10.2307/j.ctt5hjqnj.57

Banerji, A. and Distante, I. (2009) An intimate ethnography. *Women & Performance: A Journal of Feminist Theory* 19 (1), 35–60.

Bonfiglio, T.P. (2007) Language, racism, and ethnicity. In M. Hellinger and A. Pauwels (eds) *Handbook of Language and Communication: Diversity and Change* (pp. 619–650). Berlin: De Gruyter Mouton.

Bonfiglio, T.P. (2010) *Mother Tongues and Nations.* Berlin: De Gruyter. https://doi.org/10.1515/9781934078266

Cabral, R.R. and Smith, T.B. (2011) Racial/ethnic matching of clients and therapists in mental health services: A meta-analytic review of preferences, perceptions, and outcomes. *Journal of Counseling Psychology* 58 (4), 537–554.

Carini, P.F. (2001) *Starting Strong: A Different Look at Children, Schools, and Standards.* New York: Teachers College Press.

Charlo, A. (2015) Indigenous language revitalization [Video file]. YouTube. TedxUMontana. See https://www.youtube.com/watch?v=6kuC_IemiCs&t=442s.

Chávez-Moreno, L. (2020) U.S. Empire and an immigrant's counternarrative: Conceptualizing imperial privilege. *Journal of Teacher Education* 72 (2),1–14. https://doi.org/10.1177/0022487120919928

Collins, P. (1986) Learning from the outsider within: The sociological significance of black feminist thought. *Social Problems* 6 (33), 14–32. https://doi.org/10.2307/800672

Corbin Dwyer, S. and Buckle, J.L. (2009) Reflection/commentary on a past article: 'The space between: On being an insider-outsider in qualitative research'. *International Journal of Qualitative Methods* 17 (1), 54–63. https://doi.org/10.1177/1609406918788176

Cormier, G. (2018) The language variable in educational research: An exploration of researcher positionality, translation, and interpretation. *International Journal of Research and Method in Education* 41 (3), 328–341. https://doi.org/10.1080/1743727X.2017.1307335

Court, D. and Abbas, R. (2013) Whose interview is it, anyway? Methodological and ethical challenges of insider–outsider research, multiple languages, and dual-researcher cooperation. *Qualitative Inquiry* 19 (6), 480–488.

Deiri (Diri-Rieder), Y. (2018) Finding way just like an ant: Racialized bodies reading and writing themselves. Unpublished doctoral dissertation, The Ohio State University.

Deiri, Y. (2021) Teaching Arabic to children and youth: Between love and indictment. *International Journal of Bilingualism and Bilingual Education*, 1–13. https://doi.org/10.1080/13670050.2021.1989372

Diversi, M. and Moreira, C. (2018) *Betweener Autoethnographies: A Path towards Social Justice.* Abingdon: Routledge.

Fine, M., Tuck, E. and Zeller-Kerkman, S. (2008) Do you believe in Geneva? Methods and ethics at the global–local nexus. In N. Denzin, Y. Lincoln and L.T. Smith (eds) *The Handbook of Critical and Indigenous Methodologies* (pp. 157–179). London: Sage.

Flores, N. (2016) A tale of two visions: Hegemonic whiteness and bilingual education. *Educational Policy* 30 (1), 13–38. https://doi.org/10.1177/0895904815616482

Gaudry, A. (2015) Researching the resurgence: Insurgent research and community engaged methodologies in 21st century academic inquiry. In S. Strega and L.A. Brown (eds) *Research as Resistance* (pp. 243–267). Toronto: Canadian Scholars' Press.

hooks, b. (1989) Choosing the margin as a space of radical openness. *Framework: The Journal of Cinema and Media* 36, 15–23. https://www.jstor.org/stable/44111660?seq=1#metadata_info_tab_contents

Kovach, M. (2017) Doing indigenous methodologies. In N.K. Denzin and Y.S. Lincoln (eds) *The SAGE Handbook of Qualitative Research* (5th edn, pp. 383–406). Thousand Oaks, CA: Sage.

Lerum, K. (2001) Subjects of desire: Academic armor, intimate ethnography, and the production of critical knowledge. *Qualitative Inquiry* 7 (4), 466–483.

Lessard, S., Kootenay, I., Whiskeyjack, F., Chung, S., Clandinin, J. and Caine, V. (2020) Working with indigenous elders in narrative inquiry: Reflections and key considerations. *Qualitative Inquiry* 11 (2), 93–108. https://doi.org/10.1177/1077800419898498

Macedo, D. (2000) The colonialism of the English only movement. *Educational Researcher* 29 (3), 15–24. https://doi.org/10.3102/0013189X029003015

Morris, J. (2016) Intimate ethnography and cross-cultural research. In J. Morris (ed.) *Everyday Post-Socialism* (pp. 215–231). London: Palgrave Macmillan.

Pope, E.M. and deMarrais, K.P. (2017) *An Intimate Ethnography: A Review of My Father's Wars: Migration, Memory, and the Violence of a Century*. New York: Taylor & Francis.

Ruíz, R. (1984) Orientations in language planning. *NABE Journal* 8 (2), 15–34. https://doi.org/10.1080/08855072.1984.10668464

Said, E.W. (1979) *Orientalism*. New York: Vintage.

Sarroub, L.K. (2002) In-betweenness: Religion and conflicting visions of literacy. *Reading Research Quarterly* 37 (2), 130–148.

Sarroub, L.K. (2013) *All American Yemeni Girls: Being Muslim in a Public School*. Philadelphia, PA: University of Pennsylvania Press.

Smith, G.H. (2011) Protecting and respecting indigenous knowledge. In M. Battiste (ed.) *Reclaiming Indigenous Voice and Vision* (pp. 209–224). Vancouver: UBC Press.

Tuck, E. (2010) Breaking up with Deleuze: Desire and valuing the irreconcilable. *International Journal of Qualitative Studies in Education* 23 (5), 635–650. https://doi.org/10.1080/09518398.2010.500633

Tuck, E. and Yang, K.W. (2018) Building things not to last forever. *Critical Ethnic Studies* 4 (2), 1–12. https://doi.org/10.5749/jcritethnstud.4.2.0001

Urrieta, L. (2010) *Working from Within: Chicana and Chicano Activist Educators in Whitestream Schools*. Tucson, AZ: University of Arizona Press.

Waterston, A. (2019) Intimate ethnography and the anthropological imagination: Dialectical aspects of the personal and political in my father's wars. *American Ethnologist* 46 (1), 7–19. https://doi.org/10.1111/amet.12730

Waterston, A. and Rylko-Bauer, B. (2006) Out of the shadows of history and memory: Personal family narratives in ethnographies of rediscovery. *American Ethnologist* 33 (3), 397–412.

Wilson, S. (2008) *Research is Ceremony: Indigenous Research Methods*. Winnipeg: Fernwood Publishing.

Yancy, G. (2008) *Black Bodies, White Gazes: The Continuing Significance of Race in America*. Lanham, MD: Rowman & Littlefield Publishers.

Part 2

Rethinking Reflexivity and Positionality

4 Race Reflexivity: Examining the Unconscious for a Critical Race Ethnography

Laura C. Chávez-Moreno

Research about race in schools (and arguably other inquiries as well) requires a researcher to engage with their personal, educational and scholarly training about race and racism. This chapter takes readers on my journey as a scholar in learning race scholarship, particularly in employing critical race theory (CRT), and some of the reflexivity I engaged in. To start, I briefly situate the ethnographic tradition in which I locate my study, and I summarize my inquiry into a two-way dual-language (DL) program. The chapter's main section describes the race-reflexivity typology: the three levels of race reflexivity in relation to my learning about, and use of, CRT and other race theories. More specifically, I provide scholars with an example of using the typology of race reflexive modes of thought outlined by sociologists Mustafa Emirbayer and Matthew Desmond (2012) and extended by sociologist Wendy Moore's (2012) critique of Emirbayer and Desmond's article. As such, the chapter contributes a scholar's race reflexivity, an example of considering one's knowledge acquisition and unconscious when conducting a Critical Race ethnography to study White supremacy, race and racism in schooling contexts.

Critical Race Ethnography in Education

I selected ethnography as my study's mode of inquiry because it encourages thick description about everyday cultural practices and interactions between people in their lived environment, for example, institutional activities in schools. Many rich ethnographies examine questions centering race and racism (Bartlett & Brayboy, 2005; Carter, 2005; Haddix, 2012; Lee, 2009; Pollock, 2009) by asking, for example, how the complexities of race/racism in schooling influence the interactions between teachers, youth and other school community members (Lewis, 2011; Valenzuela, 1999). My study follows this tradition by utilizing a specific type of ethnography: 'Critical Race ethnography' (Duncan, 2005; Vaught, 2011; see also Coles, this volume). While this chapter explores reflexivity and does not aim to offer an example of how to conduct a Critical Race ethnography or elaborate on this as a methodology, I briefly mention below some key features of Critical Race ethnography in order to situate the study for readers.

A Critical Race ethnography is similar to ethnographies that contribute insights into and thick description of how race operates as a stratifying force in localized school contexts and thus larger society. However, a Critical Race ethnography goes further, as Sabina Vaught (2011: 24) elaborates – it is not just attention to race and racism that makes a Critical Race ethnography, but its adherence to and development of 'central conceptual arguments of CRT'. The central concepts from CRT's legal tradition are, like all concepts, decided on by each researcher, and I suggest some of the most influential in education have been interest convergence (e.g. Alemán & Alemán, 2010; Castagno, 2014; Milner, 2008), intersectionality (e.g. Harris & Leonardo, 2018; Harris & Patton, 2019; Pérez Huber, 2010) and Whiteness as property (e.g. Annamma, 2015; Powell, 2018). The fundamental difference between a critical ethnography and a Critical Race ethnography is the latter's aim of explaining the observed sociocultural practices through CRT and, through this, then expounding on CRT concepts.

I aimed for my study to advance as the theoretical and analytical framework the concept of Whiteness as property (Harris, 1993), a choice guided by the rationale of focusing on the material consequences of race. Following Vaught, I capitalize Critical Race ethnography to differentiate it from critical ethnographies that study race/racism and to signal that my project advances a key concept from CRT. Next, I briefly describe the context of the Critical Race ethnography I conducted.

The Study

My investigation took place in a two-way DL bilingual education program, which is a bilingual model said to improve students' academic achievement and to develop biliteracy by balancing a classroom's number of English-dominant students and (in my context) Spanish-dominant students. I focused on two racially diverse schools with DL programs, a high school and its feeder middle school. Almost all the youth had participated in DL since early elementary school. The DL elementary school's logic of labeling students as either Spanish dominant (in this case Latinxs[1]) or English dominant continued to organize the secondary-level classrooms, even though the adolescents mostly self-identified as bilingual. Reflecting its midwestern public school district's issue with racial disparities, the DL program faced tensions between the program objective of focusing on Latinxs (many of whom were labeled 'English language learners') and that of teaching White youth, who comprised most of the English-dominant half. My ethnography explores the policies, program practices, pedagogy and ideologies of the DL program. For example, I examined the teachers' practices in regard to culturally relevant pedagogy's sociopolitical consciousness (Ladson-Billings, 2014). I also examined how the policies and program practices attended to equity for Latinxs. The study intervened in the fields of bilingual education and race studies in education by showing how a DL program perpetuates Whites' inequitable material accumulation and the superiority of a White racial identity. I found that DL whitewashed bilingual education through policies benefiting Whites while excluding many Latinx students and other students of color from a bilingual education (Chávez-Moreno, 2018; see also Heiman & Yanes, this volume).

The next section comprises the chapter's main argument and contribution, that of describing a type of race reflexivity and providing examples of this reflexivity.

Race Reflexivity

Unlike post-positivist attempts to sanitize the researcher's influence from the study, critical research paradigms and ethnographic traditions consider the researcher as determinative to the study (e.g. Banks, 1998; Carspecken, 1996; Madison, 2019; Villenas, 1996). I understood myself as formative to the inquiry and therefore an instrumental part of the study. This stance requires considering my own positionality and engaging in reflexivity practices to help me account for my interpretations when conducting fieldwork in the analytical description and interpretation of the data. Furthermore, because racial ideologies are pervasive yet invisibilized in US society, I submit that to conduct research that examines race requires a researcher to engage in reflexivity about race – that is, their unconscious ideas, assumptions and scholarly training about race.

For my Critical Race ethnography, I sought theoretical guidance for a rigorous practice of reflexivity for race scholars. I decided to adapt the race reflexive thinking suggested by sociologists Emirbayer and Desmond (2012) and extended by Moore's (2012) push to attend to the systemic racism and White normativity within academia. I mention my choice not to suggest that, in order to do a Critical Race ethnography, one must follow the race reflexivity recommended by these particular scholars. Rather, after considering several reflexivity conceptualizations, I chose this approach as the one most appropriate for my situation and research. I anticipated this approach would help me be explicit about the assumptions guiding my decisions for my study for several reasons. For one, like Emirbayer and Desmond, I disagree that a scholar's racial vantage point and/or identity *in and of itself* leads to scholarly advances.

Reflexivity can help scholars from different racial standpoints to provide constructive theories that advance race scholarship (see also May & Caldas, this volume). Another reason I chose this approach was because

I did not initially understand and/or (ultimately) agree with all of Emirbayer and Desmond's points (which I describe below). Meaning, I chose this approach in order to not engage with the obvious and/or an 'easy' reflexivity practice, but to embark on a practice that would challenge me into reading more about new ideas.

Emirbayer and Desmond (2012) argue that advancing race scholarship requires scholars from across fields to share practical knowledge on race reflexivity in order to (1) grow scientific knowledge of racial structures and practices, (2) develop ways to theorize and address racial injustice and (3) promote appreciation of racial differences without resorting to essentialized platitudes that reify race. Scholars should not narrate their life-history, but rather engage in 'rigorous institutional analyses of the social and historical structures that condition one's thinking and inner experience' (Emirbayer & Desmond, 2012: 591). In so doing, they should 'pass on to one another their accumulated practical knowledge regarding the multifarious ways in which the academic unconscious shapes seemingly even innocuous "choices" such as the selection of research questions or the crafting of objects of study' (Emirbayer & Desmond, 2012: 591), the latter of which I do elsewhere (Chávez-Moreno, 2018). Emirbayer and Desmond (2012) note that individuals are products of institutions, like schools and universities, and thus they argue that reflecting on different dimensions of reflexivity is not to establish legitimacy or be an exercise in navel-gazing, but to benefit one's study and advance social science. Moore (2012) reminds us that the academy was founded on, and still engages in, White supremacist ideologies and practices, and that it behooves race scholars to analyze the contexts and institutional structures and processes that formed their ideas.

Basing their conception of race reflexivity on Pierre Bourdieu's ideas on reflexivity, Emirbayer and Desmond (2012) describe three levels of the unconscious a scholar should consider when engaging in race theory scholarship: the social unconscious; the disciplinary unconscious; and the scholastic unconscious. The following three sections each describe one level of reflexivity and provide examples of the reflexivity I engaged in for my study of race in a DL program. To do the latter, I weave into each of the three levels of reflexivity identified by Emirbayer and Desmond (2012) my reflections on the beliefs which informed my research's aims and my researcher decisions. These reflections touch on how I adapted the three levels for my own situation and learning, how I learned about race theory and how various learnings came to influence my goals for my Critical Race ethnography. My description of the disciplinary reflexivity level is lengthier than the other two because I believe reflexive thinking about how one's academic traditions conceive of race is the most underexplored in educational scholarship.

The Social Unconscious

The first level of reflexivity, the social, involves a scholar recognizing their racial vantage points and their view as limited. Emirbayer and Desmond (2012) call for race scholars to consider their location(s) in society's racial order and the impact of Whiteness, either alone or, depending on what is germane for the particular study, in some combination with gender, class, religion and so forth, and to consider their particular trajectories across spaces, as well as the trajectories that have led to their position(s). Emirbayer and Desmond (2012) claim that the most common form of reflexivity is exploring how identity and background have influenced one's vision of the world – which is necessary yet insufficient. Moore (2012) adds that the difficulty of the reflexivity process is caused by White normativity being ingrained in our social institutions, and thus some scholars' reflexivity wants for nuance.

I heeded the call to consider the social unconscious, and thus share relevant parts of my personal background, perspective, assumptions and social agenda in relation to my study. While I engaged in an intersectional analyses (e.g. of gender, education, class, religion and sexuality) of my multiple identities (e.g. woman of color, (im)migrant and Chicana), below I largely focus on significant points from my institutional schooling experience regarding race, White normativity, language and literacy because my Critical Race ethnography is of a DL program.

I grew up in Sonora/Arizona border cities and became a Mexican (im)migrant to the United States when I was eight years old. Given that I knew almost no English when I was enrolled in an Arizona elementary school, I would have been labeled an 'English as a second language' (ESL) student, but my father refused to disclose that we spoke Spanish at home because he heard that ESL classes treated students like tontos (*à la* the Lone Ranger). Consequently, I suffered through elementary school and required several interventions in order to not 'sink' in my English-only classes.

The Title 1 border schools I attended had more than 85% Mexican heritage students and had many of the issues that are frequently documented for youth such as myself. For example, I see many parallels in my schooling experiences with Angela Valenzuela's (1999) description of 'subtractive schooling', in which she suggests that systemic problems for US-Mexican youth in education include: discounting alternate definitions of education; assimilating youths' culture and language; and disregarding the importance of care as an essential element in schooling. My schooling had very culturally and linguistically subtractive assimilationist practices, such as having an education that did not develop our bilingualism and biliteracy but did teach us how to square dance (for a racialized and gendered history of square dancing, see Pennacchia, 2017).

As a middle-school student seeking to improve my Spanish literacy, I enrolled in the only Spanish courses available, even though they were designed for English speakers. I became frustrated that my schooling did not provide a rigorous education, and that I had to maintain my Spanish through interactions with family and friends instead. As I progressed through middle and high school, I ascended to the higher-tracked courses that had an over-representation of White students compared to my previous classes. There, I noticed a clear pattern of White students being preferred by teachers and regarded as 'smart', despite how I saw many Mexican students just as academically capable.

In high school, I decided to become a secondary-level teacher to help adolescents like me develop their biliteracy and have a better education than mine. As a teacher of Spanish in Philadelphia public schools, I ended up teaching Spanish as a foreign language to classes of mostly White and Black students because secondary-level bilingual programs were (and remain) uncommon. The schools where I taught did have Latinx students from Spanish-speaking homes who were interested in learning and improving their Spanish literacy; however, the schools did not use resources for Spanish heritage language courses. As a teacher, I advocated for these classes to be offered, but was unsuccessful in expanding the school's course offerings. Needless to say, I was disturbed by the inequitable distribution of resources and attention to students who looked and sounded like me. This discomfort motivated me to begin my graduate studies and, once there, I became interested in racial formation and the materiality of race in the lives of students of color.

In my trajectory, I experienced various economic class statuses, private/public schooling both in Mexico and the United States, being seen as an exceptional learner or an 'at risk ESL immigrant' and moving back and forth between countries and languages. I have crossed in and out of statuses as a student and as a teacher of both 'gifted' and 'at-risk' students, and have seen the sameness in their intellectual potential, except for their class/racial positioning. These crossings have changed my positioning in society's racial order and given me an understanding of 'race' as constructed not only from color, but also from other markers, such as language.

Concerning my assumptions about language, I start by mentioning that Spanish is a colonizer language that has eradicated some Indigenous languages and continues to marginalize and/or invisibilize others (e.g. Mexico's Nahuatl, Zapotec, Maya, Otomí, Purépecha), which perpetuates the erasure of Indigeneity (Calderon & Urrieta, 2019; see also McCarty, this volume). I also see the Spanish language in the United States as being a foundational characteristic, for better and for worse, of the social construction of the 'Latinx' racialized group (Chávez-Moreno, 2021), which has helped form the racial coalition 'Hispanic/Latinx' (Mora, 2014). The Spanish language also assists Latinxs in holding on to, and passing down, history in order to understand present injustices. For example, Richard Delgado (2009) argues that lynchings of Mexican Americans in the Southwest are not better known because the accounts of these atrocities were in Spanish newspapers. Thus, language and literacy loss contribute to being disconnected from written histories and other knowledges.

My struggles with providing youth with a biliterate, culturally relevant education thus inform my understanding of the district where my ethnographic study takes place as providing a rare and promising opportunity for some of its language-minoritized youth to receive that education. As a researcher, when I sat in most of the classes I studied, I wished I had had this type of education, or even this particular teacher and course. I would have benefited greatly from having a bilingual education program that shifted from a subtractive to an additive model of schooling in my schools, both as a student and as a teacher. However, while I recognize the potential of the DL program I examined, given my understanding of racial realism, I still wondered how such an opportunity can cause unintended consequences and/or perpetuate White supremacy.

This section shows how my research agenda grew from my social identity, which explores issues in the intersection of race and language in the tradition of contributing a robust critique of societal structures that maintain and/or challenge oppression.

The Disciplinary Unconscious

Emirbayer and Desmond's (2012) second reflexivity level involves the scholar acknowledging both that the cultural knowledge they produce is informed by their discipline or larger social-scientific field (e.g. education, an interdisciplinary field), and that their academic tradition places limits on their understanding of the questions and solutions they explore (see also Deiri, May & Caldas, this volume). Drawing from Bourdieu's 'academic unconscious', Emirbayer and Desmond note that each academic tradition has national peculiarities, shared beliefs and common sense, lines of thought that may exist in mutual antagonism, presuppositions stemming from the speciality's history, unavoidable problematics, constructions of what counts as evidence, censorship and constraints on publishing certain findings.

Emirbayer and Desmond recommend scholars learn their academic tradition's particularities and how the field/discipline expresses racial knowledges in order to appreciate earlier conceptions and frameworks of race and to understand what new frameworks are constructed. Toward this end, Emirbayer and Desmond argue for the need to read, rather than dismiss, the cast-aside theories that have informed the discipline's collective memory (e.g. Ogbu's 1978 oppositional culture from *Minority Education and Caste*). On the one hand, serious study allows a race scholar to recognize their position within their academic tradition, and to see the openings and constraints for innovative scholarship, which significantly informs how scholars engage in their scholarly work. On the other hand, Moore (2012: 617) cogently rejoins that, while there is a need for scholars to read and understand the work we critique, spending time studying foundational works that express White supremacist and imperialist views would not only have scholars of color legitimizing (even if indirectly) 'scholarship that pathologizes and dehumanizes' their communities, but it also takes time away from exploring and advancing anti-racist alternatives (see also Deiri, this volume).

Along a different line, Emirbayer and Desmond (2012: 584) also note the importance of crossing into other disciplinary spaces, and they call for great skepticism of 'academic tendencies toward parochialism and overspecialization', such as specifically focusing on one single racial group, which 'propagate[s] a distorted view of the social world wherein (reified) racial groups exist in relative isolation from one another' (2012: 585).

Disciplinary reflexivity for my study means discussing my exploration of what it means to be a scholar of race trained in education, which I later came to understand as an interdisciplinary field (and one at the bottom of the academic hierarchy; Lagemann, 2000). I learned early on in my graduate training that the field of US education is historically founded on psychology and is influenced by that discipline's preoccupation with wanting to be regarded as a rigorous science (Lagemann, 2000). Knowing this foundation and psychology's scientific racism allows me to better appreciate connections to education's research on racial difference (Skiba, 2012), testing and eugenics (Stoskopf, 1999) and the learning style ideas ethnocentric origins (Fallace, 2019). As a result, I also learned about and gravitated more toward CRT (see also Coles, this volume). Below, I weave in my learning about CRT in order to explain how CRT and its foundational discipline – legal studies – influenced my understanding of race.

As previously mentioned, I used CRT in education, founded by legal scholars as a critique of liberalism, as my study's framework. Thanks to Gloria Ladson-Billings and William Tate (1995), CRT has given education scholars the language with which we talk about race in education (e.g. Dixson & Rousseau, 2005; Leonardo, 2013; Lynn & Dixson, 2013; Solórzano & Yosso, 2001; Tran, 2019). As I read about CRT during my Boston College graduate studies and thought of the possibility of adapting CRT for my research, I heeded Ladson-Billings' (1998: 22) advice to 'study and understand the legal literature in which it is situated [... and be] serious about intense study and careful rethinking of race and education'. Because my training is in teaching and curriculum studies, not legal studies, I enrolled in my university's law school course, 'Education Law and Public Policy'. There, I read court decisions and learned about the fundamentals of the legal tradition such as the structure of the US system of laws and the nature of legal analysis by which legal decisions are made. This foundation helped me better understand CRT legal scholars' claims about the limits of the law in occasioning social justice – for example, their critique of the idea of incremental progress eventually leading toward justice. I continued to learn about CRT scholars' critiques, along with their calls for changing or even discarding, for example, the US Constitution (an argument I heard developed in the 2015 LatCrit Conference of legal scholars, with the theme 'Critical Constitutionalism'[2]). I learned about how the legal discipline has historically conceptualized race, oppositions to its traditional conceptions of race and what questions are asked about race.[3] In addition to knowing how laws are interpreted, CRT readings helped me obtain a deeper appreciation for the implications of the US legal tradition's construction of race as an immutable characteristic and of the limits of strict scrutiny toward achieving justice (e.g. Carbado & Gulati, 2000; Haney López, 1997, 2006; Perea, 1997, 2004; Tehranian, 2019).

Legal studies' construction of race left me wanting a more robust theory of race. As I learned more about CRT, Zeus Leonardo's (2013) claim that race in CRT is assumed and not defined and that CRT did not have a 'racial theory' became more pronounced. Looking to sociology became fruitful for learning about race theory, an approach later validated by other scholars (Cabrera, 2019; Lewis *et al.*, 2019). Delving into sociology, I found a spirited debate with nuanced theorizations of race that most influenced my understanding of race (e.g. Bonilla-Silva, 1997, 2004, 2010; Desmond & Emirbayer, 2009; Fields & Fields, 2014; Golash-Boza, 2016; Omi & Winant, 2015; Roth, 2016; Twine, 2004; Winant, 2000). This literature helped me move beyond the trite precept of race as a social construction to seeing race as ill-defined in education (Leonardo, 2013), and later recognizing CRT in education as largely focused on examining racism and not on contributing to racial theories (Cabrera, 2018). I found it useful, as an education scholar, to look toward sociology's advances on racial theory to understanding race, as suggested by Lewis *et al.* (2019). With these understandings, my research study's scope included inquiring into Latinidad as a shifting racial category and into the role of bilingual education in racialization, something mostly ignored in scholarship (Chávez-Moreno, 2019).

On the subject of my inquiry's scope, I return to Emirbayer and Desmond's (2012) call for scholars to eschew studying just one single racial group – advice I was more hesitant to accept than their other suggestions. One of my interests and intentions for my research was to contribute to advancing the education field's understanding of equity issues in secondary-level DL schooling, specifically concerning Latinxs. Setting aside my reluctance, I opened my study to consider Whiteness and Blackness in relation to my questions and my inquiry into what Latinidad means.

While readers will judge for themselves, I believe this provided my study with more theoretical nuance than a narrower lens would have afforded.

Traversing disciplines such as psychology, law and sociology gave me an appreciation of the nuanced differences in academic currents, and allowed me to see more clearly the affordances and limitations of my own academic tradition. For example, not until reading debates of sociologists of race, which featured openly antagonistic criticisms explicitly naming the limitations of other scholars' ideas, did I appreciate how education was a 'nice' field, as described by Ladson-Billings (1998), where critiques are more indirect and muted. Although I had already understood that race was historically seen as a biological attribute across academic traditions, exploring other disciplines' conceptions of race helped me to situate my analysis within the field of social sciences more broadly, an important insight given the social sciences' significant role in developing and extending CRT (Crenshaw, 2010; Zuberi, 2011).

The Scholastic Unconscious

Emirbayer and Desmond's (2012: 578) third level of reflexivity, the scholastic, involves scholars recognizing the 'invisible determinations inherent in the intellectual posture itself, in the scholarly gaze that [one] casts upon the social world'. The authors critique academia's *modus operandi* of studying and explaining, (1) with a disinclination to concede that scholars' position from academia limits their understanding of the issues under inquiry, and (2) without an inclination to affect the material conditions of people. Emirbayer and Desmond contend that this level of reflexivity is the least practiced by scholars and leads to scholars engaging in an intellectual posture of withdrawing from the experiential and the practical, forgetting existing material inequities and overlooking the faults of people of color, which is another form of dehumanizing people along with attributing nothing good. Moore's (2012) rejoinder emphasizes that CRT has a tradition of engaging the reflexivity championed by Emirbayer and Desmond and adds that the authors should have paid more attention to the way institutional arrangements (my example is tenure evaluations that do not validate activism on a par with publishing scholarship) are influenced by White supremacist systems and by who has power to negotiate these arrangements.

For my study, I had to be conscious of not dismissing Emirbayer and Desmond's (2012) claims even though I understood (1) education as a 'practical' field that works on and proposes how to improve the schooling, learning and lives of youth and children; and (2) CRT scholars have called for much of the reflexive knowledge advocated by Emirbayer and Desmond (Harris, 2019; Moore, 2012). Connecting the two points, CRT education scholars have proposed not only critiquing the cherished victories from the civil rights movement (Ladson-Billings & Tate, 1995) and exposing incidents of racism (Hylton, 2012; Ladson-Billings, 2009; Ladson-Billings & Donnor, 2005) but *also* imagining and proposing radical solutions for the education field's aim of improving the schooling and learning of youth (Ladson-Billings, 1998) – a practical goal differentiating education from sociology.

As someone who has suffered through subtractive schooling and is trained in critical theories that see truths as constituted from sociopolitical power (Lather, 2006), my scholarly gaze has been influenced to see my cultural production of research as needing to attend to the two aims of uncovering unintended consequences and of proposing radical solutions. For the first aim, I saw my study as illuminating the role of schooling in the reproduction of inequality. I believe that, to improve policies and programs intended to advance equity, the unintended or negative consequences of an intervention that affect communities of color – even in what is perceived as beneficial programs, like bilingual education – must be exposed in order to understand whether the interventions are actually combating racial inequities and addressing racial inequities (see also Heiman & Yanes, this volume). While some bilingual education models serving bilingual youth of color have been on shaky ground because of racist policies (e.g. Gándara & Hopkins, 2010; Gutiérrez *et al.*, 2002; Viesca, 2013), I still see it as necessary to critique how asset-based approaches to education are working, while also carefully explicating nuances and complexities. The social implications of my research study add to a push for a more explicit accounting of race and racism by bilingual education and teacher training programs.

Regarding the second aim, my personal and professional experience impact my sense of urgency to correct injustices that youth continue to face and inform my proclivity toward seeing a researcher's goal as that of ameliorating injustices (Lather, 1986b), as well as serving the public interest (Ladson-Billings, 2006). Thus, I kept in mind that ethnographic studies in the critical tradition should also respond to the social implications of the cultural description and the social usefulness of the research (Carspecken, 1996), and, as Patti Lather (1986a) argues, that openly ideological research should consider how the research engages in participants' own critical consciousness (Freire, 2000 [1970]; cf. Heiman & Yanes, this volume). Although I believe studying and theorizing injustices are necessary, my theory of change is informed by action research (Cammarota & Fine, 2008; Cochran-Smith & Lytle, 2009), which prevents me from believing that calling attention to societal wrongs necessarily leads to emancipatory change (see also May & Caldas, this volume). That is, while scholarship can inspire folks toward critical consciousness and/or action, critique does not, by itself, advance justice. Acknowledging this led me to recognize one of my study's limitations: engaging in the cultural production of critiquing without working with those most affected by the oppressive structures to think of, and act toward, radical solutions. One of the radical proposals I offered is not that different from what education theorists have been proposing for decades: an education that historicizes and that liberates the mind from dominant ideologies (Freire, 2000 [1970]; Illich, 2012 [1970]; Woodson, 2009 [1933]). Another radical (and perhaps unpopular) solution I proposed is to keep monies and resources intended for students from marginalized groups to serve these students (Chávez-Moreno, 2018).

My study did engage teacher participants in reflecting on their own practice, which pushed their conscientization. For example, a few teachers expressed relief in talking about the DL program's shortcomings in regard to equity and Latinx youth, and these teachers felt the study's findings validated their concerns. Additionally, other participants shared that they had never thought much about race and racism. Through the interview process and our informal discussions, they reflected that they shied away from including social justice teaching because of not knowing how to address topics like race/racism while being sensitive to students' perspectives. Through the process of thinking about justice and race, some participants were pushed to reflect on sociopolitical consciousness, an often forgotten aspect of culturally relevant pedagogy (Ladson-Billings, 2014) – although, admittedly, reflection is insufficient if not acted upon (see e.g. Chávez-Moreno, in press).

Lastly, I understand that the racial order is fraught with tension between groups of color. Thus, I attended to tensions caused by Whiteness and Blackness between Latinx and Black communities, the latter of which is the second largest group of color in the school district and DL program. At times, these tensions seemed to reveal grievances stemming from hegemonic ideologies, which may be uncomfortable to expose. However, ignoring the unintended and/or negative consequences of implementing bilingual education programs that do not lead to educational equity for all groups of color will not permit stakeholders to see clearly the issues in order to improve them, and instead may contribute to silences, such as erasing tensions and/or alliances between the Latinx and Black communities (Johnson, 2013; Vaca, 2004). I also later noticed the invisible presence of Indigenous folks in my inquiry, and I decided to rectify this in a subsequent study by engaging with questions about their invisible presence in Spanish/English DL programs.

Concluding Reflections on the Unconscious

The ability to perform the principles of CRT justice is more than just using the CRT framework as a lens to understand a problem, or merely stating that CRT (or another critical framework) encourages reflexivity. Thus, this chapter invites education researchers of race (and, arguably, even those not engaged in race scholarship) to broaden beyond identity reflexivity to understand the positioning of their scholarly training and academic gaze.

My account of contemplating Emirbayer and Desmond's (2012) reflexivity typology and Moore's (2012) extensions serves as an example of an education scholar of race considering her own work. I continually engaged in a reflexive approach throughout the study's fieldwork and analyses by reflecting on my potential biases and assumptions, and, when needed, seeking feedback from colleagues who are familiar with the topics under study. Adopting a race-reflexivity approach for me means excavating my own biases, backgrounds and intersectional identities (e.g. race, ethnicity, class, gender, region and scholarship) both in, and after, the fieldwork, and acknowledging the ways these shape my research and cultural representations.

Adopting a race-reflexivity approach also means continuing to reflect on the three levels of the unconscious – even after one's empirical study is completed. This ongoing reflection and learning may lead to one's ideas having changed from those ideas in a manuscript in the publication process. For example, when this chapter was in the copyediting stage, I recognized a disciplinary unconsciousness to my thinking related to the education field's race-as-a-social-construction view. This disciplinary unconsciousness had not allowed me to grasp, as a graduate student, the nuances in other critical perspectives on 'race' and racialization that I now understand upon new readings (e.g. Hochman, 2019) and re-reading work I had read as a student (e.g. Darder & Torres, 2003). For me, engaging in race reflexivity will undoubtably lead to more changes to my perspectives on race, racism and racialization.

So, while I thought, as I finished my 'final' draft of this chapter, that engaging in race reflexivity helped me approach an in-depth understanding of how my positionality and gaze affect my study, I am again reminded that the human condition is one of learning and changing. And I am again reminded of the value in inquiry and reflection, especially given that I, like all people in our society, have grown up with hegemonic ideologies made invisible to me and which are worth uncovering and challenging.

Notes

(1) My use of Latinx includes Latina/Latino/Latine and is a political move to upset gender binaries and patriarchy. I use the term Latinxs to refer to a racialized group of people who reside in the United States, are imagined having a connection to the Spanish language and who suffer the effects of the histories of multiple colonialisms, specifically, Spanish colonialism, American colonialism and American imperialism (Chávez-Moreno, 2021).

(2) See https://latcrit.org/latcrit-conferences/.

(3) For readers interested in how disciplines like psychology, anthropology, law and/or sociology conceptualize race and engage with race questions, refer to the special issue of *Equity & Excellence in Education* (Leonardo, 2019).

References

Alemán, E. and Alemán, S.M. (2010) 'Do Latin@ interests always have to 'converge' with White interests?': (Re)claiming racial realism and interest-convergence in critical race theory praxis. *Race Ethnicity & Education* 13 (1), 1–21. https://doi.org/10.1080/13613320903549644

Annamma, S.A. (2015) Whiteness as property: Innocence and ability in teacher education. *Urban Review* 47 (2), 293–316. https://doi.org/10.1007/s11256-014-0293-6

Banks, J.A. (1998) The lives and values of researchers: Implications for educating citizens in a multicultural society. *Educational Researcher* 27 (7), 4–17.

Bartlett, L. and Brayboy, B.M.J. (2005) Race and schooling: Theories and ethnographies. *Urban Review* 37 (5), 361–374. https://doi.org/10.1007/s11256-005-0021-3

Bonilla-Silva, E. (1997) Rethinking racism: Toward a structural interpretation. *American Sociological Review* 62 (3), 465–480.

Bonilla-Silva, E. (2004) From bi-racial to tri-racial: Towards a new system of racial stratification in the USA. *Ethnic & Racial Studies* 27 (6), 931–950. https://doi.org/10.1080/0141987042000268530

Bonilla-Silva, E. (2010) *Racism without Racists: Color-Blind Racism and the Persistence of Racial Inequality in the United States* (3rd edn). Lanham, MD: Rowman & Littlefield Publishers.

Cabrera, N.L. (2018) Where is the racial theory in critical race theory?: A constructive criticism of the Crits. *Review of Higher Education* 42 (1), 209–233.

Cabrera, N.L. (2019) Critical race theory v. deficit models. *Equity & Excellence in Education* 52 (1), 47–54.

Calderon, D. and Urrieta, L. (2019) Studying in relation: Critical Latinx indigeneities and education. *Equity & Excellence in Education* 52 (2–3), 219–238. https://doi.org/10.1080/10665684.2019.1672591

Cammarota, J. and Fine, M. (2008) *Revolutionizing Education: Youth Participatory Action Research in Motion*. New York: Routledge.

Carbado, D.W. and Gulati, M. (2000) The fifth black woman. *Journal of Contemporary Legal Issues* 11, 701–729.

Carspecken, P.F. (1996) *Critical Ethnography in Educational Research: A Theoretical and Practical Guide*. London: Routledge.

Carter, P.L. (2005) *Keepin' it Real: School Success beyond Black and White*. Oxford: Oxford University Press.

Castagno, A.E. (2014) *Educated in Whiteness: Good Intentions and Diversity in Schools*. Minneapolis, MN: University of Minnesota Press.

Chávez-Moreno, L.C. (2018) A critical race ethnography examining dual-language education in the new Latinx diaspora: Reinforcing and resisting bilingual education's racial roots. Unpublished doctoral dissertation, University of Wisconsin-Madison.

Chávez-Moreno, L.C. (2019) Researching Latinxs, racism, and white supremacy in bilingual education: A literature review. *Critical Inquiry in Language Studies* 17 (2), 101–120. https://doi.org/10.1080/15427587.2019.1624966

Chávez-Moreno, L.C. (2021) The problem with Latinx as a racial construct vis-à-vis language and bilingualism: Toward recognizing multiple colonialisms in the racialization of Latinidad. In E.G. Murillo Jr (ed.) *The Handbook of Latinos & Education: Theory, Research, and Practice* (2nd edn, pp. 164–180). New York: Routledge.

Chávez-Moreno, L.C. (in press) The continuum of racial literacies: Teacher practices countering whitestream bilingual education. *Research in the Teaching of English*.

Cochran-Smith, M. and Lytle, S.L. (2009) *Inquiry as Stance: Practitioner Research for the Next Generation*. New York: Teachers College Press.

Crenshaw, K.W. (2010) Twenty years of critical race theory: Looking back to move forward. *Connecticut Law Review* 43 (5), 1253–1352.

Darder, A. and Torres, R.D. (2003) Shattering the 'race' lens: Toward a critical theory of racism. In A. Darder, M. Baltodano and R.D. Torres (eds) *The Critical Pedagogy Reader* (pp. 245–261). New York: Routledge.

Delgado, R. (2009) The law of the noose: A history of Latino lynching. *Harvard Civil Rights – Civil Liberties Law Review* 44, 298–312.

Desmond, M. and Emirbayer, M. (2009) What is racial domination? *Du Bois Review* 6 (2), 335–355. https://doi.org/10.1017/S1742058X09990166

Dixson, A.D. and Rousseau, C.K. (2005) And we are still not saved: Critical race theory in education ten years later. *Race Ethnicity & Education* 8 (1), 7–27. https://doi.org/10.1080/1361332052000340971

Duncan, G.A. (2005) Critical race ethnography in education: Narrative, inequality and the problem of epistemology. *Race Ethnicity & Education* 8 (1), 93–114. https://doi.org/10.1080/1361332052000341015

Emirbayer, M. and Desmond, M. (2012) Race and reflexivity. *Ethnic & Racial Studies* 35 (4), 574–599. https://doi.org/10.1080/01419870.2011.606910

Fallace, T. (2019) The ethnocentric origins of the learning style idea. *Educational Researcher* 48 (6), 349–355. https://doi.org/10.3102/0013189X19858086

Fields, K.E. and Fields, B.J. (2014) *Racecraft: The Soul of Inequality in American Life*. New York: Verso Trade.

Freire, P. (2000 [1970]) *Pedagogy of the Oppressed* (30th anniversary edn). New York: Continuum.

Gándara, P. and Hopkins, M. (eds) (2010) *Forbidden Language: English Learners and Restrictive Language Policies*. New York: Teachers College Press.

Golash-Boza, T. (2016) A critical and comprehensive sociological theory of race and racism. *Sociology of Race and Ethnicity* 2 (2), 129–141. https://doi.org/10.1177/2332649216632242

Gutiérrez, K.D., Asato, J., Pacheco, M., Moll, L.C., Olson, K., Horng, E.L., Ruiz, R., Garcia, E. and McCarty, T.L. (2002) 'Sounding American': The consequences of new reforms on English language learners. *Reading Research Quarterly* 37 (3), 328–343.

Haddix, M. (2012) Talkin' in the company of my sistas: The counterlanguages and deliberate silences of Black female students in teacher education. *Linguistics and Education* 23 (2), 169–181. https://doi.org/10.1016/j.linged.2012.01.003

Haney López, I.F. (1997) Race, ethnicity, erasure: The salience of race to LatCrit theory. *California Law Review* 85 (5), 1143–1211. https://doi.org/10.2307/3481058

Haney López, I.F. (2006) *White by Law: The Legal Construction of Race* (2nd edn). New York: New York University Press.

Harris, A. (2019) Racing law: Legal scholarship and the critical race revolution. *Equity & Excellence in Education* 52 (1), 12–23.

Harris, A. and Leonardo, Z. (2018) Intersectionality, race-gender subordination, and education. *Review of Research in Education* 42 (1), 1–27.

Harris, C.I. (1993) Whiteness as property. *Harvard Law Review* 106 (8), 1707–1791. https://doi.org/10.2307/1341787

Harris, J.C. and Patton, L.D. (2019) Un/doing intersectionality through higher education research. *The Journal of Higher Education* 90 (3), 347–372.

Hochman, A. (2019) Racialization: A defense of the concept. *Ethnic and Racial Studies* 42 (8), 1245–1262.

Hylton, K. (2012) Talk the talk, walk the walk: Defining critical race theory in research. *Race Ethnicity & Education* 15 (1), 23–41. https://doi.org/10.1080/13613324.2012.638862

Illich, I. (2012 [1970]) *Deschooling Society*. London: Marion Boyars.

Johnson, G.T. (2013) *Spaces of Conflict, Sounds of Solidarity: Music, Race, and Spatial Entitlement in Los Angeles*. Berkeley, CA: University of California Press.

Ladson-Billings, G. (1998) Just what is critical race theory and what's it doing in a nice field like education? *International Journal of Qualitative Studies in Education* 11 (1), 7–24. https://doi.org/10.1080/095183998236863

Ladson-Billings, G. (2006) Introduction. In G. Ladson-Billings and W.F. Tate (eds) *Education Research in the Public Interest: Social Justice, Action, and Policy* (pp. 1–16). New York: Teachers College Press.
Ladson-Billings, G. (2009) Race still matters: Critical race theory in education. In M. Apple, W. Au and L.A. Gandin (eds) *The Routledge International Handbook of Critical Education* (pp. 110–122). New York: Routledge.
Ladson-Billings, G. (2014) Culturally relevant pedagogy 2.0: A.K.A. the remix. *Harvard Educational Review* 84 (1), 74–84.
Ladson-Billings, G. and Tate, W.F. (1995) Toward a critical race theory of education. *Teachers College Record* 97 (1), 47–68.
Ladson-Billings, G. and Donnor, J. (2005) The moral activist role of critical race theory scholarship. In N.K. Denzin and Y.S. Lincoln (eds) *The Sage Handbook of Qualitative Research* (pp. 279–301). Thousand Oaks, CA: Sage.
Lagemann, E.C. (2000) *An Elusive Science: The Troubling History of Education Research.* Chicago, IL: University of Chicago Press.
Lather, P. (1986a) Issues of validity in openly ideological research: Between a rock and a soft place. *Interchange* 17 (4), 63–84.
Lather, P. (1986b) Research as praxis. *Harvard Educational Review* 56 (3), 257–277.
Lather, P. (2006) Paradigm proliferation as a good thing to think with: Teaching research in education as a wild profusion. *International Journal of Qualitative Studies in Education* 19 (1), 35–57. https://doi.org/10.1080/09518390500450144
Lee, S.J. (2009) *Unraveling the 'Model Minority' Stereotype: Listening to Asian American Youth* (2nd edn). New York: Teachers College Press.
Leonardo, Z. (2013) *Race Frameworks: A Multidimensional Theory of Racism and Education.* New York: Teachers College Press.
Leonardo, Z. (2019) Race(ing) across the disciplines: An introduction. *Equity & Excellence in Education* 52 (1), 7–11.
Lewis, A.E. (2011) *Race in the Schoolyard: Negotiating the Color Line in Classrooms and Communities.* New Brunswick, NJ: Rutgers University Press.
Lewis, A.E., Hagerman, M.A. and Forman, T.A. (2019) The sociology of race and racism: Key concepts, contributions & debates. *Equity & Excellence in Education* 52 (1), 29–46.
Lynn, M. and Dixson, A.D. (2013) *Handbook of Critical Race Theory in Education.* New York: Routledge.
Madison, D.S. (2019) *Critical Ethnography: Method, Ethics, and Performance* (3rd edn). Thousand Oaks, CA: Sage.
Milner, H.R. (2008) Critical race theory and interest convergence as analytic tools in teacher education policies and practices. *Journal of Teacher Education* 59 (4), 332–346. https://doi.org/10.1177/0022487108321884
Moore, W.L. (2012) Reflexivity, power, and systemic racism. *Ethnic & Racial Studies* 35 (4), 614–619. https://doi.org/10.1080/01419870.2011.630097
Mora, G.C. (2014) *Making Hispanics: How Activists, Bureaucrats, and Media Constructed a New American.* Chicago, IL: University of Chicago Press.
Ogbu, J. (1978) *Minority Education and Caste: The American System in Cross-Cultural Perspective.* New York: Academic Press.
Omi, M. and Winant, H. (2015) *Racial Formation in the United States* (3rd edn). New York: Routledge.
Pennacchia, R. (2017) America's wholesome square dancing tradition is a tool of white supremacy. *Quartz.* See https://qz.com/1153516/americas-wholesome-square-dancing-tradition-is-a-tool-of-white-supremacy/ (accessed 25 March 2020).
Perea, J.F. (1997) The Black/White binary paradigm of race: The normal science of American racial thought. *California Law Journal* 10, 127–172.
Perea, J.F. (2004) Buscando América: Why integration and equal protection fail to protect Latinos. *Harvard Law Review* 117 (5), 1420–1469.

Pérez Huber, L. (2010) Using Latina/o critical race theory (LatCrit) and racist nativism to explore intersectionality in the educational experiences of undocumented Chicana college students. *Journal of Educational Foundations* 24 (1/2), 77–96.
Pollock, M. (2009) *Colormute: Race Talk Dilemmas In an American School.* Princeton, NJ: Princeton University Press.
Powell, S.N. (2018) The paradox of a credit-recovery program: Alleviating and exacerbating racial inequity. *Race Ethnicity & Education* 23 (6), 784–799.
Roth, W.D. (2016) The multiple dimensions of race. *Ethnic & Racial Studies* 39 (8), 1310–1338. https://doi.org/10.1080/01419870.2016.1140793
Skiba, R. (2012) 'As nature has formed them': The history and current status of racial difference research. *Teachers College Record* 114 (5), 1–49.
Solórzano, D. and Yosso, T.J. (2001) From racial stereotyping and deficit discourse toward a critical race theory in teacher education. *Multicultural Education* 9 (1), 2–8.
Stoskopf, A. (1999) The forgotten history of eugenics. *Rethinking Schools* 13 (3), 12–13.
Tehranian, J. (2019) Changing race: Fluidity, immutability and the evolution of equal-protection jurisprudence. *University of Pennsylvania Journal of Constitutional Law* 22, 1–80.
Tran, H.V. (2019) Seeing the racial elephant: CRT and the focus of educational scholarship. *Equity & Excellence in Education* 52 (1), 24–28.
Twine, F.W. (2004) A white side of black Britain: The concept of racial literacy. *Ethnic & Racial Studies* 27 (6), 878–907. https://doi.org/10.1080/0141987042000268512
Vaca, N.C. (2004) *The Presumed Alliance: The Unspoken Conflict between Latinos and Blacks and What It Means for America.* New York: Harper Collins.
Valenzuela, A. (1999) *Subtractive Schooling: U.S.-Mexican Youth & Politics of Caring.* New York: SUNY.
Vaught, S.E. (2011) *Racism, Public Schooling, and the Entrenchment of White Supremacy: A Critical Race Ethnography.* New York: SUNY Press.
Viesca, K.M. (2013) Linguicism and racism in Massachusetts educational policy. *Education Policy Analysis Archives* 21 (52), 1–34. https://doi.org/10.14507/epaa.v21n52.2013
Villenas, S.A. (1996) The colonizer/colonized Chicana ethnographer: Identity, marginalization, and co-optation in the field. *Harvard Educational Review* 66 (4), 711–732.
Winant, H. (2000) Race and race theory. *Annual Review of Sociology* 26 (1), 169–185.
Woodson, C.G. (2009 [1933]) *The Mis-education of the Negro.* Radford, VA: Wilder Publications.
Zuberi, T. (2011) Critical race theory of society. *Connecticut Law Review* 43, 1573–1591.

5 Interrogating Our Interpretations and Positionalities: Chicanx Researchers as Scholar Activists in Solidarity with Our Communities

Idalia Nuñez and Suzanne García-Mateus

After attending sessions at the American Educational Research Association (AERA) 2019 Annual Conference, Suzanne García-Mateus (Author 2) and I, Idalia Nuñez (Author 1), engaged in a conversation where we noticed the lack of acknowledging positionality by researchers doing research with communities of color.[1] Our concern was grounded in our shared perspective that research with communities of color, or our communities, is complex due to the varied histories of marginalization and oppression that they have faced, particularly in the US. As Chicana education researchers, our commitment is to serve and address the needs of bi/multilingual students and communities of color who continue to be disenfranchised by deeply ingrained social and institutional policies and practices. In the process of critical research, we (the researchers) often find ourselves informed by our histories and multiple identities and, at the same time, constrained and conflicted by our privilege (Calderón *et al.*, 2012; Cervantes-Soon, 2014). Acknowledging and interrogating who we are is significant when conducting any research, but even more so when we work with our own communities (Ortega, 2005). We argue that this process is necessary in order to reveal how positionality can diverge and/or converge from the stories and/or experiences of participants, and thus can possibly alter the interpretations and the knowledge generated about participants (see also Coles, May & Caldas, this volume).

In this chapter, we first review the literature that discusses the role of researchers' positionality when doing research with communities of color. Then we draw on Chicana feminist epistemology (CFE) to examine how, as Chicana scholars from the borderlands, we were informed about and/or constrained by our own interpretations at the time of data collection and data analysis. Our data sets are derived from two separate contexts. Author 1 examined transfronterizxs language and literacy experiences and Author 2 focused on a study of a two-way immersion bilingual education (TWBE) program examining the interactional co-construction of identity. Finally, we conclude the chapter with a discussion of the significance in naming our positionalities when working with our communities and the practical and sensible ways to reflect on our own positionalities throughout the research process.

Researcher Positionality

Researcher positionality refers to how a researcher's position within the social and ideological placement impacts the way they see and understand the world (Glesne, 2011). A researcher's background, personal experiences, perspectives and values influence what is being observed, collected and analyzed when engaged in research (D'Silva *et al.*, 2016). Scholars focused on qualitative methods (Glesne, 2011; Merriam, 2002) have made the argument that researchers cannot separate themselves from their research, but they can be aware of their 'self' or subjectivities through the process of reflexivity (Glesne, 2011). According to Lincoln and Guba (2000: 200), reflexivity is a process of 'reflecting critically on the self as researcher, the "human as instrument"'. Through this process of reflection, researchers become more aware of their own biases, perspectives and dispositions in relation to the participants, data and the research process. To push this further, other scholars (Merriam, 2002) have argued for the need to also disclose researchers' positionalities in order to better understand the research at hand and the interpretation of the data; this, however, is a more pressing issue when discussing communities of color.

Questions on who should conduct research with and alongside our communities have been a central conversation among researchers in the field of social sciences. As Dillard (2000) and Milner (2007: 389) explain: 'People of color are not white[2] people with pigmented or colored skin'. Unlike white people, the nature of their everyday experiences is shaped by their racial and cultural backgrounds; this also results in a different way of seeing, perceiving and understanding the world (Ladson-Billings, 2003). Milner (2007) explains that, for researchers, it can be difficult to center on the voices of those who have been marginalized and interpret and capture their experiences in ways that are humanizing. Scholars of color (Delgado Bernal, 1998; Vélez-Ibáñez, 1996; Villenas, 1996) have become critical in disrupting deficit-based research on communities of color and offering ways to (re)conceptualize research practices in these communities. As research continues that focuses on the practices and experiences of our communities, there is a growing responsibility to our communities to make all researchers accountable for their approach to research when studying, analyzing and reporting on their participants' cultural and racial experiences.

Chicanx Researchers and Methodology

As part of broader efforts to decolonize standard research approaches and enactments, Chicanx researchers have provided alternative methodologies and/or unique research practices for studying our communities and their diverse experiences (Cervantes-Soon, 2014, this volume; Delgado Bernal, 1998). Delgado Bernal (1998), for example, introduces the term *cultural intuition* to name and explain the role of Chicana researchers' personal experiences, histories, intuitions and insights as contributing to the research process and analysis. *Confianza*[3] (Vélez-Ibáñez, 1996) is another practice to engage with our communities, to embody *respeto*[4] (Valdés, 1996) and to reach and learn from participants through *platicas*[5] and *encuentros*[6] (González, 1998). Latinx scholars also draw from *neplanta* (Anzaldúa, 1987: 517) to navigate their multiple identities by 'living between multiple worlds or beliefs' to explain issues of power and to 'develop transformational pedagogical spaces in education'. *Testimonios*[7] offer a way to break down power dynamics between 'subject' and researcher, but are also rooted in storytelling traditions in our communities (Cruz, 2006). These practices center on the nuanced perspective that scholars of color bring to the process of doing research with our communities. It brings our Chicanx *ways of being* into the research process. This is significant to the field of academia because it challenges traditional research practices and (re)positions the practices of our communities as methodologically valuable. While researchers of color strive to decolonize the research process and engage in humanizing approaches, we are not absolved from falling prey to the larger dominant discourses that have historically depicted communities of color negatively (Villenas, 1996; cf. May & Caldas, this volume). Zamudio *et al.* (2009: 460) remind us that all people experience oppression and privilege in some way or another and these experiences occur through the 'lens of the master narrative'. Therefore, one must continue to challenge and question our own selves as we share or generate understandings of the various communities with which we work.

Saavedra (2011) shares the notion of *destrenzando*[8] as a way to deconstruct our assumptions as we approach the research. This involves being vigilant of how we (researchers) interpret and generate the knowledge of our participants. For Saavedra, questions about her identity and her research with Mexican immigrant *mujeres* were crucial to challenging or *destrenzar* Westernized ways of conducting research. The research process is not neutral, it carries colonized methodologies and practices that potentially (re)construct or (re)produce ideas of 'the other'

(Saavedra, 2011: 292). Therefore, Saavedra argues for researchers, especially researchers of color, to develop and sustain a critical perspective that can always be used to question what is done in research. Delgado-Gaitan (1993) explains that even researchers who share similar ethnic backgrounds or experiences to their participants cannot make claims of being more knowledgeable regarding the participants' experiences. Following this argument, we, as Chicana scholars doing research with and for our communities, were interested in understanding what are the connections and disconnections experienced by researchers studying their own communities? How can researchers interrogate their own positionality to uncover the connections and disconnections they experience throughout the research process? How do our connections/disconnections impact our interpretations or understanding of the data? What are the implications for doing this kind of interrogation?

Who We Are: Our Historias

We are Chicana researchers from the borderlands working with Latinx communities and in bilingual school contexts. We are also faculty of schools of education at two different higher education institutions where we work with both undergraduate and graduate students seeking to become (bilingual) educators. Our social, political and cultural convictions to work with, and for, Latinx communities are rooted in our upbringing and our identity as immigrants of color. We share who we are by centering on our families' immigration stories. These are the stories and testimonies that we carry on our back and that have guided our own experiences and perspectives in our everyday life and our work as researchers. It is important to note that stories of immigration vary and speak to the individual and/or their family's immigration experience. What unites our stories includes a shared experience in physically and spiritually crossing borders, which can transcend generations, as they have for us.

Idalia's historia

I (Idalia Nuñez) identify as a Mexican border crosser or *transfronteriza* (Relaño Pastor, 2007). I was born in Mexico and grew up on the Texas–Tamaulipas borderlands. My parents are Mexicanos, born and raised in a rural town in Mexico. They both come from low-income families, and did not get a schooling experience beyond second grade. Early in their lives they had to learn to work to contribute much needed financial support to their families. My mother started working in the fields of California at the age of seven. She started by taking care of younger children from other immigrant families working in the fields. Once she was allowed to work in the fields, she worked picking tomatoes, strawberries and grapes alongside her parents and her six older siblings; and later in her life, she worked cleaning hotel rooms in California. They traveled across the US–Mexico border based on the seasonal work available to them. My father, at the age of six, started working in livestock in local ranches in a rural community in Mexico with his father and four brothers. Later, at the age of 13, he started working in the US for dredging companies filtering out the oil from bodies of water such as the Gulf of Mexico. Sharing their *historias* and *testimonios* of their experiences as immigrants was their way of instilling values, a sense of responsibility and *respeto* for our family, our elders and our culture.

Our life on the *borderlands* (Anzaldúa, 1987) was not easy. My father continued to work for dredging companies and my mother took care of children in our home. My two brothers and I grew up understanding that our main responsibilities included taking care of our home and family, and getting an education. I grew up both in Mexico and the US. In Mexico, I had a home, our extended family (ti@s, prim@s, abuel@s, etc.), friends, church, doctors, dentist, etc. In the US, I had a home, school, friends and community. As a border crosser, I learned how to navigate nation-states, languages, cultures and more. I learned to help my parents by being a language and cultural broker. I remember translating material from school, such as notes, announcements and grades. I also translated medical and bank letters from English to Spanish. But the most difficult experience was when I was only nine years old and my mom experienced a car accident where she had been pushed out of the highway by a company truck. I remember having to translate a conversation between three lawyers and my mother. I had to figure out how to translate the formal documents they were making her sign. I felt not only a strong sense of responsibility, but also fear; I wasn't sure I knew English well enough to translate such important conversations and documents. But I did it anyway. These experiences taught me the value of knowing more than one language, and about the disadvantages that people such as my parents who do not speak English faced in an English-dominant society, even in places such as the US border. It is because of these border-crossing experiences that today I am a multilingual and an advocate for bi/multilingualism.

Suzanne's historia

I (Suzanne) identify as a second-generation Mexican immigrant. My parents immigrated from Tamaulipas, Mexico, as teenagers in the 1960s with their designated families. As is the case with many immigrant families, the way my parents arrived '*al otro lado*' includes more than one version. As I have understood my family members' stories, my maternal *abuelita*, Catalina, crossed the Texas–Mexico border for many years in order to work '*sin papeles*'. She was crossing over to do various jobs in order to support herself and her four children. After several life-changing events and working, as she oftentimes described to me growing up as '*mojada*', she arranged for a marriage and was able to receive a green card. My paternal *abuelita* was born in the US at a time (1940s) when many Mexicanos crossed the border frequently and with minimal surveillance. She eventually had to register her birth on US soil in order to 'prove' she was a US citizen. Her status as a US citizen then gave my paternal *abuelito* the ability (or right) to also become a US citizen, as did their children as adults. My paternal grandparents were also able to cross over to the US prior to receiving their citizenship because my *abuelito* worked for a US-based construction company.

Once on the other side, my parents were enrolled in public schools in Brownsville, Texas, where my father was placed two grades below his actual level because he did not speak English and my mother would face being retained a grade level in middle school due to not speaking English. These sort of deficit practices placed my parents at a disadvantage, which took a toll on their bilingual and academic identities. My father stopped attending high school to pursue his general education development (GED) test and took some classes at a local community college while working. My mother would also stop attending high school to marry my father and would eventually pursue her GED. When I was born, my father worked as a fumigator and years later worked his way up to become a foreman for a local newspaper in Southern California. He would, at the young age of 36, experience a fatal cerebral aneurysm while at work. My mother would work different jobs, depending on whether she was staying home to care for my sisters and me, or earning extra money for the family. She would later become a widow with three children at the age of 32. Both my parents worked what are considered blue collar or working-class jobs, but we had a stable and loving home. My parents were part of their local Catholic church and Mexican community where we participated in cultural events like *posadas*, *quinceañeras* and *carne asadas*. I distinctly remember my parents inviting Mexicano youth from our church to our home for *carne asadas*. They were also involved with a local nonprofit called Hermandad Mexicana Nacional that advocates for issues of interest to the immigrant community. For example, we would join them for meetings and protests that sought to improve tenant rights for immigrants.

My grandparents took on the largest burden of physically immigrating, establishing a new life in a new country and learning how to 'make it' here. My grandparents also took on the hardship of making sure their children had documents in this new country. They laid the foundation and paved the way and made it 'so much easier' for me as part of the second generation in the US. In fact, their sacrifices make the structural inequities I have had to face as a first-generation college student seem easy; I feel privileged in many ways.

Due to my parents' negative experiences in US public schools as Spanish-speaking immigrants from Mexico, they purposely indicated on school forms that their three daughters spoke only English at home. I grew up in Southern California in a bilingual and Latinx community. Our home was bilingual in that my parents spoke Spanish with each other and with us it was a mix of Spanish and English. My two sisters and I would respond primarily in English, although we drew on our bilingualism to communicate with various community members. As an adult, I have revitalized my Spanish socially, as a bilingual teacher and as a parent raising bilingual daughters. These experiences and stories of hardship, resistance and immigration shared by my family members have made an impression on my bilingual and Chicana soul. It is for immigrant students like my parents that I continue to advocate for socially just and equitable bilingual education programs.

Turning to Chicana feminist epistemology

Our chapter draws from a CFE to examine the ways in which our identities and experiences, as bilingual Chicana scholars from the borderlands, informed and/or constrained our own interpretations at the time of data collection and data analysis. Delgado Bernal (1998: 2) describes that a CFE is necessary as a sort of 'for us and by us' epistemology because 'traditional patriarchal and liberal educational scholarship' has essentially failed us. A CFE draws from the work of Chicana feminists and '…is also grounded in the life experiences of Chicanas and involves Chicana research participants in analyzing how their lives are being interpreted, documented, and reported, while acknowledging that many Chicanas lead lives with significantly different opportunity structures than men or white women' (Delgado Bernal, 1998: 1). Aligned with the tenets of a CFE, we included Latinx participants and their voices by interviewing them about their experiences in becoming bilingual (Author 2) or their use of biliteracy in and outside of school (Author 1). As a theoretical framework, a CFE serves multiple purposes in our work as educational scholars. A CFE can be a form of both resistance and decolonization of research from 'traditional paradigms', which undermine the experiences and funds of knowledge of Chicanas (as cited in Delgado Bernal, 1998: 555–582). A CFE allows us to consider our common experiences with our research participants, which have historically marginalized our shared communities. Some of these experiences include issues related to immigration, migration, generational status and bilingualism (Delgado Bernal, 1998).

Description of Data

We drew from two separate previously collected ethnographic data sets to pay attention to how our positionality informed and shaped our interpretation of the data as Chicana researchers doing research on Latinx communities. The first author's (Idalia Nuñez) data set derives from a study with *transfronterizo* children and families that examined their language and literacy border-crossings (Nuñez, 2018). The second author's (Suzanne García-Mateus) data set derives from a study of a TWBE program examining the interactional co-construction of identity (García-Mateus, 2016). Data sources include fieldnotes and analytic/reflective memos as windows to our researcher voices during the process of collecting and interpreting the participants' data.

Drawing on lived experiences to understand

From revisiting and reviewing our data sets, we recognized how, throughout our initial interpretations, we were drawing from our *lived experiences* to better *understand* the experiences of our participants. We also recognized how our *outsider perspectives* came through when we were *struggling to understand* our participants' experiences or perceptions. The following are examples that illustrate how our identities and experiences influenced our way of thinking during the data collection process.

Observing through our lived experiences

We use *lived experience* to refer to our shared historical, cultural and political experiences with the Latinx community in the US context. Specifically, this involves connecting these *lived experiences* with what Delgado Bernal (1998) refers to as *cultural intuition* to name and explain how our (shared) histories contribute to the research process and analysis. For example, after Suzanne collected data, she would compose analytic memos to make sense of what she observed. In the following quote, Suzanne is connecting her own experience of having to navigate an institution, just like her focal student, Elizabeth (bilingual Latinx) was navigating a piloted TWBE program. Elizabeth was considered a second-generation US-born immigrant after her parents had immigrated from Mexico. Elizabeth was part of a decreasing demographic of students at her elementary school. Latinx families originally made up the majority of the community prior to the gentrification of the surrounding neighborhood (Heiman & Yanes, 2018, this volume). Her working-class and diverse linguistic and ethnic background reflected the local community that the school had been serving for many years. When she entered kindergarten, she would use an invented language and proclaim she was actually speaking English:

> I can relate to Elizabeth in more than one way. Her experience in kindergarten and now in 1st grade remind me of how I struggled as an undergrad: not knowing the cultural norms, not knowing how to make

> it through an institution like The University (a pseudonym), my mom didn't know how to teach me; how to advise [me] about how to make it at The University. For example, throughout my entire three years there, she sent me fifty dollars, not because she didn't know I needed more but because she didn't have the money. That is just one example of how I came from a home that did not have the 'resources' to make it at an institution like The University, studying alongside peers that came from homes that had different resources or learned how to make it. Elizabeth, like me, is making her way and learning how to 'make it'. (Reflection memo, 2010)

In this reflection, Suzanne was connecting her *lived experiences* as a first-generation college student, by describing the challenges she experienced in navigating a large institution, to the experiences of her focal student in a TWBE program. Elizabeth started out in the TWBE program as dominant in Spanish and each subsequent year she acquired more English. The challenges she faced as a person of color and from a working-class background contributed to the ways her identity was co-constructed, and in the challenges she faced as she navigated her public school institution (García-Mateus, 2016).

Similarly, Idalia also experienced moments in which her personal experiences in the context served to ground her understanding of her observations during the time in the field. The following fieldnote is a representative example that reflects the parallels between her personal experience and her participant's experience at the time of the study:

> The US Custom official was holding Luis's passport in his left hand. 'Luis?' he asked. Luis made eye contact with the official. Then the official moved Luis's passport to his right hand and opened the next one. Luis looked away from the official and looked towards his younger brother Alvaro. 'Alvaro?' the official asked…
>
> Researcher's note: Luis knows that you can answer to these inspections with more than using verbal words. He ensured his presence was known when the inspector called out his name by making eye contact. And then he knew when the inspector was satisfied with his response when he stopped making eye contact. Luis was demonstrating an alternative way to responding to the inspector. From my experience as a border crosser, I know that depending on how the inspector asks you can respond verbally, you can make eye contact, you can nod, or even raise your hand.

In this example, Idalia's personal experience provided a foundation for the particular attention she gave to the embodied practices that Luis used in his brief interaction with the US Custom official or border inspector. The observation noted the eye and body movements of the participants as a way of participating in the particular interaction with the inspector. She also commented that Luis used eye contact as a way of communicating. This interpretation was possible because she has engaged in this practice or way of communicating. Idalia drew on her lived experiences as a surveilled border crosser who has experienced inspections, and provided insights about the various ways in which border crossers respond to border inspectors. It is important for us to note that, although this was a short moment and happened in a matter of seconds, this interaction and the practices that Luis engaged in carried a lot of risks. If Luis's response was not acceptable to the border agent, this could have had serious consequences for not only Luis, but everyone in the vehicle attempting to cross the border. Based on the fieldnotes, Luis was able to respond in an acceptable manner avoiding any risks of being detained at the border.

Beyond our connections, our lived experiences also provided a foundation for *trying to understand the experiences* of our Latinx participants. In the following section, the authors pinpoint with examples how as (ethnic and linguistic) insiders their lives as graduate students (a privilege only few can pursue), at the time of their studies, obscured their understanding of what it means to be in a setting that once seemed very familiar.

The outsider's lens: Struggling to understand

In interrogating our identity, it was important to recognize when our outsider's perspective played a role as well. An outsider's perspective became evident in those moments when we struggled to understand the normal practices, situations or perspectives that take place when documenting and/or making sense of the participants' experiences. We contest that these struggles are rooted in the privileged positionality that distances the researchers from the current situated conditions that participants are facing. For example, in the following fieldnote, Idalia documents a conversation with a participant whose comments are addressing the changes in the community, specifically the children, as a result of the cartel violence on the Mexican borderlands. In this note, although the participant speaks directly to the sociocultural and economic context, Idalia is making note of her struggles that set her apart from her participants – an outsider's perspective.

> Rene's tía was a pre-K teacher in Mexico. 'It's not the same anymore, families do not have money or work. In terms of behavior, they [children] don't listen to us… But it has to do with the corrupt politicians and violence. These children were born seeing this as reality, like this is normal and it's not'.
>
> Researcher's note: She just made me realize the difference between me and the participants that I was struggling to understand. All three of the

> participants have been born into this environment of surveillance, which is why they don't react the way I do to the military presence. I need to explore this and keep it in mind as I think about the data. (Author 1, fieldnote, 6/13/2016)

Although Idalia knows the context because she grew up in the area, there is a *struggle to understand* the experiences of the participants with whom she is dealing. Furthermore, this struggle, rather than being ignored, indexed the disconnection between Idalia and her participants. Instead of assuming that she understands her Latinx participants' reactions to the heightened surveillance, she recognizes that the border context has changed, and her own changing identity was challenging her understanding. Delgado Bernal (1998) explains that Chicanx researchers draw on their *cultural intuition* and *personal experience* to recognize both the insights to connections and disconnections making space to continue the search and struggle for accurately interpreting the experiences of Chicanx/Latinx communities. In this case, her participants do not react to the presence of the military on the borderlands the way she does. Particularly, Idalia was experiencing the normalization, and the participants' emotional and physical acceptance of the military in this context, as an outsider who has not lived in the border context for a period of time. Her own reflection and realization of this difference are significant to the process of interpreting the cultural everyday experiences of her participants.

The following example is from Suzanne. She was describing and reflecting on what she noticed about the student interactions in a TWBE kindergarten classroom:

> The three children at this table continued conversing randomly… the Anglo smiled at the Hispanic male student, he smiled back and she proclaimed, 'You have a lot of fillings!'
>
> [Researcher reflecting]: She had a point. This is one of the first things I noticed about my students, as a former bilingual teacher, on the east side of Ostin (a pseudonym). They did have a lot of caps on their teeth. I'm not sure if their parents weren't educated about dental hygiene, couldn't afford dental insurance, or if it was some sort of cultural statement. When I volunteered in Honduras for 6 weeks I learned that people got caps on at least one of their teeth as a statement of [having] wealth. (Author 2, fieldnotes, 2010)

In this example, Suzanne noticed, and later reflected on in writing, a white student's comment about the amount of fillings a Latinx student had in their mouth, which was visibly evident by the number of caps on their teeth. Even though Suzanne shared a similar ethnic background with the Latinx participant, she revealed her disconnections and her privilege in this reflective note, which consequently also marked her outsider's perspective. She noted from her experiences as a bilingual teacher in Ostin, that her students also had fillings, but she did not understand why that was a common practice. In her struggle to make sense of this practice, she mentioned several rationalizations and then made a connection to her volunteer experience in Honduras and the similar observations with that particular culture. Even with her rationalizations and the connection she made, there was still a sense of uncertainty in the fieldnote. In other words, she was not able to fully arrive at an answer regarding this practice. This example is important because it allowed us to deeply reflect on how our positionality, and how the lenses that we bring, can influence the ways in which we see and understand (or do not understand) our participants and the data collected. Here, the lack of an insider's perspective left a lingering question for the researcher. In this case, we see this as a useful approach to handling an observation from an outsider's perspective. Rather than immediately making claims or assumptions about this student in her reflective note, Suzanne limited herself to attempting to make sense of the observation. As we engaged in this, we were reminded of how important it is to always go into the research process knowing that not all questions are answered, or all observations clearly understood and interpreted.

Discussion

> This 'native' ethnographer is potentially both the colonizer, in her university cloak, and the colonized, as a member of the very community that is made 'other' in her research. (Villenas, 1996: 712)

We recognize that being able to engage in research, step in and out of our own community spaces and examine our own work are all privileges afforded by our positions as researchers of color participating in research institutions. We are, as Villenas (1996) discusses, the colonized and colonizer. Because of our privileged positions, we contend it is our responsibility to continue to struggle with and through these contradictions – our personal borderlands (Anzaldúa, 1987). As Chicana researchers, our personal and professional worlds collide when we do research, challenging us to make sense of what it means to be a person of color, or a person of our community, doing research with and alongside our people.

It is crucial that we critically examine our 'self' in relation to participants, the data and research to reveal how our positionality and privilege seep throughout the research process. This process involves acknowledging who we are both inside and outside the field, and, in many ways, disclosing the most vulnerable moments of our lives that impact the way we experience (physically and intellectually), perceive and understand the practices and identities of the communities we study. Engaging in this process has important contributions to the academic field by potentially identifying the areas in which we, as researchers, connect and disconnect from our participants' experiences, especially when we discuss and generate knowledge about 'our comunidades' (Saavedra, 2011: 296). Belonging to the communities we study does not warrant complete understanding or connection to the stories and lives of our participants, but it can provide enough insight to know how and when to question our positionalities within the research. As we demonstrate in the examples, we were able to recognize when we were struggling to understand and connect to what we were observing or learning from our participants. By engaging in this struggle, we resisted framing our 'researcher self' as the knower and producer of knowledge. This process allowed us to learn more about our participants within our ever-changing communities, and about our 'self'.

Conclusion

We have described how part of our work as scholars of color aims toward decolonizing the research process that has historically centered on theories and methodologies that privilege members of the dominant group. We continue to contemplate whether research can be 'decolonized', as it is rooted in structural inequities which seep into the contexts where data are collected. By shedding light on the need for mindful and equitable research practices (Orellana, 2019), we are also making a call for scholars who come from white and/or privileged backgrounds to engage in critical reflection where they name their positionality and privilege in relation to the communities they are 'studying' (see also May & Caldas, this volume). It is through this naming and acknowledging that we can begin the process of deconstructing and *destrenzando* (Saavedra, 2011) the social inequities that are part of doing research. This also applies to researchers of color doing work with their communities. A researcher's positionality can experience insider and outsider perspectives, as we described, that are important to recognize, especially when working with communities who have experienced marginalization (Delgado-Gaitan, 1993).

Moving forward, this chapter contributes to the ways in which interrogating our interpretations and positionalities as scholars can either align us with the urgent and critical work needed in communities of color or contribute to structural inequities that further marginalize people of color. Our positionalities as researchers need to be constantly examined and challenged in relation to what we are seeing in the experiences of our communities. As Delgado-Gaitan (1993: 390) shares, this work matters because 'it impacts the nature of the research we conduct' and the knowledge we produce about our communities. This is not to be taken lightly. It is a great responsibility to ensure that the stories and interpretations shared of our communities are truly representative of their voice, their *sentimientos*[9] and their everyday, lived, experience.

Notes

(1) Communities of color (COC) is used interchangeably with 'our communities', but also to denote that we stand in solidarity with COC we are not members of in order to continue to advocate for equitable and inclusive research methods.
(2) The authors use a lowercase 'w' for the label white to problematize and challenge representations of white supremacy in society and in school settings.
(3) *Confianza* [Trust].
(4) *Respeto* [Respect].
(5) *Platicas* [Conversations].
(6) *Encuentros* [Gatherings].
(7) *Testimonios* [Testimonies].
(8) *Destrenzando* [Unbraiding].
(9) *Sentimientos* [Feelings].

References

Anzaldúa, G. (1987) *Borderlands/La frontera: The New Mestiza*. San Francisco, CA: Aunt Lute Books.

Calderón, D., Delgado Bernal, D., Pérez Huber, L., Malagón, M. and Vélez, V.D. (2012) A Chicana feminist epistemology revisited: Cultivating ideas a generation later. *Harvard Educational Review* 82 (4), 513–539.

Cervantes-Soon, C. (2014) The U.S.–Mexico border-crossing Chicana researcher: Theory in the flesh and the politics of identity in critical ethnography. *Journal of Latino/Latin American Studies* 6 (2), 97–112.

Cruz, C. (2006) 'Toward an epistemology of a Brown body'. In D. Delgado Bernal, C.A. Elenes, F.E. Godinez and S. Villenas (eds) *Chicana/Latina Education in Everyday Life: Feminista Perspectives on Pedagogy and Epistemology* (pp. 59–75). Albany, NY: SUNY Press.

Delgado Bernal, D. (1998) Using a Chicana feminist epistemology in educational research. *Harvard Educational Review* 68 (4), 555–579.

Delgado-Gaitan, C. (1993) Researching change and changing the researcher. *Harvard Educational Review* 63 (4), 389–412.

Dillard, C.B. (2000) The substance of things hoped for, the evidence of things not seen: Examining an endarkened feminist epistemology in educational research and leadership. *International Journal of Qualitative Studies in Education* 13 (6), 661–681.

D'Silva, M.U., Smith, S.E., Della, L.J., Potter, D.A., Rajack-Talley, T.A. and Best, L. (2016) Reflexivity and positionality in researching African-American communities: Lessons from the field. *Intercultural Communication Studies* 25 (1), 94–109.

García-Mateus, S. (2016) 'She was born speaking English and Spanish!' Co-constructing identities and exploring children's bilingual language practices in a two-way immersion program in central Texas. Unpublished doctoral dissertation, University of Texas at Austin.

Glesne, C. (2011) *Becoming Qualitative Researchers: An Introduction* (4th edn). Boston, MA: Pearson Education.

González, F.F. (1998) The formations of Mexicannes: Trenzas de identidades multiples [The development of womanhood among young Mexicanas: Braids of multiple identities]. Unpublished doctoral dissertation, University of California, Davis.

Heiman, D. and Yanes, M. (2018) Centering the fourth pillar in times of TWBE gentrification: 'Spanish, love, content, not in that order'. *International Multilingual Research Journal* 12 (3), 173–187.

Ladson-Billings, G. (2003) It's your world, I'm just trying to explain it: Understanding our epistemological and methodological challenges. *Qualitative Inquiry* 9 (1), 5–12.

Lincoln, Y.S. and Guba, E.G. (2000) Paradigmatic controversies, contradictions, and emerging confluences. In N.K. Denzin and Y.S. Lincoln (eds) *The Handbook of Qualitative Research* (2nd edn, pp. 163–188). Los Angeles, CA: Sage

Merriam, S.B. (1998) *Qualitative Research and Case Study Applications in Education*. San Francisco, CA: Jossey-Bass.

Merriam, S.B. (2002) Introduction to qualitative research. In S.B. Merriam and R.S. Grenier (eds) *Qualitative Research in Practice: Examples for Discussion and Analysis* (pp. 3–18). San Francisco, CA: Jossey Bass.

Milner IV, H.R. (2007) Race, culture, and researcher positionality: Working through dangers seen, unseen, and unforeseen. *Educational Researcher* 36 (7), 388–400.

Nuñez, I. (2018) Literacies of surveillance: Transfronterizo children translanguaging identity across borders, inspectors and surveillance. Unpublished doctoral dissertation, University of Texas at Austin.

Orellana, M.F. (2019) *Mindful Ethnography: Mind, Heart and Activity for Transformative Social Research*. New York: Routledge.

Ortega, L. (2005) For what and for who is our research? The ethical as a transformative lens in instructed SLA. *The Modern Language Journal* 89 (3), 427–443.

Relaño Pastor, A.M. (2007) On border identities. 'Transfronterizo' students in San Diego. *Diskurs Kindheits-und Jugendforschung* 2 (3), 263–277.

Saavedra, C.M. (2011) De-academizing early childhood research: Wanderings of a Chicana/Latina feminist researcher. *Journal of Latinos and Education* 10, 286–298.

Valdés, G. (1996) *Con respeto: Bridging the Distances between Culturally Diverse Families and Schools: An Ethnographic Portrait*. New York: Teachers College Press.

Vélez-Ibáñez, C. (1996) *Border Visions: Mexican Cultures of the Southwest United States*. Tucson, AZ: University of Arizona Press.

Villenas, S. (1996) The colonizer/colonized Chicana ethnographer: Identity, marginalization, and co-optation in the field. *Harvard Educational Review* 66 (4), 711–732.

Zamudio, M., Bridgeman, J., Russell, C. and Rios, F. (2009) Developing a critical consciousness: Positionality, pedagogy, and problems. *Race Ethnicity and Education* 12 (4), 455–472.

6 Toward Reflexive Engagement: Critical Ethnography's Challenge to Linguistic Homogeneity and Binary Relationships

Julie S. Byrd Clark

In this chapter, drawing upon critical ethnographic research, I investigate the potential of developing critical intercultural language awareness, or what I refer to as 'reflexive engagement', for future language teachers and researchers (Byrd Clark, 2020). In doing so, I explore some of the experiences and complex positionings of bi/multilingual teacher education students who took part in a two-year intensive Bachelor of Education (B.Ed) program in Ontario, Canada, and who, likewise, participated in a virtual international exchange in French as part of their coursework. With the continued rise of neoliberal discourses and the marketization of education, along with processes of globalization, transnational mobility, immigration and rapid change, the need for critically aware professional language educators, open and supportive of diversities, remains paramount. Such processes and discourses have brought about an increased importance for language student teachers and teachers in today's world to develop and refine their linguistic and intercultural practices concerning the inclusivity of diversities in varied contexts, and for overall communicative effectiveness.

In Canada, as elsewhere, the conceptualizations of how language, identity and community are experienced have been continually undergoing transformation. This has been particularly evident at the tertiary level, namely in urban and suburban French language teacher education programs, comprising youth with increasingly complex linguistic repertoires and social backgrounds. However, one of the biggest challenges perceived in some of the Canadian provinces (e.g. British Columbia, Alberta, Ontario) that provide French language teaching and learning programs (historically referred to as French as a second language [FSL] programs), has been a lack of support for the integration of, and engagement with, social variation and diversities. Despite the increased value of multilingualism as a practical norm in competitive national and international markets, educational policies and curricula in FSL, particularly French immersion (FI), are just beginning to contemplate what it might mean to include the explicit development of multilingual repertoires or societal multilingualism in their classrooms (Byrd Clark, 2012, 2016; Byrd Clark & Roy, 2018).

As more diversity is present in French language education classrooms in Canada, we can no longer look at bi/multilingualism in the same way – nor can we continue to view linguistic or social identities as static. Furthermore, in order to develop an openness to social variation, and to be able to thrive in different contexts, contemporary professional language teachers need to be both reflexive and mindful of their own social and linguistic practices as well as others' interactions and ways of communicating. In these transnational times, we need the 'critical ability to question the implicit and explicit assumptions behind cultural claims and the power dynamics that they may be concealing' (Breidenbach & Nyíri, 2009: 343–345), specifically language ideologies. That said, there needs to be an increased critical awareness of the varieties of English and French spoken within different Canadian communities. As we shall see, developing a deeper, reflexive awareness could destigmatize certain varieties, as well as speakers of those languages.

Drawing upon a three-year critical ethnography incorporating multimodality, discourse analysis and transdisciplinarity (Blommaert, 2010; Byrd Clark, 2016), this chapter underscores the significance of critical ethnography and how it may lead to developing *reflexivity or reflexive engagement* (see Byrd Clark, 2020). Combining a critical ethnographic approach with a discourse analytic framing (Blommaert, 2010) in this study facilitated a way to be able to capture some of the complexities that a qualitative coding tool like Nvivo would normally miss, or not be able to decipher. This combined approach provided a rich and detailed account of future language teachers (and researchers) participating in an international exchange. Accordingly, I selected some data samples gathered through online, interactive discussion groups, and from semi-structured interviews, as well as focus groups of student teachers from different classes, participating in a French language teacher education program in the province of Ontario. Thus, the analysis for the data in this chapter reveals a more in-depth, thick description of the participants' understandings of what it means to be/become bi/multilingual and a French language teacher in contemporary times and, at the same time, sheds light on the kinds of messages student teachers receive concerning their social and linguistic practices.

That said, the findings presented in the upcoming sections of this chapter advocate for the support and employment of critical ethnography as a method, particularly in a world currently dominated by data-driven, 'evidenced-based' research, which often subscribes to positivist and post-positivist views of reality. That is to say, the findings here challenge black-and-white binaries or fixed, static, dualistic views of reality, and instead show some of the multiple, complex, relational and contradictory positionings and practices of youth through their interactions and varied positionings. At the same time, this approach could foster a means to become aware of one's own use of language and ideological attachments. This is significant because each of us has our own ways of seeing, relating with and being/becoming in the world – we all have our own complex processes for interpreting the world and one another. Nevertheless, without any awareness of such interpretive processes, we each begin to believe that our own way of seeing the world, and interpreting it, equals the *real, right, correct* way or *the truth*. Yet, when employing critical ethnography, we may begin to see that there is no singular, fixed *common-sense* truth. Instead, there are multiple, multidimensional and often contradictory ways of seeing, interpreting, understanding and engaging with the world. Bringing about this awareness, in this case, could additionally help to destigmatize certain linguistic varieties of French, and English in the Canadian context, in this instance. Certainly, critical ethnography has its own epistemology and/or historical, philosophical underpinnings (see Giroux, 2011) principally concerned with the emancipation of a marginalized oppressed group from a dominant oppressor (the socially constructed *Us vs. Them* paradigm, see Gumperz, 1982). However, critical ethnography and the development of criticality can potentially lead toward reflexive engagement (see Byrd Clark, 2020; cf. May & Caldas, this volume) which destabilizes and dismantles dualistic, binary ways of thinking. For example, when analyzing the interviews and online discussion groups, I drew upon discourse analysis and critical ethnography to get at some kind of understanding of the *how* and *why* of the student teachers' positionings, as well as some of the instabilities and inconsistencies that emerge when researching heterogeneous representations of multilingualism and multilinguals. Critical ethnography provides a space here for those whose voices have both gone unheard and need to be heard. With critical ethnography and discourse analysis, we uncover how some of the relations of power and injustice operate. Yet, at the same time, this combined approach illuminates the ways in which knowledge is co-constructed, as well as the contradictions and instabilities of our everyday practices that would (again) go largely unnoticed or ignored in other research methodologies (e.g. surveys, questionnaires, statistical analyses). Additionally, this combined approach has led me to uncover the *who* involved throughout this complex process – in other words, some of my own ways of interpreting and framing (for a more detailed account, see the Methods section).

Research Questions

Some of the main questions which guide this particular research are:

(1) What does French mean to the participants? And has this positioning of French shifted, or evolved, over time?
(2) What kinds of messages do the participants receive in relation to their social and linguistic positionings and practices?
(3) What does it mean to become mindful or more aware of one's positionings, language use and practices? Why does this matter?

As a researcher who advocates for reflexive engagement, I ask myself the same questions, simultaneously reflecting upon my own intentions, interpretations and representations, which are included and weaved throughout this chapter. I do this for several reasons. First, to become aware of, and acknowledge, my own biases. Second, to come clean about how the intersections of my own lived experiences and perceived interpretations come up, resonate and evoke judgments when working with participants in the field. Third, by becoming aware of the judgments and thoughts that enter my mind when interacting with participants, I can 'get out of my own way', so to speak, in order to attune and listen more deeply to my participants and to hear their stories and experiences with more clarity. Practicing and asking the same questions of myself allow me to notice and examine my own beliefs, emotional energies, ways of embodying, assumptions and concepts in a non-judgmental way and, in turn, this reflexivity helps me to appreciate the wisdom and insight of each offering (without necessarily feeling I have to give up my own views or suppress dissent). This reflexive process is very helpful when doing critical work, in that we become *critical* of the critical, so to speak, which reveals our interconnectedness as humans and, at the same time, highlights the particularities of individual experience(s).

Context/Background

> Awareness of histories helps our understanding of how things have come to be the way they are; it helps us understand the continuities and discontinuities in individuals' lives as well as in the social organization of these lives. (Saint-Georges & Weber, 2013: 7)

Before going into the data samples, it is important to understand some of the historical context and background for this research. Under the administration and legislation of the then Canadian Prime Minister (Premier) Pierre Elliot Trudeau and the Official Languages Act (1969) that his administration ushered in, Canada has been represented as an officially bilingual country for just over 50 years with French language programs, especially FI, serving as a hallmark of Canadian education. These programs have since been heralded as the inspiration for many bilingual education programs across the globe. At the same time, Canada has been widely recognized for its policy on multiculturalism (e.g. Canadian Multicultural Acts, 1971, 1985). With immigration accounting for two thirds of its population growth, Canada has become one of the most linguistically and culturally diverse countries in the Western world. According to Statistics Canada (2011), one out of five children speaks a language at home other than English or French. However, it is important to understand that Canadian English/French bilingualism operates differently at the federal level than at the provincial level. As such, there is an unevenness in one's access to being and becoming a certain kind of bilingual, as linguistic and social resources are not as uniformly or evenly distributed across Canada's 10 provinces and three territories (as we shall see with the upcoming example of the province of Ontario). Equally important to note is that the Canadian government has operated and continues to operate in a dualistic, fixed manner, by embodying the language-nation-state ideology (one language/one people) adopted from the 1960s and 1970s bilingual legislation. This understanding perpetuates both the use and social categories of Anglophones and Francophones as separate, homogeneous and founding groups, all the while completely ignoring the fact that neither of these so-called homogeneous 'two solitude' groups were the first people to live in Canada (reconciliation efforts have only recently begun with First Nations people in Canada, see revised Official Languages Act, 2019).[1]

Nevertheless, during the 1960s and 1970s, the Canadian government sought to balance a way to maintain individual rights (universalistic), and likewise set up a pluralist framework to give recognition to both multicultural groups (those groups who speak neither English nor French as a first language [L1]) and English and French minoritized communities[2] (particularistic), thus recognizing the specificity of the cultural and linguistic community to which individuals belong. However, the notion of community has become increasingly blurred (Byrd Clark, 2010; Flores, 2017). As Quell (2000) reminds us, recognizing difference as linked to one linguistic and cultural community has become problematic because, as we can see, an individual may claim belonging to, or membership of, several cultural and linguistic communities, and more importantly, not all groups (or languages for that matter) are perfectly homogeneous (Marcellesi, 1979). This blurring and/or complexity has been an important feature of my study, as multilingual students with complex transnational identities and linguistic practices obscure such claims of belonging to a specific ethnolinguistic community. Nonetheless, many Canadian studies still tend to research Anglophones and Francophones as separate groups in education (e.g. Gérin-Lajoie, 2010; Swain & Lapkin, 1995). For example, one does not often hear of the term *Franglophones*, even though this term seems to capture the real, complex, heterogeneous social reality for Canadians in contemporary times.

Ontario

For being and becoming bilingual in Ontario, there are three main program options for acquiring French/English bilingualism (of course, there are always options within the options, see e.g. intensive French/*Français Intensif*). I have listed the programs in Table 6.1 in order to show some of the main distinctions between the different French language learning options.

The goal of core French is to develop students' functional communication skills in French (Ministry of Education and Training, 1998, 1999). However, the second FSL program option, called FI, is a more intensive program as students are immersed in French for at least half (50%) of the school day, thereby having half their school subjects taught exclusively in French. There are several types of immersion programs (early, middle, late as well as full or partial). The third option in the chart, established under Charter 23 of the *Charter of Rights and Freedom* in 1982, is *l'école de langue française* (Labrie & Lamoureux, 2003), or a Francophone school (also referred to as French as an L1), which constitutionally guarantees minority language educational rights to French-speaking communities outside Québec, where all subjects are taught in French. English is offered as a core subject for approximately 50 minutes a day (although this can vary).

Each option produces its own possibilities and constraints, although each program's goal is to teach French in a universal, objective, standardized way. Nevertheless, the distribution of resources (in this case, access to a certain kind of French instruction) is unequal across and among the programs throughout different school boards and regions.

In regard to becoming a French language teacher in Ontario, there are 18 teacher education programs. However, only 30% of the province's publicly funded higher education programs are, in fact, available in French, mostly at the Cité Collégiale and the Université d'Ottawa in Ottawa, and at the Collège Boréal and l'Université Laurentienne in Sudbury, with some programs at York University's Glendon College in Toronto, the Collège Dominicain and the Université St-Paul in Ottawa, Guelph's Collège Alfred in Eastern Ontario and the Collège Universitaire de Hearst in northeastern Ontario.[3] Interestingly, within the French language teacher education program and classes in Ontario, and aside from

Table 6.1 Program options

Program	Core French	French immersion	École de langue française
Mandatory	Yes, from Grade 4 to Grade 8 (some boards can offer core French in Grade 1)	No. Intensive program and a choice by parents	No, a linguistic choice and right
Hours	600 hours of French instruction	A minimum of 1260 hours	All instruction is in French

beginning undergraduate university French courses, this is generally one of the first places where students from all of the French language education programs come together (e.g. students from a core French background, students from an FI background and students from French as an L1 schools) with inevitably varied linguistic proficiency and competence.

Insights from the Literature and Context

> Despite immigration, increased mobility, and the emergence of trans-global identities, official educational policies and curriculum have not yet expanded to include the explicit development of multilingual repertoires or societal multilingualism in [Canadian] classrooms. (Byrd Clark, 2011: 110)

Although recent initiatives in the literature have begun to open up the teaching of national standard languages to sociolinguistic variation, translation practices, multimodal activities, translanguaging and transdisciplinarity (e.g. Byrd Clark, 2016; Canagarajah, 2013; García & Li, 2014; Warner, 2019), FSL and FI in particular have lagged behind due to particular ideological and historical underpinnings about language: viewing language as an idealized form to be mastered, along with official educational policies that continue to reproduce solutions based on the language-nation-state ideology (e.g. one language, one people; see Hobsbawm, 1990), rather than including *real-life* heterogeneous translingual practices performed by people in their everyday lives (see Byrd Clark, 2012).

In the upcoming section, I review certain facets of how French/English bilingual education has evolved, and some of the major epistemological framings that have dominated FSL learning and teaching in Canadian provinces such as Ontario.

From systems to social practices: Rethinking bi/multilingualism

Most of the research in FSL has historically been established for middle-class Anglophone (English-speaking) students and has centered on their learning in FI education contexts[4] (Genesee, 1987; Tarone & Swain, 1995). These studies have also tended to be more Anglo dominant in their conceptualizations of bilingualism and have not addressed some of the social and economic realities of FI (e.g. the experiences of immigrant youth; see Dagenais & Berron, 2001); children from lower socioeconomic backgrounds participating in the programs, as well as the inclusion of children with exceptionalities participating in these programs (see Arnett & Mady, 2013). Bilingualism conceived as two separate linguistic systems (L1 and second language [L2]) inevitably causes inequalities, as many individuals do not have access to or the possibility of learning to be/become bilingual that way. Even if practices are challenged by recent debates concerning the inclusion of translanguaging (García & Li, 2014), teaching practices still reveal a monolingual and monocultural approach, especially in FI, where we witness the continued use of skills-based competence models which treat learners as homogeneous, static, commonsensical entities with an over-emphasis on teacher centeredness, grammar and textbook language. These prescriptive norms or ideological representations of language do not reflect the social realities or heterogeneous everyday linguistic practices of Canadian youth. However, they have, at the same time, very real consequences, particularly for students and future language teachers of French. For example, many students and teachers alike have claimed that their French is not good enough, and experience what has been referred to as 'linguistic insecurity' (see Byrd Clark *et al.*, 2013). Yet, at the same time, there are paradoxes because if students and teachers are not prepared to compete for university and/or job placements and, for whatever reason, do not manage or adapt to such linguistic norms (e.g. in attaining this imagined, idealized standard variety of French), there are also *real* social and economic consequences concerning life chances and career advancement (see Precarious Positionings section).

Tensions, misconceptions and contradictions continue to ensue in today's FSL classrooms as highlighted, for example, by Roy (2015), who looked at FI in Alberta and discovered nationalist and linguistic ideologies that likewise marginalized students who wished to learn French and be part of Francophone communities. Galiev (2013) also found that, when talking about French in Canada, students of immigrant origin appear to be absent from discussions – whereas Mady (2010), in a similar vein, discovered that many multilingual students (whom she refers to as *Allophones*) would like to take French but instead have been discouraged from doing so because of their limited English language proficiency. In this regard, the learning of French in FI by students of immigrant origin is treated as a deficit model. This deficit approach has been a very common practice (unfortunately) in other countries that have adopted bilingual education. For example, the two-way immersion model (adapted from Canada) in the United States has had similar issues with allowing immigrant children to take advantage of these programs (cf. Chávez-Moreno, Heiman & Yanes, this volume). In other words, the same excuse has been used regarding English proficiency to exclude immigrant students from these programs (see e.g. Flores, 2017).

Several authors (de Souza, 2019; May, 2014, 2019) have worked on deconstructing the notion of the monolingual bias which presumes that learners of languages should be equally proficient and competent in each of their languages. The monolingual bias of bilingualism (two separate monolingual linguistic systems) has enabled a deficit notion of being/becoming bilinguals and multilinguals for decades. Some researchers (Coste, 2002; Moore & Gajo, 2009) have found the term *plurilingual* to be more appropriate than *bilingual* since people have varying levels of competence in more than one linguistic variety, while others have proposed *translingualism* (see Canagarajah, 2013). Such alternative conceptualizations reflect the evolving and dynamic relationship between languages, as well as the ways in which people use and negotiate identities and meanings through language. Languages, in this sense, are always heterogeneous and dynamic, drawing on multiple resources.

Consequently, Byrd Clark (2009) found that a large number of university students studying French at post-secondary level in the Greater Toronto Area claimed to be of Italian origin, and additionally Byrd Clark *et al.* (2014) found that the majority of teacher education candidates in three FSL teacher education programs comprised multilingual students (speaking languages at home other than English and/or French). Thus, 'as more diversity is present in French second language classrooms [in Canada], we cannot continue to look at these programs in the same way anymore' (Byrd Clark & Roy, 2018: 4). Multilingual students with complex transnational identities and linguistic practices obscure such claims of belonging to a specific ethnolinguistic community. Nonetheless, because of the intersections between nation and the ideological representation of an idealized language(s) in the form of a standard variety, language teachers (in particular) remain under an enormous amount of pressure from society to 'fit within the norm' regarding their linguistic proficiency and competence.

Precarious positionings

Becoming a teacher in transnational times means developing the flexibility to navigate and discern between (and in-between) dominant ideological discourses, societal norms and contradictions to such norms; in other words, between and in-between structure(s) and agency/ies. Student teachers thus find themselves in precarious and challenging positions when having to fulfill the theoretical, philosophical and multimodal demands of teacher education programs that promote the development of critical thinking, only to then go out and teach (in most public schools) where Western Cartesian structuralist approaches (dualistic – 'cause and effect', 'this or that' approaches, such as evidenced-based testing measures and national standards for language teaching) to learning, teaching and curriculum still dominate.

At the same time, Canadian teachers are often critiqued and under scrutiny by other teachers, parents and students if they happen to speak another linguistic variety of French or speak French with a 'different' accent other than what is ideologically deemed the standard linguistic variety (Byrd Clark, 2009, 2012; Byrd Clark *et al.*, 2013) or *langue légitime* (see Bourdieu, 1977). Shohamy (2006) explained that educational institutions have often been required to subscribe to the 'ideological aspiration' of monolingual competence, which completely disregards the diversity and variety of languages spoken by bi/multilinguals.

Finally, from my own reflections and research, teachers (and researchers, for that matter) have also been held accountable and in many ways, expected to be and become perfect – that is, teachers must appear to be all things to everyone (students, parents, other teachers, administrators, taxpayers, school board members, government, researchers, etc.). It is thus no surprise that teacher attrition continues to be on the rise, and a significant need for qualified teachers, especially French language teachers in Canada, remains. The representation of a *good teacher* is an idealized representation in the same way that language has been idealized. But this demand for an ideal, perfect language teacher, who has idealized mastery and fluency, is often not reality – and, even if this happens to be the case, this idealized mastery of a language holds no guarantee that this interlocutor can actually teach or connect with students.

Theoretical Framing

Rather than position language as an idealized form, an object in nature that one must master (Chomsky, 1965; Saussure, 1966) and, in order to complement a critical ethnographic, sociolinguistic and discourse analytic conceptual approach, my research draws upon postmodern approaches to language, culture and identity, such as reflexivity and transdisciplinarity (see Byrd Clark, 2016, 2020; Byrd Clark & Dervin, 2014) and views language as a social activity (Bourdieu, 1977; Pennycook, 2010), a discourse, a product of practice and an in-between-ness of multidimensional, complex meshings between self and other. The moment we speak, our words become representations, open to others for their interpretation (and reinterpretation) of how we will be seen, heard, recognized, valued as certain kinds of people (low status, high status, Francophone, African American, Chinese Canadian, etc.). While linguistic practices exist within structures (e.g. school, family), they are not determined by them (e.g. Butler, 1997; Byrd Clark, 2016; Giddens, 1984).

As such, this research employs Blommaert's (2010) critical sociolinguistic argument to examine languages as both repertoires (varieties, accents, multicompetencies) and as resources (linguistic and cultural) from an historical point of view, from specific contexts. An historical view permits us to see the ways in which history has influenced how we use languages in the present and how language ideologies (beliefs, attitudes, perceptions) are transmitted and become natural, primordial or common-sense-like.

Accordingly, we can see for (at least) the past 30 years, that this common-sense, monolingual approach to languages and identities has been challenged via an emphasis on critical, social approaches to bi/multilingualism (e.g. May, 2014; Pennycook, 2010), theories on multicompetence (Cook, 1992), social identity (LePage & Tabouret-Keller, 1985; Norton Pierce, 1995), interculturality (Holliday, 2010), plurilingualism (Choi & Ollerhead, 2018; Coste, 2002; Lin, 2020; Moore & Gajo, 2009) and, most recently, translanguaging (García, 2009; García & Li, 2014; García & Otheguy, 2020).

Originating from the Council of Europe, the term *plurilingualism* was established as a means to celebrate linguistic diversity and build cultural tolerance throughout Europe. The *pluri* in plurilingualism intends to acknowledge the overlappings and intersections happening between the linguistic parts of an individual's holistic linguistic repertoire, making the argument that linguistic competence is not unidimensional, nor does it develop uniformly. In fact, the goal of plurilingualism should be partial competence in multiple languages, rather than full competence in two or three (see Hélot & Cavalli, 2017). Nonetheless, there is still an emphasis on dualistic approaches in plurilingual education, advocating that, although code-switching no longer represents a stigmatized, reviled, deviant form of behavior (see Labov, 1972), plurilingual students must learn the dominant monolingual ways of being multilingual at school, and yet develop an awareness of linguistic hierarchies – so again, 'this and that'. The dominant ways (or structures) continue to be viewed as fixed, static, homogeneous entities, and thus the focus in plurilingualism has been on turning monolingual speakers into multilinguals.

Dualisms are not bad, by any means, and surely, as Lin (2020) argued, they can exist side by side, rather than as an either/or binary approach. Moreover, we do need to understand and be able to function with them in society – because certainly we know there are consequences of not being able to navigate dominant discourses. But dualisms limit what students and teachers and we humans can do with our language use, and who we can become, particularly when we focus on *the navigating* in-between structures and agencies. Dualisms perpetuate fixed homogeneous entities (black and white; good and bad; Anglophone and Francophone; monolingual and multilingual, etc.), rather than fluid, embodied, heterogeneous ones.

In alignment with García (2009) and Flores (2017), my theoretical framing calls for transdisciplinary approaches to language and teaching, which inextricably draws upon translanguaging conceptualizations, but expands to include the disciplinary crossings and connections involved (applied linguistics, multilingual education, French language pedagogy, sociolinguistics, etc.). 'Transdisciplinary approaches lend themselves to the re-imagining of multidimensional ways of meaning making (e.g. translanguaging, translating, gesturing) that are fluid, but also and more importantly, valued and encouraged' (Byrd Clark, 2016: 5). For example, with regard to translanguaging, García (2009) has argued that bilinguals do not switch codes like two monolinguals within a single individual, rather they use both codes in an integrated, interconnected manner, and in doing so, invent a new way of communicating (and a new language, for that matter). More importantly, García and Otheguy (2020: 32) assert that 'translanguaging offers the potential to transform minoritized communities' sense of self that the concept of plurilingualism may not always do'. By the same token, transdisciplinarity transforms our ways of thinking about the disciplinary divides between multilingualism, multiculturalism, multicompetence, etc., all the while highlighting an individual's potential for creativity, openness and criticality (see Perrin & Kramsch, 2018). As Byrd Clark (2016) reminds us, ideas are not tied to any one discipline – just as making meaning is not tied exclusively to one linguistic code – and that disciplines are not separate static entities (i.e. they overlap, inform and intersect with one another). Thus, we are permitted to observe the complexities and fluid practices that transcend socially constructed language systems and structures. In the navigating of in-between-ness and through the embodying of languages, we find creativity, resourcefulness, multiple meaning-making and complexities that destabilize social frames, dismantle boundaries and nation-state language ideologies.

Complex positionings: Who is the researcher or the 'I' here?[5]

My ways of identifying (and life experiences) are about as complex and complicated as anyone else's. Perhaps the processes of being and becoming a multilingual have helped to make such complexities appear more visible, but certainly do not make me better or superior in any way, shape or form. Yet, we each have our own stories, experiences and life trajectories. In my case, I grew up with particular kinds of adversities in life (e.g. difficult childhood, surviving loss, trauma and tragedy at a young age). At the same time, I lived between Protestant and Catholic faiths, between Mediterranean, Celtic, Native American and British heritage, between Italian dialect and English[6] (and later French)[7] and between working-class Italian immigrants and middle-class Americans. Additionally, I have worked with students from lower socioeconomic backgrounds as a K-12 language teacher in the US (e.g. in Baltimore, Maryland) and, at the same time, studied languages alongside students from elite, upper social class backgrounds (e.g. Middlebury College; La Sorbonne). Of course, this in-between-ness has had a huge influence on my ways of relating to the world, and how I've come to understand, engage with and see the world. I suppose as Julie Byrd Clark, I have never been satisfied with being seen or recognized as *one* thing, nor have I been able to accept a *singular way* of seeing reality (or knowledge for that matter). To this day, I live between countries (dual citizen of Canada and the United States), live in-between languages, including *translanguaging* (Italiese, Franglais, Frantaliano, Spanglish, etc.) and, though I appear to have a privileged lifestyle as a professor (in North America), you would be hard pressed to take away my modest, no-nonsense upbringing (for which I remain indebted to my *Italian* grandparents). Alas, these experiences have both broadened and at the same time caused blind spots for Julie Byrd Clark.

> Nevertheless, these experiences of in-between-ness have drawn me to reflexivity. Reflexivity interrupts or problematizes dichotomous ways of thinking, as it involves a constant shifting and navigating between the interconnected, complex meshings of self and other, of *being and becoming*. We see this complex shifting, dependent upon or intersecting with different contexts, situations, preferences, and conditioning. Thus, such experiences of in-between-ness cannot help but be present in my everyday encounters, interactions, and performances. (Byrd Clark, 2020: 89)

Critical Ethnography and Reflexive Engagement

One of the greatest functions of critical ethnography lies in its ability to unmask and make visible processes such as symbolic violence (Bourdieu, 1991) and hegemony (Gramsci, 1971), allowing people to see how power and hegemonic discourses operate and circulate in the social world. As such, criticality aims to demystify power structures, namely from the perspective of 'those that suffer' (Fairclough & Wodak, 1997: 258), representing the voices of those who have been marginalized, at the periphery of the social world (see Giddens, 1991). Many critical scholars in applied linguistics, intercultural education and linguistic minority education (e.g. see Giampapa, 2019; Norton Pierce, 1995) have drawn upon critical ethnography to produce highly influential work, revealing unequal relations between dominant and marginalized groups in society (in other words, *the haves and the have-nots*). This is important because, as researchers and human beings, we want to take a stand against social injustices, especially in lieu of significant crimes against humanity when dominant groups are killing historically marginalized groups because of racial hatred (e.g. police brutality and killings in the US, see Kendi, 2016; Muhammad, 2011); residential schooling of First Nations people in Canada (see Metatawabin & Shimo, 2014); genocides in Rwanda and Nazi Germany.

Critical ethnography thus emerged largely from critical theory, which was initially a movement to overcome oppression from dominant objective, scientific and/or positivist ways of thinking about reality and knowledge. In other words, there are multiple ways to interpret and represent reality(ies) – and more importantly, that we are not born with a social identity, that is we actually become an 'identity' or 'identities' through complex social conditioning, socialization and constant repetition. Nonetheless, the *critical* in critical ethnography has tended to focus on the outside world and its impact on the constructed, imagined *other* (e.g. the construction of social difference), thus producing the dualistic 'Us vs. Them' binary. With this *critical* in ethnography, there are more than likely two opposing sides (e.g. positivist vs. social constructivist; structuralist vs. poststructuralist; and native vs. non-native). Many established scholars' work exudes this kind of criticality, focusing on the tensions and unequal relations of power with emphasis on the materiality of social processes, the distribution of resources (be they linguistic, social, material, symbolic), social and political order, hegemony and/or hegemonic processes, to name just a few (e.g. Fairclough, 2006; Heller, 2011). However, most of us academics and researchers still 'appear unreflexive as regards our own ideological attachments as well as positionings (positions of power) and in the material conditions' (Byrd Clark & Dervin, 2014: 15) that enabled/afforded us the opportunities to produce such critical work in the first place.

I want to stress that *reflexive engagement* does not abandon criticality. On the contrary, we, as researchers and research participants, need to begin by questioning and becoming aware of the subjective, social situated-ness of reality/ies and people. Critical ethnography, in this case, serves a necessary and vital *point de départ* (entry point) in developing/practicing reflexivity, for it is only the questioning of reality, a constant skepticism, that may lead us to not only witness the instabilities, contradictions and multiplicities in the constructing of the social world (such as political binaries) but also (perhaps, more shockingly) within what constitutes our own sense of *selves*.

Data Collection

The majority of the data presented in this chapter come from a three-year critical ethnographic study, including interviews and online forum discussions, which took place in London, Ontario, Canada.

In London, I selected from the research I had done with 53 student teachers enrolled in a one year (at the time) post-secondary teacher education program to become professionally certified and specialized in FSL in this particular province (being able to teach in core French, intensive French, extended French and FI programs). It is important to note that all the student teacher candidates had already completed a first undergraduate degree (in different disciplines) before gaining entry to the B.Ed teacher education program. The selected data passages reflect individual interviews and small-group, online discussions with fellow student teacher candidates from class, as well as with student teacher candidates participating in a professional master in teaching program from France (part of an online virtual collaboration).

Participants

The majority of the participants ranged from 21 to 28 years old and were representative of diverse social, linguistic and geographical backgrounds – having different life trajectories and French language learning experiences. Some of the participants self-identified as having hyphenated identities (e.g. Italian-Canadian, Korean-Canadian), although in varied ways, such as 'bilinguals', 'Franco-Ontarians' and 'Canadians', with multidimensional engagements (multiple purposes) in pursuing French at the post-secondary level.

Data analysis

For data analysis, I used an interpretivist approach (which does not accept 'reality' at face value, acknowledging the subjective nature of interpretation). As a reflexive researcher with complex positionings, I acknowledge the different ways of interpreting as well as how my interpretations intersect with some of my experiences and represent some of my own ontological and epistemological framings. That said, I had many conversations about the ways of interpreting the data with the student teachers. These exchanges presented different dimensions or angles to consider which, in the end not only reflect a polyphonic, multilingual analysis of the data, but also a more in-depth and transdisciplinary (transforming in-between-ness) account (see Byrd Clark, 2016).

Interviews were recorded and transcribed to highlight themes and important passages, reflective of the research questions. The data were then manually coded according to recurring themes and discursive patterns.

Three themes emerged from this discursive data analysis: (1) *complex positionings, authenticity and legitimacy, and representations of French*; (2) *ideological messages and complex practices*; and (3) *challenges of ideologies and moving toward reflexive awareness*. Each of these themes will be represented in the data presentation section. In what follows, I reflect upon the research questions and present themes that came from the analysis of interviews and online forum discussions to shed light on both the impact of ideologies and the complex, contradictory positionings of the multilingual participants.

Complex positionings, authenticity and legitimacy, and representations of French

In this first theme, we consider how student teachers make sense of what it means to be and become bi/multilingual. In other words, what does it mean for them to become French language teachers, particularly as concerns their ways of looking and sounding (e.g. speaking, accent and linguistic variety), and in different contexts, such as the classroom, and in one case, within different Canadian provinces.

Student teachers in B.Ed program in London (Ontario)

- **Julie:** So, tell me a little about your French language learning experiences, maybe you were… mentioning that you were in French Immersion, how was that // what was it like?

- **Brad Zakamoto:** In my French immersion program, like the entire program, Grade 9–12, I was the only Asian in the program. The other kids called me 'Monsieur Chang or Monsieur Wang' …they were playful but it was offensive. Even in my Master's classes, you know you walk in, and I guess I've gotten used to that, but you know they say, 'Oh, you speak French?' So being Asian and pursuing French is kind of not the norm here.

***

- **Julie:** OK Christopher, it's funny to hear you in English! [laughs]. Ok, so can you tell me a little bit about your own ways of identifying, and maybe a little more about some of your teaching and learning experiences before coming to Canada?
- **Christopher:** Well… I'm not sure how I identify these days. I'm British… I taught in La Réunion and in France for the past four years, and met my wife, who is from Montréal… and now live in Ontario, Canada… most of the time, people think I'm from France, they don't know that I'm British, until I switch to English. And it's quite funny to see their reactions… I think it's safer actually if they think I'm French! [laughs]

These two different samples represent some of the complex identities and positionings of student teachers in French, as well as how social difference gets constructed. Both participants' samples challenge traditional boundaries of who or what gets recognized as an authentic, legitimate speaker of French, though at varied degrees. At the same time, we can see some of the messages (and discourses) and ways that others have positioned both Brad and Christopher. Brad is of Korean origin, so being called Monsieur Wang/Chang is offensive not only in being stigmatized or represented as being the only Asian in class, but also for being positioned as Chinese rather than Korean (as if they are the same). There is also a racist discourse here on who gets recognized as an authentic and legitimate speaker/learner of French. Although he experiences being racialized, Brad's complex positioning simultaneously challenges this discourse of authenticity and legitimacy. Christopher, on the other hand, seems to experience more ease with his complex positionings (see next sample). However, he jokes at the end when saying that 'it's safer if they think I'm French!' and goes on to recount how people threw garbage at him and his wife while driving in Montréal, Québec, with Ontario license plates (with the irony being that his wife is from Montréal). So being seen as French is perhaps cool in Ontario for Christopher, but perhaps takes on a different value in Québec, when driving with Ontario license plates.

In addition, I would like to reflect on my own positioning and language use, initially being surprised at hearing Christopher speak in

English. Prior to our interview, Christopher and I had only ever spoken in French together and, unlike some of the other students, he would only speak French both in and outside of class. So, this interview was the first time I actually heard him speak in English, and it was a pleasant surprise, even for someone who is used to navigating multiple ways of communicating. I can see how my frames became destabilized, so to speak, and how my mind had gotten used to seeing and hearing Christopher in a certain way – and then, *voilà*, there he was speaking in English with a British accent. It is important to note that the interviews were conducted mostly in English for transcription purposes (issues of access).

In this next sample, we further see that complex identities can sometimes destabilize social frames and temporarily disrupt our ideologies (or ways of being, thinking), in particular interactions and contexts. Christopher's (from above) complex positionings obscure the socially constructed dualism 'Us and Them', as he participates in an online synchronous video discussion with two students, Melanie and Céline from France, who have mistaken him for French and are shocked to learn that he's originally from the United Kingdom.

- **Céline:** Tu sais Christophe, il y a beaucoup de choses qui se passent en France maintenant avec l'élection, comme toujours…
- **Melanie:** Oui, on le sait bien, n'est-ce pas Chris? Par hasard, tu es né où en France?
- **Christopher:** Aaa, je ne suis pas né en France, effectivement.
- **Céline:** Ah non? Mais tu as grandit ici, n'est-ce pas? Ou est-ce que tu as grandit au Québec?
- **Christopher:** Non, je suis né en Angleterre, et j'ai grandit là, plus ou moins.
- **Melanie:** Oh my God ! Comment, mais comment c'est possible?
- **Céline:** Ça m'étonne aussi… vraiment? J'ai pensé que tu étais *un de nous*.

In this first theme, I also revisited the question, 'What place does French hold (past, present and future) in the student teachers' lives?' and found that many of the participants' investments in French had shifted, for example, from being seen as a lucrative possession/commodity, as linguistic capital leading to upward social and economic mobility, to a more affective, embodied, emotional attachment or symbolic affiliation. For some, it represented a possibility or way to be seen as something 'other', as in the sample with Brad. What's more, Brad reflects on his learning of French as having had an impact on kindling his interest to engage and reassess his *Koreanness*.

- **Brad Zakamoto:** I embraced French, it's a big part of my life. I would have liked to have diversif[ied] the curriculum more, it was heavily grammar based. And not interdisciplinary [...] I find it bizarre that only a handful of us (my friends) continued French at university. French, for me, is a huge part of my life, it's played a huge and multiple kind of role, I've taken it since Grade 4, and would like to be a model of a Canadian who speaks both official languages. Becoming a teacher of French would allow me to be part of that process, cultivating new young Canadians, Korean Canadians, all different backgrounds, if they have the desire and ambition, I want to support them. And I want for people not to worry so much about speaking, that they know it's OK to make mistakes, and I want them to feel comfortable and not think that their French is not good enough. Hopefully, I can be an inspiration to my students, as I've had to break through a lot of social barriers to get to this point, and I want to share my experiences. French was always something that made me feel more Canadian. Like it wasn't English, it wasn't Korean, it was something that allowed me to create // or carve out my own space as an individual, and I think that's important.

- **Julie:** Yes, I understand and can relate [laughs]. Do you think learning and studying French has had any impact on your English, and Korean?
- **Brad:** Oh, well, *bonne question!*[8] [laughs, pause] Actually, I went to Korea for the first time four years ago, after I graduated from university (with a degree in French literature), and it was like amazing and intimidating at the same time, but I would say yes... I never really thought much about it, but studying French, I would say, has affected my vocabulary in English and writing for sure! Hahaha... and yeah, since studying French, I have developed a profound interest in claiming err reclaiming my Korean heritage, being able to travel to Korea and see that there's a whole world you know of people speaking and living in Korean, and not just like one block in my neighborhood or one church community in London. Korean became alive for me, and not just something I was targeted as or labeled because of my family.

This sample reflects the question as to what place French holds in their lives. As we can see, Brad's engagement with French in this particular moment appears to go beyond economics or cognitive benefits, and reflects affective, experiential and subjective dimensions. Brad has explained that:

(1) French was always something that he was good at.
(2) French represents something that made him feel *more* Canadian.
(3) French allowed him to feel he could carve out his own space as an individual.

Interestingly, this sample illustrates the interconnection of French with English and Korean. Brad did not seem to have considered the impact of his personal linguistic and social repertoire – particularly that studying French may have opened up the possibility for him to explore his Koreanness, his desire to go to Korea and (re)claim a Korean identity. French also appears to represent a transdisciplinary or an in-between space for Brad, as he does not have to be confined to the dualistic roles of being Canadian and being Korean, his hybrid, multiple identities can shift in becoming seen as Canadian, Korean Canadian, French as well as a bi/multilingual Canadian or all of the above, in different contexts, situations and interactions.

Ideological messages

Considering the second research question, regarding certain messages and representations of language and identity from different people and contexts, and whether such messages have an impact on the student teachers' perceptions, it becomes clear that ideological representations of French (and language, in general) do, indeed, have an impact. Looking at the deficit-binary model of language education (incorporating the Chomskian conception of language), the notion of the 'idealized native speaker' intersects with positivist ways of understanding language as an abstract static object that is rational, universal, cognitive, neutral and organized. When we look at fields, such as second language acquisition (SLA), we can see that formalist (cognitive psychometric) and Cartesian structuralist approaches to languages have tended to dominate ways of 'either-or' thinking about language teaching and learning (particularly in schools). Recently, sociolinguistic and postmodern approaches have begun to have an impact on the field of language teaching and, in particular, on what constitutes or represents a 'professional language teacher' (Byrd Clark, 2012). The following two samples, for example, reflect and reproduce such mono-ideological representations (e.g. l'interlocuteur natif = the native speaker). At the same time, they demonstrate how powerful such discourses are for student teachers (in particular) who are in the midst of working in a competence skills-based domain (grammar-rule based). This domain exudes a monolingual view of languages, that is, an idealized mastery of two separate linguistic systems, while simultaneously trying to incorporate linguistic diversity (inclusive of their own).

- **Angela:** Madame, Prof BC, j'ai essayé de créer une leçon qui inclut les diversités des identités et les multilittéracies que vous nous avez montré dans notre cours à Western, mais le prof à mon école m'a dit que ces choses ne sont pas liées au curriculum du FSL, et **je dois me concentrer plutôt sur expliquer la grammaire et les régles aux élèves.**

- **Fiora** (in teacher education class): I didn't know what to do, my Associate teacher was like correcting my French, she sat at the back of the room, writing down every mistake… it made me so nervous, and then she told me that I really need to lose my Italian accent when I speak French, she said that I would be transferring it onto the kids, and that would not be good. I didn't know I had an Italian accent when I speak French?!? [pause] and well, maybe I do? …I guess I don't speak 'proper' French… I went to French Immersion, go figure?

This conception of bringing students to 'native speaker' level, including the attainment of a native to near-native speaker accent, is still represented as the ultimate goal for teachers, student teachers, even multilinguals, to reach prior to teaching. Nonetheless, while certain dominant discourses and ideologies abound throughout the exchanges and perceptions of the student teachers, there are also some compelling samples of moments where the student teachers challenge traditional and dominant ways of thinking, including their own (as we shall see in the upcoming examples).

Complex practices, challenges of ideologies and moving toward reflexive awareness

When discussing code-switching and multilingualism with the student teachers, many of them had never heard of code-switching or, if they had, they had heard that it was bad, and did not seem consciously aware of their own bi/multilingual practices. In the two discussions: the first between Lise and Yolanda (two Canadian students) in early fall/autumn at the beginning of the term; and then the second between Veronique (from France) and Yolanda in late fall/autumn, at the end of term, we see some of their impressions of translanguaging (which they refer to as code-switching)[9] in relation to teaching French in the classroom, as well as some of the contradictory shifts in their ideological positionings.

Lise: I think code-switching would be OK to use in class, I had a prof that called it 'Franglais' and we used words like 'Hello' 'party' and 'weekend'.

Yolanda: I wouldn't use code-switching, I think of code-switching in terms of showing the different registers of the French language. In my opinion, it's very important for FSL students to know that there is **only one correct version of the French language**.

Lise: Well, je pense qu'on a plusieurs variétés du français, pas une seule version correcte, on a bien sûr français parisien, québécois, haitien, mauricien, franco-ontarien.

In this first online exchange, Lise seems more accepting of code-switching than Yolanda, and challenges the ideological notion that there is only one correct version of the French language, where she is reflective of heterogeneity and aware of the different linguistic varieties of French.

Yolanda, who grew up in a Francophone community in southwestern Ontario, had recounted having difficult experiences when attending French language schools, being corrected and made to feel that she was not a legitimate or authentic member.

In the following sample (which took place three months later), we see Yolanda in an online exchange with Veronique. Ironically, Yolanda's positioning on code-switching appears to have shifted, as in this excerpt, she challenges Veronique's understanding of code-switching (as well as her own previously) to show that this is not a practice exclusive to Canada. Her shift also demonstrates her transdisciplinary (in-between-ness) positioning, as she translanguages between French, Spanish and English in one interaction.

- **Veronique:** Is there a difference between the French in Ontario and in Québec?
- **Yolanda:** Ouais, il y a une différence [...]
- **Veronique: Nous n'avons pas ce *code switching* en France.**
- **Yolanda: *¡ Oh dios mio* ! Vous n'avez pas les musiciens qui chantent en français avec les mots des autres langues ? What about Manu-Chao?**
- **Veronique:** Ah si, on a ça, bien sûr, **mais je veux dire, pas dans la salle de classe.** (Online discussion between students in Canada and student in France)

This sample was taken from an online discussion (synchronous) between a Canadian student, Yolanda, and a student, Veronique, from France. Yolanda grew up speaking Spanish, French and English. Her parents moved to southwestern Ontario, Canada, to a Francophone community when she was six years old. Before entering the teacher education program, Yolanda had lived in France with her boyfriend for three years, in a Paris suburb. It is important to note this because it is not common knowledge for many Canadians (outside Québec) to know or be familiar with French singers from France, particularly Manu Chao (who translanguages mainly between Spanish, Arabic and French). But the fact that Yolanda did have this information was a way for her to challenge Veronique's views of code-switching in the classroom (as well as her own previously held views!). Her complex discursive practices pose a paradox or a contradiction, especially in France, which is well known for having its *l'Academie Française* discourse, on keeping the French language 'pure'.

Ironically, the two women are having a conversation about code-switching, informally, online, but what is compelling is that Yolanda actually translanguages in this exchange, using '*Dios mio*' (in Spanish) and '*What about Manu Chao?*' (in English), just as if she is speaking one language, effortlessly. Perhaps the Spanish could be seen as an affinity for the singer Manu Chao (being multilingual and a fellow speaker of Spanish)? Interestingly, Veronique starts the conversation in English, but then finishes in French. This conversation happened after a couple of months – in the beginning the students were quite nervous and cautious about their writing (as well as expressing their ideas) in French and wanting to use more formal language, illustrating more traditional ideas about teaching and learning. However, once they appeared more comfortable with one another, they began using more colloquial yet complex, everyday language. The language use in this data sample challenges our notions of language as separate, fixed, binary systems, revealing instead the fluidity, affective (emotional) dimensions and heterogeneity when *doing* language.

When conducting the study, many of the students became interested in learning more about language ideologies. We watched segments of *My Fair Lady* and *Bienvenue chez les Ch'tis* (*Welcome to the Sticks*) to discuss social variation, the imposition of one linguistic variety over another and how certain ideologies or ways of thinking become powerful and, at the same time, linked with one's social class, gender, ethnicity and race. In the following excerpt, I met with Josephine, who was in the midst of completing her teaching practicum in an FI high school. During this phase of our interview, I was catching up and asking how things were going with her teaching placement and associate teacher (or cooperating teacher), the teacher who accepted Josephine to be a student teacher in her classroom.

Josephine: ...you know how we were like talking about ideologies that people have about speaking language, like accent [Julie: yes] well she corrected me in front of the whole class the other day, and told me that I had a strong accent, and I really need to work on perfecting my French. Then she went on to ask me where I was from [Julie: Really?] yeah, yeah, and I said I'm from Canada, and she was like No, **WHERE** are you **REALLY** from? [Julie: Raised eyebrows, surprised], yeah like I'm not Canadian.

Julie: How did that make you feel?

Josephine: Terrible, at first, really, you know like I'm some kind of imposter or something! [laughs] ...I mean the only thing, I mean something that helped me was I remembered what we were talking about the other day, being mindful about how people get so attached to certain beliefs or ways of seeing other people that they actually cause inequality or discrimination, and suffering, subconsciously. She couldn't really see 'me' you know cuz she was so blinded by her ah own ideologies, you know what I mean?

Julie: Yes, I do, for sure. What did you do… did you say anything to her?

Josephine: Oh yeah, I told her I was born here, in Canada, and then I asked her where she was from (laughs), really from… she didn't like that too much! (laughs) (Julie: Laughs, good for you!) She just stared at me and then walked away. I didn't take it personal, you know? It felt good to not be afraid and ask her the same question back – at least she might have a chance to think about it.

This exchange was a powerful one for me, and at the same time, representative of a larger discourse I've heard from many participants before – though with particular examples – and that is a racist, colonialist discourse on who or what gets to look and sound Canadian – on who can be seen and heard as an authentic, legitimate Canadian. As the youngest child, Josephine was born in Canada and grew up with her Haitian grandparents, as both her parents had been killed in a car accident when she was very young. She speaks a mixture or goes in-between Créole French and English at home. The irony here is that Josephine speaks French, from Haiti, and once again, we see that anything that appears different from the ideologically deemed 'standard norm' gets treated as a problem, rather than as an asset. Both Josephine's complex positioning and linguistic variety challenge the mono-ideological norms of school and the colonialist views of the associate teacher – who questions her in front of the class, 'Where are you REALLY from?' as if Josephine cannot claim a Canadian identity because of the way she looks and sounds. This is why dualism ('this and that') and binary ('this or that') ways of conceiving the world are problematic and perpetuate narrow-minded, limited understandings *and* why youth with complex identities and heterogeneous linguistic practices challenge, contradict and destabilize such perceived fixed, impermeable ideologies.

What is noteworthy (and admirable) is Josephine's response, in that she challenges the associate teacher, by simply returning and asking the same question to the associate teacher, who then turns and walks away. This sample shows reflexive engagement on Josephine's part in that she was willing to critically engage with the associate teacher, and to resist the deficit perspective being imposed on her by the teacher, despite the teacher walking away. More importantly, she did not allow the teacher's preconceived notions and beliefs to cause her to suffer or stop her from teaching in the classroom. Her complex positionings and linguistic variety disrupt the teacher's colonialist discourse and power representational system and, at the same time, offer a significant model for the students in the classroom – to show that being Canadian and a French language teacher does not belong exclusively to one singular identity or a particular group of people.

The critical ethnographic observations of online discussions and interviews have provided a unique lens that permits us to see how perceptions, meanings and representations are adhered to, negotiated and challenged. Many of the samples and data demonstrate a serious need to rethink these political binaries ('either-or', Anglophone or Francophone) as well as some of the older, more traditional, formal and reductionist (deficit) models of thinking about bilingualism, and institutional policies, in order to develop and foster an openness to (and an adaptability to) social and linguistic variation, thereby helping all of us to develop multiple ways of communicating and comprehending flexibly, rather than only in one singular, unidimensional way.

Discussion and Conclusion

To recapitulate then, critical ethnography (sociolinguistic reflexive ethnographic research) creates spaces for us to become reflexive of our linguistic practices, of our own ideological investments and of our own identifications as well as others' interpretations of us in different spaces, times and places. We can become more aware of how and why we think, speak and act in the ways that we do, in particular settings and with particular people. This is important, as we can no longer look, categorize or treat learners/citizens/individuals as homogeneous, static, sedentary or unidimensional entities. We look much more at how individuals construct their humanity, their ways of being, doing and thinking through discourse (or their social and linguistic practices), and how these shift in contexts, interactions and moments, as they did for the participants in this study. We need to think about the ways in which we have been labeled or categorized and get in touch with our own ideological attachments and investments, so that we can take action and create new public policies, to imagine a social reality that offers more opportunities and fewer constraints. More importantly, insofar as what I have presented here, we can see how what happens in the social world – as in how socialization has an impact on our own investments, and how we come to think about things; how we internalize such things; in other words, how daily life is achieved. This can lead to an understanding of how complex social processes and relations operate, demonstrating that languages and identities cannot be categorized into neat, separate compartments with delineated boundaries in the brain (Firth & Wagner, 1997). It can also thus lead us to think differently about language via a reconceptualization of multilingualism where heterogeneity is valued. We must look at the diversity of meanings rather than the diversity of languages (in terms of enumerating languages). Can we practice pedagogy and create public policies that treat diversity, human agency, heterogeneity and multimodality as the norm?

More importantly, the critical ethnographic research I have presented in this chapter provides one way for us to understand how and why (future) language teachers do the things that they do, how they see themselves, how they are seen by others in certain contexts and how certain representations therein become meaningful or symbolic (Moscovici, 1984). The creation of new policies means more than taking account of unequal power relationships, more than an oppressor/oppressed deficit model – it means creatively finding alternative ways to support diversities and more opportunities for equal access to education.

Therefore, we need to continue to challenge and break through the deep-rooted political binaries which continue to perpetuate a mono-ideological, deficit-based model, to shift these dominant ideologies and focus more on what youth actually do and can do, rather than focusing only on what they cannot do. On the ground, we need to work on strategies and transdisciplinary approaches that may enable future teachers – of French in Canada, in this instance – to become reflexive of their practices (especially now), as well as the ways they invest in certain representations of languages, identities and power. Focusing on the *doing* may lead to alternative approaches to learning, understanding and engaging – as well as an openness to social variation – and perhaps a deeper understanding of what it means to be and become multilingual and multicultural (Byrd Clark, 2012).

My hope is that (1) this research will inspire new ways of imagining, engaging and rethinking such policies surrounding what it means to be and become a multilingual language teacher; and (2) it will help to inspire more students to become critical ethnographers, developing reflexive engagement and giving way to new frontiers of dialogic, interculturally aware, transdisciplinary and multidimensional understandings of teaching and learning. Critical ethnography represents one key way to use such approaches and practices going forward in challenging theoretical and political binaries in contemporary times.

Notes

(1) In 2019, the Official Language Act was revised (https://www.clo-ocol.gc.ca/en/publications/other/2019/modernizing-ola-recommendations) and the Indigenous Languages Act, which is intended to support the reclamation, revitalization, maintaining and strengthening of Indigenous languages in Canada received Royal Assent on 21 June 2019 (https://www.canada.ca/en/canadian-heritage/campaigns/celebrate-indigenous-languages/legislation.html).

(2) English minoritized communities in the province of Québec (where French is the dominant language used in society) and French minoritized communities in all provinces outside of Québec.

(3) A brand new university, the University of French Ontario/l'université de l'Ontario Français, is slated to open in Toronto, Ontario, in the next few years.

(4) French immersion being represented and renowned worldwide as Canada's exemplar bilingual education program.

(5) Portions of this section of the chapter appear in the *Routledge Handbook of Language and Intercultural Communication* (vol. 2, 2020).

(6) American mid-Western, upstate New York and Hibernian varieties.
(7) Parisian, Québecois and Franco-Ontarian varieties.
(8) Bold and italics have been used in the participants' quotes to highlight emphasis, both in intonation and discursive significance (the importance of larger discourses found in the participants' discursive samples).
(9) Please note: Code-switching and translanguaging are not the same. However, at the time of this study, my students were only becoming aware of code-switching for the first time. In my analysis, I believe they were translanguaging (using different codes from one linguistic system) though, rather than code-switching (drawing from two or more separate linguistic codes from two or more different linguistic systems).

References

Arnett, K. and Mady, C. (2013) *Minority Populations in Canadian Second Language Education*. Bristol: Multilingual Matters.

Blommaert, J. (2010) *The Sociolinguistics of Globalization*. New York: Cambridge University Press.

Bourdieu, P. (1977) *Outline of a Theory of Practice* (trans. R. Nice). Cambridge: Cambridge University Press.

Bourdieu, P. (1991) *Language and Symbolic Power*. Cambridge, MA: Harvard University Press.

Breidenbach, J. and Nyíri. P (2009) *Seeing Culture Everywhere: From Genocide to Consumer Habits*. Seattle, WA: University of Washington Press.

Butler, J. (1997) *Excitable Speech: A Politics of the Performative*. New York: Routledge.

Byrd Clark, J.S. (2009) *Multilingualism, Citizenship, and Identity: Voices of Youth and Symbolic Investments in an Urban, Globalized World*. London: Continuum.

Byrd Clark, J.S. (2010) Making 'wiggle room' in French as a second language/Français langue seconde: Reconfiguring identity, language, and policy. *Canadian Journal of Education* 33 (2), 379–406.

Byrd Clark, J.S. (2011) La signification du plurilinguisme et la voix de jeunes italo-canadiens [The meaning of plurilingualism and the voice of young Italo-Canadians]. *Cahiers d'ILOB (Institut des langues officielles et du bilinguisme)* (Vol. 2, pp. 1001–1021). University of Ottawa Press.

Byrd Clark, J.S. (2012) Heterogeneity and a sociolinguistics of multilingualism: Reconfiguring French language pedagogy. *Language and Linguistics Compass Blackwell Online Journal* 6 (3), 143–161.

Byrd Clark, J. (2016) Transdisciplinary approaches for language learning and teaching in transnational times. *L2 Journal* 4, 3–19.

Byrd Clark, J.S. (2020) Reflexivity and criticality in language and intercultural communication. In J. Jackson (ed.) *The Routledge International Handbook of Language and Intercultural Communication* (2nd edn, pp. 86–106). London: Routledge.

Byrd Clark, J.S. and Dervin, F. (2014) *Reflexivity in Language Education: Rethinking Multilingualism and Interculturality*. New York: Routledge.

Byrd Clark, J.S. and Roy, S.M. (2018) *French for New Social Realities in Transnational, Contemporary Time*. Insight Grant Award, J.S. Byrd Clark (principal investigator); S. Roy (co-investigator), 2018–2024 (pp. 1–45). Social Sciences and Humanities Research Council of Canada (SSHRC).

Byrd Clark, J.S., Lamoureux, S. and Stratilaki, S. (2013) Apprendre et enseigner le français dans l'Ontario, Canada: Entre dualité linguistique et réalités plurielles et complexes [Learning and teaching French in Ontario, Canada: Between linguistic duality and plural and complex realities]. *Journal of Cahiers d'ACÉDLE* 10 (3), 37–54.

Byrd Clark, J.S., Mady, C. and Vanthuyne, A. (2014) Exploring reflexivity, multiple identities, and multilingualism in three postsecondary French language teacher education programs. *Canadian Journal of Applied Linguistics* 17 (1), 129–155.

Canagarajah, S. (2013) *Translingual Practice: Global Englishes and Cosmopolitan Relations*. London: Routledge.

Choi, J., Ollerhead, S. and French, M. (2018) Introduction. In J. Choi and S. Ollerhead (eds) *Plurilingualism in Learning and Teaching: Complexities across Contexts* (pp. 1–17). London: Routledge.

Chomsky, N. (1965) *Aspects of the Theory of Syntax*. Cambridge, MA: Massachusetts Institute of Technology Press.

Cook, V.J. (1992) Evidence for multi-competence. *Language Learning* 42 (4), 557–591.

Coste, D. (2002) *Compétence à communiquer et compétence plurilingue* [*Communication Skills and Plurilingual Competence*]. Notions en Questions, 6 (pp. 115–123). Lyon: ENS Éditions.

Dagenais, D. and Berron, C. (2001) Promoting multilingualism through French immersion and language maintenance in three immigrant families. *Language, Culture & Curriculum* 14 (2), 142–155.

de Souza, L.M.T.M. (2019) Glolocal languages, coloniality and globalization from below. In M. Guilherme and L.M.T.M. de Souza (eds) *Glocal Languages and Critical Intercultural Awareness: The South Answers Back* (pp. 17–41). London: Routledge.

Fairclough, N. (2006) *Language and Globalization*. London: Routledge.

Fairclough, N. and Wodak, R. (1997) Critical discourse analysis. In T. van Dijk (ed.) *Discourse Studies: A Multidisciplinary Introduction* (2nd edn, pp. 258–284). London: Sage.

Firth, A. and Wagner, J. (1997) On discourse, communication, and (some) fundamental concepts in SLA research. *The Modern Language Journal* 81 (3), 285–300.

Flores, N. (2017) From language-as-resource to language-as-struggle: Resisting the Coke-ification of bilingual education. In M.-C. Flubacher and A. Del Percio (eds) *Language, Education and Neoliberalism: Critical Studies in Sociolinguistics* (pp. 62–81). Bristol: Multilingual Matters.

Galiev, A. (2013) Official bilingualism and immigrants: Perceptions, experiences and practices. Unpublished doctoral dissertation, University of Calgary.

García, O. (2009) Education, multilingualism and translanguaging in the 21st century. In A. Mohanty, M. Panda, R. Phillipson and T. Skutnabb-Kangas (eds) *Multilingual Education for Social Justice: Globalising the Local* (pp. 128–145). Hyderabad: Orient Blackswan.

García, O. and Li, W. (2014) *Translanguaging: Language, Bilingualism, and Education*. Basingstoke: Palgrave MacMillan.

García, O. and Otheguy, R. (2020) Plurilingualism and translanguaging: Commonalities and divergences. *International Journal of Bilingual Education and Bilingualism* 23 (1), 17–35.

Genesee, F. (1987) *Learning through Two Languages: Studies in Immersion and Bilingual Education*. Cambridge, MA: Newbury House.

Gérin-Lajoie, D. (2010) Le discours du personnel enseignant sur leur travail en milieu scolaire francophone minoritaire [Teachers' discourse on their work in French-language minority schools] [Special issue]. *Canadian Journal of Education* 33 (2), 356–378.

Giampapa, F. (2019) An unfinished critical ethnographic journey: Collaborative reframing and repositioning of relationships in the field. *Foro de Educacíon* 17 (27), 167–184.

Giddens, A. (1984) *The Constitution of Society: Outline of the Theory of Structuration*. Berkeley, CA: University of California Press.

Giddens, A. (1991) *Modernity and Self-Identity. Self and Society in the Late Modern Age*. Cambridge: Polity.

Giroux, H. (2011) *On Critical Pedagogy*. London: Bloomsbury Academic.

Gramsci, A. (1971) *Selections from the Prison Notebooks*. New York: International Publishers.

Gumperz, J.J. (1982) *Discourse Strategies*. Cambridge: Cambridge University Press.

Heller, M. (2011) *Paths to Post-Nationalism. A Critical Ethnography of Language and Identity*. New York: Oxford University Press.

Hélot, C. and Cavalli, M. (2017) Bilingual education in Europe: Dominant languages. In O. García, A. Lin and S. May (eds) *Bilingual and Multilingual Education* (pp. 471–488). New York: Springer.

Hobsbawm, E. (1990) *Nations and Nationalism since 1780: Programme, Myth, Reality*. Cambridge: Cambridge University Press.

Holliday, A. (2010) Complexity in cultural identity. *Language and Intercultural Communication* 10 (2), 165–177.

Kendi, I.X. (2016) *Stamped from the Beginning: The Definitive History of Racist Ideas in America*. New York: Nation Books.

Labov, W. (1972) *Sociolinguistic Patterns*. Philadelphia, PA: University of Pennsylvania Press.

Labrie, N. and Lamoureux, S. (2003) *L'éducation de langue française en Ontario: Enjeux et processus sociaux*. Sudbury, ON: Prise de Parole.

LePage, R. and Tabouret-Keller, A. (1985) *Acts of Identity: Creole-Based Approaches to Language and Ethnicity*. Cambridge: Cambridge University Press.

Lin, A.M.Y. (2020) From deficit-based teaching to asset-based teaching in higher education in BANA countries: Cutting through 'either-or' binaries with a heteroglossic plurilingual lens. *Language, Culture and Curriculum* 33 (2), 203–212.

Mady, C. (2010) Motivation to study core French: Comparing recent immigrants and Canadian-born secondary school students. *Canadian Journal of Education* 33 (3), 564–587.

Marcellesi, J.B. (1979) Quelques problèmes de l'hégémonie culturelle en France: Langue nationale et langues régionales. *International Journal of the Sociology of Language* 21, 63–80.

May, S. (2014) *The Multilingual Turn: Implications for SLA, TESOL and Bilingual Education*. New York: Routledge.

May, S. (2019) Negotiating the multilingual turn in SLA. *The Modern Language Journal* 103, 122–129.

Metatawabin, E. and Shimo, A. (2014) *Up Ghost River: A Chief's Journey through the Turbulent Waters of Native History*. New York: Penguin Random House.

Ministry of Education and Training (1998) The Ontario curriculum. French as a second language: Core French. Grades 4–8. Toronto: Queen's Printer for Ontario. See http://www.edu.gov.on.ca/eng/curriculum/elementary/fsl48curr.pdf (accessed 9 May 2010).

Ministry of Education and Training (1999) The Ontario Curriculum. Grades 9 and 10. French as a second language: Core, extended, and immersion French. Toronto: Queen's Printer for Ontario. See http://www.edu.gov.on.ca/eng/curriculum/secondary/fsl910curr.pdf (accessed 9 May 2010).

Moore, D. and Gajo, L. (2009) French voices on plurilingualism and pluriculturalism: Theory, significance and perspectives. *International Journal of Multilingualism and Multiculturalism* 6 (2), 137–153.

Moscovici, S. (1984) The phenomenon of social representations. In R.M. Farr and S. Moscovici (eds) *Social Representations* (pp. 3–70). Cambridge: Cambridge University Press.

Muhammad, K.G. (2011) *The Condemnation of Blackness: Race, Crime, and the Making of Modern Urban America*. Cambridge, MA: Harvard University Press.

Norton Pierce, B. (1995) Social identity, investment, and language learning. *TESOL Quarterly* 29 (1), 9–31.

Pennycook, A. (2010) *Language as a Local Practice*. London: Routledge.

Perrin, D. and Kramsch, C. (2018) Transdisciplinarity in applied linguistics. *AILA Review* 31 (1), 1–13.
Quell, C. (2000) Speaking the languages of citizenship. Unpublished doctoral dissertation, Ontario Institute for Studies in Education of the University of Toronto.
Roy, S. (2015) Discours et idéologies en immersion française. *Revue canadienne de linguistique appliquée* [*Canadian Journal of Applied Linguistics*] 18 (2), 125–143.
Saint-Georges, I. and Weber, J. (2013) *Multilingualism and Multimodality: Current Challenges for Educational Studies*. Rotterdam: Sense.
Saussure, F. (1966) *Course in General Linguistics* (C. Bally and A. Sechehaye [eds], trans. W. Baskin). New York: McGraw-Hill.
Shohamy, E. (2006) *Language Policies: Hidden Agendas and New Approaches*. London: Routledge.
Statistics Canada (2017) Linguistic diversity and multilingualism in Canadian homes. See http://www12.statcan.gc.ca/census-recensement/2016/as-sa/98-200-x/2016010/98-200-x2016010-eng.cfm (accessed 5 October 2017).
Swain, M. and Lapkin, S. (1995) Problems in output and the cognitive processes they generate: A step towards second language learning. *Applied Linguistics* 16, 371–391.
Tarone, E. and Swain, M. (1995) A sociolinguistic perspective on second language use in immersion classrooms. *La revue canadienne des langues vivantes* 79 (2), 166–171.
Warner, C. (2019) Transdisciplinarity across two-tiers: The case of applied linguistics and literary studies in U.S. foreign language departments. *AILA Review* 31 (2018), 29–52.

7 Dialogical Relationships and Critical Reflexivity as Emancipatory Praxis in a Community-Based Educational Program

Randy Clinton Bell, Manuel Martinez and Brenda Rubio

In this chapter, we engage critical ethnography and decolonial theory as we consider Academia Cuauhtli, a unique cultural and linguistic revitalization program for Latinx, Spanish/English, bilingual/bicultural elementary school students. We do so in order to address the subjective possibilities, constraints and refusals among Academia Cuauhtli community members involved in the teaching, learning and research with this out-of-school program. We situate ourselves – the students, researchers, community and partners – in relation to the material, ideological and discursive regimes of power through which, and against, the Academia Cuauhtli (Valenzuela, 2017; Valenzuela *et al.*, 2015) project makes sense as an educational space poised – in the collective words of an Academia Cuauhtli educator – to '[h]onor our community's cultural heritage, foster a social justice consciousness, and reclaim our collective identities in pursuit of educational freedom' (see Gautier, 2016). Reading and writing critical ethnography through decolonial theories, we attend to the local and temporal exigencies of social justice work as we consider the productive possibilities and limitations of working and doing research within colonizing grammars of imperialist nation-state geographies. We engage and complicate critical ethnography's call for critical reflexivity as we address our collective and individual privileges and responsibilities within the contested geographies of the research setting. As part of this effort, we name and confront pervasive hegemonic forces as we attempt to disrupt Western transcendent approaches to research that divorce knowledge production from communities. We propose possibilities to delink from assumed epistemological vantages of Western Eurocentric science and geography, and instead locate the voices of knowers/learners/

community/researchers in the colonized lands of the current study. A goal of this effort is to name and decenter the assumed white epistemological subject of research design and curriculum development. We present findings from our collective work and ethnographic research with the Academia Cuauhtli program, demonstrating how the Cuauhtli community engages subjective possibilities through curriculum and pedagogy within, and against, contemporary discursive, ideological and material regimes.

Critical Reflexivity

Proponents of critical ethnography center interrogations of power as an integral part of the research process (May, 1997; Thomas, 1993). Madison (2019) places emphasis on the need for researchers and research participants to co-construct meaning based on lived inequities and oppressions, putting the onus directly on researchers to account for their privileges and the ways their work may further inequities. Anderson (1989) conceptualizes critical reflexivity as a heuristic by which ethnographic researchers should consider their place in the research process in relation to sociohistorical and geopolitical contexts. This process is distinct from positionality statements, as critical reflexivity requires a serious epistemological consideration of one's subjective privileges and solidarities within broader sociohistorical realms, as well as in particular research settings. Part of this consideration includes how researchers come to know research communities and spaces. Cary (2006: 3) states it succinctly: '[b]asically it's all about knowing others and how that "getting to know" is informed by the subject position we assume the other inhabits and knowing ourselves (research positionality that is more than a confession)'. This effort should not be confused with researcher positionality statements. Rather, as May (1997: 200) states, reflexivity 'is not to be misunderstood here as the mere self-reflection of the researcher. Rather, reflexivity involves a complex dialectic between the researcher, the research process, and the research outcome(s)' (see also May & Caldas, this volume). In the following sections, we attend to these calls for more engaged critical reflexivity on the parts of researchers as we consider our varying subjective positionalities within the particular research locale of Academia Cuauhtli. Specifically, we respond to Anderson's (1989: 255) call for critical ethnography to engage 'the structural and historical forces that inform and shape the social setting under study'.

We initiate our response to calls for critical reflexivity by acknowledging and troubling the ideological underpinnings of the work we do with ethnography as historically embedded in colonial flows of power. We situate the ethnographic impulse within settler colonialism (Tuck & Yang, 2012) as a primary sociohistorical and geopolitical force of accumulation in the lands we (un)learn and (un)teach as the US state of Texas. This place-based recognition presents unique challenges and opportunities to think differently about the work we seek to do in response to the constant threats of violence facing our research community from ongoing colonizing projects, such as Immigration and Customs Enforcement (ICE) raids. We seek to address the very real oppressions and inequities facing students within colonizing institutions and geographies with an eye toward epistemic delinking and the refusal of the grammars making such critiques possible. That is, the grammars of critical ethnography place us within colonizing constructions of race, citizenship, language and gender as they function within white, Western, Eurocentric, modernist geographies and political economic histories. This means we must attend to the implications of our work as, in some ways, furthering colonizing projects, even as grammars of social justice frame intelligible discursive responses to ongoing and immediate marginalizations of our communities (cf. Deiri, this volume). In what follows, we (re)imagine critical ethnography as a process of unlearning and decentering grammars of colonialism.

Locations

Further situating ourselves within 'historical and structural forces' (Anderson, 1989), we locate ourselves within geopolitical and colonial matrices of power (Mignolo, 2007a, 2007b; Valenzuela, 2019). Quijano (2007), in articulating the concept of coloniality of power, links the machinations of racialization, labor and the state with knowledge production and geographic relations. Here we name white supremacy and capitalism as pervasive forces working alongside, and with, settler colonialism to shape the day-to-day material and relational encounters in our lives with students and communities as we work, learn and teach together. This recognition necessarily implicates us, the authors as researchers, in oppressive institutional projects while, at the same time, providing frameworks by which we might disrupt the impulses and systems that further these projects (Paperson, 2017). With this in mind, we take seriously our collective and individual interpellations into socially and professionally prescribed ideologies, discourses and material configurations mediating our differences and belongings with researched communities. The very distinction between researcher and researched is, for us, simultaneously a constraining social relation of potential othering within the scientism of modernity/colonialism, and a needed and productive heuristic through which we come to distinguish our privileges, differences, understandings and advocacies. In other words, working within the discourse of critical ethnography as methodology provides us with a grammatical, but not neutral, framework in which to make sense. To this point, we have sought to engage these tensions as productive intellectual spaces in which to rethink and unlearn the discursive limitations of ethnographic research. In what follows, we respond to, and work toward, the undoing of the invisible, white epistemological subject as locationless arbiter of knowledge in research and curriculum.

Decolonial theorists have called for the reintroduction of spatial relations as part of an epistemological shift advocated by Maldonado-Torres (2004). Mignolo (2011) advocates a shift in the 'geography of reasoning' as a necessary and conscious move toward epistemic delinking. Extending May's (1997) problematization of the 'power relations' within ethnographic research design, we locate and name the supposedly neutral and universal 'modest witness' (Haraway, 1997) of traditional ethnography as an extension and (re)inscriber of colonizing formations. Specifically, we articulate and locate the detached observer of traditional ethnography as the white European male of the Enlightenment whose work, over time, has produced and (re)inscribed the social constructions and grammars of race, social class, gender, national identities and language(s) that provide the palimpsest over which we (re)write social justice around issues such as democracy, justice and humanization. In seeking to disrupt and relocate the locus of enunciation (Mignolo, 2007a; Sugiharto, 2020), from the hegemonic white European male subjective position, we engage the geographically subaltern epistemologies (Spivak, 1988) of those living and working in the in-between spaces of race, language, nationality, culture and gender in the physical, relational and theoretical spaces of Academia Cuauhtli. The current work interrogates a particular manifestation of the white epistemological subject as it prefigures the English monolingual, male, citizen knower/learner of the K-12 Texas public school curriculum. The teaching and learning presented later respond to the mis- and non-representations of Latinx, Spanish-speaking, immigrant subjectivities within the official state curriculum of Texas. Sugiharto (2020) posits the importance of explicit loci of enunciation ideologies situating geopolitical and body-political speech and action from Global South positionalities not only as valuable epistemological perspectives, but also as an overtly political tactic of resistance by which to confront epistemological racism and to decolonize knowledge production.

In our collective work to situate knowledge construction spatially against colonizing geographies of Western nation-state subjectivities, we are especially indebted to the work of Gloria Anzaldúa (2012 [1987]) and the new mestiza consciousness of Chicana/Latina feminisms (cf. Nuñez & García-Mateus, this volume). In their articulation of Nepantla as an interstitial subjectivity, Anzaldúa renders the realities of mestiza life in the physical, psychological, gendered and spiritual borderlands of the Texas-US Southwest/Mexico. Key to understanding the new mestiza consciousness is an engagement with the linguistic, cultural, racial, gendered and national tensions experienced by those living in and between Indigenous, colonizing nation-states and cultural/linguistic geographies. As a geographically situated epistemology, the new mestiza consciousness calls for a productive, but uncomfortable, engagement with ambiguity based in these complex subjectivities of place. Addressing the new mestiza consciousness, Anzaldúa states:

> *La mestiza* constantly has to shift out of habitual formations; from convergent thinking, analytical reasoning that tends to use rationality to move toward a single goal (a Western mode), to divergent thinking, characterized by movement away from set patterns and goals and toward a more whole perspective, one that includes rather than excludes. (Anzaldúa, 2012 [1987]: 79)

We, the authors, apply this productive understanding of ambiguity to our struggles to work within and against traditional, Western, ways of doing research that prefigure the discursive and ideological limitations and possibilities of critical ethnography. Furthermore, living in Nepantla allows for simultaneous understandings of subjective positionings and experiences that, from a Western perspective, may seem incompatible or contradictory. The new mestiza consciousness as epistemic delinking (Mignolo, 2011) provides a refusal of the colonizing logics that normalize particular hegemonic subjectivities – such as the detached white, male, 'modest witness' (Haraway, 1997) of traditional ethnographic research.

Dialogic Relationalities

Collectively, we conceive of the different subjective constraints, possibilities and privileges we experience personally in relation to white supremacy, capitalism and settler colonialism. These 'historical and structural forces' (Anderson, 1989) frame the discursive, ideological and material realms in which we make sense of one another and our research communities and settings. In this section, we consider the relational and dialogic becomings that brought the three of us together in our work with Academia Cuauhtli and this publication.

Manuel and Randy met as bilingual elementary school teachers through a unique master's program at the University of Texas at Austin designed for practicing bilingual teachers. Through the program, Proyecto Maestría (Palmer, 2018), Randy and Manuel dialogued and learned with one another about historical and political issues influencing bilingual education in the United States and developed critical understandings and approaches to curriculum and pedagogies with linguistically othered students. Through this process, Randy and Manuel developed a shared commitment to culturally and linguistically relevant curriculums and pedagogies that were responsive to the experiences and strengths of the Latinx, Spanish/English, bilingual/bicultural students they served as practicing bilingual teachers in the local school district. Through the Proyecto Maestría graduate program, Randy and Manuel also became involved in a project to develop a Tejano history social studies curriculum based on the Grade 4 Texas Essential Knowledge and Skills (TEKS) standards about Texas history, but retold from the perspectives, contributions and experiences of Tejanos. (See below for a description of the particular lesson from the Tejano history curriculum that is the focus of the current work.) Manuel now works as a technology specialist in the local school district. Brenda was a founding member of Nuestro Grupo, the community-based organization that originally proposed the Academia Cuauhtli. Brenda and Randy conducted their dissertations at Academia Cuauhtli and collaborate frequently on issues of educational leadership/policy and curriculum and instruction. The three of us came to work together in January 2015 for the inaugural year of Academia Cuauhtli – Brenda as coordinator of the program, and Manuel and Randy as program teachers.

Randy identifies as a middle-class, cisgender white man and sequential bilingual. My entrance and participation in Academia Cuauhtli is mediated by my experience as a former elementary school bilingual teacher. I perceive the students of Academia Cuauhtli through past relational experiences with the Latinx, bilingual/bicultural (Spanish/English) students I served in public school classrooms. My perceptions of Latinx bilingual students are limited as a result of the privileges I experience in whiteness. For example, I do not experience the linguistic discrimination facing bilingual students of color in public schools. In contrast, I recognize the positive reactions to my bilingualism as intersecting with racial and national ideologies and expectations. On the other hand, I have experienced the ways the public school system racializes and discriminates against bilingual students of color as others in need of remediation against white norms; such as in the official classification of bilingual students as English language learners (ELLs) and the under-representation of Latinxs in the official curriculum. I also understand, through my experiences teaching middle elementary grade levels, the hegemonic pull of English for students at the fourth-grade target level of the program, even within dual immersion programs designed to foster and sustain bilingualism, biculturalism and biliteracy (Cervantes-Soon *et al.*, 2017). That is, I have witnessed firsthand the Spanish language loss of eight- to 10-year-olds through the confluence of white school cultures, standardized testing and age-level influences. It is in response to these pressures and experiences that I became involved with Academia Cuauhtli through work to develop a culturally and linguistically responsive social studies curriculum (see Tejano history curriculum below) with other practicing bilingual teachers. My roles at the academy have included instructor, curriculum developer, coordinator/liaison and researcher.

Manuel identifies as Mexican immigrant; my first language is Spanish. Upon coming to the United States, I began learning English in order to learn how to navigate the system. Unfortunately, I also began acculturating myself to the dominant culture. I remember that, on many occasions, I actively sought to improve my accent as a way to prove that my ideas were valuable just because they were expressed in the language of the dominant culture. All this without giving importance to the beauty and richness of my first language, which had helped me acquire the knowledge that I now possessed. Expressing my ideas was only a matter of language technicalities and not of ability. I also remember the lack of desire to go back to Mexico because I considered that the way of living in the United States was better and more valuable than the way of living in Mexico. Proyecto Maestría made me aware of this reality, which helped me reclaim my language and my identity. After Proyecto Maestría, I started feeling proud of who I was – embracing my first language, my accent and my identity. Proyecto was a transformative experience in my life.

Although I feel proud of who I am, the fact that bilingualism is neither celebrated nor encouraged in schools has contributed to the racialization of bilingual immigrants. The fact that state-mandated tests either focus on English acquisition, or do not include or value immigrants' culture as well as their repertoires, makes Spanish lose value compared to English. Students who have been in bilingual or dual-language programs for many years and never experience recognition for their performance in Spanish receive the subliminal message that their native language is not an asset. The mission and vision of Academia Cuauhtli, which focuses on the revitalization of the students' native language, make us very intentional to not only include Spanish in the lessons, but also value and incorporate the high levels of students' linguistic repertoires in both languages exhibited by them, and the rich vocabulary that they have acquired throughout their lives. The issue of racialization surfaces in my workplace as well. When providing professional development, in many instances I feel that I have to prove to the audience that my accent is not a handicap in order to get my message across and that my ideas are worth listening to.

Brenda identifies as a Mexican immigrant woman. My first language is Spanish but I was enrolled in English-only classes once I started attending school. This decision was made by my parents, both out of wanting to support my academic development and out of fear that I would be somehow targeted otherwise. This was a fear so deeply ingrained in me and supported by my lived experiences and environment that it continues to follow me, despite years of deconstructing my perspective. While I had already begun exploring my experiences when I first moved to Austin, I still recall the immediate sense of danger I felt inhabiting mostly white spaces on the university campus and around my neighborhood.

Genealogy of Academia Cuauhtli

In this section, we locate the Academia Cuauhtli program within the geopolitical and local forces that led to its creation as a response to political and educational inequities facing bilingual/bicultural, Spanish/English, Latinx students in the local public schools of the research setting. Academia Cuauhtli opened as an out-of-school Saturday program at the Mexican-American cultural center in downtown Austin in January 2015. The program was designed by community members, certified bilingual teachers and university faculty and students to serve fourth-grade bilingual/bicultural (Spanish/English) students from three local public schools. The impetus for the program grew out of the collective frustration of local Latinx educational activists and community members who recognized the vast under- and misrepresentation of Latinxs in school curriculum generally, and children's literature specifically. Brenda Rubio (2018: 14) details the coming together of 'public educators, administrators, advocates, scholars, librarians, historians, parents, students, and other community members' at an event hosted by the Texas Center for Educational Policy to address these invisibilities. Out of this public conversation, a community-based organization formed as Nuestro Grupo, with the explicit goal of 'cultural and linguistic revitalization for the city's Mexican and Latino/a community' (Rubio, 2018: 16). Academia Cuauhtli emerged through these ongoing dialogues as a community-based educational response to these issues.

Crucial to the conversation and call to action was, and continues to be, the alarming rate of gentrification of the historically Mexican-American interior neighborhoods of Austin's east side. Academia Cuauhtli takes place at the Mexican-American cultural center, located in a historically Mexican-American neighborhood that has undergone substantial gentrification over the past 10 plus years. Due to its location in downtown Austin, the homes in this neighborhood, once owned by Mexican-American families, have been purchased by developers and converted into high-end restaurants, bars and luxury apartments. The impact of gentrification on the historically Mexican-American neighborhood schools of Austin has been severe. Bilingual education programs, originally designed for working-class Latinx families and students, struggle with systemic gentrification as two-way immersion (TWI) programs are marketed to middle/upper-class white, monolingual, English families. Building on the scholarship and caution articulated by Valdés (1997) regarding the potential harm of what Flores (2015) frames as the 'discovery' of TWI programs by privileged and dominant groups, Heiman and Yanes (2018, this volume) detail local school administrator responses to the gentrification of TWI programs in the local district in which Academia Cuauhtli teachers and students work and learn. At the time of this writing, Academia Cuauhtli students who regularly attend one of the neighborhood schools are displaced to another campus while their school is being repurposed. As the growing gentrification displaces the traditional Mexican-American working-class residents, there is a growing fear of school closures as the local school district moves to consolidate a dwindling public school demographic. It is within, and in response to these realities, that Academia Cuauhtli works to provide culturally and linguistically appropriate, antiracist, educational spaces for teachers (Bonilla, 2017), students and community.

Data Collection and Analysis

Thinking with critical ethnography and decolonial frameworks, we consider data collected through traditional ethnographic methods, while also attending to the relational and unofficial processes by which we co-construct knowledge with one another and the Cuauhtli community. In the case of Brenda and Randy, respectively, the experiences, histories, voices and interpretations included in this piece are drawn from larger individual dissertation research projects. Typical ethnographic data-gathering methods included field notes, audio-visual recordings, interviews and frequent member checks. Manuel Martinez contributes his expertise as one of the lead educators of Academia Cuauhtli who has worked on various initiatives, including curricular lesson design, teaching the children during Saturday sessions and collaborating with Academia Cuauhtli parents. These collaborations with parents are based in Freirean circles in which the parents pose problems in the group and are supported by the teachers, volunteers and community activists also present. For example, addressing the concern of parents regarding magnet schools in the local school district and the application process, we organized a series of one-to-one supporting sessions for them. Such sessions were held on Saturdays at the same time students were participating in Academia Cuauhtli.

Beyond just an account of our experiences as they might be cataloged as part of a positionality statement within a traditional ethnography, we acknowledge and engage our social, affective and transpersonal collective experiences as a troubling of traditional data collection and analysis protocols based in representationalist logics of objectivity/subjectivity and accumulation that work in tandem with doxas of white supremacy, capitalism and settler colonialism to disenfranchise. This effort aligns with our desire to understand ourselves geohistorically and locally within the logics and forces of power in our lives and in the lives of our communities. While the current format precludes a full ethnographic account (were such a thing possible), we focus specifically on a particular curricular lesson and the encounters it inspired. Our research question becomes: How does the Cuauhtli community of bilingual teachers, students, family members and researchers take up and reject discourses, ideologies and material regimes around narratives of civil rights?

For the purposes of this project, we focus on a lesson from the Tejano history curriculum (Salinas *et al.*, 2015) implemented at Academia Cuauhtli as part of a curricular unit dedicated to Latino civil rights.

The Tejano history curriculum was originally designed as a social studies curriculum based in the Grade 4 state of Texas standards (TEKS), which focus on Texas history as part of a collaboration. The curriculum provides a culturally and linguistically relevant alternative narrative to the whitestream, patriarchal and statist narrative found in the TEKS, and instead focuses on the histories and experiences of Latinx peoples of Mexican descent and their contributions to Texas histories. The specific lesson was taught on four separate occasions by Manuel. The focus of the lesson is Emma Tenayuca, a civil rights activist whose leadership on behalf of the Mexican-American pecan shellers of the Southern Pecan Shelling Company in 1938 led to a raise in wages for workers after the company proposed wage deductions. Utilizing the book *¡No es justo!* by Tafolla and Teneyuca (2008), Manuel conducted the lesson in Spanish in the spring semesters of 2016, 2017, 2018 and 2019 with different groups of fourth-grade students, along with some of the students' family members. Randy was also present on all four occasions in his varying roles as curriculum developer, coordinator and researcher. Data collected and considered include the following:

- Audio/video transcripts of lessons.
- Video and transcription of 2019 lesson.
- Individual and collective memories.
- Interview transcript between Manuel and Randy.
- Publicly available demographic information.
- Brenda's interviews with teachers including Manuel.
- Conversations between the authors.

Analysis took place individually and collectively. Individually, each of us reviewed transcripts and watched videos as we considered the subjective productions and resistances of Academia Cuauhtli community members as expressed in the pedagogical moments of the lessons. Collectively, we participated in ongoing conversations together in person, over the phone and via text messaging. Thinking of ourselves simultaneously as Academia Cuauhtli community members and researchers, we frequently checked our understandings with one another in a reciprocal process that led us to the following findings.

Findings

Complexity of 'rights' discourses across subjectivities

Issues of justice and fairness often emerged during the classes Manuel taught on Emma Tenayuca. Students' and family members' responses to Manuel's question of what justice signifies to them bridged discourses of national civil and global human rights. In one classroom exchange, the question of justice led to student-initiated conversations concerning issues of civil and human rights as tied to understandings of justice. In the following exchange, Manuel mediates a discussion in which Cuauhtli students co-construct their understanding of justice as rights.

Spanish (original)	English (translation)
Manuel: ¿Qué todos tengan los mismos *derechos*, verdad? Pues estamos hablando la palabra tener lo mismo y estamos escuchando la palabra derechos. Todos tenemos *derechos*. **Student:** ...*derechos civiles...* **Manuel:** ...Estamos aprendiendo... me puedes decir mas de lo que estamos aprendiendo? Excelente, buenas ideas. **Student:** La justicia es que tengan las mismas cosas y todos sean amables con las otras personas... como *derechos humanos.*	**Manuel:** Everyone has the same rights, correct? So we're saying everyone has the same and we're hearing the word rights. Everyone has *rights.* **Student:** ...*civil rights...* **Manuel:** ...We're learning... can you tell me more about what we're learning? Excellent, good ideas. **Student:** Justice means everyone has the same things and everyone is nice to one another... like *human rights.*

Voting, education, working, living, having a family, having one's voice heard and fun were among the specific rights students went on to name explicitly. Manuel contributed to these conversations by reminding students of the importance of the right to education and what that means in the day-to-day lives of students with their teachers.

Spanish (original)	English (translation)
Manuel: Esto es un *derecho* que tienen los niños. La maestra no te está haciendo un favor con educarte. Es un *derecho* que tú tienes.	**Manuel:** This is a *right* that all children have. The teacher isn't doing a favor by educating you. It's a *right* that you have.

Racializing rights

Beyond students' discursive familiarity with rights-based understandings of justice as nation-state and/or universal juridical imperatives, they further interrogated this discourse by engaging issues of race. For example, immediately after the previous exchange in which Manuel reinforces education as a right of all children, a student brought up the subject of race in relation to civil and human rights.

Spanish (original)	English (translation)
Student: ...la piel **Manuel:** la que? Dime. **Student:** ...el color. **Manuel:** El co... o sea... **Student:** ...de la piel... **Manuel:** Pues no importa el color de tu piel, verdad? El color de tu piel puede ser que sea, tu tienes los mismos derechos. Si, excelente, ya ven? Como Martin Luther King, su piel era más oscura que la nuestra y él luchaba para que todos tuvieron los mismos derechos.	**Student:** ...skin **Manuel:** What? Say it. **Student:** ...the color... **Manuel:** The co... or like... **Student:** ...of the skin... **Manuel:** So it doesn't matter the color of your skin, right? The color of your skin can be whatever, you have the same rights. Yes, excellent, you see? Like Martin Luther King, his skin was darker than ours and he fought so that everyone had the same rights.

Manuel's invocation of Martin Luther King situates Cuauhtli students' experiences within the US civil rights movement and in solidarity with historical efforts by Blacks to desegregate US schools. This connection was part of a strategic effort within the Cuauhtli curriculum to draw on students' knowledge of civil rights leaders typically taught in public schools so as to engage prior knowledge before introducing under-represented Latinx civil rights advocates such as Emma Tenayuca.

Racializing class, nationality, gender and Indigeneity

In participating in a read-aloud of the book *¡No es justo!* (Tafolla & Teneyuca, 2008), the Cuauhtli community confronted intersections of social class, nationality, gender and Indigeneity with race. Responding to a scene in the book, in which the poverty of the majority female Mexican-American pecan shellers is portrayed, students quickly make connections to race and Manuel moves to expand the dialogue to include other subjectivities.

Spanish (original)	English (translation)
Manuel: ¿Qué piensan Uds. de estas palabras que dicen, '¿Qué importa que viven en la miseria? Son mexicanos'. ¿Les enojan estas palabras igual que a mi? ¿O no?	**Manuel:** What do you all think of these words that say 'So what if they live in misery? They're Mexican'. Does it make you mad like it does me? Or no?
Estudiante 1: Sí	**Student 1:** Yes.
Manuel: Hablan con sus compañeros. ¿Qué piensan de estas palabras?	**Manuel:** Talk to your classmates. What do you think of these words?
(Estudiantes hablan en grupos pequeños)	(Students talk in small groups)
Estudiante 2: ¿Como se dice racista?	**Student 2:** How do you say racist?
Manuel: Si, eso es ser racista.	**Manuel:** Yes, this is being racist.
Estudiante 2: Racista...	**Student 2:** Racist...
Estudiante 3: Está...	**Student 3:** It's...
Manuel: Discriminando. ¿Por qué está discriminando?	**Manuel:** Discriminating. Why is it discriminating?
Estudiante 4: Ellos no saben cómo se han tratado, por eso deben de abrir los ojos bien para que vean cómo los están tratando.	**Student 4:** They don't know how they've been treated, that's why they should open their eyes to see how they are treated.
Manuel: Deberían de abrir los ojos mejor para verlos como les están tratando... estas palabras no suenan bien, ¿verdad? Es como, por ejemplo, a veces en México a los indígena no les dan un buen trato, 'son indígenas, no son personas', ¿Hay unas personas mas importantes que otras? Por ejemplo, tendrá que ver que seas de México o las personas de aquí? Uds. son más importantes que los niños de México? No. Todos somos iguales, verdad, no importa de donde seamos.	**Manuel:** They should open their eyes to see them, how they're being treated, right? It's like, for example, sometimes in Mexico the Indigenous aren't given a good deal, 'they're Indigenous, they're not people'. Are there people that are more important than others? For example, does this have anything to do with if you're from Mexico or if you're from here? Are you all more important than the children in/from Mexico? No. We're all equal, right? It doesn't matter where we're from.

Here, the Cuauhtli community addresses the complexities of economic discrimination in the US in response to the national subjectivities of the pecan shellers as Mexican-origin women. A student quickly points out that the discrimination is not only based on nationality and economic status, but also results, in part, from the racism of the pecan-shelling business owners. Manuel makes further connections by asking students to consider their respective privileges as being of Mexican descent living in the US in relation to the Indigenous peoples and children living in

Mexico. It is within these classroom dialogues that the Cuauhtli community is able to respond, both historically and in the moment, to contemporary intersections of discrimination across geopolitical landscapes in and out of nation-state boundaries.

Discussion

Subjective constraints and possibilities

In order to engage the productive tensions between critical ethnography and the decolonial disruptions presented in this piece, we have worked together to situate our collective and individual privileges and experiences in relation to the ideological, discursive and material forces we simultaneously take up and resist. We acknowledge and resist the complexity of working inside colonizing grammars of race, citizenship and gender, even as we put these subjective constraints to use in social justice efforts. This process led us to attend to the subjective possibilities, alternatives and refusals of the Academia Cuauhtli community in response to hegemonic mis- and non-representations of Latinx, linguistically and racially othered students in abstract curricular spaces and immediately gentrifying physical spaces.

Drawing on our collective and individual experiences with the institution of public schooling in which Cuauhtli elementary-level students live so much of their lives, we also consider our own complicities and refusals of official labels so often applied to othered US school-age children in policy, and curriculum and instruction research. As part of the current disruption, we consider how Cuauhtli students are typically positioned and written in research, using systemic terminology such as 'economically disadvantaged', 'low socioeconomic status' (SES) and 'English language learners'. We attend to these labels in our collective understandings of Cuauhtli students as both productive and limiting as they animate our work. That is to say, we acknowledge and trouble these labels as only making sense within ongoing colonizing grammars whereby Cuauhtli students are positioned as others, even in local institutions in which they are the majority. We accept and refuse 'low SES' and 'ELL' labels as they operate in the here and now of income inequality and the need for skills accumulation (English) within the current neoliberal hellscape. We are not arguing that approximations of white English by students of color ensures economic success, only that we recognize this raciolinguistic ideology (Flores, 2016; Flores & Rosa, 2015; Rosa, 2019) as the historical starting point of US bilingual education. At the same time, we acknowledge 'low SES' and 'ELL' as deficit terms (Valencia, 2010), framing students in terms of lack within global capitalism and racist national ideals of English monolingualism. Against these hegemonic labels, and the discourses they work within, we juxtapose the more complex subjective possibilities that the Academia Cuauhtli teachers engage in with students and community. These engagements push us to listen even closer to the expertise of bilingual educators as we move to delink from a state-sponsored curriculum.

Conclusion

As we consider the sense-making of the Academia Cuauhtli community in response to questions of subjective affiliations and refusals, we are struck by the complexity of classroom dialogues and understandings. The fourth-grade students were quick to make connections between Western, liberal humanism ideals of justice, and discourses and ideologies of civil and human rights. Students exhibited an understanding of particular civil rights within the US as a nation-state guaranteeing the right to vote and access to public education. An issue not addressed was the students' understanding of citizenship in relation to these civil rights within the US. The students also dialogued around broader desires by invoking discourses of human rights, such as when they named the rights to life, family, having one's voice heard and fun. In these ways, the Cuauhtli community provides a space in which students are able to make sense of themselves subjectively through appeals to historically and geographically located nation-state civil rights' discourses, and within more universal and abstract ideologies of human rights. Students demonstrate a critical awareness of themselves as the desiring subjects and participants in these rights as they exist in their lives.

To the question of how the Cuauhtli community rejects certain subjectivities, we see how Manuel works with, and against, strict notions of nationality and belonging. For example, in his simultaneous positioning of students as Mexican and non-Mexican, when he asks students if it makes them mad that a character from the book rationalizes the poverty of the pecan shellers as justifiable since they are Mexicans, and shortly thereafter when he asks the students if they are better than the children in Mexico. The fluidity of what it means to be Mexican in the borderlands of US/Mexico for Latinx, bilingual/bicultural, Spanish/English children, many of whom are of Mexican descent, finds expression here as Manuel presents a transnational subjective possibility (see Urrieta, 2016). Although not developed extensively, the possibilities for transnational subjective understandings are also invoked in Manuel's inclusion of the discrimination faced by the Indigenous peoples of Mexico. We are left to wonder how Cuauhtli students make sense of Indigenous subjectivity within the rights' discourses and ideologies with which they are familiar. Future studies might further address transnational subjectivities that ask students to try on complex, and at times, competing subjective positionings (cf. Byrd Clark, this volume).

A concluding question we ask ourselves concerns the ultimate goals of critical theory and decolonial theories. We take seriously

Mignolo's (2009) distinctions between decolonial options and de-Westernizing options. Mignolo (2009: 161) argues that de-Westernizing options 'do not question the "civilization of death" hidden under the rhetoric of modernization and prosperity, of the improvement of modern institutions (e.g. liberal democracy and an economy propelled by the principle of growth and prosperity)'. We understand the grammars of the de-Westernizing option to include modernist questions of citizenship, human and civil rights, and public versus private notions of education (among other things) that require ideological, discursive and material foundations in Western, Eurocentric and racist flows of colonialism and capitalism. Relative to the critical aspects of critical ethnography, we consider the dialogic and emancipatory possibilities and limitations of teaching within a habitus that takes colonial nation-state histories and geographies as the starting points by which we (teachers, researchers, students) make sense of the world and push toward equity. Alternatively, Mignolo (2009: 161) proposes decolonial options that 'start from the principle that the *regeneration* of life shall prevail over primacy of the *production and reproduction* of goods at the cost of life' (emphasis in the original). Calling for radical reframings emerging from the decolonial option, Mignolo urges a conscious interrogation of Western zero-sum epistemologies in which control of knowledge goes unconsidered and uncontested. The Academia Cuauhtli community seeks to disrupt these controls.

References

Anderson, G. (1989) Critical ethnography in education: Origins, current status, and new directions. *Review of Educational Research* 59, 249–270.

Anzaldúa, G. (2012 [1987]) *Borderlands/La frontera: The New Mestiza* (4th edn, 25th anniversary). San Francisco, CA: Aunt Lute Books.

Bonilla, C.M. (2017) Relational professionalism in a bilingual teacher association: Promoting occupational identities and pedagogic agency. *Bilingual Research Journal* 40 (3), 304–317. https://doi.org/10.1080/15235882.2017.1351009

Cary, L.J. (2006) *Curriculum Spaces: Discourse, Postmodern Theory and Educational Research*. New York: Peter Lang.

Cervantes-Soon, C.G., Dorner, L., Palmer, D., Heiman, D., Schwerdtfeger, R. and Choi, J. (2017) Combating inequalities in two-way language immersion programs: Toward critical consciousness in bilingual education spaces. *Review of Research in Education* 41 (1), 403–427.

Flores, N. (2015) Re: Columbusing bilingual education [Web log comment]. See https://educationallinguist.wordpress.com/2015/01/25/columbising-bilingual-education/.

Flores, N. (2016) A tale of two visions: Hegemonic whiteness and bilingual education. *Educational Policy* 30 (1), 13–38. https://doi.org/10.1177/0895904815616482

Flores, N. and Rosa, J. (2015) Undoing appropriateness: Raciolinguistic ideologies and language diversity in education. *Harvard Educational Review* 85 (2), 149–171. https://doi.org/10.17763/0017-8055.85.2.149

Gautier, A. (2016) New Hispanic enrichment program to teach students about their roots. *Statesmen News Network*, 24 September. See https://www.statesman.com/NEWS/

20160924/New-Hispanic-enrichment-program-to-teach-students-about-their-roots (accessed 3 September 2018).

Haraway, D.J. (1997) *Modest_Witness@Second_Millennium.FemaleMan_Meets_OncoMouse*. London: Routledge.

Heiman, D. and Yanes, M. (2018) Centering the fourth pillar in times of TWBE gentrification: 'Spanish, love, content, not in that order'. *International Multilingual Research Journal* 12 (3), 173–187.

Madison, D.S. (2019) *Critical Ethnography: Method, Ethics, and Performance* (3rd edn). New York: Sage.

Maldonado-Torres, N. (2004) The topology of being and the geopolitics of knowledge. *City: Analysis of Urban Trends, Culture, Theory, Policy, Action* 8 (1), 29–56.

May, S.A. (1997) Critical ethnography. In N.H. Hornberger and D. Corson (eds) *Encyclopedia of Language and Education: Research Methods in Language and Education* (pp. 197–206). Dordrecht: Kluwer. https://doi.org/10.1007/978-94-011-4535-0_19

Mignolo, W.D. (2007a) Delinking. *Cultural Studies* 21, 449–514.

Mignolo, W.D. (2007b) Introduction: Coloniality of power and de-colonial thinking. *Cultural Studies* 21, 155–167.

Mignolo, W.D. (2009) Epistemic disobedience, independent thought and decolonial freedom. *Theory, Culture & Society* 26 (7–8), 159–181. https://doi.org/10.1177/0263276409349275

Mignolo, W.D. (2011) Epistemic disobedience and the decolonial option: A manifesto. *Transmodernity* 1, 3–23.

Palmer, D.K. (2018) *Teacher Leadership for Social Change in Bilingual and Bicultural Education*. Bristol: Multilingual Matters.

Paperson, L. (2017) *A Third University is Possible*. Minneapolis, MN: University of Minnesota Press.

Quijano, A. (2007) Coloniality and modernity/rationality. *Cultural Studies* 21, 168–178.

Rosa, J. (2019) *Looking Like a Language, Sounding Like a Race: Raciolinguistic Ideologies and the Learning of Latinidad*. Oxford: Oxford University Press.

Rubio, B. (2018) Academia Cuauhtli teachers: Additive teaching in subtractive contexts. Unpublished doctoral dissertation, the University of Texas at Austin.

Salinas, C., Rodríguez, N.N. and Lewis, B.A. (2015) The Tejano History Curriculum Project: Creating a space for authoring Tejanas/os into the social studies curriculum. *Bilingual Research Journal* 38 (2), 172–189. https://doi.org/10.1080/15235882.2015.1066275

Spivak, G.C. (1988) *Can the Subaltern Speak?* Basingstoke: Macmillan.

Sugiharto, S. (2020) Enacting the locus of enunciation as a resistant tactic to confront epistemological racism and decolonize scholarly knowledge. *Applied Linguistics* 43 (1), 196–202. https://doi.org/10.1093/applin/amaa023

Tafolla, C. and Teneyuca, S. (2008) *That's Not Fair!/¡No es justo!: Emma Tenayuca's Struggle for Justice/La lucha de Emma Tenayuca por la justicia* (Spanish and English edn). Sant Antonio, TX: Wings Press.

Thomas, J. (1993) *Doing Critical Ethnography*. Newbury Park, CA: Sage.

Tuck, E. and Yang, K.W. (2012) Decolonization is not a metaphor. *Decolonization: Indigeneity, Education & Society* 1 (1), 1–40. http://decolonization.org/index.php/des/article/download/18630

Urrieta, L. (2016) Diasporic community smartness: Saberes (knowings) beyond schooling and borders. *Race Ethnicity and Education* 19 (6), 1186–1199. https://doi.org/10.1080/13613324.2016.1168541

Valdés, G. (1997) Dual-language immersion programs: A cautionary note concerning the education of language-minority students. *Harvard Educational Review* 67 (3), 391–429.

Valencia, R.R. (2010) *Dismantling Contemporary Deficit Thinking: Educational Thought and Practice*. New York: Routledge.

Valenzuela, A. (2017) Academia Cuauhtli: (Re)locating the spiritual, if crooked, path to social justice. *International Journal of Qualitative Studies in Education* 30 (10), 906–911. https://doi.org/10.1080/09518398.2017.1312610

Valenzuela, A. (2019) The struggle to decolonize official knowledge in Texas' State curriculum: Side-stepping the colonial matrix of power. *Equity & Excellence in Education* 52 (2–3), 1–19.

Valenzuela, A., Zamora, E. and Rubio, B. (2015) Academia Cuauhtli and the eagle: 'Danza Mexica' and the epistemology of the circle. *Voices in Urban Education* 41, 46–56.

Part 3
Conflicts, Collaborations and Community

8 Critical Ethnographic Monitoring and Chronic Raciolinguistic Panic: Problems, Possibilities and Dreams[1]

Teresa L. McCarty

In 2001, linguistic anthropologist Jane Hill introduced the notion of language panics – media-fueled hyperbolic reactions in response to racialized language practices. Language panics are not about language but rather about race, Hill (2001: 245) argued, 'the single most important category of social organization in the United States'. She illustrated this with the 1996–1997 Ebonics controversy in Oakland, California. After the Oakland School Board passed a 'moderately worded resolution' promoting African-American vernacular (Ebonics) as a medium of instruction for African-American students, alongside 'standard English', the national media and internet exploded with a flurry of racist cartoons, pundit commentaries and 'Mock Ebonics' websites. The Oakland school superintendent and leading linguists were summoned to testify before the US Senate Subcommittee on Labor, Health and Human Services, and Education Appropriations, and a California legislator introduced a bill banning the use of state or federal funds for teaching anything but '*the* English language' (Hill, 2001: 250–251; my emphasis). Hill (2001: 251) wrote: '[I]t is precisely the media-firestorm... quality of language panics that suggests their discourse touches deeper cultural concerns than technical issues about language'.

By definition, panic is an acute rather than a chronic condition, associated with uncontrollable fear and irrational response. Yet, in the US, raciolinguistic panic has been chronic, dating from early bans on Indigenous languages in colonial schools to myriad contemporary language-restrictive policies (Gándara & Hopkins, 2010; Lomawaima & McCarty, 2006). Writing nearly a decade-and-a-half after Hill (2001), Nelson Flores and Jonathan Rosa (2015: 161) analyzed ideologies of linguistic standardization that position the heteroglossic practices of students of color as inferior, simultaneously normalizing monoglossia and 'the' English language. Rosa (2016: 163, 165) further described these processes as guided by 'a racialized ideology of languagelessness' and 'monoglot standardization', which normalizes 'the policing of language use for racialized signs of deviance'. A theme developed in this chapter is that such language policing is designed to preserve what Frederick Douglass (1881) and W.E.B. Du Bois (2004 [1913]) more than a century ago called the color line and is a naturalized response to chronic raciolinguistic panic.

A growing body of scholarship reveals the complex ways in which language is 'raced' and race is 'languaged' (Alim, 2009, 2016; Alim *et al.*, 2020). By 'analyzing language and race together rather than as discrete and unconnected social processes', this scholarship shows how socially constructed racial categories become laminated with particular linguistic forms (Alim, 2016: 5). Alim *et al.* (2020: 4) have defined this field of study as 'language and race', noting the 'powerful insights that emerge when race and language are analyzed together as dynamic processes rather than fixed objects'.

In this chapter, I explore how raciolinguistic processes operate within the social terrain of schooling. To do so, I draw on Dell Hymes's (1980: 105) notion of ethnographic monitoring, 'a disciplined way of looking, asking, recording, reflecting, comparing, and reporting' that relies on a suite of complementary methods: participant and non-participant observation, in-depth interviews and the analysis of cultural artifacts, including *de jure* and *de facto* language policies. A hallmark of ethnographic monitoring is that it is undertaken in collaboration with stakeholders (De Korne & Hornberger, 2017; Hymes, 1980; Van der Aa & Blommaert, 2017). As Hymes (1980: 100) noted, ethnography reveals the ways in which language education policies play out in state-sponsored schooling 'to define a certain proportion of people as inferior, even to convince them that they are so, and to do this *on the seemingly neutral ground of language*' (emphasis in original). Understanding – and challenging – these processes require not simply observation and description, Hymes (1980: 104) stressed, but 'critical evaluation' guided by 'values and goals'. Allan Luke (1996: vii) points out that this values orientation positions ethnography as a 'science of activism and intervention', what I have called a 'way of being' a researcher (McCarty, 2015; see also Martin-Jones & Da Costa Cabral, 2018). As Haley De Korne and Nancy H. Hornberger (2017: 247) write, 'Ethnographic monitoring is a paradigm for researchers of multilingualism in support of social justice'.

A critically conscious ethnography is distinguished by researcher reflexivity, 'the systematic assessment of [one's own] identity, positionality, and subjectivity' as these influence our analyses, interpretations and ethnographic accounts (Ravitch & Carl, 2021: 15; see Part 2 of this book). I come to this work as a White woman of Irish settler heritage, trained in cultural and educational anthropology and committed to scholarship that investigates and seeks to remediate enduring social, educational and linguistic inequities. What I share in this chapter grows out of my long-term collaborative work with Native American and other Indigenous communities and schools. I also draw on ethnographic monitoring undertaken by researchers aligned with the Civil Rights Project/ Proyecto Derechos Civiles at the University of California, Los Angeles.

In what follows, I offer three critical ethnographic accounts that not only illuminate the problems of chronic raciolinguistic panic, but also the possibilities and dreams for raciolinguistic equity and justice. The first two accounts focus on the level of the classroom, a setting Hymes (1996: 74) described as vitally 'important to the life chances of children'. 'A key question in the classroom', Hymes (1996: 74) noted, 'is what the teacher may make of the attitudes and values toward language use brought by the children'. What transpires in minute-by-minute classroom interaction brings into sharp relief larger sociolinguistic and sociopolitical processes – in particular, how official and covert language policies work to regulate and naturalize raciolinguistic containment.

But Hymes (1996: 63) also recognized the need for macro-level analyses that are 'concrete yet comparative, cumulative, yet critical'. This level of analysis, he suggested, has the potential not only to explain but also to transform social-linguistic inequalities. Here, Hymes (1996: 64) pointed toward a vision – a dream – of sociolinguistic equality: 'What ideal or vision can we entertain in terms of language?' he asked. He framed that vision as *freedom of voice*: 'freedom from denial of opportunity due to something linguistic,... [and] freedom to have one's voice heard, freedom to develop a voice worth hearing' (Hymes, 1996: 65; cf. May, this volume). Bilingual education scholar-activist Richard Ruiz (1991: 222, 224) equated voice with agency – the power to act – and stressed that empowerment is not 'a gift from those in power to those out', but is people realizing their own power so that individual voices are joined 'to effect social action on behalf of the community'.

My third account, then, is at the level of intertwined Indigenous sociolinguistic and educational movements aimed toward realizing the dream of freedom of voice (cf. Eagle Shield *et al.*, 2020). These movements originated locally but are connected within a genealogy of a larger Indigenous language and culture reclamation movement. For this account, I draw on my longstanding involvement as an invited witness, co-inquirer and 'allied other' (Kaomea, 2001) in the local movements and the larger movement of which they are part. I conclude with a reflection on the possibilities these movements raise for interrupting enduring (i.e. chronic) raciolinguistic panic, and the role of ethnographic monitoring in surfacing and leveraging those possibilities. I also consider what can be learned from the specific position of Indigenous education, which, as Lumbee scholar Bryan McKinley Jones Brayboy (2005) outlines in his seminal introduction of tribal critical race theory, must attend to the role of race and racism in the context of endemic (chronic) colonization.

Language Policy Context: 'Ground Zero'

The first two ethnographic accounts derive from research within the state of Arizona, described by Beatriz Arias and Chris Faltis (2012: xix) and Terrence Wiley (2012: xix) as 'ground zero for the most restrictive language policies' in the US (see also Moore, 2014). Of the state's approximately 1.1 million K-12 public school students, approximately 40% are Latinx, most of Mexican heritage (Combs *et al.*, 2011). What is now known as Arizona is the autochthonous homeland of 22 Native American nations. The state's public schools enroll 11% of all American Indian public school students in the US (García, 2008). All of these students are represented among the thousands of students labeled 'English learners' (ELs).

In this demo-linguistic context, Arizona voters in 2000 passed Proposition 203, 'English for the Children', a state ballot initiative that dismantled existing bilingual education programs and replaced them with 'structured English immersion' (SEI). SEI uses 'a structured syllabus to focus on grammar and vocabulary, without attention to the academic content for which students will be held responsible' (Long & Adamson, 2012: 39). Although Proposition 203 targeted Spanish-speaking immigrant students, its effects have been felt by all schools serving students labeled EL, including the public, federal and tribal-community schools serving diverse Native American students (Combs & Nicholas, 2012).

When Proposition 203 passed, funding for EL programs was being litigated in a 1992 case called *Flores v. Arizona*, which claimed that 'the state was violating federal law by failing to adequately fund' these programs (Lillie *et al.*, 2010: 3). In an attempt to comply with the *Flores* judgment requiring a defined but unspecified 'language program for ELs with adequate funding' (Lillie & Markos, 2014: 133), in 2006 the state legislature passed House Hill (HB) 2064, whereby all students identified as ELs must be placed in English-only classrooms for four hours of 'concentrated' English language development (ELD). 'In effect', writes Mary Carol Combs (2012: 66), a close observer of these policy processes, HB 2064 'transformed SEI classrooms into four-hour [English] grammar blocks', a core element of which was 'the segregation of [ELs] from non-[ELs]'.

Federal language policies added another layer of linguistic restriction to this policy environment. Education policy in the US is guided by the various programs authorized by the 1965 Elementary and Secondary Education Act (ESEA), reauthorized in 2001 as the No Child Left Behind (NCLB) Act and in 2015 as the Every Student Succeeds Act (ESSA). Under NCLB (and continued under ESSA), ESEA-funded bilingual education programs were eliminated. The former Office of Bilingual Education and Language Minority Affairs was replaced with the Office of English Language Acquisition; the National Clearinghouse for Bilingual Education was replaced with the National Clearinghouse for English Language Acquisition; and the Bilingual Education Act was renamed the English Language Acquisition, Language Enhancement and Academic Achievement Act. In addition to eliminating a prime source of bilingual education funding, NCLB's high-stakes English-only testing requirements created intense pressures to teach to the test, crowding out 'low-stakes' curricular content such as Native American language and culture programs (Beaulieu *et al.*, 2005; McCarty, 2009; Menken, 2008; Wyman *et al.*, 2010). In Arizona, the effects of these anti-bilingual federal policies were heightened by state-level English-only policies. This is the political and educational context for the first two ethnographic cases presented here.

Ethnographic Account 1: 'We're Totally Segregated Out Here'

As the four-hour ELD block mandate unfolded, the Civil Rights Project/Proyecto Derechos Civiles at the University of California, Los Angeles, commissioned a series of studies to investigate the policy's implementation. In the first and most extensive ethnographic study of the ELD block, Karen Lillie, Amy Markos and their associates studied nine schools representing five Arizona public school districts and 18 classrooms in which 30%–40% of the students were identified as ELs (Lillie & Markos, 2014; Lillie *et al.*, 2010). Of the students in these schools, 60%–80% were eligible for free or reduced-cost lunch, a federal indicator of poverty status. The researchers recorded 264 observation hours in ELD classrooms; conducted in-depth interviews with the 18 ELD teachers and with EL coordinators and school principals; and collected classroom artifacts such as lesson plans, copies of instructional materials, student language proficiency data and teacher certification information. (For a full discussion of the study's data collection and analysis methods, see Lillie & Markos, 2014.)

Lillie and Markos (2014: 140) point out that, 'Nowhere in the policy on SEI programs does the state call for segregating ELs'; instead, the policy calls for placing ELs in ELD classrooms 'for four hours and then [integrating them] into mainstream classes for the remainder of the school day'. Yet, their study showed that the 'most important difference' in instruction for EL students was their virtually complete physical, social, linguistic and educational isolation from their English-proficient peers. 'Day in and day out', Lillie *et al.* (2010: 12) write, ELs spent most of the day interacting with 'the same students who [were] also limited in their English proficiency'.

For example, in the seventh- and eighth-grade classes observed, placement in the ELD block prevented students 'from the typical middle school practice of changing teachers and classrooms throughout the day, an essential socializing activity... for transition to high school' (Lillie &

Markos, 2014: 141). EL classrooms were isolated from the rest of the school; work areas were 'relegated to a back corner… and visibly different in …academic content from that of non-EL students' (Lillie *et al.*, 2010: 11). In one district, high school ELD classes were located in a separate building alongside technical and vocational classes, leading one ELD teacher to remark that teachers felt 'surrounded by special classes' and 'totally segregated out here' (Lillie & Markos, 2014: 145). Even during lunch period, 'the one time of the day most ELs and English-speakers of the same grade level are accessible to each other' (Lillie & Markos, 2014: 141), assigned seating practices meant that ELs sat with students from the ELD block. As one ELD coach told the researchers: '[Students] are always separated; they don't get a chance to interact. That makes it harder and harder. Students get used to being with other ELs and the mainstream kids know nothing about ELs…' (Lillie & Markos, 2014: 142).

Subject matter content in ELD classrooms was also segregated and contained. The assumption underlying HB 2064 is that EL students should develop sufficient proficiency in English to succeed academically in English-only classrooms within one year – an assumption that runs counter to decades of second language acquisition research (Baker & Wright, 2021; Collier, 1989; Crawford, 2004; Cummins, 2021; Genesee *et al.*, 2006; May, 2017; Thomas & Collier, 1997). The pressure for students to become 'academically proficient' in English within a year meant that instruction in ELD classrooms was focused almost exclusively on English reading, writing, grammar, vocabulary and oral language (Lillie *et al.*, 2010). Thus, ELs had limited exposure to core grade-level content in math, science and social studies, and that age-appropriate materials were often lacking. In one high school classroom, for example, students were using a beginning reader for five-year-olds, while non-EL students read Shakespeare and young adult books (Lillie & Markos, 2014: 146). Some ELD classrooms had no textbooks at all (Lillie *et al.*, 2010).

The containment of EL student bodies, curriculum and instruction meant that EL students fell progressively behind their grade-level peers, sharply curtailing the likelihood that they would ever 'catch up'. ELs often lacked the necessary credits to graduate from high school. 'For every year these students spend in an ELD classroom, where instructional time is hyper-focused on language learning, they fall further behind their grade-level peers in content area academic knowledge and abilities', Lillie and Markos (2014: 144) wrote. Often, EL students reclassified as English proficient, when placed in mainstream classrooms, were not provided access to linguistic and pedagogic scaffolding and support. As a consequence, many ended up being reclassified, acquiring a new stigmatizing label: English language learner after reclassification (ELLAR) (Lillie *et al.*, 2010).

Within the ELD block, students' linguistic and cultural assets were also contained and policed. ELD classrooms featured prominent displays that represented EL students as deficient and different: 'Practice your English 24/7!', 'English only!' (Lillie *et al.*, 2010: 13). Some teachers 'made it taboo for students to use their primary language' (Lillie *et al.*, 2010: 22), asking students to patrol their peers and report 'unwanted use of the native language' (Lillie & Markos, 2014: 147). When one EL student observed to his teacher that the English word collar was also a word in Spanish (*collar* or necklace), he was scolded: 'You may think that is a Spanish word; but it is not; we only have English words in this room' (Lillie *et al.*, 2010: 22). As Lillie *et al.* (2010: 22) summed up these practices, EL students 'appeared to be forced to *surrender* their cultural and linguistic knowledge... at the door of the ELD classroom'.

Especially telling about the language 'panic' quality in this account is its location within a larger system of raciolinguistic containment and control. In 2010, the Arizona legislature passed Senate Bill 1070 ('Support Our Law Enforcement and Safe Neighborhoods Act'), an anti-immigrant measure that a federal judge later ruled encouraged racial profiling. On the same day, the legislature approved HB 2281, a ban on ethnic studies (specifically Mexican-American studies) in public schools (specifically the Tucson Unified School District near the US–Mexico border), on the grounds that such classes 'promote resentment toward a race or class or people' (i.e. Whites). The week that these measures were approved, the state superintendent of public instruction instructed school districts to remove teachers with 'accents' from teaching English. Together, these containment policies provide troubling evidence of the ways in which language policy in education recements the unequal distribution of power and resources along racial lines, doing so 'on the *seemingly neutral ground of language*' (Hymes, 1980: 110).

Arizona is an extreme case ('ground zero') but it is not unique. In an ethnographic study within a predominantly Latinx Chicago public high school, Jonathan Rosa (2019) notes that when he first began working at the school as a tutor, 'I was troubled by a noticeable pattern':

> In one classroom after another, students who were officially designated as English Language Learners (ELLs) sat in the corners of the classroom, usually closest to or farthest from the door. ...whereas mainstreamed students (i.e., students not designated as ELLs) interacted freely among groups, students designated as ELLs seemed to be cut off from general classroom affairs. (Rosa, 2019: 127)

And in a longitudinal qualitative case study of ELs in a large suburban high school in Pennsylvania, Yasuko Kanno and Sara Kangas (2014: 23) found that ELs 'almost always exited to remedial-level courses', isolating them from high-track classes and sometimes graduation – regardless of their past performance in segregated 'sheltered' English classes. Across the US, say Patricia Gándara and Gary Orfield (2010: 30),

'English learners are more likely to attend large failing urban schools in which they are segregated with other English learners'. The next ethnographic example shows that these school failures extend to both teachers and students of color and to rural and urban schools.

Ethnographic Account 2: 'It's Like the Native Teacher Doesn't Exist'

Native American education is a test case of chronic language panic. Indigenous language eradication and the erasure of Indigenous sovereignty and peoplehood is a key mechanism of settler colonialism employed 'to clear [Indigenous inhabitants] from valuable land' (Tuck & Yang, 2014: 224). Punitive and often violent English-only policies carried out in government boarding schools were central to this quest. As Alutiiq scholar Eve Tuck and K. Wayne Yang (2014: 224) write, in tandem with chattel slavery, such efforts at Indigenous erasure constitute 'the basis of the formation of Whiteness in settler colonial nation-states'.

To examine these processes, I draw on research with Cochiti scholar Mary Eunice Romero-Little and Tohono O'odham scholar Ofelia Zepeda (McCarty *et al.*, 2014; Romero-Little *et al.*, 2007) from a five-year (2001–2006) study of Indigenous youth language ideologies and practices in the Southwestern US. The purpose of the study was to explore how Indigenous language loss and revitalization were experienced in the everyday lives of Native American youth and the impacts on their linguistic, cultural and academic identities. Seven Indigenous-serving schools participated in the study, representing a cross-section of rural and urban settings and multiple Indigenous languages, Englishes and Spanishes. Altogether, the participating schools enrolled 2039 Native American students.

Critical ethnographic monitoring in collaboration with local Indigenous educators was central to the study. This included 212 in-depth interviews, 22 extended classroom observations and 80 site visits to seven participating schools. Sociolinguistic questionnaires ($n = 500$), analyses of district- and state-collected test data and document analysis (e.g. lesson plans, school mission statements and student writing samples) were also part of the study.

Under NCLB, five of the seven participating schools were under some form of federally mandated 'corrective action', subjecting students and teachers to scripted English phonics-based reading instruction. This also placed the schools in a high-stakes environment in which the sole measure of achievement was English language standardized tests. Together, these policies fostered the marginalization of 'low-stakes' curricular content, including Indigenous language and culture instruction. The following ethnographic vignette is representative of these processes.

The observation reported here took place at an elementary school located on Indigenous lands adjacent to a large metropolitan area. On the morning of our arrival, Ms M, the Native language and culture teacher and an esteemed community elder, awaited our arrival. We would soon learn that high stakes testing pressures had reduced Native language and culture instruction to one-half hour each week for each class; Ms M taught all these classes. Greeting us at the school entrance, she guided us to her classroom in a portable building at the edge of the campus – the furthest building from the entry to the school. This is significant not only in terms of the building's physical segregation from the rest of the school, but also because Ms M uses a wheelchair.

Ms M had arranged her classroom with long tables grouped adjacent to each other at the center of the room. In addition to enabling students to face one another, this configuration enabled Ms M to move freely around the room, facilitating her own close interaction with students. Bulletin boards around the room featured illustrations of human body parts, animals, and colors labeled in the local Indigenous language. Shortly after we settled into chairs on one side of the room, the White first-grade teacher escorted her 16 Native students single-file into the classroom. Ms M explained to us that although most students' primary language is English, most had been identified as English learners. Once students took their seats, Ms M wheeled to one side of the tables and said, 'OK, class, today we are going to go over parts of the body'. This routine followed:

Ms M: OK, we all have a paper now. We are going to go over our (speaking the term in the Indigenous language and indicating her face). What's this? [head]. This is [head] too (points to hair). What do we use our [head] for?

Student (S): Thinking.

Ms M: What do we use this for? (indicating hair) The next one down is this (pulls her ear). Say [ear].

Multiple students (Ss): [Ear].

Ms M continued with vocabulary on facial features, instructing students to follow along on a worksheet. Students appeared restless, moving in their seats and whispering (in English) among each other. Finally, Ms M said, 'OK, I know you're all getting bored'.

Ss: Can we color?

Ms M: Yes, you're going to color.... OK, you can get the crayons.

After about 15 minutes of coloring, the first-grade teacher returned to take her students back to their self-contained classroom. Later in the day, as we were interviewing another Native teacher at the school, she related this:

> I think Ms. M is not a priority [for the school]. It's like she doesn't exist. There is no support, even down to her disability. I just see her as not existing at the school. She's there, but they [non-Native classroom teachers] don't pay attention to her. They never ask what she's working on or tell her what they're working on to help her integrate her lessons with classroom lessons. Teachers say time in Ms. M's class is lost time. 'What's the point? They just go there to color'. (Field notes, 3 November 2005)

In this ethnographic vignette, the Native language and knowledge system were physically and symbolically peripheralized and contained. Language learning was similarly constricted and constrained, stripped of context, content and meaning. This occurred through the exclusion of adequate material resources, professional support and physical access for the Indigenous teacher. Students' language learning was rendered pointless, time lost to the more 'important' tasks of learning English and mainstream content; their teacher was dismissed as 'non-existent'.

The effect of these practices was to segregate what 'counts' as legitimate language and knowledge along racial and social class lines. Native students were subjected to pedagogies that even their teachers described as boring and pointless, while students advantaged by Whiteness and social class, who attended more affluent schools in the nearby metropolitan area benefited from asset-based pedagogies. These differential learning opportunities demarcate a racialized 'language line' (Hopson, 2003). Rosa (2016, 2019) relates this to intertwined ideologies of standardization and 'languagelessness', in which minoritized and racialized languages and language users (i.e. Ms M) are rendered incompetent and illegitimate; they are, in effect, erased ('What's the point?'). In writing about Spanish–English bilingual education in the US more than 40 years ago, Hymes (1980: 111) made a similar observation: 'One hears of teachers saying to a child,... you have no language at all'.

Ethnographic Account 3: A Movement of 'Like-Minded People Who Somehow Survived Attempted Language Annihilation'

In this final account, I expand the ethnographic lens to offer what Hymes (1980: 101) described as a comparative ethnological perspective. 'Such an interdependence between general and particular inquiry is essential', he noted, 'as the contribution ethnography ought to make to education'. In contrast to the previous two accounts, my goal in this section is to center counter-possibilities to raciolinguistic containment and erasure by tracing a genealogy of Indigenous language, culture and education reclamation movements. The account draws on more than three decades of my own and others' ethnographic monitoring, including firsthand participant and non-participant observation, interviews, formal and informal conversations and meetings and extant literature and documents. Together, these methods illuminate a genealogy of local resurgence movements deeply rooted in place, yet part of a larger Indigenous de/anticolonization movement. The individuals who have charted the movements know and support one another; their local language efforts are intertwined. As Hermes and Kawai'ae'e (2014: 104) write, this is a relational movement involving a 'transnational network of like-minded people... who somehow survived attempted language annihilation'. At the heart of these movements is what myaamia (Miami) linguist Wesley Leonard (2017: 16) calls 'language work': 'language documentation, description, teaching, advocacy, and resource development'.

As is true of all genealogies, this one has no finite starting or ending point. I begin with three of the earliest contemporary efforts: Kanien'kehá:ka (Mohawk), Diné (Navajo) and Kanaka Maoli (Hawaiian). This is necessarily an attenuated account; I cannot do justice to, nor do I claim to offer a full account of these movements. And it is perspectival, based on my position as an observer, (co)researcher and collaborator in the work. I begin with Kanien'kehá:ka and the Akwesasne Freedom School.

The Akwesasne Mohawk Nation – the Land where the Partridge Drums, also known as St Regis – lies along the St Lawrence Seaway. Akwesasne is 'the only federally recognized tribe with contiguous territory in both the United States and Canada' (Boyer, 2018: 1). The self-referential term, Kanien'kehá:ka, People of the Flint, refers to flint deposits used for tool-making in what is known in English as Mohawk Valley, New York. Mohawk is a Haudenosaunee (Iroquoian) language spoken by people Indigenous to what is known in English as upstate New York, southern Québec and eastern Ontario.

In her ethnographic study, *Free to be Mohawk*, Kanien'keha scholar Louellyn White (2015: 50) recounts the Mohawk's 1968 blockade of the St Lawrence River – a fight for free passage across Mohawk lands and waterways bifurcated by colonial borders – which laid a 'foundation for a language and education reclamation movement'. That movement materialized in a three-year struggle between Akwesasne citizens who opposed settler state-influenced governance and those who supported the elected tribal council. Between 1979 and 1982, hundreds of people remained barricaded in an encampment on the land of tribal leader Loran Thompson, at a place called Raquette Point (Boyer, 2018). As White (2015: 56) describes, 'living communally, sharing space, cooking and eating together, having a ceremony each morning' united the group in 'a determination to keep Mohawk culture alive'.

The Akwesasne Freedom School was born out of this struggle, as parents in the encampment refused to send their children to assimilative state-sponsored schools. Threatened by the New York school system that they would be jailed if they did not enroll their children in the public schools, the parents 'stood their ground', holding classes 'in barns, living rooms, and trailers until a small building could be constructed' (White, 2015: 56). 'I couldn't imagine sending my daughter to public school', recalled Beverly Cook, a resident of the encampment; 'it was really important for us to know our kids were going to know who they were... and why their parents were behind a barricade' (cited in Boyer, 2018: 11). Writing 15 years after the barricades came down, long-time Mohawk language educator-activist Dorothy Lazore described the initial development of the Freedom School: 'Over a period of ten years, the Mohawk language program continued into every grade level from nursery... through to Grade 6. Every subject and concept... was taught via the Mohawk language. Indian Control of Education is a reality' (cited in Freeman *et al.*, 1995: 65).

At the time of this writing, the Akwesasne Freedom School serves approximately 75 students in pre-K through Grade 8. Housed in a main facility built by parents and community volunteers to resemble a Haudenosaunee longhouse and other nearby structures, the school's curriculum revolves around the Mohawk language and the Ohenton Kariwahtekwen or Thanksgiving Address (White, 2015). It is 'not the school's mission to follow the Western curriculum or justify their work against current school reform mandates', writes Paul Boyer in a 2018 National Science Foundation 'Voices of Language' report. This 'is an entirely different non-English and Mohawk-led paradigm for teaching and learning', states the Harvard Project on American Indian Economic Development (2005), which made the school its 2005 'Honoring Nations' awardee.

As the language work at Akwesasne took root, another influential language, culture and education reclamation movement emerged within the Navajo Nation in what is now the Southwestern United States. In 1966, community leaders in the small community of Tsé Ch'ízhí (Rough Rock, Navajo Nation, Arizona) signed an unprecedented contract with the Bureau of Indian Affairs (BIA) and the Navajo tribe to take control of a newly built but unstaffed local BIA school. Like Akwesasne, this was not to be a school in the conventional sense. As the school's first director, Dr Robert A. Roessel Jr, described it: 'We brought the entire community into the school.... This was what the school was all about' (cited in McCarty, 2002: 84).

Additional communities within the Navajo Nation soon signed similar contracts, ushering in the American Indian community-controlled school movement. Bilingual-bicultural education propelled the movement. In a 1996 oral history interview with me, Diné education leader Agnes Holm described racialized ideologies of English supremacy that reverberated from the federal boarding school era: 'Nobody *ever* suggested using Navajo in the school to learn.... School is to learn English' (cited in McCarty, 2002: 113). Out of this movement came the most significant federal Indian education legislation of the 20th century: the

Indian Education Act (1972), which provided for bilingual-bicultural curriculum development, teacher preparation and parent–community engagement; the Indian Self-Determination and Educational Assistance Act (1975), which created a mechanism for Native nations and communities to contract with the BIA to operate their own schools and social services; and the Tribally Controlled Community College Act (1978), designed to establish and improve tribal colleges and universities (TCUs).

At the time of this writing there are 130 tribally operated Native American schools and 32 tribal colleges and universities attended by nearly 20,000 students. Many Navajo Nation public schools and Head Start preschools offer Diné immersion programs, and Diné immersion programs operate in off-reservation public schools in Arizona and New Mexico (for a discussion of the latter, see Lee & McCarty, 2017). Many students in these programs and in TCUs have returned to their home communities and tribal nations as teachers and administrators, and contribute to the continued development of these Indigenous institutions and movements (Roessel, 2011).

Diné bilingual education, Akwesasne and many other Native American language and culture reclamation initiatives have been influenced by and allied with Hawaiian-medium schooling, the most comprehensive system of full Indigenous language medium education in the US. Native Hawaiian scholar-activist Sam L. No'eau Warner (2001: 135) traces the beginnings of this movement to a late 1960s 'cultural revolution' among younger Hawaiians centering on music and dance. Out of this 'first renaissance' grew a 'new group of second-language Hawaiian speakers who would become Hawaiian language educators' (Warner, 2001: 135). These educators helped secure a 1978 state constitutional amendment making Hawaiian an official language of the state. By this time, writes Hawaiian language scholar-activist Noelani Iokepa-Guerrero (2016: 232), 'there were fewer than 50 Hawaiian-language speakers under 18 years of age'. With support from Māori language educators and activists from Aotearoa, New Zealand, a small group of college students established the nonprofit 'Aha Pūnana Leo' ('Nest of Voices') Hawaiian-medium preschools. Pūnana Leo cofounder William H. Wilson (2014: 221–222) writes: 'Our small nucleus of families then moved into the public school system of education through Hawaiian, referred to by the Hawaiian term *Kaiapuni Hawai'i* (Hawaiian environment) and by the English term *Hawaiian language immersion*'.

Establishing Hawaiian-medium education faced stiff challenges, including overturning an 1896 ban on the Hawaiian language. Much like the families at Akwesasne, Pūnana Leo parents boycotted state-sponsored schooling, establishing their own Hawaiian-medium kindergarten until the state department of education created a Hawaiian-medium track in the public schools. Hawaiian educator-activists found allies among other Indigenous language resurgence movements. Mohawk educator Dorothy

Lazore, for example (cited above), provided teacher training and state-level advocacy for Hawaiian-medium schooling. According to Wilson (2014: 222), the movement also 'built from the work of previous generations' in documenting and teaching Hawaiian as a 'foreign language in English-medium educational entities'.

The Kaiapuni schools (numbering 25 in 2021) have been instrumental in increasing Hawaiian language speakers of all ages, estimated at 10,000–24,000 throughout the US (Hermes & Kawai'ae'a, 2014: 315; Wilson, 2014: 25). This includes approximately 4000 Hawaiian-speaking children under age 18, most of whom attend or attended Kaiapuni schools (Iokepa-Guerrero, 2016: 237).

Each of these movements illuminates the ways in which new 'ideological and implementational spaces' (Hornberger, 2006) have been wedged open as small groups have interacted with wider social, cultural, educational and political processes (for a host of additional case examples, see Hinton, 2013; Hinton & Hale, 2001; Hinton *et al.*, 2018; May, 2013). The wider processes include the creation and mobilization of organizations such as the American Indian Language Development Institute (AILDI), founded in 1978 by Hualapai educator Lucille J. Watahomigie and linguists Leanne Hinton and Akira Y. Yamamoto (https://aildi.arizona.edu); the National Coalition of Native American Language Schools and Programs, which 'advocate[s] for the use of Indigenous languages as the medium of instruction' (http://www.ncnalsp.org/about); the Breath of Life Institute and the National Breath of Life Archival Institute for Indigenous Languages, founded by the Advocates for Indigenous California Language Survival (https://aicls.org/breath-of-life-institute/); and the Stabilizing Indigenous Languages Symposium (SILS), launched in a series of roundtables in 1994–1995 to bring together 'tribal educators and experts on linguistics, language renewal, and language teaching to lay out a blueprint of policy changes, educational reforms, and community initiatives to stabilize and revitalize American Indian and Alaska Native languages' (Cantoni, 1996: vi; see Reyhner, 2018, for a history of SILS). Individuals and groups in these organizations were instrumental in securing passage of the 1990/1992 Native American Languages Act (NALA), the 2007 Esther Martinez Native American Languages Preservation Act and provisions for Native American language and culture revitalization within multiple reauthorizations of the ESEA. Alongside this wave of 'counterpoised' bottom-up and top-down movements (López, 2008), there has been a growing body of scholarship on Indigenous language revitalization and reclamation that eschews damaging metaphors of language 'death' and 'extinction', calling for de/anticolonial approaches that (re)center language and culture vitalities and Indigenous community-based perspectives on what 'counts' as transformative 'language work' (Leonard, 2011, 2017; Perley, 2011).

This local/global activism 'rejects marginalized [and racialized] status' (Sherris & Penfield, 2020), pushing back against language and culture endangerment and equally, pushing *for* radically different possibilities and dreams (McCarty, 2020). (Re)claiming voice – the power to act – is central to these language and culture projects. Critical ethnographic monitoring reveals the ways in which Indigenous educators, parents, elders and youth are doing this by repurposing school spaces in ways that explicitly counter ideologies of minoritized bilingualism (Rosa, 2016) and settler-sanctioned notions of 'appropriate' language practices. These Indigenous movements imagine and are realizing an education process that nurtures the co-participation of families and communities across generations, reclaims cultural knowledge and identity rooted in place and takes control over communities' language futures, knowledges and nationhood. Describing the Akwesasne Freedom School, Kanien'kehá:ka educator and language activist Elvera Sargent puts it this way: The Freedom School is a place 'where we can learn our language and culture, learn who we are as Onkwehonwe people [Original People]. ...That to me is the *key* for us to be strong people' (Jacobs & Bonaparte, 2020).

Beyond and through Chronic Raciolinguistic Panic

In this chapter, I have offered three ethnographic accounts of overt and covert language education policies in action. The accounts show the ways in which the policies are negotiated, accommodated and sometimes resisted, as they are made and remade in social practice (McCarty, 2011). Within and across the accounts, critical ethnographic monitoring helps tease out these processes and 'the workings of multiple, intersecting and conflicting power structures which are local but tied to non-local systems' of governmentality and control (Shore & Wright, 1997: 13). Bryan Brayboy's (2005) exposition of tribal critical race theory makes clear that a 'culturally nuanced' ethnographic analysis must attend to both endemic (chronic) racism and endemic (chronic) coloniality in understanding those structures and their implications for language and culture survivance.

As the third account shows, ethnographic monitoring also surfaces the possibilities for re-envisioning and transforming the conjoined power structures of race/ism and colonialism. We can think of the movement(s) profiled in this account as guides toward the longstanding vision of communities of color for freedom from raciolinguistic oppression and the freedom to be, speak, read, write and learn on community-defined terms. The Akwesasne Freedom School frames this as the 'freedom to walk and think in [multiple] worlds, to survive in the larger society and to have a strong sense of self' (Jacobs & Bonaparte, 2020). In collaboration with local stakeholders, ethnographic monitoring can peer into and leverage the cracks and spaces in the system where such freedom can emerge and grow. By critically examining how power and authority ripple through language policy processes, and the ways in which people 'undo' racialized authority and appropriateness (Flores & Rosa, 2015), ethnographic monitoring offers a pathway toward realizing community-based language, culture and education dreams.

Note

(1) This chapter was completed within the settler-occupied homelands of the Gabrielino-Tongva and Muwekma Ohlone peoples (respectively, in Spanish and English, the Los Angeles Basin and Channel Islands and the San Francisco Bay Area). I recognize and respect Tongva and Ohlone sovereignty over these lands. Parts of this chapter are adapted from McCarty (2018) and McCarty *et al.* (2012, 2021).

References

Alim, H.S. (2009) Creating 'an empire within an empire': Critical hip hop language pedagogies and the role of sociolinguistics. In H.S. Alim, A. Ibrahim and A. Pennycook (eds) *Global Linguistic Flows: Hip Hop Culture, Youth Identities, and the Politics of Language* (pp. 213–230). London: Routledge.

Alim, H.S. (2016) Introducing raciolinguistics: Racing language and languaging race in hyperracial times. In H.S. Alim, J.R. Rickford and A.F. Ball (eds) *Raciolinguistics: How Language Shapes Our Ideas about Race* (pp. 1–30). Oxford: Oxford University Press.

Alim, H.S., Reyes, A. and Kroskrity, P.V. (2020) The field of language and race: A linguistic anthropological approach to race, racism, and racialization. In H.S. Alim, A. Reyes and P.V. Kroskrity (eds) *The Oxford Handbook of Language and Race* (pp. 1–21). Oxford: Oxford University Press.

Arias, M.B. and Faltis, C. (2012) Introduction. In M.B. Arias and C. Faltis (eds) *Implementing Educational Language Policy in Arizona: Legal, Historical and Current Practices in SEI* (pp. xxiii–xxviii). Bristol: Multilingual Matters.

Baker, C. and Wright, W.E. (2021) *Foundations of Bilingual Education and Bilingualism* (7th edn). Bristol: Multilingual Matters.

Beaulieu, D., Sparks, L. and Alonzo, M. (2005) *Preliminary Report on No Child Left Behind in Indian Country*. Washington, DC: National Indian Education Association.

Boyer, P. (2018) *Language Connects Us: Maintaining the Mohawk Language in the St. Regis Reservation*. Ithaca, NY: Native Science Report Press.

Brayboy, B.M.J. (2005) Toward a Tribal Critical Race Theory in education. *The Urban Review* 37 (5), 425–446. doi: 10.1007/s11256-005-0018-y

Cantoni, G. (1996) Introduction. In G. Cantoni (ed.) *Stabilizing Indigenous Languages* (p. vi). Flagstaff, AZ: Northern Arizona Center for Excellence in Education.

Collier, V.P. (1989) How long? A synthesis of research on academic achievement in a second language. *TESOL Quarterly* 23 (3), 509–531.

Combs, M.C. (2012) Everything on its head: How Arizona's structured English immersion policy re-invents theory and practice. In M.B. Arias and C. Faltis (eds) *Implementing Educational Language Policy in Arizona: Legal, Historical and Current Practices in SEI* (pp. 59–85). Bristol: Multilingual Matters.

Combs, M.C. and Nicholas, S.E. (2012) The effect of Arizona language policies on Arizona Indigenous students. *Language Policy* 11 (1), 101–118.

Combs, M.C., González, N. and Moll, L.D. (2011) US Latinos and the learning of English: The metonymy of language policy. In T.L. McCarty (ed.) *Ethnography and Language Policy* (pp. 184–203). New York: Routledge.

Crawford, J. (2004) *Educating English Learners: Language Diversity in the Classroom* (5th edn). Los Angeles, CA: Bilingual Education Services.

Cummins, J. (2021) *Rethinking the Education of Multilingual Learners: A Critical Analysis of Theoretical Concepts*. Bristol: Multilingual Matters.

De Korne, H. and Hornberger, N.H. (2017) Countering unequal multilingualism through ethnographic monitoring. In M. Martin-Jones and D. Martin (eds) *Researching Multilingualism: Critical and Ethnographic Perspectives* (pp. 248–258). London: Routledge.

Douglass, F. (1881) The color line. *North American Review*. See https://americanliterature.com/author/frederick-douglass/essay/the-color-line (accessed 16 August 2021).

Du Bois, W.E.B. (2004 [1913]) *The Souls of Black Folk*. Boulder, CO: Paradigm.

Eagle Shield, A., Paris, D., Paris, R. and San Pedro, T. (2020) *Education in Movement Spaces: Standing Rock to Chicago Freedom Square*. New York: Routledge.

Flores, N. and Rosa, J. (2015) Undoing appropriateness: Raciolinguistic ideologies and language diversity in education. *Harvard Educational Review* 85 (2), 149–171.

Freeman, K., Stairs, A., Corbiére, E. and Lazore, D. (1995) Ojibway, Mohawk, and Inuktitut alive and well? Issues of identity, ownership, and change. *The Bilingual Research Journal* 19 (1), 39–69. https://doi.org/10.1080/15235882.1995.10668590

Gándara, P. and Hopkins, M. (eds) (2010) *Forbidden Language: English Learners and Restrictive Language Policies*. New York: Teachers College Press.

Gándara, P. and Orfield, G. (2010) *A Return to the 'Mexican Room': The Segregation of Arizona's English Learners*. Los Angeles, CA: The Civil Rights Project/Proyecto Derechos Civiles.

García, D.R. (2008) Mixed messages: American Indian achievement before and since the implementation of *No Child Left Behind*. *Journal of American Indian Education* 47 (1), 136–154.

Genesee, F., Lindholm-Leary, K., Saunders, W. and Christian, D. (2006) *Educating English Language Learners*. Cambridge: Cambridge University Press.

Harvard Project on American Indian Economic Development (2005) *Honoring Nations: Akwesasne Freedom School*. Harvard, MA: John F. Kennedy School of Government, Harvard University.

Hermes, M. and Kawai'ae'e, K. (2014) Revitalizing Indigenous languages through Indigenous immersion education. *Journal of Immersion and Content-Based Language Education* 2 (2), 303–322. https://doi.org/10/1075/jlcb.2.2.10her

Hill, J.H. (2001) The racializing function of language panics. In R.D. González and I. Melis (eds) *Language Ideologies: Critical Perspectives on the Official English Movement, Vol. 2: History, Theory, and Policy* (pp. 245–267). Urbana, IL/Mahwah, NJ: National Council of Teachers of English/Lawrence Erlbaum.

Hinton, L. (ed.) (2013) *Bringing Our Languages Home: Language Revitalization for Families*. Berkeley, CA: Heyday Books.

Hinton, L. and Hale, K. (eds) (2001) *The Green Book of Language Revitalization in Practice*. San Diego, CA: Academic Press.

Hinton, L., Huss, L. and Roche, G. (eds) (2018) *The Routledge Handbook of Language Vitalization*. Abingdon: Routledge.

Hopson, R. (2003) The problem of the language line: Cultural and social reproduction of hegemonic structures for learners of African descent in the USA. *Race, Ethnicity and Education* 6 (3), 227–245.

Hornberger, N.H. (2006) Nichols to NCLB: Local and global perspectives on US language education policy. In O. García, T. Skutnabb-Kangas and M.E. Torres-Guzmán (eds) *Imagining Multilingual Schools: Languages in Education and Glocalization* (pp. 232–237). Clevedon: Multilingual Matters.

Hymes, D. (1980) *Language in Education: Ethnolinguistic Essays*. Washington, DC: Center for Applied Linguistics.

Hymes, D. (1996) *Ethnography, Linguistics, Narrative Inequality: Toward an Understanding of Voice*. London: Taylor & Francis.

Iokepa-Guerrero, N. (2016) Revitalization programs and impacts in the USA and Canada. In S.M. Coronel-Molina and T.L. McCarty (eds) *Indigenous Language Revitalization in the Americas* (pp. 227–246). New York: Routledge.

Jacobs, R. (executive producer) and Bonaparte, B. (director and producer) (2020) Akwesasne Freedom School. Akwesasne TV. See https://www.youtube.com/watch?v=85xidcNwLQM (accessed 25 July 2022).

Kanno, Y. and Kangas, S.E.N. (2014) 'I'm not going to be, like, for the AP': English language learners' limited access to advanced college preparatory courses in high school. *American Educational Research Journal* 51 (5), 1–31.

Kaomea, J. (2001) Dilemmas of an Indigenous academic: A Native Hawaiian story. *Contemporary Issues in Early Childhood* 2 (1), 67–82. doi:10.2304/ciec.2001.2.1.9

Lee, T.S. and McCarty, T.L. (2017) Upholding Indigenous education sovereignty through critical culturally sustaining/revitalization pedagogy. In D. Paris and H.S. Alim (eds) *Culturally Sustaining Pedagogy: Teaching and Learning for Justice in a Changing World* (pp. 61–82). New York: Teachers College Press.

Leonard, W.Y. (2011) Challenging 'extinction through modern Miami language practices. *American Indian Culture and Research Journal* 35 (2), 135–160. doi:10.17953/aicr.35.2.f3r173r46m261884

Leonard, W.Y. (2017) Producing language reclamation by decolonizing 'language'. In W.Y. Leonard and H. De Korne (eds) *Language Documentation and Description* (pp. 15–26). London: EL Publishing.

Lillie, K.E. and Markos, A. (2014) The four-hour block: SEI in classrooms. In S.C.K. Moore (ed.) *Language Policy Processes and Consequences: Arizona Case Studies* (pp. 133–155). Bristol: Multilingual Matters.

Lillie, K.E., Markos, A., Estrella, A., Nguyen, T., Trifiro, A., Arias, M.B., Wiley, T.G., Peer, K. and Pérez, K. (2010) *Policy in Practice: The Implementation of Structured English Immersion in Arizona*. Los Angeles, CA: The Civil Rights Project/Proyecto Derechos Civiles.

Lomawaima, K.T. and McCarty, T.L. (2006) *'To Remain an Indian': Lessons in Democracy from a Century of Native American Education*. New York: Teachers College Press.

Long, M.H. and Adamson, H.D. (2012) SLA research and Arizona's structured English immersion policies. In M.B. Arias and C. Faltis (eds) *Implementing Educational Language Policy in Arizona: Legal, Historical and Current Practices in SEI* (pp. 39–55). Bristol: Multilingual Matters.

López, L.E. (2008) Top-down and bottom-up: Counterpoised visions of bilingual intercultural education in Latin America. In N.H. Hornberger (ed.) *Can Schools Save Indigenous Languages? Policy and Practice on Four Continents* (pp. 42–65). Houndsmill: Palgrave Macmillan.

Luke, A. (1996) Series editor's introduction. In D. Hymes (ed.) *Ethnography, Linguistics, Narrative Inequality: Toward an Understanding of Voice* (pp. vi–ix). London: Taylor & Francis.

Martin-Jones, M. and Da Costa Cabral, I. (2018) The critical ethnographic turn in research on language policy and planning. In J. Tollefson and M. Pérez-Milans (eds) *The Oxford Handbook of Language Policy and Planning* (pp. 71–92). Oxford: Oxford University Press. https://doi.org/10.1093/oxfordhb/9780190458898.013.3

May, S. (2013) Indigenous immersion education: International developments. *Journal of Immersion and Content-Based Education* 1 (1), 34–69.

May, S. (2017) Bilingual education: What the research tells us. In O. García, A. Lin and S. May (eds) *Bilingual/Multilingual Education. Encyclopedia of Language and Education* (3rd edn, pp. 81–100). New York: Springer.

McCarty, T.L. (2002) *A Place to be Navajo: Rough Rock and the Struggle for Self-Determination in Indigenous Schooling*. Mahwah, NJ: Lawrence Erlbaum.

McCarty, T.L. (2009) The impact of high-stakes accountability policies on Native American learners: Evidence from research. *Teaching Education* 20 (1), 1–23.

McCarty, T.L. (ed.) (2011) *Ethnography and Language Policy*. New York: Routledge.

McCarty, T.L. (2015) Ethnography in language planning and policy research. In F.J. Hult and D.C. Johnson (eds) *Research Methods in Language Policy and Planning: A Practical Guide* (pp. 81–93). Malden, MA: Wiley Blackwell.

McCarty, T.L. (2018) So that any child may succeed: Indigenous pathways toward justice and the promise of Brown. *Educational Researcher* 47 (5), 271–293.

McCarty, T.L. (2020) Coda. 'Fight back and fight on' – Reflections on education projects for the continuance of Indigenous, tribal and minoritized languages and cultures. In A. Sherris and S.D. Penfield (eds) *Rejecting Marginalized Status of Minority Languages: Education Projects Pushing Back against Language Endangerment* (pp. 152–161). Bristol: Multilingual Matters.

McCarty, T.L., Collins, J. and Hopson, R.K. (2012) Dell Hymes and the New Language Policy Studies: Update from an underdeveloped country. *Anthropology and Education Quarterly* 12 (4), 335–363.

McCarty, T.L., Romero-Little, M.E., Warhol, L. and Zepeda, O. (2014) Genealogies of language loss and recovery: Native youth language practices and cultural continuance. In L.T. Wyman, T.L. McCarty and S.E. Nicholas (eds) *Indigenous Youth and Multilingualism: Language Identity, Ideology, and Practice in Dynamic Cultural Worlds* (pp. 26–47). New York: Routledge.

McCarty, T.L., Noguera, J., Lee, T.S. and Nicholas, S.E. (2021) 'A viable path for education': Indigenous language immersion and sustainable self-determination. *Journal of Language, Identity and Education* 20 (5), 340–354.

Menken, K. (2008) *English Learners Left Behind: Standardized Testing as Language Policy*. Clevedon: Multilingual Matters.

Moore, S.C.K. (ed.) (2014) *Language Policy Processes and Consequences: Arizona Case Studies*. Bristol: Multilingual Matters.

Perley, B. (2011) *Defying Maliseet Language Death: Emergent Vitalities of Language, Culture, and Identity in Eastern Canada*. Lincoln: University of Nebraska Press.

Ravitch, S.M. and Carl, N.M. (2021) *Qualitative Research: Bridging the Conceptual, Theoretical, and Methodological* (2nd edn). Thousand Oaks, CA: Sage.

Reyhner, J. (2018) Brief History of the Stabilizing Indigenous Languages Symposium. Northern Arizona University. See https://jan.ucc.nau.edu/~jar/History.html (accessed 25 July 2022).

Roessel, M. (2011) Keynote address. 'Preparing the past to secure the future': The Center for Indian Education – the next 50 years. *Journal of American Indian Education* 50 (2), 13–23.

Romero-Little, M.E., McCarty, T.L., Warhol, L. and Zepeda, O. (2007) Language policies in practice: Preliminary findings from a large-scale national study of Native American language shift. *TESOL Quarterly* 41 (3), 607–618. https://doi.org/10.2307/40264393

Rosa, J.D. (2016) Standardization, racialization, languagelessness: Raciolinguistic ideologies across communicative contexts. *Journal of Linguistic Anthropology* 26 (2), 162–183.

Rosa, J.D. (2019) *Looking Like a Language, Sounding Like a Race: Raciolinguistic Ideologies and the Learning of Latinidad*. Oxford: Oxford University Press.

Ruiz, R. (1991) The empowerment of language-minority students. In C. Sleeter (ed.) *Empowerment through Multicultural Education* (pp. 217–227). Albany, NY: SUNY Press.

Sherris, A. and Penfield, S.D. (eds) (2020) *Rejecting the Marginalized Status of Minority Languages: Educational Projects Pushing Back against Language Endangerment*. Bristol: Multilingual Matters.

Shore, C. and Wright, S. (1997) Policy: A new field of anthropology. In C. Shore and S. Wright (eds) *Anthropology of Policy: Critical Perspectives on Governance and Power* (pp. 3–39). London: Routledge.

Thomas, W.P. and Collier, V. (1997) *School Effectiveness for Language Minority Students*. Washington, DC: National Clearinghouse for Bilingual Education.

Tuck, E. and Yang, K.W. (2014) R-words: Refusing research. In D. Paris and M.T. Winn (eds) *Humanizing Research: Decolonizing Qualitative Inquiry with Youth and Communities* (pp. 223–247). Los Angeles, CA: Sage.

Van der Aa, J. and Blommaert, J. (2017) Ethnographic monitoring and the study of complexity. In M. Martin-Jones and D. Martin (eds) *Researching Multilingualism: Critical and Ethnographic Perspectives* (pp. 259–271). London: Routledge.

Warner, S.L. (2001) The movement to revitalize Hawaiian language and culture. In L. Hinton and K. Hale (eds) *The Green Book of Language Revitalization in Practice* (pp. 133–144). New York: Academic Press.

White, L. (2015) *Free to be Mohawk: Indigenous Education at the Akwesasne Freedom School*. Norman, OK: University of Oklahoma Press.

Wiley, T.G. (2012) Foreword: From restrictive SEI to imagining better. In M.B. Arias and C. Faltis (eds) *Implementing Educational Language Policy in Arizona: Legal, Historical and Current Practices in SEI* (pp. xiii–xxii). Bristol: Multilingual Matters.

Wilson, W.H. (2014) Hawaiian: A Native American language official for a state. In T.G. Wiley, J.K. Peyton, D. Christian, S.C.K. Moore and N. Liu (eds) *Handbook of Heritage, Community, and Native American Languages in the United States: Research, Policy, and Educational Practice* (pp. 219–228). Washington, DC: Center for Applied Linguistics and Routledge.

Wyman, L.T., Marlow, P., Andrew, C.F., Miller, G., Nicholai, C.R. and Reardon. Y.N. (2010) High stakes testing, bilingual education and language endangerment: A Yup'ik example. *International Journal of Bilingual Education and Bilingualism* 13, 701–721.

9 Unequal Language Policy, Deficit Language Ideology and Social Injustice: A Critical Ethnography of Language Education Policies in Nepal

Prem Phyak

Researchers have long been critical about the role of language education policies in reproducing social inequalities. Tollefson's (2002, 2013) works have greatly contributed to the understanding of how language education policies are deeply embedded in structural inequalities and power relations. Tollefson (2002: x) argues that language education policies 'must be understood in connection with broad social, political, and economic forces' because they are 'not merely about choice of language as medium of instruction, but instead are often central to a host of social processes'. Scholars working with Indigenous and minoritized communities have unpacked how the language education policies of nation-states have contributed to erasing Indigenous and minoritized languages from the public spheres. McCarty (2003, this volume) and Hornberger (2006), among others, have discussed that Indigenous communities face multiple challenges to make their languages visible in the dominant public sphere. Such challenges include broader hegemonic political ideologies that support colonialism, neoliberalism and nationalism, and local issues such as policymakers' lack of ideological awareness about and support for Indigenous communities (Davis & Phyak, 2017; De Korne *et al.*, 2019; May & Hill, 2008). At the center of critical language policy studies remain language ideologies and sociopolitical inequalities. While analyzing language ideologies and inequalities, this approach considers schooling as a sociopolitical space that reproduces dominant language ideologies through language policies and practices. More importantly, critical scholars take schools as part of the state mechanism which supports dominant ideologies that disregard the value of Indigenous languages.

Building on a critical and engaged approach (Davis & Phyak, 2017; Tollefson, 2013), this chapter analyzes deficit language ideologies and their contributions to the erasure of Indigenous languages in education in Nepal. Drawing on the data from my ethnographic study in a public school in Eastern Nepal, I explore how schools are creating and promoting language hierarchies and invisibilizing the space for Indigenous languages while perpetuating a deficit language ideology. I use 'linguicism' (Skutnabb-Kangas, 1988) as a major theory to interpret the case of the language education policy I have selected to analyze in this chapter.

Linguicism and Linguistic Injustice in Education

Critical scholars have argued that language policies in education should be investigated in relation to their broader sociopolitical conditions. For Tollefson (2013), language education policies are the embodiment of sociopolitical inequalities and mechanisms for reproducing social, cultural and linguistic injustices. Considering schools as a social space, critical language policy approaches pay attention to how schools can create and implement language policies to support or resist the ideologies, interests and beliefs of specific sociocultural groups. In other words, for critical scholars, schools represent the broader sociopolitical structures and practices which eventually support a particular knowledge system and ideology, mostly of the dominant public sphere. Language issues are critical components of such unequal structures and practices in education.

Skutnabb-Kangas (1988) uses the concept of *linguicism* to unpack the role of language in the construction and reproduction of social injustices. She defines linguicism as 'ideologies, structures and practices which are used to legitimate, effectuate, regulate and reproduce an unequal division of power and resources (both material and immaterial) between groups which are defined on the basis of language' (Skutnabb-Kangas, 1988: 13). Language ideology is central to the creation of unequal language policies. Linguistic anthropologists and critical applied linguists have defined language ideology as a set of assumptions about language and language use (Kroskrity, 2004; Woolard, 1992). Language ideology represents the aesthetics, identities, perceptions and power relations of people from different linguistic backgrounds (Kroskrity, 2010). It embodies the sociopolitical, economic and cultural conditions of languages and language practices. In mainstream (dominant language) schooling, monolingual and monoglossic language ideologies become the norm, supporting the sociopolitical, economic and cultural values of dominant languages, while devaluing the importance of local multilingualism. Studies have shown that the monolingual ideology that discursively constructs multilingualism as a problem plays the most influential role in reinforcing language-related discriminations in multilingual contexts (Piller, 2016).

This kind of monolingual ideology is historically rooted in the colonial European ideology of linguistic nationalism which defines nation-states as an *imagined community* of the people speaking (usually) the one 'national language' (Anderson, 1991).

Other ideologies that exacerbate language discriminations are the standard language ideology and neoliberal ideology. The standard language ideology defines language as a fixed and autonomous entity, which is based on homogeneous rules and norms (Milroy, 2001). This ideology reproduces language discriminations in two ways: (a) by recognizing the legitimacy of language used by a particular group, mostly middle-upper class; and (b) by erasing the non-standard and oral language practices of multilingual and ethnic minoritized speakers (Lippi-Green, 1997). In the same way, neoliberal ideology, the assumption that the value and legitimization of language are shaped by a competitive and free market (Block *et al.*, 2013), also creates unequal language policies and practices. This ideology constructs and naturalizes a hierarchy of languages by letting the free market 'decide' which languages should or should not be given space. In other words, it assumes that languages that do not have exchange values, in terms of currency, receive insignificant space in public spheres. As a global capitalist ideology, neoliberalism thus defines the role and place of language as a commodity in a free market (Heller, 2010).

The structure of state mechanisms further promotes the language ideologies that strengthen language discriminations. One explicit example of such structures, in the case of Nepal, is the English as a medium of instruction (EMI) policy, which denies the use of mother tongues, including Nepali, in schools. This policy is historically linked with the neoliberalization of education in Nepal, which has contributed to increasing the number of state-deregulated private schools. Such schools have been promoting EMI as one key part of their competitive and market-based education. Speaking languages other than English is strictly prohibited in these private schools, and students are punished for not speaking English (Khati, 2011). Such discriminatory school language policies are shaped by broader sociopolitical structures and discourses. As neoliberal ideologies become hegemonic in dominant public discourses, minoritized languages are not recognized as a legitimate medium of instruction in education. Consequently, minoritized language speakers feel excluded and invisibilized in school spaces (Phyak, 2013).

These unequal structures produce unequal language practices. If institutions adopt educational practices that allocate unequal access to power and resources on the basis of language, the communities and individuals who speak minoritized languages are often discriminated against. For Skutnabb-Kangas (2015), unequal access is largely produced through three processes: *glorification*, *stigmatization* and *rationalization*. Glorification is the process of idolizing the value and importance of the dominant languages and language practices through three major claims:

(a) what the languages *are*—for example, logical, rich, able to describe everything (e.g., in science, because of their large vocabularies);
(b) what they *have*—for example, grammars, dictionaries, teaching materials, well-trained teachers; and
(c) what they can *do* for you—such as open doors, function as a window onto the world, enable you to talk to many people, get a good job, and so on.

(Skutnabb-Kangas, 2015: 13; italics in original)

Such glorification leads to the related stigmatization of minoritized languages as 'traditional, backward, not able to adapt to an advanced capitalist technological information society, and so forth' (Skutnabb-Kangas, 2015: 13). Rationalization is another process that reproduces language-based discriminations. It refers to the process of normalizing unequal relationships between dominant and minoritized languages through economic, political, educational, sociological and linguistic justifications of how dominant language(s) are necessary for *civilizing*, *modernizing* and *teaching democracy* (Skutnabb-Kangas, 2015). The normalization of linguistic inequalities contributes to the unequal participation of minoritized language speakers in the public sphere. Defining such inequality as linguistic injustice, Piller (2016) argues that linguistic discriminations are closely linked with the cultural and political power of dominant language speakers. For her, linguistic injustices are normalized by blaming the minoritized language speakers for not being able to speak dominant languages. She further argues that:

> Disadvantaged speakers are typically seen as the agents of their own exclusion and it is assumed that the barriers they face are due to inadequate proficiency in the dominant language. However, it is social arrangements that exacerbate linguistic disadvantage or, alternatively, enable participation. (Piller, 2016: 162)

Social arrangements include national, local and regional policies regarding education, healthcare and the military, among others. In this chapter, I consider school spaces as part of the broader social arrangement and discuss how they reproduce unequal language policies that exacerbate discriminations against language minoritized groups. Next, I discuss the context of language education policy in Nepal.

Language Education Policy in Nepal

Nepal's identity as a multilingual, multiethnic and multicultural country has been articulated in the 2015 constitution. The constitution states that the nation-state should adopt a multilingual policy and has guaranteed the right of each ethnic community to preserve and promote their languages. More specifically, the constitution makes the following major provisions related specifically to multilingualism and language education policy:

- Each community residing in Nepal shall have the right to obtain education in their mother tongue and, for that purpose, to open and operate schools and educational institutes, as per the law.
- Each citizen and individual and community shall have the right to use their mother tongues.
- Each citizen and community shall have the right to participate in the cultural life of their communities.
- All communities shall have the right to preserve and promote their mother tongues, scripts, cultures, cultural civilizations and heritages.

More importantly, the constitution guarantees that 'the nation-state shall not discriminate [against] citizens on the grounds of origin, religion, race, caste, tribe, sex, economic condition, language, region, ideology or on the similar other grounds' (Nepal Law Commission, 2016: 6). However, this 'rhetoric of multilingualism' (Phyak & Ojha, 2019), as stated in the constitution, has hardly been enacted in actual practice. Although the constitution has the provision of 'the right to obtain education in their mother tongue', the visibility and meaningful use of local mother tongues in school spaces, both inside and outside the classroom, are limited (Phyak, 2016a). Rather than putting efforts into ensuring the use of children's home languages, government (both local and federal) and schools are instead creating an environment where local languages, including Nepali (mainly in private schools), are systematically displaced and undervalued in education (Seel *et al.*, 2015). Following the private schools' policy, the public schools throughout the country are now adopting an EMI policy. This policy has been supported by the local government representatives who are responsible for looking after education. Studies have shown that local governments and public schools are adopting an EMI policy to compete with the private schools and 'improve' the quality of public schools (Khati, 2015; Sah & Li, 2018). These assumptions have not only misrecognized the importance of children's home languages in learning literacy and academic subjects, but they have also created challenges for promoting the use of local Indigenous languages in schools.

Nepali communities and schools are linguistically and culturally diverse. The 2012 census has identified 123 languages, and the recent study by the Nepal Language Commission has found six new languages. Among these languages, Nepali is the dominant language spoken by some 44% of the population. Although Nepali is the mother tongue of the dominant caste groups, Khas-Arya, it is used as a lingua franca and *de facto* official language throughout the country. In the dominant public discourse, Nepali is considered a symbol of Nepali nationalism (Phyak & Ojha, 2019). Until the early 1990s, languages other than Nepali were banned from education and other public spheres, such as government offices (Weinberg, 2013). Citizens could not defend their cases in court in their mother tongues, and the local Indigenous languages were banned in schools. There are 59 different Indigenous groups, as scheduled by the Nepali government, that have their own unique languages and cultural practices. These languages are in a critical situation as their domains are narrowing due to the increasingly widespread use of Nepali and English in the public sphere, particularly in education and official businesses (Yadava, 2007).

Although English is rarely used in interpersonal communications, it has a strong symbolic value in Nepal's public sphere. Historically, it is known as the language of elites and middle- to high-class people (Phyak, 2013). While languages other than Nepali were banned in schools until the 1990s, the state had promoted English to cater to the needs of high-class elites (Giri, 2010). In addition, the elites used to send their children to various parts of India, such as Darjeeling and Gangtok, for an English-medium education. After the 1990s, the Nepali nation-state adopted a neoliberal ideology in its policies and allowed private companies and individuals to open private schools (Phyak, 2016b). English is the *de facto* medium of instruction in these private schools. More strikingly, these schools do not follow the state's language education policies. Regarding the medium of instruction, the Ministry of Education created an unclear and dubious policy in 2006. On the one hand, it states that the medium of instruction for school education should be 'Nepali or English, or both'; on the other hand, it mentions that the '[Indigenous] mother tongues can be the medium of instruction at the basic level of education'. This policy not only legitimizes the use of EMI in private schools but also creates a hierarchy of languages. Moreover, this policy statement has created a backdoor route for private schools to legitimize their illegal anti-multilingual education policy. Despite the recognition of Nepali and Indigenous mother tongue education, the new policy has, in effect, given public schools the forced choice to select English as the medium of instruction. Consequently, there is now an increasing trend of EMI in public schools. Local governments and public schools defend the adoption of the EMI policy 'as the demand of time' to compete with private schools (Phyak, 2016b). However, Seel *et al.* (2015) contend that the 'ad-hoc switching' from Nepali to EMI is an example of 'weak governance' and lack of public awareness about the value of multilingual education.

The Nepali Ministry of Education has recently published a national education policy and reiterated that Nepali and local mother tongues should be the medium of instruction in basic education (Grades 1–8). The policy further states that mathematics and science subjects can also be taught in English (Ministry of Education, Science and Technology,

2019: 19). At the same time, the policy focuses on adopting a mother tongue-based multilingual education (MTB-MLE) in multilingual classes. According to the MTB-MLE policy, the children's mother tongues should be used as a medium of instruction in the early grades to teach academic content subjects (Phyak, 2013). More importantly, the policy includes the following provisions to promote the use of mother tongues:

- Mother tongues should be given a *significant space* in school curricula and textbooks to preserve and promote mother tongues.
- Federal, provincial and local governments could organize special programs to develop audio-visual, communicative and educational materials in mother tongues.

These policies are promising in their textual forms, but they are hardly implemented in practice. Although the rhetoric of these policies shows the Nepali nation-state's commitment to recognizing the value of local mother tongues, the plans for structural transformations and support for teachers, communities and schools are neglected. Due to a lack of training and education, schools and teachers are not fully aware of how local Indigenous languages can be used as a pedagogical resource in teaching–learning activities. In this situation, local Indigenous languages are continually displaced from school spaces (Poudel & Choi, 2020). In this chapter, I thus focus on how public schools in Nepal are creating and reproducing unequal language policies that devalue the importance of Indigenous languages in education. More specifically, I analyze how schools construct and promote deficit language ideologies and linguistic inequalities through their language policies. My analytical perspectives are informed by the notion of linguicism (Skutnabb-Kangas, 1988), as discussed earlier, which provides insights into analyzing the ideologies, structures and practices that support linguistic inequalities and hierarchies in this context.

Critical Ethnography as the Method of the Study

This chapter is based on a critical ethnographic study of language education policy and practices in a public school, River School (pseudonym), in a rural village in Eastern Nepal. Critical ethnography builds on the assumption that language education policies are sociocultural practices that are embedded in wider political and economic ideologies. My perspectives about critical ethnography as an engaged process are informed here by the work of Davis and Phyak (2017), who argue that critical ethnographers should engage participants in critical dialogue about the sociopolitical conditions of language policies. In theorizing the notion of 'engaged language policy', Davis and Phyak (2017) discuss the importance of engaging language policy actors in analyzing language ideologies, and their historical and political roots in ethnographically situated dialogues. They further argue that it is important to engage language policy actors, particularly those on the margins, in critical ideological dialogue to transform unequal language policies.

Considering language policy as a social construct, my critical ethnographic approach focuses on how policies create and reproduce inequalities and discriminatory ideologies. As Heller (2011: 10) claims, the power of critical ethnography lies in 'its ability to follow social processes across time and space, and to see how agency and structure engage each other under specific political economic conditions'. In this study, I thus focus on how 'the complexities of power works' (Heller, 2011: 11). In doing so, I pay close attention to how the public school in this study, River School, controls the language policy-making process, thereby creating and reproducing linguistic hierarchies, instead of creating a multilingual school space. I also do not just observe language policies and practices in this public school, but also engage teachers and parents in critical dialogue about the past, present and future of Indigenous languages in education in Nepal.

The school is located in a relatively low-income and semi-agrarian community. Historically, the livelihood of the community members relied on subsistence agriculture. However, recently, there has been an increasing trend of community members joining the foreign labor market, mostly in the Gulf. Most parents of River School children have been to *bidesh* (foreign countries) as migrant laborers to support the livelihood of their families. The *bidesh*-going culture has created a new discourse and social imagination in the community. There have been three significant changes in the community due to this emergent culture. First, most parents have started emigrating to cities for an imagined *sukhi jeevan* (a good life), a new and modern lifestyle which takes them away from their traditional, agriculture-oriented lifestyle. Second, the number of private schools has increased in the village. There are now three new private schools in the community. As the head teacher of River School observes, these private schools are catering to the interests of the parents and families who mostly are in *bidesh* and can accordingly pay the tuition fees for their children.

Established in 1986, the majority (almost 85%) of the school's students come from a Limbu Indigenous background. The students predominantly speak Limbu at home and in the community. The school was initially established via a community initiative, which built the physical infrastructure and hired teachers locally (cf. McCarty, this volume). As one of the founders of the school says 'all of us were very excited to run a school. We had a dream that no children will remain illiterate in our community'. In the beginning, the school was run in a bamboo-thatched shed. The community members collected rice from each household to pay the locally hired teachers. In an interview, one founder of the school states 'it was not easy to run the school. But we worked hard and succeeded to establish it'. Unfortunately, the current number of students is decreasing because of the presence of low-cost private schools in the village. In a series of interviews, River School's head teacher states that, within the past decade, there has been a growing 'craze' of sending children to private schools. So, the school now has only 93 students across five grades. In some classes, there are only five students. The head teacher remembers that they used to have about 300 students. Currently, there are six teachers in the school; four of them have taught for about 20 years while two have taught for five years. While two teachers can speak Limbu as their mother tongue, other teachers speak Nepali as their first language.

In order to understand the existing language policy situation, I stayed in the community episodically for about seven months between 2014 and 2019. To unravel hidden ideologies, beliefs and assumptions about languages and language policies, I observed classes and had dialogic discussions with the parents and teachers. The observations were focused on collecting information related to language practices in the classroom, school premises and the community. Field notes were taken to record the observational data. Such observational data were used as a resource for critical dialogue with the teachers and parents to analyze the ideological dimensions of the current language policies and practices in the school (see Davis & Phyak, 2017). The notion of *critique* remains at the center of data analyses and interpretations. For Heller (2011: 34), engaging in a critique involves 'describing, understanding, and explaining the relations of social difference and social inequality that shape our world'. In this study, the critique involves the analysis of 'the processes that underlie the ways in which social difference is bound up in relations of inequality' (Heller, 2011: 35) and focuses on how languages are categorized unequally, thereby contributing to linguistic stratification. In other words, I discuss how River School has given unequal social, cultural and economic values to languages in its policies, and analyze their relationships with social inequalities. While unravelling linguistic injustices and inequalities, my critical ethnographic analyses focus on the historicity and situatedness (Codó & Pérez-Milans, 2014) of River School's language policies. Situating its policies in the broader sociopolitical ideologies and discourses, I pay attention to 'challenging established views, not only of language but of symbolic capital in societies in general' (Blommaert, 2009: 266).

As an engaged ethnographer, my positionality is informed by the assumption that researchers have 'an ethical responsibility to address processes of unfairness or injustice within a particular *lived* domain' (Madison, 2019: 4; emphasis in original). For this reason, I discuss the process of my engagement with teachers and community members 'to understand, inform and transform policies and practices of language (in) learning and teaching' (Hornberger, 2013: 115). The discussion 'takes us beneath surface appearances, disrupts the status quo, and unsettles both neutrality and taken-for-granted assumptions by bringing to light underlying and obscure operations of power and control' (Madison, 2019: 4). More importantly, this process contributes to transforming unequal language policies by unravelling linguistic inequalities which are otherwise considered natural and common practices (Davis & Phyak, 2017). In the remainder of the chapter, I discuss how River School's policy has strengthened deficit languages ideologies and contributed to the erasure of Indigenous languages in the region.

Erasure and Deficit Ideologies of Indigenous Languages

In the whole district, River School was one of the first schools to introduce the Limbu (Yaakthung) language as a subject of teaching two decades ago. As claimed by the former chairperson of the school management committee (SMC) and a community leader, it was like *falaamko chiuraa chapaaeko* (chewing beaten rice of iron) to introduce the Limbu language in the school. On the one hand, it was not easy to convince the parents about the importance of the Limbu language in education. On the other hand, they did not receive much support from the district education office to hire, pay and train the teacher who was appointed to teach the Limbu language. The SMC collaborated with Yaakthung Chumlung, the national organization of the Limbu Indigenous people, to collect the textbooks for teaching Limbu. In the beginning, the teacher, who could speak Limbu, was assigned to teach the Limbu language and sent to participate in some teacher training programs organized by Yaakthung Chumlung. *Aani Paan* (Our Language) was the textbook developed by Yaakthung Chumlung in collaboration with the Curriculum Development Center (CDC).

According to the national curriculum framework, schools could either develop a 'local curriculum' or teach 'mother tongues' (CDC, 2008). The local curriculum includes topics such as agriculture, history, customs, rituals and the related content representing the local community. River School had opted for *mother tongue* to teach Limbu as a subject to all students, irrespective of their ethnic and linguistic backgrounds. Nepali and English are compulsory subjects in the existing curriculum from the first grade (CDC, 2019). However, both languages are not predominantly used in children's homes. In 2014, I had observed classes and school activities and talked with the teachers, students and parents. Even the non-Limbu-speaking students told me that they had enjoyed learning Limbu. For them, learning Limbu had helped them interact with their Limbu-speaking friends and parents in the community. However, the Limbu language class was terminated in 2018 and additional English has been introduced in the school instead. In an interview, the head teacher told me that the SMC decided to introduce additional English (replacing Limbu) and an EMI policy to help students develop their English proficiency. He had reiterated that the school committee felt this need because other schools in the village have already initiated this new policy and the Resource Center (the institution responsible for looking after the schools in the village) had also asked public schools to adopt an EMI policy.

River School's new language policy to replace Limbu with additional English and implement an EMI policy, as claimed by the teacher, found no resistance from the community members. The head teacher claims that the policy is based on parents' 'desire' to see their children proficient in English. In our initial conversations, he had argued that 'parents did not show their interest to promote mother tongue education because of the "increasing craze" of English in the community'. Since some children have already joined the low-cost private schools, recently opened in the community, the discourse regarding English and EMI has become hegemonic in the public sphere. The head teacher claims that by teaching additional English, the students will be able to develop English proficiency to facilitate the implementation of the EMI policy effectively. With this new policy, textbooks for all subjects, written in English, have been introduced from the first grade. One of the major ideologies that emerges from the discussions with the teachers and parents is that the EMI policy has been deeply hegemonic because the dominant public discourse of educational reforms glorifies English as a symbol of 'quality education' (Phyak, 2016b). The head teacher, for example, reiterates that, 'without focusing on English, parents don't believe in the quality of public schools'. He further rationalizes that they have felt an 'increased pressure' to introduce the EMI policy in the school because of growing 'demands' from parents. For him, the new policy is 'an unopposed and appropriate policy' for the school because English is the language of 'quality education', 'better future [for] children' and the 'international job market'. The valorization of English eventually contributes to the 'erasure' (Irvine & Gal, 2000) of Indigenous languages from the school (Poudel & Choi, 2020). Erasure is the process by which 'ideological outliers [...] are either discounted as being anomalous or disregarded altogether and ignored' (Andronis, 2004: 264). The space for the Limbu mother tongue has been erased from River School because knowledge of Indigenous languages is misrecognized, is considered a symbol of educational deficiency, while their visibility does not fit into the dominant discourses of the current educational reform agendas.

River School's language policy supports the valorization of the English language ideology in the public sphere which glorifies English medium as a panacea for improving public education in Nepal (see Phyak, 2016a). While doing this, River School's policy reproduces a deficit ideology of Indigenous languages and multilingual education. According to Gorski (2011: 154), a deficit ideology 'can be understood as a sort of "blame the victim" mentality applied, not to an individual person, but systemically, to an entire group of people, often based upon a single dimension of identity'. In a series of dialogic discussions, the head teacher and the members of the SMC have consistently claimed that the Indigenous communities (Limbu, in the case of River School) 'are not aware of the importance of their own languages' and do not take the initiative to promote their mother tongues. In a group discussion, for example, the chair of the SMC (and a parent) states that 'if the concerned community is not aware and active, then the school alone cannot continue mother tongue education'. In another discussion, one of the teachers said that:

> The community has not taken a serious concern about mother tongue education. If the community and parents are not aware, then the school cannot do anything. Limbu parents are sending their children to private schools. They don't seem to believe in [the] quality of public schools. If parents do not send their children to public schools, it is not possible to implement mother tongue teaching.

While rationalizing the discontinuity of Limbu in the school, the entire Limbu community is blamed for being *unaware* and *inactive* in promoting mother tongue education. More importantly, the rationalization of the EMI policy positions the community, but not the school, as the sole responsible agency for the erasure of Limbu teaching. Such an assumption supports 'the belief that inequalities result, not from unjust social conditions [...] but from intellectual, moral, cultural, and behavioral deficiencies assumed to be inherent in disenfranchised individuals and communities' (Gorski, 2011: 154). This deficit ideology ignores the historicity of structural inequalities and unequal power relations among languages. Nepal has gone through a long history of oppressive linguistic and cultural policies to support a one-nation-one-state ideology (Phyak & Ojha, 2019; Weinberg, 2013). In the pre-1990 era, Nepal's language policies were largely shaped by the ideology of monolingual nationalism, which not only constructed the symbolic identity of Nepali as the *national* and *official* language but also prohibited the use of local mother tongues in education and other public spheres (Yadava, 2007). Scholars have been critical of the negative impacts of the one-nation-one-state ideology on Nepal's linguistic diversity, particularly in Indigenous communities. Giri (2011), for example, argues that, by imposing a restrictive monolingual policy, the ruling elites performed an 'invisible politics' of privileging the Nepali language and devaluing Nepal's rich linguistic and cultural diversity. Giri's analysis shows that the ruling elites, who hold the sociopolitical power to develop and implement language policies at the national and local level, have hardly paid any attention to developing appropriate plans, or shown their commitment to ensure citizens' right to education in their mother tongues, as ostensibly enshrined in the constitution (Giri, 2011; Turin, 2007). Rather, as Giri (2011) claims, the elites have been influential in creating language policies that privilege the power of the dominant languages, Nepali and English. In this sense, the discontinuing of mother tongue teaching – as, for example, Limbu in River School – is the product of invisible politics in local language education policy with a visible impact, the erasure of Indigenous languages from school. These politics disregard the struggles and agency of the community, as seen in the past SMC chair's comments above, to introduce Indigenous languages in schools.

At the center of the invisible politics of language education policy remains the stigmatization of Indigenous languages. Although studies have shown the pedagogical, educational and social importance of multilingualism (Skutnabb-Kangas & Heugh, 2012), children's home languages, particularly Indigenous languages, are discursively stigmatized as a symbol of incompetence, disadvantage, unemployment and low sociopolitical/economic prestige. In this regard, during a focus group discussion, one of the teachers in River School claimed that:

> Nowadays, parents go to foreign countries for employment. There, they face language problems due to lack of English. They want their children to learn English so that they [the children] don't have to face any problem[s] when they go to a foreign country in the future. The craze of English has increased because of the increasing tendency to leave the village for the foreign employment. Mother tongues don't have much value in this modern society. [They are not] used in [the] job market, technology, and media. So, people don't show interest in mother tongue education.

The valorization of the EMI policy is shaped by the global neoliberal ideology, which considers English as the dominant language of a free market economy (Holborow, 2015). In the context of River School, the discourse of the EMI policy is heavily impacted by the culture of leaving the village for employment in the migrant labor market, particularly in the Gulf, and other countries such as Malaysia and South Korea. For the last two decades, the number of Nepalis joining the global labor market has been increasing. About 25,000 Nepali youth leave the country every month to join the cheap and exploitative global labor market (Government of Nepal, 2020). Most parents and/or family members in the River School community have joined the foreign labor market to 'earn money and support the livelihood of their family', as one of the parents observed. When remittances began to flow into the village, parents started to migrate to the nearby cities, mostly for their children's education. The common discourse among the villagers, as shared by a parent, is that 'with the hard-earned money they would like to send their kids to "a good school"'. For the parents, the schools that help their children develop better English language proficiency are believed to be these 'good schools'. The imagined future of securing jobs in the labor market thus glorifies the value of English as the language of employment while stigmatizing local mother tongues as the languages-of-no-value in modern society. Such stigmatization of Indigenous languages not only misrecognizes the educational and cultural values of children's home languages, but also constructs Indigenous language speakers' identity as deficient individuals, while invisibilizing their linguistic and cultural knowledge (Kovats Sánchez, 2018). In what follows, I discuss how this situation has normalized social injustice and language hierarchies in the broader national context of Nepal.

Normalizing Social Injustice and Language Hierarchies

Although Nepal's constitution and national education policies provide space for children's mother tongues in education, schools across the country are not paying much attention to creating a multilingual school environment (Phyak & Ojha, 2019). They are not only creating language hierarchies but also, and more importantly, normalizing social injustices. In the case of River School, before the implementation of the new EMI policy, students could freely communicate in Limbu with their friends and teachers at school. Since their home language was used in the school, they did not experience that speaking Limbu could be a symbol of personal deficiency. But with the implementation of the new EMI policy, the Indigenous Limbu students now feel 'uncomfortable' to speak Limbu.

Prem: Why don't you speak Limbu?
Student: Nobody speaks it in school.
Prem: Why?
Student: People don't like it.
Prem: But you speak at home, right?
Student: Yes. At home I should speak Limbu with my parents and siblings. But in school I don't speak because it is not taught in school.
Prem: Right. But you can still speak Limbu here.
Student: Yes. But I feel uncomfortable. Friends may tease us if we speak Limbu. They laugh. They say many things.

As seen in the above excerpt from an informal discussion with one of the students, the new EMI policy has a deeply negative impact on Indigenous students' confidence about speaking in their home language. As the focus of the school has shifted from a multilingual to a monolingual (English medium) policy, the students are implicitly embracing/internalizing the deficit ideology of Indigenous languages. Students, as mentioned above, when asked why they do not speak Limbu in the school, straightforwardly respond that 'people don't like it'. The new policy has created an unequal linguistic environment where the Indigenous children are teased and laughed at for using their home languages. Consequently, as one of the parents comments, the Indigenous children feel 'ashamed of speaking Limbu, thus losing their repertoire of home languages'. This situation indicates that Nepal's public schools, as part of the state apparatus, are not creating equal and safe spaces for their Indigenous children. Like River School, schools across the country are imposing an EMI policy and creating a hostile linguistic environment where Indigenous and language-minoritized children feel discriminated against for speaking their home languages. This situation is against Nepal's constitutional provisions that guarantee that its citizens are not discriminated against in terms of their linguistic, cultural and ethnic backgrounds.

The erasure of Limbu in River School is an example of how schools normalize language hierarchies and social injustice. A series of classroom observations show that the students are not fully participating in the classroom activities, which are predominantly teacher centered and textbook based. Teachers rely fully on the English language textbooks; they read the lines from the textbook and ask students to reproduce the same lines. Teachers are not able to provide explicit instructions and comprehensible input on the content related to science, social studies and other subjects, including English. The data from the ethnographic field notes show that the students in River School mostly remain silent throughout the class period and hardly ask questions of their teachers. As seen in the following excerpt, the students try to ask questions in Nepali, but teachers insist that they speak English:

Teacher: We live in a family. Where do we live?
Students: [silent]
Teacher: We live in a family. [asks students to repeat]
Students: We live in a fa-mi-ly [repeat]
Student 1: Sir family *bhaneko ghar ho*? [Sir, is family a house?]
Teacher: No. It's family. *Pariwaar* [family]. But you should speak and understand in English. We are reading an English textbook. Who are in your family?
Students: [silent]

The above excerpt is taken from one of the observation notes from a Grade 2 social studies class. The teacher is teaching about 'family' and the 'professions of parents', as mentioned in the textbook. The professions include farmer, shopkeeper, mason, teacher and official. The teacher begins the class by writing the title of the lesson and describing it in English. As seen in the above excerpt, he tells the students that 'we live in a family' and asks 'where do we live?'. However, the students remain silent, thus the teacher answers the question himself and asks them to reproduce what he says. The students try to ask questions in Nepali, but the teacher forces them to 'speak and understand in English' because they are 'reading an English textbook'. Again, the teacher asks students about their family members in English, but they remain silent. Throughout the class, the students get very few opportunities to express their opinions on the questions that the teacher asks. Teacher–student interactions hardly exist, nor do the students participate in the meaning-making processes to understand the contents of teaching due to the obvious language barrier. This kind of silence in the classroom constructs learners' identity as 'submissive subordinate' (Gilmore, 1985). King (2012) argues that silencing in the classroom symbolizes 'students' lack of power' and it works as a teacher's tool for controlling students. While silencing students' voices, the new EMI language policy in River School thus constructs and normalizes injustices through its teaching–learning processes. It restricts the students from expressing their ideas freely and diminishes the relevance of their prior linguistic knowledge.

In silencing students' voices, River School's new language policy perpetuates 'epistemic injustice' (Fricker, 2007). Epistemic injustice is a form of social injustice that 'wrongs someone in their capacity as a subject of knowledge' (Fricker, 2007: 5). Since the students in River School are not allowed to express their ideas and thoughts in their home languages, they are positioned as passive subjects that reproduce what the textbooks and teachers say. By misrecognizing students' prior knowledge, both linguistic and cultural, the new language policy positions them as non-epistemic beings (see Phyak, 2016b). Moreover, the students are dehumanized by not being allowed to speak freely, or to invest their existing knowledge and identities in learning processes. Consequently, they are not able to access the knowledge in the curricula, nor can they fully participate in classroom interactions, due to a lack of competence in English. However, the teachers and the school assume such epistemic injustice to be a natural process.

In a series of dialogues, the head teacher and other teachers have agreed that the new policy does not necessarily help their students learn effectively. In those dialogues, the teachers have been provided with the opportunities to critically reflect on their own experiences of teaching in English and to analyze how the new policy has impacted on teaching–learning activities. As the teachers reflect on their classes, they become aware of the fact that the new policy is not promoting meaningful learning and student participation in the classroom activities. For example, a social studies teacher states:

> Due to the new policy, our students are more disadvantaged [than before]. They aren't learning what we expect them to learn from the curriculum. Students aren't able to understand the content from the translated textbooks [in English]. Teaching in English is not easy for us [teachers] as well. I don't think that we have a good [enough] English proficiency to teach all the subjects in English. It isn't effective.

The community of teachers in River School agree that the new policy is less relevant for both students and teachers. Since students are learning English as a foreign language, they have not yet fully developed the English language proficiency needed to understand and invest in learning academic contents. Likewise, the teachers, except for English as a subject, are not recruited to teach in an English-medium school. In this regard, the head teacher reflects:

> This policy [EMI policy] is not realistic. The children read and write *kanikuthi* [by force] what's given in the textbook. My experience tells [me] that students aren't learning both language and content effectively. Poor students! How can they learn effectively in English? [...] they hardly understand it. The English medium policy is just for a name's sake.

As the head teacher reflects on his experiences implementing the new EMI policy, he becomes critical about how it is detrimental to effective teaching and learning. He agrees that the policy is forcing children to learn in a language (English) which they hardly understand. However, the head teacher confesses that the school was 'forced' to introduce the EMI policy because other schools had already implemented it. For him, the ongoing dominant discourse of education reform is responsible for the 'forced implementation' of the policy in the school. He argues that public schools are told to introduce the EMI policy by the authorities from the local government and 'advertise it [EMI policy] like what private schools do'.

After the second year of its implementation, the school had *gahiro chhalafal* (a serious discussion) on the relevance of the new policy. The teachers agreed that the policy was not appropriate and assessed whether they could stop implementing it. However, they decided to continue the policy because, as one of the teachers says, 'the withdrawal from the policy would give "a wrong message" to the parents and community that the school and teachers are not competent to teach in English'. He also states that 'if the school doesn't implement the EMI policy, the parents send their children to private schools'. These remarks clearly indicate that public schools are accepting and normalizing social injustice by imposing a language policy that does not necessarily help students invest their prior knowledge, identities and cognition in the learning process.

While normalizing social injustice through the EMI policy, the public schools in Nepal are further strengthening the linguistic hierarchies created by existing structural inequalities. The teaching of English as a compulsory subject begins from the first grade. In addition, most public schools, including River School, are teaching additional English by replacing a 'local subject' (which includes mother tongues). In this context, the EMI policy is another mechanism which strengthens the power of English and invisibilizes the existence and importance of local languages in education. As the head teacher argues, River School has introduced the EMI policy because English is 'widely accepted as the language of the educated people and employment. It's been known as the symbol of high social prestige. So, it is unopposed'. As Sah and Karki (2020) have argued, the EMI policy thus supports the ideological power of neoliberalism and serves the interest of existing elites. While reproducing the neoliberal ideology, River School's policy discursively positions the identity of local Indigenous languages as 'irrelevant for quality education', 'a language of the poor' and 'a language of home only'.

Conclusion

In this chapter, I have analyzed how the new language policy that focuses on English, both as an additional subject and a medium of instruction, is erasing the space and significance of Indigenous languages in education in Nepal's public schools. The critical ethnographic analyses of River School's language policy indicate that the public schools are becoming a space for strengthening what Skutnabb-Kangas (2012) calls 'linguicism' by creating the policies and practices that support language hierarchies and social injustice. At the center of linguicism lies the EMI policy, which not only glorifies English medium instruction as a way to improve the 'quality of education' but also, and most importantly, discursively stigmatizes local Indigenous languages as inappropriate and unnecessary in education. This phenomenon is closely linked with the 'ideological hegemony' (Blommaert, 2006) of English as the language of the global neoliberal market. The privatization of education and the foreign labor market are two major neoliberal forces that have contributed to creating and reinforcing the symbolic power of English in Nepal's educational policy reform discourses. The neoliberal legitimization of English as an uncontested medium of instruction is closely linked with the interests and ideologies of elites (Sah & Karki, 2020). National policies have historically promoted English as a medium and subject of teaching, even during the era of restrictive Nepali monolingual nationalism, to cater to the needs of elites.

Although the chapter analyzes language policy in only one public school, three major insights can be drawn in relation to language education policies more broadly. First, the erasure of Indigenous languages, like Limbu, in schools is the continuation of historical inequalities supported by oppressive linguistic nationalism and free-market neoliberalism. The critical ethnographic analysis of River School's language policy shows that neoliberal ideology plays a critical role in shaping the dominant discourse of what counts as a legitimate language and medium of instruction in education. Critical ethnography, as discussed in this chapter, helps to understand the situatedness and historicity of the EMI policy and unravels how it contributes to the erasure of local Indigenous languages. Second, critical ethnographic analyses provide insights into understanding the subtleties of social injustice in schools. As discussed in this chapter, the erasure of Indigenous languages diminishes and misrecognizes the identity of Indigenous language speakers as epistemic beings (Phyak, 2016b). Consequently, they are disadvantaged with respect to their freedom of expression in the learning process, as well as access to knowledge they are entitled to obtain from the curricula.

Third, and most importantly, the critical ethnographic analysis of River School's new language policy indicates that the EMI policy is an embodiment of 'ideological domestication' which, as Thomas (1993: 8) argues, 'not only leads to a form of benign ignorance, but also absolves us from certain kinds of social responsibility'. The case of River School clearly indicates that the public schools in Nepal are not taking an agentive role to disrupt unequal language policies that support linguistic hierarchies and discriminatory language ideologies. Rather, they become an ideological space that strengthens deficit ideologies about Indigenous languages by 'recycling its [their] own misperceptions, all of which justify inequalities' (Gorski, 2011: 6). The continuity of the EMI policy, despite being irrelevant in the early grades, reproduces a deficit ideology which manipulates 'popular consciousness in order to deflect attention from the systemic conditions and socio-political context that underlie or exacerbate inequities' (Gorski, 2011: 156).

That said, this chapter also shows how underlying language ideologies can be unraveled, challenged and transformed by engaging language policy actors in critical dialogue (Davis & Phyak, 2017). In sum, this chapter shows that critical ethnographers have two major responsibilities: (a) to observe, document and analyze the historicity, situatedness and political economic conditions in which (unequal) language policies are created, negotiated and implemented; and (b) to engage language policy actors, as Davis and Phyak (2017) have argued, in critical dialogues to help them analyze, understand and resist language ideologies and political conditions that shape their agency and reinforce unequal policies.

Acknowledgments

This study is funded by the project State of Social Inclusion in Nepal (SOSIN), a collaborative project between the Central Department of Anthropology, Tribhuvan University Nepal and USAID Kathmandu. I am grateful to the reviewers and the editors, Stephen May and Blanca Caldas, for their feedback on an earlier version of the chapter. Of course, any remaining errors in the chapter are mine.

References

Anderson, B. (1991) *Imagined Communities: Reflections on the Origin and Spread of Nationalism*. London: Verso.

Andronis, M.A. (2004) Iconization, fractal recursivity, and erasure: Linguistic ideologies and standardization in Quichua-speaking Ecuador. *Texas Linguist Forum* 47, 263–269.

Block, D., Gray, J. and Holborow, M. (2013) *Neoliberalism and Applied Linguistics*. London: Routledge.

Blommaert, J. (2006) Language policy and national identity. In T. Ricento (ed.) *An Introduction to Language Policy: Theory and Method* (pp. 238–254). Malden, MA: Blackwell.

Blommaert, J. (2009) Ethnography and democracy: Hymes' political theory of language. *Text & Talk* 29 (3), 257–276.

CDC (2008) *Curriculum for Primary Level*. Kirtipur: Curriculum Development Center.

CDC (2019) *National Curriculum Framework for School Education*. Kirtipur: Curriculum Development Center.

Codó, E. and Pérez-Milans, M. (2014) Multilingual discursive practices and processes of social change in globalising institutional spaces: A critical ethnographic perspective. *International Journal of Multilingualism* 11 (4), 381–388.

Davis, K.A. and Phyak, P. (2017) *Engaged Language Policy and Practices*. New York: Routledge.

De Korne, H., López Gopar, M.E. and Rios Rios, K. (2019) Changing ideological and implementational spaces for minoritised languages in higher education: Zapotequización of language education in Mexico. *Journal of Multilingual and Multicultural Development* 40 (6), 504–517.

Fricker, M. (2007) *Epistemic Injustice: Power and the Ethics of Knowing*. Oxford: Oxford University Press.

Gilmore, P. (1985) Silence and sulking: Emotional displays in the classroom. In D. Tannen and M. Saville-Troike (eds) *Perspectives on Silence* (pp. 139–162). Norwood, NJ: Ablex.

Giri, R.A. (2010) Cultural anarchism: The consequences of privileging languages in Nepal. *Journal of Multilingual and Multicultural Development* 31 (1), 87–100.

Giri, R.A. (2011) Languages and language politics: How invisible language politics produces visible results in Nepal. *Language Problems & Language Planning* 35 (3), 197–221.

Gorski, P.C. (2011) Unlearning deficit ideology and the scornful gaze: Thoughts on authenticating the class discourse in education. *Counterpoints* 402, 152–173.

Government of Nepal (2020) *Nepal Labor Migration Report – 2020*. Katmandu: Ministry of Labor, Employment and Social Security.

Heller, M. (2010) The commodification of language. *Annual Review of Anthropology* 39, 101–114.

Heller, M. (2011) *Paths to Post-Nationalism: A Critical Ethnography of Language and Identity*. Oxford: Oxford University Press.

Holborow, M. (2015) *Language and Neoliberalism*. Milton Park: Routledge.

Hornberger, N.H. (2006) Voice and biliteracy in indigenous language revitalization: Contentious educational practices in Quechua, Guarani, and Māori contexts. *Journal of Language, Identity, and Education* 5 (4), 277–292.

Hornberger, N.H. (2013) Negotiating methodological rich points in the ethnography of language policy. *International Journal of the Sociology of Language* 2013 (219), 101–122.

Irvine, J.T. and Gal, S. (2000) Language ideology and linguistic differentiation. In P. Kroskrity (ed.) *Regimes of Language* (pp. 35–83). Santa Fe, NM: School of American Research Press.

Khati, A.R. (2011) When and why of mother tongue use in English classrooms. *Journal of NELTA* 16 (1–2), 42–51.

Khati, A. (2015) EMI in Nepal: A passport to a competitive world or a commodity to sell? A case study. *ELT Choutari*. See http://eltchoutari.com/2015/08/emi-in-nepal-a-passport-to-a-competitive-world-or-a-commodity-to-sell-a-case-study/.

King, J. (2012) Silence in the second language classrooms of Japanese universities. *Applied Linguistics* 34 (3), 1–20.

Kovats Sánchez, G. (2018) Reaffirming indigenous identity: Understanding experiences of stigmatization and marginalization among Mexican Indigenous college students. *Journal of Latinos and Education* 19, 1–14.

Kroskrity, P.V. (2004) Language ideologies. In A. Duranti (ed.) *A Companion to Linguistic Anthropology* (pp. 496–517). Oxford: Blackwell Publishing.

Kroskrity, P.V. (2010) Language ideologies: Evolving perspectives. *Society and Language Use* 7 (3), 192–205.

Lippi-Green, R. (1997) *English with an Accent. Language, Ideology, and Discrimination in the United States*. London: Routledge.

Madison, D.S. (2019) *Critical Ethnography: Methods, Ethics, Performance* (3rd edn). London: Sage.

May, S. and Hill, R. (2008) Māori-medium education: Current issues and challenges. In N. Hornberger (ed.) *Can Schools Save Indigenous Languages? Policy and Practice on Four Continents* (pp. 66–98). London: Palgrave Macmillan.

McCarty, T.L. (2003) Revitalising indigenous languages in homogenising times. *Comparative Education* 39 (2), 147–163.

Milroy, J. (2001) Language ideologies and the consequences of standardization. *Journal of Sociolinguistics* 5 (4), 530–555.

Ministry of Education, Science and Technology (2019) *National Education Policy – 2019*. Kathmandu: Government of Nepal.

Nepal Law Commission (2016) *Constitution of Nepal 2015*. Kathmandu: Government of Nepal.

Phyak, P. (2013) Language ideologies and local languages as the medium-of-instruction policy: A critical ethnography of a multilingual school in Nepal. *Current Issues in Language Planning* 14 (1), 127–143.

Phyak, P. (2016a) Local–global tension in the ideological construction of English language Education policy in Nepal. In R. Kirkpatrick (ed.) *English Language Education Policy in Asia* (pp. 199–217). Heidelberg: Springer.

Phyak, P. (2016b) 'For our cho:tlung': Decolonizing language ideologies and (re)imagining multilingual education policies and practices in Nepal. Unpublished doctoral dissertation, the University of Hawai'i, Manoa.

Phyak, P. and Ojha, L.P. (2019) Language education policy and inequalities of multilingualism in Nepal. In A. Kirkpatrick and A.J. Liddicoat (eds) *The Routledge International Handbook of Language Education Policy in Asia* (pp. 341–354). London: Routledge.

Piller, I. (2016) *Linguistic Diversity and Social Justice: An Introduction to Applied Sociolinguistics*. Oxford: Oxford University Press.

Poudel, P.P. and Choi, T.H. (2020) Policymakers' agency and the structure: The case of medium of instruction policy in multilingual Nepal. *Current Issues in Language Planning* 1–20.

Sah, P.K. and Li, G. (2018) English medium instruction (EMI) as linguistic capital in Nepal: Promises and realities. *International Multilingual Research Journal* 12 (2), 109–123.

Sah, P.K. and Karki, J. (2020) Elite appropriation of English as a medium of instruction policy and epistemic inequalities in Himalayan schools. *Journal of Multilingual and Multicultural Development*. https://doi.org/10.1080/01434632.2020.1789154

Seel, A., Yadava, Y.P. and Kadel, S. (2015) *Medium of Instruction and Languages of Education (MILE): Ways Forward for Education Policy, Planning, and Practice in Nepal: Final Report*. Nepal: The Ministry of Education.

Skutnabb-Kangas, T. (1988) Multilingualism and the education of minority children. In T. Skutnabb-Kangas and J. Cummins (eds) *Minority Education: From Shame to Struggle* (pp. 9–44). Clevedon: Multilingual Matters.

Skutnabb-Kangas, T. (2015) Linguicism. In C.A. Chapelle (ed.) *The Encyclopedia of Applied Linguistics*. Hoboken, NJ: John Wiley & Sons.

Skutnabb-Kangas, T. and Heugh, K. (eds) (2012) *Multilingual Education and Sustainable Diversity Work: From Periphery to Center*. New York: Routledge.

Thomas, J. (1993) *Doing Critical Ethnography*. London: Sage.

Tollefson, J.W. (ed.) (2002) *Language Policies in Education: Critical Issues* (1st edn). Mahwah, NJ: Lawrence Erlbaum.

Tollefson, J. (2013) *Language Policies in Education: Critical Issues* (2nd edn). New York: Routledge.

Turin, M. (2007) *Linguistic Diversity and the Preservation of Endangered Languages: A Case Study from Nepal*. Katmandu: International Centre for Integrated Mountain Development.

Weinberg, M. (2013) Revisiting history in language policy: The case of medium of instruction in Nepal. *Working Papers in Educational Linguistics* 28 (1), 61–80.

Woolard, K.A. (1992) Language ideology: Issues and approaches. *Pragmatics* 2 (3), 235–249.

Yadava, Y.P. (2007, August) Linguistic diversity in Nepal: Perspectives on language policy. Paper presented at the International Seminar on Constitutionalism and Diversity in Nepal, Kathmandu, Nepal.

10 'But This Program is Not For Them!': Challenging the Gentrification of Dual Language Bilingual Education through Critical Ethnography

Dan Heiman and Michelle Yanes

> Because even though I don't go on the tours (for interested parents) and I try not to dip my toe in that, I'm there during planning time when people are checking in and I see the people who are coming in. And they're not the people I have in my classroom. So I think it's like a free McMillan (elite dual language private school in the city). (Michelle, Interview, 24 February 2016)

We begin this chapter with these words from Michelle[1] as an entry point into the current sociopolitical context of dual-language bilingual education (DLBE) in the United States. Michelle's view as a teacher of a DLBE program at Plainview Elementary that the (White) 'people' gentrifying the program were 'not the people' for whom bilingual education was designed highlights the broader gentrification of DLBE (Chaparro, 2020; Heiman & Murakami, 2019; Valdez *et al.*, 2016) amidst the explosive expansion of such programs in the US (Arias & Fee, 2018). This context provides the 'generative theme' (Freire, 1997) that ignited our particular curricular collaboration around this *same* sociopolitical context.

In this chapter, we document how critical ethnography maps wider social relationships and human experience from the local to the global (Means, 2013) and critically listens to, and advocates for, those being oppressed by processes such as gentrification (Barton, 2001; Madison, 2019). In particular, we critically examine the emergence, conceptualization and enactment of a curricular intervention around gentrification processes impacting Latinx students in '[Michelle's] classroom', while also providing yet another 'cautionary note' (Valdés, 1997) about the dangerous potential of the neoliberal exploitation of Latinx students by those 'people' who thirst for bilingualism (Cervantes-Soon, 2018; Morales & Maravilla, 2019). We believe it is urgent to examine how neoliberal processes in bilingual education that prioritize the logics of the market, individualism and the accumulation of human capital (Cervantes-Soon, 2014) take root 'on the ground' (Means, 2013) in DLBE contexts *and*, most importantly, challenge these processes by (re)centering the lives and realities of Latinx students and families through humanizing pedagogies that foment critical consciousness for all stakeholders (Palmer *et al.*, 2019). Our 'local' intervention positioned gentrification as a 'generative theme', a continuously and dialectically unfolding unresolved social problem that provides opportunities for students to engage in dialogue and struggle (Freire, 1997; Valenzuela, 2016). This local intervention in the form of a unit around gentrification talked back to 'global' processes being shaped by the recent 'discovery' (Flores, 2015), 'whitening' (Flores & García, 2017) and 'rebranding' (Katnelson & Bernstein, 2017) of DLBE at a time when 'tour[ists]' are 'checking [out]' how DLBE programs can augment one's human capital (De Lissovoy, 2015; Foucault, 2008).

Chapter Overview

We begin by providing the context and description of the critical ethnography at Plainview, along with the positionalities of Michelle (Author 2) and Dan (Author 1). We then situate the 'generative theme' in the current DLBE sociopolitical context that has brought bilingual education to the mainstream, specifically by mapping (Means, 2013) Plainview's local DLBE context to macro processes shaping DLBE at the national US level. Next, we discuss how critical scholars have addressed the current neoliberal hijacking of DLBE by highlighting the urgency of moving beyond DLBE's traditional goals of academic achievement, bilingualism/biculturalism and sociocultural competence to include a fourth goal around the development of critical consciousness (Cervantes-Soon *et al.*, 2017; Freire, 2020[2]; Palmer *et al.*, 2019). This fourth goal also has methodological implications. Due to inequities that have been documented at the policy, school, classroom and parent levels (Cervantes-Soon *et al.*, 2017), there is a pressing need to engage in humanizing research *with* stakeholders that addresses and challenges these same inequities (Paris & Winn, 2014; cf. McCarty, this volume). We then elaborate on how the critical ethnography took on new meaning as our critical listening of key stakeholders' perspectives of Plainview's transformation spurred our positioning of gentrification as a 'generative theme' (Freire, 1997) for a curricular intervention in Michelle's fifth-grade DLBE classroom (Heiman, 2021).

Context and Description of the Study

Dan carried out a year-long critical ethnography (Madison, 2019; Palmer & Caldas, 2015) at Plainview Elementary in 2015–2016. In Austin, Texas, the urban neighborhood near the city center where Plainview is located was experiencing rapid gentrification since the inception of the DLBE program in 2010. The critical ethnography at Plainview was inspired by the tremendous growth and potential gentrification of DLBE programs at the macro level, while also being focused on challenging this gentrification through the interrogation of dominant knowledges and paradigms. We find Means' (2013) perspectives around critical ethnography to be particularly insightful for the context of this study:

> Critical ethnography situates values and practices within the economic, cultural, and political forces that define and give them shape. This means that it is concerned with mapping wider social relationships and human experience from the local to the global and the universal to the particular. Rather than attempting to serve the status quo, critical ethnography seeks to interrogate and challenge existing forms of knowledge and social relations in the interest of promoting human freedom, dignity, and greater democracy in life. (Means, 2013: 50–51)

The original focus of the study was to examine how key stakeholders were experiencing and responding to gentrification processes that had turned Plainview into a 'magnet' for middle-class White families (Heiman & Murakami, 2019) and was guided by these overarching questions: (1) How did recent demographic shifts and processes shape an urban DLBE school?; and (2) How did stakeholders (administrators, teachers, parents) at the school respond to these demographic shifts and processes? During the study, Dan also spent a lot of time in Michelle's classroom, as her critical stance and pedagogy around issues of equity and social justice provided the impetus to pose a third research question: How did Michelle respond to these same shifts and processes through her pedagogy, curriculum and engagement with the community? This element transformed the study into a hopeful exploration, as the emergence of critical consciousness in her classroom took root at a time when this fourth goal of DLBE was being proposed due to rampant inequities in the field (Cervantes-Soon *et al.*, 2017).

Researcher Positionalities

The relationship between Michelle and Dan actually began the year before the critical ethnography, as they interacted at parent teacher association (PTA) meetings and other schoolwide functions where Dan oftentimes served as an interpreter. During one particular PTA meeting, he shared a *Rethinking Schools* article about inequities in parent involvement at a

DLBE school in San Francisco (Cornell Gonzáles, 2014), and it was here where Michelle voiced her critical perspectives about DLBE and how issues of equity and social justice should be front and center at Plainview. It was during this time that Dan was conceptualizing his critical ethnography, which prompted him to approach Michelle about possibly spending time in her classroom the following year due to her explicitness around centering the realities of Latinx students and families. In April 2015, he shared a lay summary (see Madison, 2019) with Michelle that outlined: (1) his rationale for researching gentrification processes at Plainview; (2) a description of the critical ethnographic methods he envisioned; and (3) how he planned to present findings to the Plainview administration and PTA. Michelle was excited about being part of the study, and her classroom became a generative space to document what DLBE's fourth goal of critical consciousness development looks like in practice. As Michelle and Dan became closer during the critical ethnography, she became an 'anthropological confidant', a participant who, due to her intimate relationships at/knowledges of the context, provides crucial insight and perspectives (Foley & Valenzuela, 2005). This relationship offered Dan a more nuanced and deeper understanding of local events and relationships at the school level and in her classroom, while also presenting her agentic opportunities to collaborate in the research process.

Michelle, who described herself as Salvadoran at heart, but Canadian in spirit (her family fled El Salvador when Michelle was age three), described her role at Plainview:

> And my job at Plainview is to be a dual language teacher, the Spanish version. So here you go, this is what I do. And I also think that it empowers my culture, and I also think it empowers my language. It empowers my culture. It empowers the parents that speak my language. So, it's a tool of empowerment to oftentimes people who have been pushed out of Plainview... So it's always Spanish first. All our newsletters, all our emails. Everything. And so that's why I got hired at Plainview and that's what I'm gonna do. (Interview, 27 April 2016)

At the time of the study, Michelle was in her eleventh year of teaching and in her second year as a DLBE teacher at Plainview, as she looped with her students from fourth grade. Her critical approach to DLBE was guided by her personal goals of 'Spanish, love, content, not in that order', and revealed on many occasions that the complex history of bilingual education meant that she was at Plainview to first and foremost serve Latinx students (Heiman & Yanes, 2018). Michelle's emphasis on the 'people who have been pushed out of Plainview' meant that Spanish was much more than a purely linguistic endeavor. It was most importantly centered on the *people* who spoke Spanish as a native language and who were most impacted by gentrification processes.

Dan's privileged positionality as a White, cisgender male, researcher, parent and activist at Plainview offered a unique and challenging vantage point that provided multiple points of access, emotions and learning. Madison (2019: 6) exhorts critical ethnographers to acknowledge their positionality, as 'it forces us to acknowledge our own power, privilege, and biases as we denounce the power structures that surround our subjects. A concern for positionality is a reflexive ethnography; it is a turning back on ourselves'. The fact that he comes from the dominant group that has become adept at 'discovering' (Flores, 2015) and 'colonizing the imagination' (De Lissovoy, 2015) of DLBE realities cannot be overlooked. Even though Dan is fluent in Spanish, was a bilingual teacher in El Paso, Texas, a teacher educator in Mexico, and is committed to issues of equity and social justice in bilingual education spaces, his Whiteness undoubtedly facilitated a sense of comfort and trust with key stakeholders at Plainview. He was, in a sense, complicit in the 'discovery' of Plainview, as even though he is married to a Mexican-American woman and is part of a bilingual/bicultural family, his son was able to transfer to the school because their neighborhood school did not offer a DLBE program. In spite of this power and privilege, he was intent on engaging in activist work at Plainview as the lead facilitator of the school's DLBE committee, and at the district level where he advocated at parent and school board meetings for the expansion of DLBE programs for Latinx communities.

Data Sources and Participants

The findings we present in this chapter highlight the myriad perspectives that Dan captured during the year-long critical ethnography. Semi-structured interviews with three veteran teachers and the principal (all of whom were at Plainview prior to DLBE and gentrification), along with two Latinx parents, are included to shed light on research questions one and two about the demographic shifts and how these key stakeholders were making sense of these shifts. Field notes from three classroom events, one initial memo and four semi-structured interviews with eight of Michelle's students specifically address how her pedagogy and curriculum were crucial in students' development of critical consciousness. Finally, Michelle's perspectives gleaned from two semi-structured interviews, transcriptions from her guest lecture in Dan's Foundations of Bilingual Education course for bilingual pre-service teachers and their presentation about the gentrification unit, a local bilingual education conference, as well as member checks, were integral in grasping the gentrification processes at Plainview, along with how she responded to these processes. In the next section we focus on one veteran teacher's perspectives of Plainview's transformation, and how they can be 'mapped' from the micro to the macro so as to offer insight about the gentrification of DLBE.

Mapping Gentrification of DLBE from the Local to the Global: Who is the Program 'Catered to?'

> I have lots of mixed feelings about dual language. Not the concept, but the way it's run within the district, or at least how I've seen it here at Plainview. I don't feel like it's programming that's great for anyone who is not on level or above level in English. I feel like it's really catered to our parents who want their kids, their native English speakers to speak Spanish, and not really catered to our bilingual students who come to us with strong Spanish needing more academic language or more rigor in their home language. So, it's been an adjustment. (Interview, Ms Alanis, 8 December 2016)

The perspectives of Ms Alanis, a veteran bilingual special education teacher at Plainview, provide an apt entry point into the macro and the micro (Plainview) reality of DLBE at a time when these programs are/were expanding in the US at astounding and often damaging speed. Her perspectives are crucial because she had a deep understanding of the Plainview community prior to the DLBE gentrification that started in 2010 when the school was 95% Latinx with a focus on transitioning students into English instead of focusing on DLBE's traditional goals of bilingualism/biliteracy, biculturalism and intercultural competence (Howard *et al.*, 2018). In turn, Ms Alanis' experience when Plainview served mainly working-class Latinx families, coupled with her experience amid dual gentrification processes that transformed both the Plainview neighborhood and bilingual education program into whiter spaces, which now ironically promoted the aforementioned goals (Heiman & Murakami, 2019), were invaluable in the study. Her perspectives about who the DLBE program was 'catered to' are of great import, as Ms Alanis was committed to a race radical vision of bilingual education (Flores, 2016) that, first and foremost, centered 'our bilingual students' who 'come to us with strong Spanish'. We argue that her 'mixed feelings' about DLBE due to how 'she has seen it here at Plainview' and not DLBE as a 'concept' reveal the dialectical macro/micro processes that were shaping/are currently shaping the DLBE imaginary at the national/local levels. As a 'concept' at the national level, DLBE is lauded due to the cognitive benefits of bilingualism (Bialystock, 2011), high levels of academic achievement and social benefits (Lindholm-Leary & Block, 2010; Rolstad *et al.*, 2005; Thomas & Collier, 2017) and potential for cross-cultural understanding (Feinauer & Howard, 2014). At the same time, this 'concept' has been framed through a 'cautionary note' (Valdés, 1997) due to inequities at the levels of policy and practice (Cervantes-Soon, 2014; Cervantes-Soon *et al.*, 2017; Delavan *et al.*, 2017; Henderson, 2019) directly impacting Latinx students (Chávez-Moreno, 2019, this volume). This critical line of inquiry in DLBE has also revealed gentrification processes that decenter, displace and commodify the original beneficiaries of bilingual education programs (Chaparro, 2020; Heiman & Murakami, 2019; Muro, 2016; Valdez *et al.*, 2016).

These macro manifestations around the DLBE 'concept' demand that we engage in critical ethnographic work that looks to 'map' micro processes to macro processes as a way to challenge normalized practices and interrogate dominant (DLBE) paradigms and knowledges to 'promot[e] human freedom, dignity, and greater democracy in life' (Means, 2013: 51). Engaging in this critical ethnography opened up space to 'map' the macro DLBE frenzy (Williams, 2017) driven by economic, cultural and political forces onto the 'local' context (Means, 2013) in a gentrifying Plainview.

By situating Ms Alanis' 'human experience' at the local level in a dialectical relationship with a field of bilingual education that has regained status due to the dominant group's newfound interest in DLBE, it is revealed how her critical consciousness around who the program should be 'catered to' was/is essential if social justice and equity are at the core in DLBE (Cervantes-Soon *et al.*, 2017; Freire, 2020; Palmer *et al.*, 2019). As a way to counter DLBE gentrification, the centering of DLBE's 'fourth goal' of critical consciousness has taken on profound significance, which emerged at Plainview through Michelle's hopeful manifestation of critical pedagogy and centering Latinx students and families during times of displacement. Specifically, Michelle offered an ethnographic window into what the fourth goal looked like on the ground as a response to DLBE gentrification at the macro and micro levels (Heiman & Yanes, 2018), which is documented in the next section.

Countering DLBE Gentrification: Urgency of the Fourth Fundamental Goal of Critical Consciousness

> I said to Ms Taylor, 'so who fought in the American Revolution during our planning'. 'Oh well the British'. 'Well why?' 'Well you know like for independence I don't even know'. 'Where were Black people?' 'I don't know'. 'They need to find that out. They need to find out what happened to Black people during the American Revolution'. 'Why I never thought about that'. 'Cuz they were on our land, Mexican people were on this land, where were they? Where were the natives?' 'Well I guess some people, but we're doing battles Michelle'. 'Wait a minute, what's our TEK [State standards in Texas]?' 'Find the causes and the effects of the American revolution'. 'Great, I could tell them the causes, they fought because they wanted independence. Great, now find the effects. So now what happened to Black people, what happened to native people what happened to Mexican people let's go there! Cuz that seems way more interesting than just figuring out the battle of Ticonderoga!'. (Foundations of Bilingual Education class, 25 March 2016)

We start off this section by highlighting Michelle describing a planning meeting between her and Ms Taylor, a monolingual White woman who taught English language arts and social studies to Michelle's students. Michelle had been invited to Dan's Foundations of Bilingual Education course for pre-service bilingual teachers to talk with students about funds of knowledge and critical pedagogy. Michelle's criticality around the 'causes and effects of the American revolution' and 'what happened to Black people' is a generative entry point into how critical scholars are conceptualizing an expansion beyond DLBE's traditional goals of academic achievement, bilingualism and biliteracy, and intercultural competence (Howard *et al.*, 2018) to include a fourth goal around the development of critical consciousness (Cervantes-Soon *et al.*, 2017; Palmer *et al.*, 2019), highlighted earlier. The recent 'frenzy' from White middle-class constituents (Williams, 2017) has fueled DLBE gentrification processes at the levels of policy (Henderson, 2019; Valdez *et al.*, 2016) and in schools experiencing rapid demographic changes (Burns, 2017; Chaparro, 2020; Heiman & Murakami, 2019; Muro, 2016). This, in turn, has revealed the urgency of centering those Latinx populations who should benefit the most from these programs.

The fourth DLBE goal augments the recent call in *Guiding Principles for Dual Language Education* to prioritize issues of social justice and equity with all stakeholders in DLBE contexts (Howard *et al.*, 2018) through critical pedagogies that interrogate power, historicize, engender critical listening and open up spaces for discomfort (Palmer *et al.*, 2019). The interrogation of the state standards' objectives of the American Revolution was the norm in Michelle's classroom. Lydia, an upper middle-class Mexicana, spoke to this when I (Dan) asked her in an interview with two other students to describe Michelle in her own words:

> Well, we didn't just learn like academics, we learned stuff like that were real world problems, things that aren't just happening in the US but like across the world, like poverty, gentrification for instance, just many things that you don't get at a lot of schools, and many teachers don't teach. (Interview, 23 May 2016)

Michelle and her students also historicized 'real world problems' such as immigration and war during a time when Donald Trump was a popular topic due to his then insertion into the presidential race. In a discussion around the book *Sylvia & Aki* (Conkling, 2013), a powerful book that documents the experience of a young girl whose family has been placed in a Japanese internment camp after the bombing of Pearl Harbor, Michelle asked students about a specific line that stated 'a threat to national security'. This led them into a conversation that offered space for students to historicize oppressive US military and immigration policies at a time when Trump was first gaining political momentum. A student proceeded to ask who Trump would send back to Mexico if elected president, which sparked this interaction:

Shawn: He would send darker students back.
Michelle: *Me mandaría a mí?* (Would he send me back?)
Students: *Sí!*
Michelle: *No soy Mexicana!* (I'm not Mexican)
Leo: He's a modern Hitler!
Aaron: That is so sad. (Field notes, 2 October 2015)

This dialogue between students, often focused on pertinent current social issues, was the norm during my time in Michelle's classroom (Heiman & Yanes, 2018). Michelle's continuous interrogation of power and historicizing was not relegated strictly to the classroom or the curriculum, as she was also explicit about her race radical vision of bilingual education that centered those Latinx families who should benefit from these programs (Flores, 2016). She was troubled by the White middle-class 'discovery' (Flores, 2015) of Plainview:

> But this program is not for them, so [laughs] so get me some Latinos! And they [White middle-class students] can learn Spanish with us, that's awesome, and they can learn our culture with us, cool. And we can also learn from them, yes. But we can't learn from eight students out of 30, cause it's not how the program's supposed to work. So that worries me, that's what keeps me up at night. How is the program really serving the people it's supposed to serve? (Interview, 27 April 2016)

Michelle, first and foremost, 'served' the Latin[x] population, and one of the ways she did this was through what she called house meetings that brought together families from both groups once a month to dialogue about pertinent issues in the classroom and beyond:

> *La situación para mi es cómo incluir a esas familias, que sus voces sean parte integral de nuestras conversaciones, en correo electrónico que a veces no tienen acceso a eso, para que sus voces puedan ser parte de nuestras conversaciones, tenemos, para que eso pueda suceder en nuestra clase tenemos cosa que se llaman house meetings. Todo es en español, mis power points son en español, si la gente americana que no habla inglés no entiende, well amigos están en un programa de DL, así que encuentran su bilingual partner porque eso va a ser en español.*
>
> The situation for me is how do I include these families, so these voices are an integral part of our conversations. Sometimes they don't have access to email. We have, so that their voices can be part of the conversation in our classroom, what we call house meetings. Everything is in Spanish. My power points are in Spanish, and if the American folks don't understand, well friends find your bilingual pair because it's going to be in Spanish. (Interview, 25 March 2016)

Michelle's house meetings 'in Spanish' were powerful counternarratives, as the 'American folks' had to 'find [their] bilingual pair' and engage in critical listening in order to be 'an integral part of [the] conversations'. Being pushed to engage in critical listening and being explicitly de-centered in these house meetings provided generative opportunities for the 'American folks' to experience discomfort, which is crucial as these programs are commodified for neoliberal aims. Michelle believed that one way to mediate the dominant group's cultural, political and economic capitals was to assure that she prioritized the realities of working-class Latinx families who had been priced out of Plainview due to gentrification. She provided space for their voices to come through with equity and social justice at the forefront, as she offered linguistic support, provided opportunities to dialogue about important classroom and school events and promoted *convivencia* across race, class, language and ethnicity. Much of the information Michelle put forth at a house meeting would be accessed through other mediums by many of the families, which Michelle recognized:

> My meeting was for this table [working-class Latinx parents]. They're [White/Latinx middle-class parents] gonna get it. Like, the rest of these tables are gonna get it, with or without me. They will find ways to contact, to talk, to communicate with me. But my tables were these, my meeting was for these moms (working-class Latinx parents). (Interview, 24 February 2016)

It should also be recognized that the group that was 'gonna get it' appreciated the convivencia during a precarious time when many parents were being pushed out to surrounding districts. This was a point of concern for them because, after six years in the program, they had witnessed how gentrification had completely altered the demographics, discourses and histories of those who 'couldn't stay put' (Lipman, 2011) as a neoliberal path took aim at Plainview. In this regard, we specifically highlight how Dan made sense of a house meeting in which Michelle invited a bilingual employee from the district to dialogue with parents around their options for middle school and how to navigate bureaucratic spaces in this transition:

> Undoubtedly there were a lot of cultural/economic/social capitals that came to the surface. Most importantly, some having the tools to navigate the middle school systems [the privileged populations], while others not having any idea about the process [Andrea's mom] nor the policies that come into play for their child [Ernesto's mom]. Nonetheless, the conversation brought necessary topics to the forefront around equity and social justice, which is why DLBE schools should require their parents to attend house meetings such as this. (Initial memo, 2 December 2015)

Palmer and Martínez (2013) emphasized the inherent complexities of DLBE spaces that offer linguistic and curricular challenges for practicing teachers when bringing together two distinct groups of students. Michelle's commitment and work with two distinct groups of *parents* only adds to these complexities, as DLBE's fourth goal should be enacted with all stakeholders. In the midst of her critical pedagogical work with students and parents, we were also critically listening to how Plainview teachers were talking about the rapid demographic changes. In the next section, we describe this critical listening as the turning point of the critical ethnography and what we argue is key when engaging in this kind of research. Through critical listening to how gentrification was impacting the community and imagination of Plainview, the emergence of gentrification as a 'generative theme' (Freire, 1997) provided an opportunity to interrogate these processes by talking back to the 'brutal rule' of neoliberalism through a critical curricular intervention (De Lissovoy, 2015).

'They're Kind of a Commodity': Critical Ethnography as Critical Listening

> The majority of my students, the vast majority of them, are not native Spanish speakers. There's a few, and I love that there's such a family, not quest, but there's such a desire in our community for these students who are English speakers, native English speakers, to learn both languages. I think that's great. But it does end up creating sort of a strange problem in and of itself with the influx of higher income families and with the way Austin [Texas] has changed, we've lost a lot of our traditional families, but the program's sort of based on having a strong population of Spanish speakers and we don't. And it's so hard to find this ever evolving, ever shifting program that people have one expectation of what it's going to be, and if it were a textbook it would be that, but it's not, because we're talking about real people and families who, their apartments are torn down, and they have to move. And now we have two Spanish speakers in a class instead of twelve, and those two Spanish speakers can be made to feel very important and very special, but at the same time it feels a little like you're taking from them, and not necessarily in a great way ... It's cool for them to get to translate and really help other kids. But at the same time I mean it does feel a little bit like taking from them. I don't know. They're kind of a commodity, we have a few of them and like we gotta keep them 'cause we need them. (Interview, Ms Baker, 14 December 2015)

Ms Baker's perspective of Plainview's transformation was a common one among those teachers who had been at the school before it gentrified and became a DLBE school in 2010. She had been at Plainview when the school mainly served working-class 'native Spanish speakers' whose Spanish was *only* tapped to facilitate their transition into all-English instruction. As was pointed out by Ms Alanis previously, many teachers were concerned about how Plainview's DLBE program was being overrun with White middle-class families, which was a stark change from pre-gentrification/DLBE. The principal, Mr González, described this different reality along with how launching the DLBE program 'rebranded' (Katnelson & Bernstein, 2017) the school:

> So. I came here in 2000. Ms Patterson was the principal here, and at the time there were about 350 kids at Plainview. And it was predominantly Hispanic, 99% Hispanic. A low SES Title 1 school. They were transferring out, cuz we had too many bilingual kids. But when we started doing the two-way dual language (DLBE), it was like a magnet to bring people in. And not only the neighborhood kids, but kids from all over. We had parents coming from the faraway circles to walkthroughs and learn about dual language and all that. It wasn't so much about Plainview, it was the opportunity for their kids to pick up a second language regardless of where they went, and they were willing to drive that far just to get their kids in the program. A lot of families had come from California and New York where there was already dual language programs and they knew about it. (Interview, 11 December 2016)

Plainview's transformation from a 'low SES Title 1 school' in 2000 to the DLBE 'magnet' in 2010 coalesced with rapid gentrification that was pushing the 'Hispanic' population out of the neighborhood, as they were not able to 'stay put' (Lipman, 2011) in a rebranded community and school that now paradoxically had privileged students 'transferring [in]' for the 'opportunity… to pick up a second language'. The 'walkthroughs' that Mr González referred to were actually scheduled tours for families interested in 'learn[ing] about dual language and all that'. At the time of the ethnographic study (2015–2016), the tours for prospective families were in high demand, and started in late October and went through January. Mr González mentioned that they 'were booked solid' (Interview, 11 December 2015), which spoke volumes about Plainview's transformation from a place 'they were transferring out of' to a highly sought-out school (Heiman & Murakami, 2019). This transformation and high demand for the tours impacted teachers on the ground, as many veteran teachers who had been at Plainview before and after the implementation of DLBE offered critical perspectives about what they were seeing. Ms Edison, a second-grade teacher who had been at Plainview for eight years and witnessed its rapid transformation, described the tours:

> Yeah, I mean, think about when I first started. Were parents gonna tour a school? No, this is the school you go to, that's it. And now it's all upper-class parents who are checking out schools and is this the school I should go to. There's definitely not a low-income Hispanic parent walking with them in the tours. It's all the same type of people. It's a little, I mean we're used to it, but it's still aggravating to have 18 to 20 parents walking

in, they just stand there in a cluster, watch you teach or watch the kids. Of course, they always come in the morning when we have that dance class that we have to do or something, so it's a little ridiculous... cause that's what Mr González wants, he wants to sell the school. I mean that's how it was when we first got dual language, right? That was one of the main reasons. There were teachers who wanted it, but they were gonna close the school. How do we keep it open? We do tours and we show that we're gonna teach Spanish to the kids. (Interview, 15 December 2015)

'No Han Tenido Ningún Cambio': Challenging Researcher Perceptions of Gentrification

At the same time, it was crucial to highlight how the gentrification of Plainview was being understood by other stakeholders, specifically working-class, Latinx parents. As a critical ethnographer, this was the facet of the study that challenged Dan to think differently about how he had originally believed that this community would respond to the rapid gentrification of the community and school. The 'rage' Dan was feeling as a parent, activist and critical ethnographer (Erickson, 1984) due to the changes he had witnessed over the previous five years, was an emotion he thought many would share, especially those families directly affected by gentrification. Mónica, a working-class Latina who had been a parent at Plainview for 18 years and had recently been priced out of the neighborhood (and who we discuss in more depth later in this chapter), talked about the changes she had seen and her experience at the school:

> *Pues para mí, no han tenido ningún cambio, yo he visto todo bien, normal, igual, lo único si es diferente fue el lenguaje dual, fue algo muy diferente eso, y muy bonito porque el que hable dos idiomas es muy bien para su futuro de ellas...Mi hija la mayor tiene veintiuno, ella vino a esa escuela cuando tenía tres añitos de edad; so prácticamente esta escuela la siento mía porque conozco todos los maestros conozco la señorita de la oficina, Mr González, todos me dan no sé confianza para yo seguir en esa escuela. Es muy buen escuela, por eso es que todas mis hijas han venido aquí, mis cuatro hijas...yo he pasado por muchas cosas bastantes fuertes con mis hijas, entonces, esa escuela más que escuela yo la veo como mi casa, porque me quedo a platicar con la maestra, me meto a la oficina.*
>
> In my opinion there have not been any changes. I see everything as good, normal, and the same. The only difference is the dual language program. That was something very different and beautiful because there is a better future for one who speaks two languages. My oldest daughter is 21, and she came to this school when she was three, so this school feels like it's mine because I know all the teachers, the women in the office, Mr González, and all of them give me reassurance for me to stay at the school. It's a great school, and that's why all my daughters have come here. I have gone through some really difficult times with my daughters, and this school,

more than a school, I see it like my house, because I hang out and chat with the teacher and I stick my head into the office. (Interview, 19 May 2016)

Lucía, a working-class Latina who had been a parent at Plainview for 10 years and had also recently been pushed out of the neighborhood, voiced similar praise about the school:

> *Me siento muy contenta muy a gusto porque siento el apoyo de los maestros, de todo el personal de la escuela. Nunca he tenido problemas. Yo he venido a pedir ayuda y siempre han estado dispuestos a ayudarme. Siempre están pendientes de los niños, que nada les pase y siempre estoy informada de todos los cambios que están ocurriendo. Entonces eso para mí es una experiencia muy buena porque me gusta estar al día con las cosas que pasa.*
>
> I am very happy and feel comfortable because I have the teachers' support, and from the rest of the school. I have never had any problems. I have come to ask for help and they are always willing to help me out. They always know what's going on with my kids, and that nothing bad happens to them. I am always aware of any changes and what's going on. So, this is a great experience for me because I like to know what's going on on a daily basis. (Interview, 31 May 2016)

Mónica's powerful history about her love and appreciation for Plainview and Lucía's great experience at the school were good reminders that, even though gentrification was a source of 'rage' and at times sadness, there was also a caring, welcoming and innovative school that was loved by many new and working-class Latinx families. We were critically listening to these stories of Plainview pre-DLBE/gentrification, the commodification of Latinx students and those stories of disconfirming evidence that added nuance to what was taking root at Plainview in 2015–2016. It was this critical listening that was the catalyst in our decision to take up gentrification as a 'generative theme' (Freire, 1997) with Michelle's fifth-grade students (Heiman, 2021), which is discussed in the next section.

Gentrification as a Generative Theme: Critical Ethnography as a Critical Curricular Intervention

In this section, we start out by centering Michelle's voice, as even though we planned the gentrification unit (see Appendix 10.1 for *unit objectives*, *essential questions* and *daily curricular focus*) together, she was the one who drove this curricular intervention. It was an emotional two and a half weeks of high student engagement, deep understanding, discomfort, hope and tears. Michelle recalled it being 'hard for me. The whole unit was really hard for me' (Interview, 27 April 2016). Freire (1997) realized that critically engaged teachers would go through these emotions when dialoguing 'with' students around issues that directly affect their ontologies and lived experiences, while at the same time being open to the unknown. In the next paragraph we are intentional about centering Michelle's voice through the use of 'I', as this offers a more robust analysis of the urgency of engaging her students in the gentrification unit.

There was an urgency for me as their teacher, for us, as a community, to do this unit. I did not live far away from the school and in the previous three years I saw my community change so drastically and I had no doubt that it affected the school. Indeed, it did. The class one grade older looked entirely different than my class, and even my class looked entirely different than the class younger than mine. By different I mean, fewer Latinx students, more White families. From speaking to the students and their families, I found they were more affluent. The majority of families had the facility to choose this school for their children and, in doing so, they were able to provide their own transportation and their own after or before care. That is, they knew how to navigate the districts and the systems in place to take full advantage of them. Not to say that the Latinx or Spanish-speaking families did not do all those things. They did! Most of the time, they knew how to navigate these systems and oftentimes they were shepherded by the principal or the teachers at the school. Seeing these shifts in our school, I knew that students saw and understood these changes in different ways. I was curious to understand with them, and to especially make space for those understandings to lead to changes. I wanted my students to understand concepts of neoliberalism that lead to gentrification, which is difficult. But more so, I wanted them to see and hear and learn from the people who are being affected by gentrification – those in their own classrooms. I wanted to handle this unit with care, because I didn't want to mine the suffering of my Latinx students who felt displaced by the incoming changing population. I wanted them to feel empowered, as if they were experts in this field, because they were. I wanted to place the parents of these students on a pedestal, and I wanted my Latinx students to know that I was with them.

'I Have Been Legally Hired by the District to Teach You': Centering Latinx Students in a Gentrifying Plainview

We highlight two specific events that poignantly reveal how Michelle carried out the gentrification unit with care, and through an explicit focus on her Latinx students and their families who were being directly affected by gentrification. As was the norm during my research, I accompanied Michelle and her students back from their music, art or physical education class that took place first thing in the morning. As we walked, she mentioned feeling very unsettled from the previous day's conversation (day two of the unit) about certain working-class Latinx apartment complexes being unsafe and more prone to robberies. One student even mentioned that her grandparents were 'robbed like a bunch' (Field notes, 5 April 2016) in this particular neighborhood. She revealed that as a result of the dangerous deficit-laden discourse, she took her Latinx kids out of the class and told them they needed to raise their voices, if not out loud then in their blogs, where they offered their perspectives on different topics in the unit. She described the event:

> I had to pull out my Latino kids and pull them into that room [points to classroom next door] while the class was doing something else and say, 'I want you to understand that I'm here for you, that I have been legally hired by the district to teach you. And yes, it's everybody's right to learn my language, but this is our language, we are together in our language and our culture, and you and I are family… but I want you to know that I am here for you, and that your voice, your thoughts, your heart matters. (Interview, 27 April 2016)

Three of the students she pulled out of class that day discussed this event when I interviewed them at the end of the unit. Michelle recommended I put certain students together for these interviews, as she thought that having Karina, Nestor and Marisa together would encourage them to open up about their experiences at Plainview. All three of them had originally lived in the Plainview neighborhood before skyrocketing rents had pushed them to more affordable neighborhoods and, for Karina and Marisa, even into another school district. We were talking about why they still wanted to come to Plainview, even though they lived outside of the neighborhood and were zoned to another school and/or district:

Dan: Why do you still come here? What makes this place so great?
Karina: Michelle.
Nestor: Our teachers.
Dan: OK tell me, she's the one that makes it so great. What has she done for you?
Marisa: She helps us and our parents.
Karina: Yeah.
Marisa: Like with the transfers.
Dan: OK.
Karina: She doesn't give up on something if she, if it doesn't go her way than she always tries to get it to go her way.
Dan: Nestor, any ideas?
Nestor: Nos apoya. (*She supports us*)
Dan: ¿Cómo te apoya? *(How does she support you?)*
Marisa: If we don't get something she helps us.
Nestor: Yeah.
Marisa: When we don't like something.
Karina: If we don't understand something she'll like pull us outside and be like OK what do you not understand, what do you want me to help you with?
Dan: Sometimes I've seen her pull you all aside, what does she tell you?

Karina: That our voice matters and that not just because we're there does it mean that we're not human beings in class. Our voice needs to be heard.
Dan: What does that mean your voice needs to be heard?
Karina: We shouldn't be quiet.
Marisa: Don't be shy anymore.
Karina: For example, somebody said that their friends are always getting break into apartments, that doesn't happen, and she told us that we need to say, cuz some of us do live in apartments or trailers or any house. (Student interview, 13 May 2016)

As an 'anthropological confidant' (Foley & Valenzuela, 2005) throughout the year-long study, Michelle consistently offered critical insight around data sources. She was such an integral change agent, and warranted such an active role, as participant involvement in data analysis is a key element of critical ethnography (Barton, 2001; Carspecken, 1996; Madison, 2019). After reading the interview transcript with Karina, Nestor and Marisa, she emailed me her perspectives of the interview and a few weeks later we talked about them:

Dan: You mentioned many times about this idea of the reason you're at that school is for the Latino kids. How do you think the other kids [White middle-class students] responded to that? Did they take it well? Cuz it seemed like in the interviews, they didn't mention it but I think they knew, they felt OK with that.
Michelle: I think they felt OK with that, yeah, they know I'm Latina [laughing].
Dan: They felt like you were intentional and deliberate in saying I'm here because, my job here is not (both laughing), I'm going to go over that data. There's a few times where you're—I'm here for these students. Cuz I asked Karina, Nestor, and Marisa about this idea of voice. I noticed a few times that she took you guys out of the classroom, why, you know this idea of that we have a voice, do you think that they felt that they had a voice?
Michelle: Yeah.
Dan: The whole time? Their voices mattered and that they felt important?
Michelle: Yeah.
Dan: Cuz you have here my kids have a voice straight up raza (Michelle's initial perspectives sent via email)!
Michelle: I do, I just read that, those kids are, those kids are the reason that I'm employed at Plainview, so that's just very clear. Without that Latino population we wouldn't have enough money to offer someone a bilingual stipend, to teach

> nobodies right? To teach non-bilingual students is what I meant not nobodies, non-ELL students, and so I made that very clear to them last year. (Michelle, 8 July 2016)

These findings were powerful examples of the importance of engaging in humanizing methodologies (Paris & Winn, 2014) with participants like Michelle who explicitly prioritized students like Karina, Nestor and Marisa in spite of gentrification processes that were pushing them to the margins. It is through humanizing critical ethnographic studies that the documentation of DLBE's fourth goal around the development of critical consciousness has greater potential to emerge (Cervantes-Soon *et al.*, 2017; Palmer *et al.*, 2019), which we pay specific attention to in the next section. Critical ethnography as a critical curricular intervention through a unit on the same gentrification processes impacting the Plainview community and the DLBE program revealed the synergy between DLBE's fourth goal and critical ethnographic methods. The resulting combination explicitly interrogates dominant power structures and knowledges, requires critical listening and seeks to historicize macro and micro processes such as gentrification and DLBE.

'Es una Voz de Alguien que Pertenece a mi Comunidad': Developing Critical Consciousness about the Generative Theme

As Michelle emphasized in conjunction with the urgency of doing this unit, she wanted the curriculum to highlight those people who were being directly affected by gentrification processes. On day five of the unit, we invited Marisa's mother, Mónica, who appeared in a previous section, to talk with students about her experience in the Plainview community during the previous 15 years. Her family had lived in the Plainview neighborhood since 2000 but had been pushed out to a surrounding district due to rapidly rising rents in 2015. Mónica had a deep sense of *confianza* with Michelle, as she and other veteran teachers accompanied her to the district office at the beginning of the school year in order to advocate for her four children to be able to remain in the district, despite now living outside the district's catchment area. In fact, Marisa was absent the first four days of school until the issue was finally resolved and the children were granted permission to attend schools in the district. Providing curricular space for Mónica was an interrogation of power and an example of pushing students to listen critically to marginalized epistemologies (Chávez-Moreno, 2019, this volume), as DLBE programs are frequently centered on the knowledges and voices of the dominant group (Palmer, 2009). Mónica conveyed the struggle her family was going through, while also historicizing her experience at Plainview as being a space that she felt intimately connected to, in spite of no longer living in the immediate neighborhood. Michelle reflected on the impact of Monica's visit a few weeks later during a presentation about this same gentrification unit at a local bilingual education conference:

Se paró y empezó a llorar. Sin nadie, nadie le preguntó nada, nada le hizo ningún comentario, pero sabía de lo que se iba a tratar, y empezó a llorar. Porque sabía que su comunidad estaba cambiando, sabía el esfuerzo que tenía que hacer con sus hijos y eso fue un impacto más grande que quizás Pedro and Natalia (school board member and community organizer who were also invited guests) porque es una voz de alguien que pertenece a mi comunidad.

She stood up and started to cry. Without anybody asking her anything, nobody made a comment, but she knew what this was going to be about, and she started to cry. Because she knew that her community was changing and the sacrifices that she had to make for her kids, and this probably had more of an impact than Pedro or Natalia [school board member and community activist who were also invited guests] because it was a voice that was part of my community. (Conference presentation, 23 April 2016)

Mónica's visit also impacted students in generative ways, as in an interview with two middle-class English language dominant students not affected by gentrification, they revealed a deeper level of critical consciousness around the generative theme of gentrification:

Holly: Well like when Marisa's mother came it really helped me understand how it was driving people who lived in Austin out of Austin, and how it was bad because...
Alina: Manor [the district Marisa and her family were now living in].
Holly: Like the houses how they're getting so expensive cuz even apartments are, the prices of what houses used to be, ten years ago, it's just crazy how fast it's all just like gentrifying, I guess. (Interview, 13 May 2016)

Critically listening to Mónica's story fomented a deeper understanding of gentrification, as it was 'driving people ... out of Austin' who were in their own classroom.

My interview with Mónica spanned myriad themes; she felt ashamed for crying in front of the students, somber about being displaced from her home of 15 years in the Plainview neighborhood, and appreciative of both Michelle's advocacy and the Plainview community as a whole. In the same conversation we highlighted above, in which Michelle reflected on the student interview transcript, she referenced my interview with Mónica and their relationship of *confianza*:

Michelle: Just like the students thought that they were solely important, the parents saw that they were important, and that they had a voice and that they were heard and that I considered them in classroom and outside of classroom decisions; you know through house meetings, and through new letters and through just having an open communication in our classroom.

Dan: It was interesting too, Marisa's mom said that she felt that not only you helped Marisa but she felt that you really helped her, too, what do you think that meant?

Michelle: She had some really rough moments in her personal life. She was going through some really hard times when she was living in an apartment and the rent was too high and it was straining her and her husband's relationship. And the fact that she could come and talk to me about that, and I don't give advice for that because I don't know. I don't know that situation so I can't say well this is what you can do and this is what you're going to do and this is how I would solve it. But really, I just had to sit and listen, and just take it in, and give her hugs and give her tissues. I can't give advice on something I don't know, but yeah when her and her husband were about to separate, I just had to sit and take it and give her hugs and say it is OK. You have a big network of support, it is OK. (Michelle, 8 July 2016)

This curricular intervention around the 'generative theme' of gentrification demonstrated how critical ethnography can be instrumental in advocating for those original beneficiaries of bilingual education who had been displaced. Michelle and I believed it was our ethical obligation to resist this neoliberal encroachment on DLBE by advocating for the oppressed (Barton, 2001; Madison, 2019), due to gentrification processes that were impacting the Plainview community. In the concluding section we offer a critical reflection on the gentrification unit as a result of critically listening to students' experiences.

'We Really Didn't See the Good Side of it I Guess': Critical Reflection about the Gentrification Unit

We were extremely proud of the students for taking on the unit with courage and being open to the new and unknown. Nonetheless, we realized we should have taken it further. Duncan-Andrade and Morrell's (2008) three goals of critical pedagogy; academic achievement, empowered identity development, and action for social change were only partially realized and we openly acknowledged that the action component should have been extended. Michelle commented on how the unit came up short during a presentation we did a few weeks later at the local bilingual education conference, mentioned previously:

> *Dan e yo nos sentamos a reflexionar cómo hubiera podido hacer esto mejor, porque siempre se puede hacer mejor. Extender la escritura hacerla como más pesadíta, darles a ellos un llamado para actuar, ir a presentar a la mesa directiva el lunes en la noche, ir a presentar a la ciudad de Austin, ir a presentar lo que ellos habían encontrado.*

> Dan and I reflected on what we could have done better, because it's always possible to do it better. Make the writing more rigorous, give students a call to action, like going to the school board on Monday evenings. Go and present to the city of Austin and show them what they had discovered. (Conference Presentation, 23 April 2016)

Michelle showed her students the Power Point presentation a few days before we presented at the conference, and elaborated about this conversation during our presentation:

> *Cuando yo les enseñé esa presentación a ellos el viernes les dije great, como más hubiéramos podido hacer esto mejor. Varios alumnos me dijeron que hubiera sido beneficioso para ellos entender de alguien que se benefició de la gentrificación. Es verdad o sea no presentamos* (laughing) *este punto de vista para nada porque es difícil encontrar a alguien que se haya beneficiado de la gentrificación sin tomar poder, y no presentamos ese punto de vista...Y estas reflexiones es importante tenerlo nosotros como escritores de currículo y ellos como consumidores de este currículo. Entonces por eso se lo di a ellos alright cómo hubiéramos podido arreglar esto, qué más hubiéramos podido tener, y ellos agregaron conversaciones. Ellos hubieran querido tener un work session con la mesa directiva del distrito y decirle, what's up? Qué like háblame, ¿por qué estamos pasando por esto?*
>
> When I showed the presentation to my students on Friday I said great, how could we have made this better. A few students told me that it would have been beneficial to hear about somebody who benefited from gentrification. It's true that we didn't present (laughing) this point of view because it's hard to find somebody who has benefited from gentrification without using their power, so we didn't present that point of view. And these reflections are important for us who write curriculum and for those who receive the curriculum. It was for that reason that I said alright, how could we fix that, what more could we have done, and they mentioned more conversations. They would have liked a work session with the district's school board, and be like what's up? Like, why are we going through this? (Conference Presentation, 23 April 2016)

Anita, an upper middle-class, native English speaker offered the following critique of the unit when I interviewed her along with a middle-class Latinx student:

Dan: How did Michelle integrate community and parents into the class?

Anita: I think yeah, she has done a lot with the community and gotten speakers and I really like that. We did a gentrification project and she got speakers and they all seemed, I think we saw one

> side of it but we didn't really see the good side of it I guess. There wasn't someone that came and was like I really like gentrification it's great! So I think maybe seeing like [laughing] both sides of that would have been helpful. (Interview, 12 May 2016)

During the same conversation around data sources we documented previously, Michelle reflected on Anita's comment about how the unit lacked balance:

Michelle: She's little so there's hope that she can see outside of her realm, you know that's how I feel. OK so there's some things that it's tough to understand, you know the whole gentrification unit how I was really one-sided according to her. You know she sees it and I can take it and I wrote in my notes I wish she would've told me those things before!
Dan: Do you feel that it was really one-sided?
Michelle: I don't, you know I brought Celeste Smith (White middle-class parent who talked about how gentrification was impacting housing prices in gentrifying areas) in for a very specific reason. Like this isn't just affecting our Latino community or people of color community.
Dan: Right, right, right.
Michelle: I did that for a reason, I was like Ms Smith I think you are pivotal in this because we have Pedro [school board member and activist] we have Natalia [activist with local interfaith group], both Latinos. We need someone who's White who's struggling with the same thing. (Michelle, 8 July 2016)

Michelle's reflections around the data sources from the gentrification unit point to the productive possibility of working collaboratively with an 'anthropological confidant' (Foley & Valenzuela, 2005), as the complexities and nuanced nature of the findings from the unit demanded she be an integral participant in making sense of the data. To conclude this section, we once again center Michelle's voice as a way to emphasize how our discussion of findings served as an informal assessment of the gentrification unit and as a window into the students' development of critical consciousness.

I thought having Dan in our classroom so that we could talk about data in this form was beneficial. Usually, to assess my teaching and my students' learning, I would have done an assessment. It would have been nearly impossible to write an assessment for this unit, because it was so subjective. So these interviews served as an assessment of sorts. The interviews helped me understand the thinking of the students and, more importantly, their development of critical consciousness.

Conclusion

In this chapter, we revealed how engaging in critical ethnography provided an opportunity to map the gentrification of Plainview's DLBE program and neighborhood to macro processes around DLBE that position this model of bilingual education through ahistorical, apolitical discourses aligned with the neoliberal logics of the market. Our findings highlighted the synergistic relationship between DLBE's fourth goal of critical consciousness development and critical ethnography as, through critical listening of key stakeholders during the research process, the generative theme of gentrification emerged and was tapped as a unit of study in a fifth-grade DLBE classroom. Michelle's explicit attention to, and centering of, the realities of Latinx families who were being directly impacted by gentrification processes through a critical curricular intervention interrogated dominant knowledges and paradigms, which is also an overarching focus of critical ethnographic work. Through the documentation of Michelle's race radical vision and historicizing of bilingual education at Plainview, we revealed the empowering potential of critical ethnography to critique, and most importantly respond to, DLBE gentrification amidst the exponential expansion of DLBE programs throughout the United States.

Notes

(1) All names in the chapter are pseudonyms *except* Michelle.
(2) Freire uses the term 'sociopolitical consciousness' interchangeably with 'critical consciousness'.

Appendix 10.1 Gentrification Unit

Objectives:

(1) Students will be able to understand and define gentrification.
(2) Students will be able to understand that gentrification is a political, social and economic change to the community.
(3) Students will be able to observe changes in population in their community.
(4) Students will be able to identify some of the local factors that have contributed to this process in their own communities (e.g. the DLBE program/community at Plainview).

Essential questions:

(1) What is gentrification?
(2) What does it look like in your school/living community?
(3) Who benefits from it?
(4) What do socioeconomic status and communities have in common?
(5) What role does race play in gentrification?

(6) How has DLBE possibly played a role in this process?
(7) What is the role of Plainview in the changing community?
(8) What are the benefits of gentrification in a community?

Daily Curricular Focus

Day	Visitors/artifacts	Key questions/topics	Prompt for student blog writing
1	'Image walk' of city's transformation of last 20 years	What are key aspects of a community?	Where do you live and why do you live there?
2	'Language of Gentrification' (NPR Podcast); excerpt from 'The Other Side of Home' (Renee Watson)	What are hipsters? What does Quique (from Podcast) mean when he says 'White babies and their brown nannies?'	What do people look like in your community?
3	Conversation with Celeste Smith (university professor); discusses appreciation values of her house in gentrifying part of city (math)	N/A	Students write about the conversation with Celeste Smith
4	PBS video about how lack of affordable housing is impacting teachers in the district	What can we do to make Austin more affordable?	Make a list (from most to least important) of how to make the city more affordable
5	Conversation with Mónica and Natalia (community activist) about how gentrification has impacted the community	What impacted you about the visits from Mónica and Natalia? What connections can you make with previous lessons in the unit?	Is gentrification good or bad?
6	Local newspaper article from 2005: 'Here today gone tomorrow' about how Plainview staff used to do block walks in apartment complexes to reach out to working-class and immigrant Latinx families before gentrification displaced them	Diversity of middle-school options (students were applying to different ones during the time of the unit)	How diverse is Plainview?
7	Newspaper article focused on community conversations about race in Boston YWCA	At Plainview what can we do to bring our Black, Latinx and White families of all social classes together?	What can we do to make our community come together?
8	Local newspaper article about diversity in district magnet schools; visit from Pedro Salazar (schoolboard member and community activist)	Discussion about how local apartment complexes raised their rents and many Plainview families had to move outside of the neighborhood	What will the city look like in 10 years?
9	Discussion with Mr Donald (special education aide) about gentrification in a formerly Black neighborhood of the city (Clarksville)	Discussion of where students live and whether they live in the Plainview catchment area or if they're transfers	Why did you come to Plainview? What do you like about Plainview?

References

Arias, M.B. and Fee, M. (eds) (2018) *Profiles of Dual Language Education in the 21st Century*. Bristol: Multilingual Matters.

Barton, A.C. (2001) Science education in urban settings: Seeking new ways of praxis through critical ethnography. *Journal of Research in Science Teaching* 38 (8), 899–917.

Bialystock, D. (2011) Reshaping the mind: The benefits of bilingualism. *Canadian Journal of Experimental Psychology/Revue canadienne de psychologie expérimentale* 65 (4), 229. doi:10.1037/a0025406

Burns, M. (2017) 'Compromises that we make': Whiteness in the dual language context. *Bilingual Research Journal* 40 (4), 339–352.

Carspecken, P.F. (1996) *Critical Ethnography in Educational Research: A Theoretical and Practical Guide*. New York: Routledge.

Cervantes-Soon, C.G. (2014) A critical look at dual language immersion in the new Latin@ diaspora. *Bilingual Research Journal* 37 (1), 64–82.

Cervantes-Soon, C.G. (2018) Using a Xicana feminist framework in bilingual teacher preparation: Toward an anticolonial path. *The Urban Review* 50 (5), 857–888.

Cervantes-Soon, C., Dorner, L., Palmer, D., Heiman, D., Schwerdtfeger, R. and Choi, J. (2017) Combating inequalities in two-way language immersion programs: Toward critical consciousness in bilingual education spaces. *Review of Research in Education* 41, 403–427.

Chaparro, S.E. (2020) Leading parallel lives: School, parents, and community in a gentrifying two-way immersion program. *International Multilingual Research Journal* 14 (1), 41–57. https://doi.org.10.1080/19313152.2019.1634957

Chávez-Moreno, L.C. (2019) Researching Latinxs, racism, and white supremacy in bilingual Education: A literature review. *Critical Inquiry in Language Studies* 17 (2), 101–120. doi:10.1080/15427587.2019.1624966

Conkling, W. (2013) *Sylvia and Aki*. New York: Random House.

Cornell Gonzáles, G. (2014) 'Aren't you on the parent Listserve?' Working for equitable family involvement in a dual-immersion elementary school. *Rethinking Schools* 29 (1). See http://www.rethinkingschools.org/archive/29_01/29_01_gonzales.shtml.

Delavan, M.G., Valdez, V.E. and Freire, J.A. (2017) Language as whose resource?: When global economics usurp the local equity potentials of dual language education. *International Multilingual Research Journal* 11 (2), 86–100.

De Lissovoy, N. (2015) *Education and Emancipation in the Neoliberal Era: Being, Teaching, and Power*. New York: Palgrave Macmillan.

Duncan-Andrade, J.M.R. and Morrell, E. (2008) *The Art of Critical Pedagogy: Possibilities for Moving from Theory to Practice in Urban Schools*. New York: Peter Lang.

Erickson, F. (1984) What makes school ethnography 'ethnographic'? *Anthropology and Education* 15 (1), 51–66.

Feinauer, E. and Howard, E. (2014) Attending to the third goal: Cross-cultural competence and identity development in two-way immersion programs. *Journal of Immersion and Content-Based Education* 2 (2), 257–272.

Flores, N. (2015) Re: Columbusing bilingual education [Web log comment]. See https://educationallinguist.wordpress.com/2015/01/25/columbising-bilingual-education/ (accessed 17 February 2017).

Flores, N. (2016) A tale of two visions: Hegemonic whiteness and bilingual education. *Educational Policy* 30 (1), 13–38.

Flores, N. and García, O. (2017) A critical review of bilingual education in the United States: From basements and pride to boutiques and profit. *Annual Review of Applied Linguistics* 37, 14–29.

Foley, D. and Valenzuela, A. (2005) Critical ethnography: The politics of collaboration. In N.K. Denzin and Y.S. Lincoln (eds) *Handbook of Qualitative Research* (pp. 217–234). Thousand Oaks, CA: Sage.

Foucault, M. (2008) *The Birth of Biopolitics*. New York: Picador.

Freire, J.A. (2020) Promoting sociopolitical consciousness and bicultural goals in dual language education: The transformational dual language educational framework. *Journal of Language, Identity, and Education* 19 (1), 56–71. https://doi.org/10.1080/15348458.2019.1672174

Freire, P. (1997) *Pedagogy of the Oppressed* (trans. M.B. Ramos). London: Continuum.

Heiman, D. (2021) 'So is gentrification good or bad?': One teacher's implementation of the fourth goal in her TWBE classroom. *Anthropology & Education Quarterly* 52 (1), 63–81.

Heiman, D. and Yanes, M. (2018) Centering the fourth pillar in times of TWBE gentrification: 'Spanish, love, content, not in that order'. *International Multilingual Research Journal* 12 (3), 173–187.

Heiman, D. and Murakami, E. (2019) 'It was like a magnet to bring people in': School administrators' responses to the gentrification of a two-way bilingual education (TWBE) program in central Texas. *Journal of School Leadership* 29 (6), 454–472.

Henderson, K.I. (2019) The danger of the dual-language enrichment narrative: Educator discourses constructing exclusionary participation structures in bilingual education. *Critical Inquiry in Language Studies* 16 (3), 155–177. https://doi.org/10.1080/15427587.2018.1492343

Howard, E., Lindholm-Leary, K., Rogers, D., Olague, N., Medina, J., Kennedy, D., Sugarman, H. and Christian, D. (2018) *Guiding Principles for Dual Language Education* (3rd edn). Washington, DC: Center for Applied Linguistics.

Katnelson, N. and Bernstein, K.A. (2017) Rebranding bilingualism: The shifting discourses of language education policy in California's 2016 election. *Linguistics & Education* 40 (1), 11–26.

Lindholm-Leary, K. and Block, N. (2010) Achievement in predominantly low SES/Hispanic dual language schools. *International Journal of Bilingual Education and Bilingualism* 13 (1), 43–60. https://doi.org/10.1080/13670050902777546

Lipman, P. (2011) *The New Political Economy of Urban Education: Neoliberalism, Race, and the Right to the City*. New York: Routledge.

Madison, D.S. (2019) *Critical Ethnography: Method, Ethics, and Performance* (3rd edn). New York: Sage.

Means, A.J. (2013) *Schooling in the Age of Austerity: Urban Education and the Struggle for Democratic Life*. New York: Palgrave Macmillan.

Morales, P.Z. and Maravilla, J.V. (2019) The problems and possibilities of interest convergence in a dual language school. *Theory Into Practice* 58 (2), 145–153.

Muro, J.A. (2016) 'Oil and water'? Latino-white relations and symbolic integration in a changing California. *Sociology of Race and Ethnicity* 2 (4), 516–530.

Palmer, D. (2009) Middle-class English speakers in a two-way immersion bilingual classroom: 'Everybody should be listening to Jonathan right now…'. *TESOL Quarterly* 43 (2), 177–202.

Palmer, D. and Martínez, R.A. (2013) Teacher agency in bilingual spaces: A fresh look at preparing teachers to educate Latina/o bilingual children. *Review of Research in Education* 37 (1), 269–297.

Palmer, D. and Caldas, B. (2015) Critical ethnography. In K. King, Y.J. Lai and S. May (eds) *Research Methods in Language and Education, Encyclopedia of Language and Education* (3rd edn, pp. 1–12). New York: Springer. https://doi.org/10.1007/978-3-319-02329-8_28-1

Palmer, D., Cervantes-Soon, C., Dorner, L. and Heiman, D. (2019) Bilingualism, biliteracy, biculturalism... and critical consciousness for all: Proposing a fourth fundamental principle for two-way dual language education. *Theory Into Practice* 58 (2), 121–133.

Paris, D. and Winn, M. (eds) (2014) *Humanizing Research: Decolonizing Qualitative Inquiry with Youth and Communities*. Thousand Oaks, CA: Sage.

Rolstad, K., Mahoney, K.S. and Glass, G.V. (2005) Weighing the evidence: A meta-analysis of bilingual education in Arizona. *Bilingual Research Journal* 29 (1), 43–67. https://doi.org/10.1080/15235882.2005.10162823

Thomas, W.P. and Collier, V.P. (2017) *Why Dual Language Schooling*. Albuquerqe, NM: Fuente Press.

Valdés, G. (1997) Dual-language immersion programs: A cautionary note concerning the education of language-minority students. *Harvard Educational Review* 67 (3), 391–429.

Valdez, V.E., Freire, J.A. and Delavan, M.G. (2016) The gentrification of dual language. *Urban Review* 48 (4), 601–627.

Valenzuela, A. (2016) *Growing Critically Conscious Teachers: A Social Justice Curriculum for Educators of Latino/a Youth*. New York: Teachers College Press.

Williams, C. (2017) The intrusion of white families into bilingual schools. *The Atlantic Daily*, 28 December. See https://www.theatlantic.com/education/archive/2017/12/the-middle-class-takeover-of-bilingual-schools/549278/ (accessed 20 March 2019).

11 Becoming an 'Avocado' – Embodied Rescriptings in Bilingual Teacher Education Settings: A Critical Performance Ethnography

Blanca Caldas

The performance critical ethnography discussed in this chapter provides a nuanced picture of the emergent advocacy identity of a group of bilingual pre-service teachers in Texas as they rehearsed their new voices through the pedagogical implementation of *Forum Theater* (Boal, 2000) to explore sociocultural and raciolinguistic (Alim *et al.*, 2016) issues utilizing translanguaging[1] (García, 2009) practices. This kind of research methodology allowed the whole community to engage and reflect on the disruption of the hegemony of English in the ivory tower by privileging the use of stigmatized intimate language practices for academic and professional purposes. However, since Theater of the Oppressed was the cornerstone of this research, the centrality of the body in the process of becoming pushed me to look not only for alternative modes of inquiry that reflected and evoked movement and change, but also other ways of dissemination. Performance ethnography provides an additional and complementary lens that privileges the embodied knowledge of the community members, the ethnographers and the audience in our own culture/identity-making. This productive vulnerability of self-reflexivity allows the researcher to be in horizontal dialogue with the community members, thus putting ourselves in line with the messiness, the same way they put themselves on the line by sharing their lives. Therefore, I created a one-person multimedia ethnodrama (Saldaña, 2011) of my ethnographic work as 'co-performance witnesses' (Madison, 2007), influenced by the work of Soyini Madison (2007, 2018, 2019) and Omi Osum Joni L. Jones (2002, 2006, 2015).

Critical performance ethnography goes beyond theorizing culture to understanding the reality of the people immersed in a given culture (Jones, 2006: 344), as it engages subjects in the actual 'doing of culture and democracy', and how such performance shapes experience, meaning and culture but, most importantly, its processes since it is continuously in the making. This methodology provides a different lens, one that is centered in the body as a source of knowledge addressing other bodies. These concrete bodies cannot be invisibilized and demand address through the body in which different experiences, meanings and cultures are inscribed, creating a confrontation that does not allow for a 'retreat into the privacy of our own limited self-serving thinking, our stereotypes and biases' (Jones, 2006: 344). Madison (2007), extending the centrality of the body in the performance ethnography to the researcher, calls them a 'co-performative witness' in that they live dialogically with the participants within their spaces and their struggles at a certain point of their sociocultural context. Placing the researcher's body on the line with the messiness aligns with notions of relational accountability (Wilson, 2008) to the community as partners in research (Jones, 2002). Performance ethnography is, then, a political act since it allows all 'co-performative witnesses' to participate in history-making. The dialogical nature of this methodology and the inclusion of a public performance consider the following elements: *witnessing*, *community accountability*, *self-reflexivity*, *audience engagement* and *open advocacy* (Jones, 2015).

According to Jones (2015), *witnessing* requires the (critical) ethnographer to incorporate the participants during the performance (Schechner, 1993) by recreating their gestures, physicality, voices and words through everyday life performance (or ELP, see Hopper, 1993). Through witnessing, the researcher does not pretend to replicate the participants but rather to bring them closer to the audience to deepen their learning about their experiences. Conquergood (1985) describes the ethical and moral responsibility of the researcher toward the researched community. Through this brand of critical performance ethnography, *accountability* is expanded by inviting community members to perform to experience, critique and provide feedback for the researcher and as a way to be held accountable for the participants' portrayal in the performance. This move away from scriptocentrism (Madison, 2019) allows the participants to learn about the researcher's work, which they may not have access to if the format were paywalled scholarly journals with inaccessible jargon. Critical performance ethnography, thus, not only helped me construct my own identity as a researcher, but also helped me hold myself accountable to the participants and, in so doing, to embrace the unknown and my own vulnerabilities.

Self-reflexivity speaks of the questions that Chilisa (2012: 236) asks researchers to ponder in the quest for self-awareness: 'Where do I stand with regard to the researched? Am I still the colonizer? Who are the researched? Are the researched still colonial subjects distinct from the colonizer because of their incapabilities, or are the researched active agents capable of generating solutions to their social challenges?'. Engaging in self-reflexivity pushes me to question and examine the coherence of my research paradigm with the way I live and relate to others, while constantly checking how I relate to the participants in my research in a vulnerable way through public performances. During the several performances of the following one-person multimedia ethnodrama, *audience engagement* was imperative in order to deepen the potential for social change, as the audience becomes physically and emotionally committed to the work presented, and to allow the audience to be part of the co-construction of the performance ethnography (Jones, 2015). Since critical (performance) ethnography can be described as the doing/performance of critical theory (Kincheloe & McLaren, 2000; Madison, 2019), it calls individuals and communities to exercise agency for transformation. The ethnographer then openly acknowledges their *advocacy* through close involvement in the community beyond an observatory stance during the performance.

Through the following chapter/script, I embody the engagement of the participants of this ethnographic study in the embodiment of the stories of experienced bilingual teachers in situations where they confront power differentials and then push them to engage in dialogue with both the author of the story and their antagonist. Through *Forum Theater* (Boal, 2000), the participants created interventions that questioned and talked back against oppressive discourses in what we called Casos de la Vida Real.[2] The participation of my students in these performance interventions was not meant to be an attempt to try on someone else's shoes because, according to Andreotti (2011: 224), individuals cannot take off their own shoes to try others' since 'cultures are context-bound and all shoes are coming from somewhere'. Therefore, the focus of the interventions was on obtaining a better understanding of the different discourses that shape our own shoes, or in this case, our own bodies.

This chapter/script thus provides an account of the participants' re-enactments of counter-stories (cf. Coles, this volume) as they became 'avocados'[3] or advocates on the stage, and on their terms using their performances and discussions during Forum Theater – captured through video recordings – participants' reflections and semi-structured conversations (Alim & American Dialect Society, 2004). The performance uses fieldnotes to recreate the fleeting moments of witnessing captured during the participants' re-enactments to represent how advocacy was imagined and constituted among the participants through embodiment and creativity. This script was first performed in front of the researched community and other bilingual educators on 28 March 2015, at the !Adelante! Conference for Bilingual & Dual Language Community in Austin-Texas. It was also performed at the National Council of Teachers of English

Conference in November 2017 in St Louis, Missouri; November 2018 at the Literacy Research Association Conference in Indian Wells, California; and April 2019 at the American Educational Research Association Conference in Toronto, Canada. Sources used for the performance and English translations are provided as endnotes.

Part 1: Context

[*The performance opens when Caldas presses play to a video projected on the screen. She is wearing a beige trench coat and high heels. There is a pair of glasses hanging from her lapel. While the video is playing, she hands out some reading parts to six audience members, which will be read when prompted. She also places the following props around the stage: boxing helmet and boxing gloves on a table on the left side of the stage; right flat shoe on the left of the chair placed near the left corner of the stage in the background; a piece of paper stuck below the screen. Once she is done with the props, she stands on the front right side of the stage, facing the audience as the video plays. The video contains the following video bites.*]

Video bite 1: When Mexico sends its people, they're not sending their best. They're sending people who have lots of problems. They're bringing drugs, they're bringing crime, they're rapists and some, I assume, are good people.[4]

Video bite 2: Driving while brown is apparently enough to get you arrested in Kentucky. One Kentucky prosecutor, John K. Carter, is coming under fire for the comments he made to a judge regarding why a suspect was arrested.[5]

Video bite 3: Then Popp spoke to them, asking them where they were from, and he and his father both answered 'Puerto Rico'. The complaint says, then the man [Popp] said 'oh, that's why you don't speak English'. When the father and son walked back from the laundry room, Popp allegedly pointed a long gun at the father, Jesus Manso-Perez, and said 'you guys gotta go'. He then allegedly shot the father as the son ran out.[6]

Video bite 4: Being Mexican American is tough. Anglos jump all over you if you don't speak English perfectly. Mexicans jump all over you if you don't speak Spanish perfectly. We have to be twice as perfect as anybody else.[7]

Video bite 5: Replace bilingual education with immersion in English, so they learn the language of prosperity, not the language of living in the ghetto.[8]

[*As soon as video bite 5 finishes, Caldas takes center stage and adopts several personas, most of them research participants. The conference presenter is not a participant, but a character Caldas created based on traditional discourses surrounding bilingual education.*]

Conference presenter: Welcome to another conference on bilingual education; thank you all for coming. According to research, the qualities of effective bilingual teachers are…

[*The conference presenter is interrupted by the audio of voices of actual bilingual teachers Caldas interviewed, superimposed on top of one another, making the audio unintelligible to the audience. She stops to listen as the audio fades. She then performs her own voice.*]

Caldas: Juan, David, Nancy, Julia, Manuel… The stories of struggle of these bilingual teachers are tired of being whispers in my ears. They want to take shape in your own body, that their words become your words, that you can complete their unfinished sentences, that you can do the things they couldn't do, to follow their steps and go beyond. You, new teacher, the fight is yours. Try their shoes; try your new shoes. What would you do? What would I do?

[*Caldas moves toward the chair on the left, takes off one high heel and puts on the right flat shoe. Limps toward the audience and gives 10 business cards to members of the audience while making small talk. At the back of the business cards, Caldas wrote the following phrases 'first-generation college student', 'español', 'immigrant', 'brown', 'Latina', 'Quechua', 'daughter', 'mestiza', 'teacher', 'woman'. When she is finished with the business cards, she moves toward the chair, takes off the jacket and hangs it on the chair. It is revealed that she is wearing a T-shirt that says 'Bilingual Education'. This T-shirt was created by the participants, who gave it to Caldas as a gift. Caldas then employs ELP techniques to adopt the posture and voice of Zully, one of her students. She takes off the shoes, puts her hair in a side ponytail, sits on the chair in lotus pose while texting on her imaginary cellphone as the following voiceover plays in the background.*]

Voiceover 1: Language education is defined as the instruction and learning of a second or foreign language. Researchers agree that early second language instruction helps promote the mastery of correct pronunciation and grammatical concepts. However, there are many situations in which second language learning cannot or does not occur. Students enrolled in schools in the United States are more and more diverse.[9]

Part 2: Emotions

[*After the voiceover is done, the following vignette shows up on the screen for 30 seconds.*]

Vignette 1: Most of the children in bilingual classes have been taught only in English last year at my school. So, when we were looking for new bilingual teachers, many of the committee members said 'why do we need a bilingual teacher? Let's hire a [English] monolingual teacher'. I ended up leaving the meeting because these people are closed-minded. Many of these children had a great potential but because they don't speak English or the school don't see bilingualism as an advantage, they end up being stigmatized.

[*Caldas, as Zully, puts the cellphone down and stares at the audience and delivers this speech taken from a video recording of one of the class performances where Zully voices her concerns.*]

Zully: It's sad they forget the reason why they became bilingual teachers. When you listen to their answers you just want to slap them, slap them [*pretends to slap*], like 'what are you thinking?' They are bilingual teachers, they're supposed to be supporting Spanish and English y no lo están haciendo.

[*Caldas stands up, walks around the chair from right to left, undoes the ponytail and puts on the* mismatched *shoes and jacket. She moves center front.*]

Caldas: They might not feel comfortable about performing Casos de la Vida Real; not that they don't like playing, they might be uncomfortable about standing up and doing it. One day, before a performance, the students asked to divide the classroom into protagonist and antagonist so that they could discuss the arguments for and against before the performance. This changes Forum Theater but that's what they want to do. [*Offering the jacket to the audience*] What would you do?

[*Voiceover starts.*]

Voiceover 2: Bilingual education is the approach to second language instruction in which students are instructed on academic subject areas in their native language while simultaneously being taught to speak and write in the second language. The type of bilingual education instruction can vary depending on the amount of language to be taught. For example, students may have limited English proficiency or limited ability to understand and communicate in oral or written English because English is not the student's native language.[10]

[*During the voiceover, Caldas leaves shoes on centerstage, hangs the jacket on the chair and move front stage. She puts on the glasses, puts her hair in a half ponytail. The following vignette shows up on the screen for 30 seconds.*]

Vignette 2: The other day a teacher came to me and told me 'I know you were absent yesterday. One of my students lost his jacket and I think one of your students stole it'. I was puzzled. She told me she waited to talk to me because he didn't understand English. I told her that student has been here for four months in the United States. So, I asked her: 'how do you know he stole it?' She said: 'because it says Abercrombie on it, your student can't afford Abercrombie'.

> [*After the vignette disappears,* a *video of a Forum Theater performance recorded during fieldwork plays in mute mode. Using ELP techniques, voice and gestures, Caldas embodies Milagros. The following text was taken from a one-on-one interview with Milagros. Caldas puts on the mismatched shoes and rehearses poses for 10 seconds.*]

Milagros: [*to imaginary interlocutor in a desperate tone*] Señorita, por qué[11]...? [*scowls and tries again*] Cómo sabe que[12]...? Ugh [*gives up and speaks to the audience*] Me sentí bien nerviosa pero a pesar de estar bien nerviosa[13]... my mind just went blank because you're just so angry at the situation that your mind doesn't like think about all the examples you can provide, all the research, because we've done a lot of reading.

> [*Caldas takes off glasses, undoes ponytail and goes back to her voice.*]

Caldas: I can understand those feelings [*moves to get the jacket and is about to put it on but instead holds it in her arm*]. To choke up and not being able to talk without yelling/crying. Yeah, this is frustrating, but I want you to feel hopeful too. How to keep cool as you mature? How to play this game? Am I making you in the class feel helpless? [*checks her pockets and reads the card*] Henry Giroux says: 'When students are told that all that matters for them is feeling good and that feeling uncomfortable is alien to learning itself, the very nature of teaching and learning is compromised'.

Part 3: Language

> [*Caldas leaves coat and glasses on the right. She crosses the stage to background left and puts on boxing gear. During this time, we can hear the following voiceover.*]

Voiceover 3: Students with limited English proficiency may be placed in transitional bilingual education classrooms, where the student native language may be used more often for instructional purposes to ensure they do not fall behind in subject areas. As the child learns more of the second language, the amount of native language instruction declines.[14]

> [*Caldas rehearses some boxing moves while the next vignette shows up on the screen.*]

Vignette 3: Some teachers opposed language mixing. Having grown up in Spanish-speaking countries, they would tell their students: 'don't mix them, don't ruin both languages'. It was not fair to limit a child who is growing up with two languages. If they can use two languages, they should use them as they see fit; that's not 'ruining' them. There is no problem in mixing languages but they need to realize that's a Texan practice, so we need to accept it as part of their culture.

[*Caldas crosses the stage diagonally to center-right and starts shadowboxing. While shadowboxing mentioning some rules to engage in arguments created by the participants in the fieldwork.*]

Caldas: Tus ideas no son válidas si no mantienes la calma.[15] Avoid raising your voice and disrespect. Cuida tu tono, eres una profesional.[16] Keep your mind open. Listen. Use theories and research, like the ones by Krashen, Cummins, Bialystok. Se lógica y amable[17]; find solutions; no name-calling. Question people about their beliefs/thoughts; this makes people think of what they are saying.

[*Caldas catches her breath. She turns around and points at a member of the audience who was given a script during the introduction. The audience member reads the part of 'Luis' while Caldas uses ELP to embody Luz, a student. The following dialogue was captured by video during one of Luz' performances. The audience member as 'Luis' reads their part in the dialogue.*]

Luis: We think students shouldn't mix languages because they can damage both; we prefer separating them.

Luz: Recent studies show that using the first language to learn a second one is really beneficial. They're transferring their knowledge to learn a new language. That's the reason why we let our students use their first language. Besides, the concept of codeswitching helps their understanding of themes and ideas they're learning.

Luis: How do we know if our students know both languages at the same level during this time? They can mix languages, but what happens if they mix languages because they don't know a word, so they say it in the other language?

Luz: Because we're looking at our students' work and we notice they're not using their first language as crutching, but as a tool to make themselves understood and they're using language in context.

Luis: I think we do know our students and that's why we don't want them to mix languages. For example, for the STAAR test, they will be evaluated in just one language. So we want them to practice separating the languages so that they don't get confused during the exam.

Luz: Some studies show that bilingual students have higher capabilities and can have better grades than monolingual students.

Part 4: Advocacy

[*Caldas mouths 'thank you' to the audience member who reads 'Luis' before going to the background to take off the boxing gear. Caldas moves the chair to the right corner in the front of the stage facing the screen. She sits down during a video of a class performance playing on the screen. The dialogue in the video is in Spanish with subtitles in English.*]

Female teacher: Juan! qué es lo que te acabo de decir?
Male student: Um, español?
Female teacher: Español. Entonces cuál debería de haber sido la palabra que dijiste?
Male student: Marrano
Female teacher: El marrano, sí. El cerdo. Entonces por qué usaste el inglés?
Male student: Porque me sentí más a gusto
Female teacher: Pero ya te he dicho que no debes de hablar en inglés en un día de español. Mejor vete a la esquina para no volverte a regañar
Male student: Pero yo sé qué significa pig: cerdo.
Female teacher: Sí, pero lo dijiste mal, ya te lo había dicho[18]
[*As soon as the video above is over, the following vignette shows up for 30 seconds.*]

Vignette 4: When the Cinco de Mayo show finished and none of the Mexican parents showed up to see their children dance, we asked the secretary what happened. She told us that since their parents didn't show a Texas ID, she didn't let them into the school.

[*During the vignette, Caldas uses ELP techniques to embody Luis, another student. The following text was taken from his video reflection. Caldas puts her hair in a bun, stands up, goes to the background left and speaks to the audience.*]

Luis: To be honest, I never considered myself as an advocate before this semester because I used to think that an advocate would usually be someone who fights to gain rights or to be treated equally. I have always felt like I have never really had to defend any of my beliefs. After this semester, I consider myself an advocate for bilingual education after learning about the history of bilingual education and the importance of standing up for what you believe in. I have engaged in advocacy by participating in Casos de la Vida Real and at times explaining to some peers why bilingual education is very important.

[A video of another Forum Theater performance plays in the background, but the audio fades within 10 seconds, though the video keeps playing on. In these first 10 seconds the audience can hear the researcher facilitating a conversation after a Forum Theater performance. During this time, she moves to front left of the stage to embody Ana Maria through ELP techniques.]

Ana Maria: It was eye-opening. It's more meaningful to do it than just reading it because whenever you read it yes, you have a reaction. But when you role-play you're actually playing your thoughts out there while someone attacks them, and you have to defend your position. It makes it more meaningful, and you actually remember what you say, and then you feel you're doing something important. It gave me another identity. My placement is in my community, and in my letter to the parents, I was open to them, and I told them I was a DACA[19] student; if you have any questions, you can reach out to me because I've been through the process and I have answers.

[Another voiceover starts.]

Voiceover 4: Multicultural education is the approach to instruction that integrates perspectives and experiences of numerous cultural groups throughout the curriculum. Multicultural education can be approached throughout a variety of strategies. Educators can incorporate books and activities that celebrate holidays or special events from other cultures. They can incorporate literature and instruction about people from diverse cultures into the existing curriculum.[20]

[During the voiceover and the next vignette, Caldas faces the screen and starts braiding her hair.]

Vignette 5: When I used the book *Sylvia & Aki* to my students, my colleagues didn't like that I taught the history that we, bilingual teachers, didn't know about; like immigration. The Westminster case is the most crucial thing that could have happened to Mexican Americans. I told my students, 'I didn't know this, nobody taught me this. You need to educate yourself'. But my colleague teachers didn't think it was necessary. They'd say: 'you're making them not like it here in the U.S.A.'. My colleagues would say: 'why are you contradicting the textbooks?'.

[After 30 seconds, Caldas moves toward the screen and takes the piece of paper below. She turns around and moves to the center-front of the stage. Caldas uses ELP techniques to embody another student, Sharon, the author of the following poem.]

I was sitting there.
We were all sitting there.
It's 9:15 am, these white walls couldn't get any dingier.
'Okay vamos, Casos de la Vida Real'.[21]
Aye, ejole otra vez[22]... I don't wanna go up there
but a part of me hopes she calls on me.
My stomach tightens, I hate acting, but I love speaking. I'm
gonna be a teacher so I have to love acting. But is it acting if
it's really who you are. Do I really even know who I am?
The case goes up: 'you're making them not like it here in the U.S.A.'
Their passive citizenry is fading away. Provoking one critical
thought at a time, one critical question, one critical answer. Students
will then be able to answer to the sultry voice of assimilations
calling as she slowly works her way into every aspect of your life,
she begins to tell you: 'that book, Sylvia and Aki, put it away;
ese libro no contiene nada, tu historia, no contiene nada.[23]
The textbook says everything you need to know.
Students can then say, *we* can then say:
Well, what does it know about Japanese internment camps
Angel Island, Dolores Huerta, Diego Rivera, socialista,
La Bestia, coyotes, working class wages, white collar crime,
Bilingual Education, Native American boarding schools, walk-outs,
gentrification, assimilation, Chicano history?
It's the Americans tapestry, where some
threads are more costly than others,
where some threads have been stretched far too thin,
whose backs have been used to construct the entire blanket
and yet they have not given into asimilación, educación.
'Why are you contradicting the textbooks?'
I read that last sentence; *We* read that last sentence.
These white walls are telling me something.
Should I say something? My palms are sweaty. *Our* palms get sweaty.
My heart beats faster. *Our* hearts beat faster.
Okay I'll go, I'll be....
And I don't listen.
My words trail off while I submerge in my thoughts.
'How will I defend my students, if my colleagues
think my students' language should be lost?'
But then I see, I feel, I think.
Something's not right here [*pointing to her mouth*], some
things are not right *here* [*pointing to her head*].
What we're doing in *here*, we should be practicing out *there*.
We don't feel hopeless; in fact we feel much *less*
intimidated by what we will confront.

We are the teachers on the forefront; armed
with research, our stories, our history.
I have revealed my voice, *We* have revealed our voice.
It's not acting if you believe in it.

[*Pause. Caldas addresses the audience as herself.*]

Caldas: [*to the audience*] These are some of the fears my students have, and I wanted to share them with you. Can you please read the card I gave you before the performance? Can you please read the first one?

[*The previously selected audience members read the five cards distributed during the introduction.*]

Audience member 1: I think it would be difficult for me to involve myself in the community because being a teacher means being very busy working.

Audience member 2: I think trying to change unfair institutional practices would be the most difficult because I'd face more opposition.

Audience member 3: It would be hard to defend bilingual education because I could risk my job if the principal doesn't share the same ideas.

Audience member 4: The same way people reject the great amount of research that supports bilingualism, I think people will also reject codeswitching in spite of the studies that show its worth in the lives of bilingual students.

Audience member 5: I feel the most difficult thing for me is to be a new teacher because there are lots of teachers working in the district for several years. I think the most difficult thing is to gain their respect to be taken seriously.

[*Caldas addresses the audience again.*]

Caldas: Will I be taken seriously too? In the world of educational research, will I be taken seriously as I conduct a performance ethnography? [*pause*] Fuck it; I'll do it anyway.

Notes

(1) The way bilingual individuals use their full linguistic repertoire – even by crossing language frontiers – in order to communicate and make sense.

(2) Translation: Real-life cases.

(3) An English–Spanish approximation one participant made when trying to say 'advocate' in Spanish. Instead, the participant translated it to 'avocado' due to its homophonic resemblance. Despite this so-called mistranslation, their classmates understood what this participant meant.

(4) From 'Fact checking Donald Trump's immigration comments' by CNN, 2 July 2015, video, 3:54. See https://www.youtube.com/watch?v=BhbOEduvA9U.
(5) From 'Racist attorney calls driving while brown a crime in video' by The Lip TV Margaret Howell, 17 October 2015, video, 3:38. See https://www.youtube.com/watch?v=NU8NJum6Zq4.
(6) From 'Man charged following triple homicide on Milwaukee's southwest side' by TMJ4 News, 10 March 2016, video, 2:35. See https://www.youtube.com/watch?v=M_Wc3ITSY74&t=14s.
(7) From 'Selena' by Gregory Nava, 1997.
(8) From 'Newt Gingrich: Spanish is the language of the ghetto'. Collective Checkup, 25 January 2012, video 0.17. See https://www.youtube.com/watch?v=_rF694NzjPU.
(9) From 'Bilingual education, immersion & multicultural education'. Study.com, 2 November 2012, video 6:10. See https://study.com/academy/lesson/bilingual-education-immersion-multicultural-education.html.
(10) From 'Bilingual education, immersion & multicultural education'. Study.com, 2 November 2012, video 6:10. See https://study.com/academy/lesson/bilingual-education-immersion-multicultural-education.html.
(11) Translation: M'am, why…?
(12) Translation: How do you know that…?
(13) Translation: I felt very nervous, but despite being nervous….
(14) From 'Bilingual education, immersion & multicultural education'. Study.com, 2 November 2012, video 6:10. See https://study.com/academy/lesson/bilingual-education-immersion-multicultural-education.html.
(15) Translation: Your ideas won't be valid if you don't keep calm.
(16) Translation: Watch your tone, you are a professional.
(17) Translation: Be logical and polite.
(18) Translation: Female teacher: Juan, what did I just told you?
Male student: In Spanish?
Female teacher: Spanish. Then what word should you have used?
Male student: Piggy, Pig
Female teacher: Piggy, yes, pig. Then why did you use English?
Male student: Because it felt good
Female teacher: I already told you today is Spanish day. Go to the corner before I tell you off again
Male student: But I know what pig means
Female teacher: Well, but you said it wrong, Juan; I told you already.
(19) Deferred Action for Childhood Arrival: A US migration policy that allows some individuals who arrived as children without proper immigration documentation to access a two-year renewable period of deferred action from deportation and a work permit.
(20) Study.com 9.
(21) Translation: Ok, let's go, Real life cases.
(22) Translation: Oh, not again.
(23) Translation: That book has nothing; your history has nothing.

References

Alim, H.S. and American Dialect Society (2004) *You Know My Steez: An Ethnographic and Sociolinguistic Study of Styleshifting in a Black American Speech Community*. Durham, NC: Duke University Press for the American Dialect Society.

Alim, S., Rickford, J. and Ball, A. (2016) *Raciolinguistics: How Language Shapes Our Ideas about Race*. Oxford: Oxford University Press.

Andreotti, V. (2011) *Actionable Postcolonial Theory in Education*. London: Palgrave Macmillan.

Boal, A. (2000) *Theater of the Oppressed*. London: Pluto.

Chilisa, B. (2012) *Indigenous Research Methodologies*. Thousand Oaks, CA: Sage.

Conquergood, D. (1985) Performing as a moral act: Ethical dimensions of the ethnography of performance. *Literature and Performance* 5 (2), 1–13.

García, O. (2009) Education, multilingualism and translanguaging in the 21st century. In A.K. Mohanty, M. Panda, R. Phillipson and T. Skutnabb-Kangas (eds) *Multilingual Education for Social Justice: Globalising the Local* (pp. 128–145). New Delhi: Orient BlackSwan.

Hopper, R. (1993) Conversational dramatism and everyday life performance. *Text and Performance Quarterly* 13, 181–183.

Jones, J.L. (2002) Performance ethnography: The role of embodiment in cultural authenticity. *Theatre Topics* 12 (1), 1–15.

Jones, J.L. (2006) Performance and ethnography, performing ethnography, performance ethnography. In D.S. Madison and J. Hamera (eds) *The Sage Handbook of Performance Studies* (pp. 339–346). Thousand Oaks, CA: Sage.

Jones, J.L. (2015, October) Performance ethnography as social change. Paper presentation. Oral History Association Annual Meeting, Tampa, Florida.

Kincheloe, N. and McLaren, P. (2000) Rethinking critical theory and qualitative research. In N. Denzin and Y. Lincoln (eds) *Handbook of Qualitative Research* (2nd edn, pp. 303–342). Thousand Oaks, CA: Sage.

Madison, S. (2007) Co-performance witnessing. *Cultural Studies* 21 (6), 826–831.

Madison, S. (2018) *Performed Ethnography and Communication: Improvisation and Embodied Experience*. Abingdon: Routledge.

Madison, S. (2019) *Critical Ethnography: Method, Ethics, and Performance* (3rd edn). Thousand Oaks, CA: Sage.

Saldaña, J. (2011) *Ethnotheatre: Research from Page to Stage*. Walnut Creek, CA: Left Coast Press.

Schechner, R. (1993) Anna Deavere Smith: Acting as incorporation. *Tdr* 37 (4), 63–64.

Wilson, S. (2008) *Research is Ceremony: Indigenous Research Methods*. Halifax, NS: Fernwood Publications.

Index

Abu-Lughod, L. 80
academia 93–4, 97–102
Academia Cuauhtli 152–68
academic writing 67–8, 75, 82, 85
accent 33, 131, 144, 158, 177
acculturation 157–8
action research 22, 101
additive bilingualism 21, 22, 31, 32
advocacy 242, 248–51
African American English 28, 32, 34, 50, 171
Aiello, J. 70
Akwesasne Freedom School 181–2, 185
Alim, H.S. 24, 30, 33, 34, 36, 172, 240, 242
American Association of Applied Linguistics (AAAL) Annual Conference 11
American Educational Research Association (AERA) 108
Anders, A. 4
Anderson, B. 193
Anderson, G. 153, 154, 156
Andreotti, V. 242
Andronis, M.A. 201
'anthropological confidant' 216, 229, 234
anthropology 2
antiblackness 42–64
Anzaldúa, G. 4, 50, 70, 75, 81, 110, 112, 119, 155, 156
Aotearoa New Zealand 31, 183
Arabic 69, 74, 75, 86
Arias, B. 174
Arizona, US 174–5
Asian English 33, 34
Asian-American identity 34
asset pedagogies 30, 180
assimilationism 27, 95
assumptions, deconstruction of 110–11, 200
Atkinson, P. 5
authenticity 137–41
autoethnography 50, 81
axiology, researchers' 67, 82

Baker-Bell, A. 48, 50
Bakhtin, M. 33
'balanced' bilingualism 32
Banerji, A. 79
Barad, K. 5, 9
Barton, A.C. 213
Baszile, D.T. 58
Bauman, R. 25
Bell, D. 4, 54, 57
Berlant, L. 5, 23
Bialystock, D. 218
bias, awareness of 126 *see also* positionality
Biesta, G.J. 10
bilingual education *see also* dual-language programs
–Canada 126–7
–as counternarrative to monolingual ideologies 31
–critical performance 240–53
–inequality 101
–language, race/ism and in/equity 21–37
–Latinx education 152–68, 214, 216, 219–35
–mother tongue-based multilingual education (MTB-MLE) 197, 200, 202
–New Zealand 21
–race reflexivity 93

–rethinking 129–31
–Spanish-English dual-language programs 31, 92–3, 95–103, 116
–subtractive bilingual education 95, 101
–Texas 159
–two-way immersion bilingual education (TWBE) program 109, 115, 118, 130, 159
–US 213–39
biliteracy 32, 97
bi/multilingualism
–bi/multilingual competencies 26
–Canada 127
–cognitive benefits of 218
–conceived as two separate linguistic systems 129
–dynamic bi/multilingualism 23, 24, 27, 32–4
–in ESL classrooms 27
–language policy 32
Black English 28, 29, 32, 34, 50
Black Literacies 52
Black Storywork 56–9
Black Youth Voice 42–64
BlackCrit 4, 24, 42–64
#BlackLivesMatter 52
Block, D. 193
Blommaert, J. 26, 35, 124, 132, 199, 208
Boal, A. 240, 242
body epistemologies 49
Bonaparte, B. 185
Bonfiglio, T.P. 74, 85
Bonilla, C.M. 160
border crossing 111, 112, 115, 116–17
borderlands 108–9, 111, 112, 119, 165
Bourdieu, P. 2, 7, 22, 24, 31, 44–5, 94, 97, 131, 132, 135
Boyer, P. 181, 182
Brayboy, B.M.J. 173, 185
Breidenbach, J. 124
Briggs, C. 25
Britzman, D.P. 3
Bucholtz, M. 33–4
Butler, J. 3, 28, 49, 132
Byrd Clark, J.S. 123, 124, 125, 127, 129, 130, 131, 132, 133, 134, 135, 136, 137, 141, 147
Caldas, B. xi, 6, 10, 35, 215
Calderón, D. 108
Camangian, P. 50–1
Cammarota, J. 101
Canada 28, 32, 123–51, 181
Canagarajah, S. 129, 131
capital 24, 214
capitalism 154, 160 *see also* neoliberalism
Caribbean-based Creole 33
Carspecken, P. 1, 101, 229
Carstens, D. 5
Cary, L.J. 153
Cervantes-Soon, C. 108, 110, 157, 214, 215, 218, 219, 220
change, addressing 10
change facilitation 49
Charlo, A. 84
Chávez-Moreno, L. 84, 93, 94, 99, 102, 130, 218, 230
Chicago, US 177
Chicana feminist epistemology (CFE) 108–9, 114, 155
Chicanx researchers 108–22
Chilisa, B. 241–2
Choi, T.-H. 197
Chomsky, N. 132, 141
citizenship 165
civil rights movements 42, 58, 100, 160–1, 162, 165
class 28, 96, 134, 159, 163, 193, 196 *see also* gentrification
Clifford, J. 8
Cockney 33
co-construction of knowledge 125, 160, 162
co-construction of meaning 153
co-created communities 56–7
code-switching 50, 133, 142–4, 247 *see also* translanguaging
Coles, J.A. 44, 45, 46, 47, 48, 51, 58
collective action 51, 56–7, 173
colonialism
–decentering colonialism 154
–decolonial theory 152, 155, 165–6
–decolonization 110, 120, 155, 181, 184
–empire-centric gaze 71–2, 76, 77
–ethnographic studies 70–2

–language as a site of struggle 76
–monolingual ideologies 193
–and multilingualism 66
–power flows 153–4
–research methods 110
–Spanish 96
–standard language varieties 75
–standard norms as ideologies 144–5
–and traditional ethnography 155
Combs, M.C. 174
communicative competence 27, 128
community belonging 120, 127
comparative ethnological perspectives 180–5
compressed time mode 8
confianza 110, 230, 231
Conquergood, D. 241
consejos 30
Conwill, K.H. 44
co-performance witnesses 240, 241
co-researchers 9
Cormier, G. 67, 70, 74
Cornell Gonzáles, G. 216
Council of Europe 133
counter-narratives/stories 36, 47, 51, 57–8, 242
Cree 73
Crenshaw, K. 4, 100
crimes against humanity 135
critical consciousness 101, 102, 214, 219–23, 230–2
critical feminism 3
critical intercultural language awareness 123–51
critical listening 222, 223–5
critical multiculturalism 21, 22
critical pedagogy 49, 220
critical performance 240–53
critical race ethnography 91–107
critical social theory 5
critical sociolinguistics 132
critical theory 3, 24, 35, 135, 165–6, 242
CRT (critical race theory)
–and antiblackness 52–3
–asset pedagogies 30
–bi/multilingualism 34–5
–and BlackCrit 52–4
–and education 91–2, 98–9
–Latinx studies 24
–leveraging of voice 47
–non-Black researchers 59
–postcritical ethnographies 3–4
–silencing 47
–voice-of-color thesis 57
cultural communication 8–9
cultural heritage 152
cultural intuition 110, 115, 118
cultural knowledge 97
cultural pluralism 30, 35, 127
cultural production of research 101
cultural reclamation 173, 185
cultural repertoires of practice 30
cultural resources 132
cultural understanding 8–9
culturally relevant pedagogy 102
Curtis, C.A. 47

Davis, K.A. 191, 192, 197, 199, 200, 209
De Korne, N. 172, 191
De Lissovoy, N. 217, 223
de Souza, L.M.T.M. 130
decentering colonialism 154
decolonial theory 152, 155, 165–6
decolonization 110, 120, 155, 181, 184
deep hanging out 8, 9
deficit approaches
–to bilingual education in US 164
–Canada 130
–diversity 26–7
–education 113
–ESL programs 27, 29
–immersion education 28
–Indigenous education 192, 200–4
–to linguistic diversity 26–7
–monolingual ideologies 23
–structured English immersion (SEI) 177
dehumanization 50, 72, 98, 100, 206
Deiri, Y. 70, 74
Delamont, S. 9
Deleuze, G. 3
Delgado, R. 57, 97
Delgado Bernal, D. 109, 110, 114, 115, 118
Delgado-Gaitan, C. 111, 120
democratization 26, 194

Dervin, F. 132, 136
Desmond, M. 91, 93, 94, 95, 97, 98, 99, 100, 103
destrenzando 110–11, 120
dialogic approach 7
dialogical relationships 152–68, 202, 241
Dillard, C.B. 109
Diné (Navajo) 182–3
disciplinary unconscious 94, 97–100
discourse analysis 31, 34, 36, 124, 125
discrete, bounded entities, languages as 32, 127, 144, 193
Distante, I. 79
Donnor, J. 101
Douglass, F. 172
Du Bois, W.E.B. 4, 172
dual-language programs 21, 31, 92–3, 95–103, 158, 213–39 *see also* bilingual education
Dumas, M.J. 45, 46, 53, 54
Duncan, G.A. 52, 53–4, 55, 91
Duncan-Andrade, J.M.R. 232
dynamic bi/multilingualism 23, 24, 27, 32–4

Ebonics 171
editorial censorship 85
ELL (English Language Learners) 92, 157, 164, 174, 175–8
emancipatory praxis 152–68
embodied rescriptings 240–53
Emirbayer, M. 91, 93, 94, 95, 97, 98, 99, 100, 103
emotions in research 77
empire-centric gaze 71–2, 76, 77
Enciso, P. 51
'engaged language policy' 197–8
English
 –academic writing 68
 –Canada 32, 124, 125, 128
 –ELL (English Language Learners) 92, 157, 164, 174, 175–8
 –English as a medium of instruction (EMI) 193, 196, 200–2
 –English language learner after reclassification (ELLAR) 176
 –English-only movements 73, 77, 193
 –ESL/EFL teaching industries 25
 –globalization of 25
 –hegemony of 37, 50
 –in Latinx settings 157
 –linguistic discrimination in ESL 27–9
 –London English 33
 –neoliberalism 203, 208
 –Nepal 200
 –Received Pronunciation 33
 –as reference point for deficit views 23
 –and research design 68–9
 –standard language varieties 33–4, 75, 171
epistemic delinking 155, 156
epistemic injustice 206
epistemology, researchers' 67, 70, 82, 137, 153, 155, 166
erasure 96, 201
ethico-onto-epistemology 5–6, 9, 11
ethnic identity 35
ethnic studies, bans on 177
ethnodrama 240
ethnographic monitoring 172–3, 175–85
ethnography of performance 28
Eurocentrism 85, 152, 154, 166
everyday language practices 32–4, 47, 49
everyday life performance 241
exoticization, in traditional anthropology 2

Fairclough, N. 135, 136
Faltis, C. 174
Fanon, F. 4
feminist poststructuralist ethnographies of education 3
feminist scholarship 114, 155
fields 24
fieldwork 2, 9–10, 160 *see also* research methods
Fine, M. 1, 5, 6, 10, 49–50, 101
First Nations people 127, 135
Firth, A. 146
Fitzpatrick, K. 2, 4, 11, 22, 23, 24
Flores, N. 24, 35, 74, 127, 130, 133, 159, 164, 171–2, 186, 214, 217, 221
Flores v Arizona 174

flowed texts 35
focus group methods 57
Foley, D. 2, 5, 216, 229, 234
Forum Theater 240, 242
Foucault, M. 3
Franglophones 127
freedom of voice 173
Freeman, R. 31
Freire, P. 2, 49, 101, 102, 160, 213, 214, 219, 223, 226
Freirean circles 160
French 27–8, 32, 123–51
French as a Second Language (FSL) 123–51
French Immersion (FI) 124, 126–7, 128, 129–30
Fricker, M. 206
friends as research participants 69, 81
funds of knowledge 24, 30

Gal, S. 201
Galiev, A. 130
Gándara, P. 177–8
García, O. 24, 35, 129, 130, 133, 134, 214, 240
García-Mateus, S. 115, 116
Gaudry, A. 84
Geerts, E. 5
Geertz, C. 2, 8, 9
'generative themes' 213–14, 223, 226–7, 232
Genesee, F. 129
gentrification 115, 159, 213–39
geopolitical context 153–4, 155, 158–9
Giddens, A. 132, 135
Gilmore, P. 206
Giri, R.A. 202–3
Giroux, H. 125
Givens, J.R. 48
Glesne, C. 109
Global South 155
globalization 25–6, 37, 123, 193
glorification processes 193–4
Gorski, P.C. 201, 202, 209
Gramling, D. 23, 25
Gramsci, A. 135
Grenfell, M. 24
Guattari, F. 3
Guba, E.G. 109
Gumperz, J.J. 125
Gutierrez, K. 30

habitus 24
Haraway, D. 4, 155, 156
Harlins, Latasha 44
Harris, A. 100
Harris, C.I. 92
Hawaiian (Kanaka Maoli) 183–5
Heath, S.B. 28, 29
Heiman, D. 115, 130, 159, 213, 215, 216, 218, 219, 221, 224, 226
Heller, M. 25, 32, 136, 198, 199
helping/saving narratives 67
Hermes, M. 181
hierarchies of prestige 25, 37, 196, 202
Hill, J. 171
Hill, R. 31, 36, 191
Hinton, L. 184
hip hop 28, 34
historias 30, 36, 111–14
Hobsbawm, E. 129
homogenization 25, 80, 123–51
hooks, b. 76, 77
Hopson, R. 180
Hornberger, N. 32, 172, 184, 191, 199
Howard, E. 218, 220
Howard, T.C. 47
human capital 214
human rights 162, 165
humanizing research stance 35–6, 230
Hylton, K. 101
Hymes, D. 26, 28, 172, 173, 177, 180

Ibrahim, A. 27–8, 32–3
idealization of language 132
idealized native speaker model 141
identity
  –co-construction of 115
  –community belonging 127
  –complex positionings 137–41
  –counter-insurgent forms of 27
  –critical theory 135
  –embracing 158
  –ethnic identity 35
  –hyphenated identities 137
  –ideological messages 141–2
  –multiple 110, 141
  –outsider lens 117

–reflexivity 95
–standard norms as ideologies 145
–transnational 131
ideological domestication 209
ideological hegemony 208
Illich, I. 102
imagined communities 193
immersion education
–deficit approaches 28
–French Immersion (FI) 124, 126–7, 128, 129–30
–language, race/ism and in/equity 21, 27–8
–in Latinx settings 157
–Māori language 31–2
–partial immersion approaches 21
–raciolinguistics 174–8, 183
–structured English immersion (SEI) 174, 175–8
–two-way immersion bilingual education (TWBE) program 109, 115, 118, 130, 159
inbetweener, researcher as 70, 81
in-between-ness of positionality 134–5, 137, 143
Indian Education Act (1972) 183
Indigenous education 24, 31, 173, 178–85, 191–212
Indigenous epistemologies 24, 73, 80
Indigenous languages 96, 178, 180–5, 191, 196–7
Indigenous scholarship 6–7, 79, 84
Indigenous subjectivity 165
inequality 101, 164, 173, 191, 207–8
in/equity
–colonialism 154
–dual-language programs 220
–in education 19–41, 101
–key tenets of critical ethnography 4–5
–raciolinguistics 173
in/justice 4–5, 101, 192–4, 206 *see also* social justice
insider accounts 7, 115–20
interactional sociolinguistics 24, 33
interconnectedness 66, 76, 80, 81, 126
interculturality 123–51, 218, 220
interdisciplinarity 23–4, 97, 98, 100
internalized oppression 49
interpretivist approaches 2, 137
intersectionality 3, 29, 95, 163
interview methods 36, 57, 124, 136, 160
intimacy 65–6, 72–5, 77, 78, 81
intimate ethnography 78
intra-action 9
intuition 65–6, 110, 115, 118
invisibilization 192, 202
invited lens, using an 66–7, 173
Iokepa-Guerrero, N. 183, 184
Irvine, J.T. 201

Jacobs, R. 185
Jeffrey, B. 8
Johnson, G.T. 102
Johnson, L.L. 48, 57
Jones, O.O.J.L. 240, 241, 242

Kaiapuni schools 183–4
Kanaka Maoli (Hawaiian) 183–5
Kangas, S. 177
Kanien'kehá:ka (Mohawk) 181–2, 185
Kanno, Y. 177
Kaomea, J. 173
Karki, J. 208
Kashua, S. 66
Kawai'ae'e, K. 181
key tenets of critical ethnography 4–10
Khas-Arya 195
Khati, A. 193, 195
King, J. 206
King, Martin Luther 162–3
Kinloch, V. 51
Kirkland, D.E. 45, 47
Knaus, C.B. 47
Kovach, M. 79, 80, 81, 84
Kroskrity, P.V. 192

Labov, W. 133
Ladson-Billings, G. 52, 93, 98, 100, 101, 102, 109
Lagemann, E.C. 98
language annihilation 180–5
language crossing 33–4, 35
language hierarchies 192, 196, 202, 204–8, 209
language panics 171–90
language policy
–bilingual education 32

–BlackCrit 49
–Indigenous education 31
–language panics 174–86
–nation-state 37
–Nepal 191–212
–power 185, 198
–raciolinguistics 172, 173
language purity ideologies 85, 143
language sharing 35
'language work' 181, 184
languagelessness 172, 180
language-nation-state ideology 127, 129, 131, 202
languages as discrete entities 32, 127, 144, 193
LatCrit 4, 24
Lather, P. 3, 4, 5, 101
Latinx education 152–68, 214, 216, 219–35
Latinx studies 24, 96, 111
Laughton, J. 21
Lazore, D. 182, 184
legal tradition 99
legitimacy 137–41, 180, 185
Leonard, W. 181, 184
Leonardo, Z. 54, 99
Lessard, S. 73
Li Wei 24, 35, 129, 130
liberalism 98, 165 *see also* neoliberalism
Liddicoat, A.J. 25
Lillie, K. 174, 175–8
Limbu 198, 199, 200–1, 202, 204, 205
Lin, A.M.Y. 133
Lincoln, Y.S. 109
linguicism 192–4, 208
linguistic capital 139
linguistic discrimination 157
linguistic insecurity 130
linguistic repertoires 26, 28, 132, 141
linguistic resources 75, 127, 132
linguistic supremacy, internalization of 75
linguistic terrorism 50
Lippi-Green, R. 193
literacy
–academic writing 68
–bilingual education 96
–biliteracy 32, 97
–BlackCrit 56
–and slavery 50
–urban BlackCrit ethnography 46, 47, 51
lived experiences 46, 48–9, 57–8, 91, 109, 115–17, 126, 226–7
London English 33
'low SES' 164, 224
Luke, A. 172
Lysicott, J. 46

Macedo, D. 66, 73, 77
Madison, D.S. 5, 7, 8, 153, 199, 200, 213, 215, 217, 229
Madison, S. 240, 241, 242
Mady, C. 130
Maldonado-Torres, N. 155
Māori language 19, 20, 21–2, 31, 183
Marable, M. 44
Marcellesi, J.B. 127
marginalized epistemologies 230 *see also* Indigenous epistemologies
Markos, A. 174, 175–8
Martin, Trayvon 44, 52, 53
Martin, W.E. 50
Martínez, R.A. 223
materiality 5
May, S. xi, 2, 8, 11, 21, 22, 23, 24, 25, 31, 32, 36, 130, 153, 155, 176, 184, 191
McCarty, T. 31, 32, 178, 182, 184, 185, 191
McLaren, P. 1
meaningful question setting 6
Means, A.J. 213, 214, 215, 219
Merriam, S.B. 109
mestiza consciousness 155–6
metanarratives 47
Mexican-American families 30, 95–103, 111–14, 115, 152–68
middle class language, as norm 29
Mignolo, W. 13, 154, 155, 156, 166
migration
–Canada 127, 130
–Nepal 198, 203
–to US from Asia 34
–to US from Mexico 95, 96, 111–12, 115, 157
–to US from Syria 68
–violence of 78
Milner, I.V. 109

Milroy, J. 193
modernism 166
Moll, L.C. 30
monoculturalism 130
monolingual ideologies
–academic writing 67–8, 75, 78, 85
–as aspiration 132
–bias of bilingualism 130–1
–and bilingual education 31, 36–7
–code-switching 133
–colonialism 76
–creating language hierarchies 204
–English-only movements 73, 77
–in ESL classrooms 27
–FI (French Immersion) 130
–idealized native speaker model 141
–languages as discrete entities 32
–linguicism 192–3
–New Zealand 22–3
–normalization of 25
–race/ism 164
–shifting away from 147
–standardization ideologies 172
–troubling the monolingual gaze 81–5
Montoya, M.E. 47, 48
Moore, W. 91, 94, 95, 98, 100, 103
Morrell, E. 232
Morris, J. 78–9
Moscovici, S. 147
mother tongue-based multilingual education (MTB-MLE) 197, 200, 202
multicompetence 133
multiculturalism 127, 249
multiethnic spaces 35
multilingual radical intimate ethnography (MRIE) 65–88
multilingualism 194–5 *see also* bi/multilingualism
multimodality 56, 124, 146
multiscalar approaches, critical ethnography offers 25
Murakami, E. 213, 215, 218, 219, 224
Myers, E. 44

Nakagawa, S. 53
National Museum of African American History and Culture (NMAAHC) 42–4, 52
nationalism 25, 130, 196, 202
Native American students 24, 29, 31, 174, 178–80
native-like competence 142
Navajo (Diné) 31, 182–3
Navarro, O. 47
neocolonialism 77
neoliberalism 54, 123, 193, 196, 203, 208, 214, 222–3, 227, 232
neo-Marxist approaches 1, 2–3
Nepal 191–212
Nepali 193, 195–6, 199, 200, 202–3, 205
nepantla 110, 155
Nero, S.J. 70
'new ethnography' 3
new materialism 5
No Child Left Behind (NCLB) 174–5
non-linearity 73
non-verbal communication 116–17
Nuestro Grupo 157, 159
Nuñez, I. 115
Nyíri, P. 124

Oakland, California 171
official language status 126, 195
Ojha, L.P. 195, 202, 204
omnidirectional microphones 33, 36
online forum discussions, as data source 136
ontology 5–6, 67, 82, 137
Orellana, M.F. 120
Orfield, G. 177–8
orientalism 75, 82
origins and developments of critical ethnography 2–4
Ortega, L. 108
Otheguy, R. 134
othering 2, 67, 110, 154, 164
outsider lens 117–19, 120
Oyster Bilingual School, Washington DC 31

Paechter, C. 7
Palmer, D. xi, 1, 6, 10, 24, 214, 215, 219, 220, 223, 230
Paperson, L. 154
parental engagement 222–3
Paris, D. 24, 30, 34, 35–6, 230

partial immersion approaches 21
participant observation 2, 9
pathologization 29, 98
Pennycook, A. 132
performance critical ethnography 240–53
performativity 28, 35
Philadelphia 46, 96
Philips, S. 28, 29
Phillipson, R. 25
Phyak, P. 191, 192, 193, 195, 196, 197, 199, 200, 201, 202, 204, 206, 209
Piedmont Carolinas study 28
Piller, I. 194
place (key tenets of critical ethnography) 5
Plainview Elementary 213–39
plurilingualism 130–1, 133
political activism, overlap with critical ethnography 5
political nature of language 74, 81
politics of representation 79
positionality
 –addressing injustice 199
 –of chapter authors 13
 –Chicanx researchers 108–22
 –compared to critical reflexivity 153
 –innovative research methods 36
 –insider/outsider considerations 69–70
 –key tenets of critical ethnography 6, 7–8
 –multilingual radical intimate ethnography (MRIE) 65–6
 –non-Black researchers and BlackCrit 59
 –post-qualitative methodologies 3
 –privileged 217
 –questions to interrogate 74
 –race reflexivity 93
 –of the reader 67
 –researcher's relationship to language 67, 72–5
 –scholar activism 108–22
 –weaving through process 81
 –White ethnic majority researchers 23
positivism 125, 135, 136
postcolonialism 2, 3, 23, 70, 76–7, 84
postcritical ethnographies 3–4, 5
posthumanism 2
postmodernism 2, 132, 141
post-positivism 93, 125
post-qualitative methodologies 3, 5
poststructuralism 3, 5, 136
Poudel, P.P. 197
Powell, T. 58
power
 –change facilitation 49
 –and colonialism 23, 153, 154
 –concealed dynamics of 124
 –interrogating 153
 –key tenets of critical ethnography 4–5, 7
 –language hierarchies 73
 –language policy 185, 198
 –legitimization of majority speech norms 29
 –linguicism 192
 –multilingual radical intimate ethnography (MRIE) 78
 –perspective of 'those who suffer' 135
 –race/ism 177, 185
 –and research design 155
 –and researcher positionality 74
 –silencing 50, 206
 –support for diversity 147
 –symbolic power 136, 147, 196, 199
 –in transcription 81
 –and voice 10
pragmatic competence 27
Price-Dennis, D. 51
Proposition 203 'English for the Children' (Arizona) 174
Proyecto Maestría 156, 158
psychology 98
Pūnana Leo 183
Puno, Peru 32

quantitative research 36
Québec 138
Quechua 32
Quell, C. 127
Quijano, A. 154

race reflexivity 91–107
race/ism

–anti-Black linguistic racism 50
–antiblackness 42–64
–authenticity 138
–bilingual education 101
–Ebonics 171
–examining the unconscious 91–107
–language, race/ism and in/equity 19–41
–racializing rights 162–3
–US 24, 47, 52–4, 93
racialization 25–6, 74, 99, 154, 158, 162–4
raciolinguistics 4, 24, 35, 164, 171–90
radical, definition of 76
radical intimacy of multilingualism 65–88
radical language education 75–7
Rakaumangamanga 31
Rampton, B. 24, 33, 35, 36
rap/hip-hop 28, 35
Rasmussen, M.L. 5
reciprocity 6–7, 36, 161
recolonization 6
recurrent time mode 8
reflexivity and reflection
–about gentrification 232–4
–critical performance 241–2
–critical reflexivity 120, 152–68
–key tenets of critical ethnography 7–8
–race reflexivity 91–107
–reflexive engagement 123–51
–self-reflexivity 241–2
register shifting 34, 144
relationalities, relationships and reciprocity 6–7
relationship, language as 65–6, 72–5
repertoires, linguistic 26, 28, 132, 141
research from the heart 65
research methods
–BlackCrit 54–6
–innovations 35–7
–interview methods 36, 57, 124, 136, 160
–key tenets of critical ethnography 9–10
–multilingual radical intimate ethnography (MRIE) 67, 69–70
–traditional ethnography 160
researcher-researched distinction 154
resource pedagogies 30
resources, linguistic 26–7
respect 27, 110
responsiveness 5
retrospective participant commentaries 36
revitalization 32, 152–68, 178, 184
Reyes, A. 29, 33, 34
Richardson, E. 49
Richmond Road Primary School, New Zealand 21, 22, 23, 31
'rights' discourses 161–2
Rogoff, B. 30
Rolón-Dow, R. 58
Romero-Little, M.E. 178
Rosa, J. 24, 35, 164, 171–2, 177, 180, 185, 186
Ross, K.M. 45, 53, 54
Rough Rock Demonstration School 31
Roy, S. 130, 131
Rubio, B. 159
Ruíz, R. 75, 173
Rylko-Bauer, B. 78

Saavedra, C.M. 110–11, 119, 120
Sah, P.K. 208
Said, E. 70, 75, 82
Saint-Georges, I. 126
Saldaña, J. 240
San Francisco, US 34
Sargent, E. 185
Saussure, F. de 132
scholar activism 108–22
scholastic unconscious 94, 100–2
second language acquisition (SLA) 141, 176
Seel, A. 195, 196
self-reflexivity 241–2
self-sovereignty 69–72, 76
semi-structured conversations (SSCs) 36
Shohamy, E. 131
Shore, C. 185
silencing 35, 37, 45–50, 59, 205, 206
sites of survivance 50
situatedness 3–4, 23, 80, 154, 155, 199
skills-based competence models 130, 141
Skutnabb-Kangas, T. 192, 193–4, 197, 203, 208

slavery 49–50, 53, 58, 178
Smith, L.T. 6
social activism, overlap with critical ethnography 5
social constructivism 136
social justice 23, 47, 99, 135, 152, 154, 172, 204–8, 219–20
social theory and ontology 5–6
social unconscious 94, 95–7
social variation 144
sociocultural background 23, 192
sociohistorical context 23, 73, 153, 160
sociolinguistics 141
sociology 2, 99, 101
Soja, E.W. 51
Solórzano, D.J. 58
South Vista, California 34–5
space (key tenets of critical ethnography) 5
space-making 51–2, 58–9
Spanish
–Academia Cuauhtli 152–68
–Arizona, US 174
–code-switching 143–4
–critical performance 243–5
–dual-language programs 216
–Mexican-American families 30, 95–103, 111–14, 115, 152–68
–Spanish-English dual-language programs 31, 92–3, 95–103, 116
Spivak, G.C. 155
square dancing 95
St Pierre, E. 5
standard language varieties 33–4, 75, 131, 145, 171–2, 193
standardized testing 178–9
stereotypes 34, 138
stigmatization 138, 193–4, 203–4, 240
storytelling, as research method 56–9
structuralism 131, 136
structured English immersion (SEI) 174, 175–8
struggle to understand 118
style shifting 34
stylization 33
subaltern epistemologies 155 *see also* Indigenous epistemologies
subtractive bilingual education 95, 101
Sugiharto, S. 155
Sunnyside High, California 34
superdiversity 35
surveillance 68, 70, 74, 81, 85
Swain, M. 129
symbolic power 136, 147, 196, 199
symbolic violence 44–5, 135
Syria 69

Tafolla, C. 161, 163
Talmy, S. 27, 29
Tarone, E. 129
Tate, W. 52, 98, 100
Te Whānau Whāriki (WW) 19, 22
teachers
–critical consciousness 102
–in English-medium settings 204–8
–monolingual ideologies 245
–teacher education 123–51, 198
–teacher professional development 158
Tejano history 156–7, 160–1
Tenayuca, Emma 161, 163
Teneyuca, S. 161, 163
testimonios 36, 110, 112
testing/assessment 178–9, 247
Texas 240–53
Theater of the Oppressed 240
thick description 2, 91, 92, 124
Thomas, J. 2, 153, 209
Thompson, K. 44
Till, Emmett 42–3, 52, 53
time, ethnography takes 8
Tollefson, J.W. 191, 192
traditional ethnography 155, 160
transcription 81, 139
transdisciplinarity 124, 132, 133–4, 137, 143, 147
translanguaging 24, 35, 130, 133–4, 142–3, 240, 247
translingualism 131
transnational cultural practices 30
transnational subjective understandings 165
transnational teachers 131–2
Trevino, A.J. 47
tribal critical race theory 24
Troman, G. 8
troubling the questions 6
troubling the researchers' gaze 81

trust 66, 74, 76
Tuck, E. 153, 178
two-way immersion bilingual education (TWBE) program 109, 115, 118, 130, 159

Ubiles, J.R. 56
unconscious, examining the 91–107
unlearning 154
urban BlackCrit ethnography 46
Urrieta, L. 70, 165
US
–Academia Cuauhtli 152–68
–antiblackness 42–4, 46
–Arizona 174–5
–Chicago 177
–Chicanx researchers 108–22
–education field 98
–English privilege in 80
–ethnographic studies 28–9
–gentrification of dual language bilingual education 213–39
–Indigenous languages 180–5
–language crossing 33–4
–language panics 171
–language policy 174–8
–Mexican-American families 30, 95–103, 111–14, 115, 152–68
–migrants 69
–race/ism 24, 47, 52–4, 93
–San Francisco 34
–Spanish language 96
–US Constitution 99
–Warms Springs, Oregon 29
Us and Them 125, 136, 139

Valdés, G. 159, 218
Valencia, R.R. 164
Valenzuela, A. 95, 152, 154, 214, 216, 229, 234
Vaught, S.E. 55, 91, 92
Vélez-Ibáñez, C. 109, 110
Vertovec, S. 35
Villenas, S. 109, 110, 119
Vizenor, G. 50
voice 10, 26, 173, 185

Wacquant, L. 8
Wagner, J. 146
Warm Springs, Oregon 29
Warner, S.L.N. 183
Watahomigie, L.J. 184
Waterston, A. 78
ways of being 110
'ways of speaking' 26, 28
Weber, J. 126
Weis, L. 1
Western bias 4, 67, 77–8, 82, 131, 154, 155, 156, 166
Western gaze, troubling the 81–5
Western research methods 110, 131, 152, 156
Whānau Whāriki (WW) 19, 22
White, L. 181, 182
White Mainstream English (WME) 50
white supremacy 48, 53, 86, 94, 98, 100, 154, 160
Whiteness as property 92
who-am-I-to do-this-work 6, 10
Wiley, T. 174
Williams, P. 48, 50
Willis, P. 1
Wilson, S. 67, 71, 241
Wilson, W.H. 183, 184
Winn, M.T. 56, 230
witnessing 56–7, 241
Wodak, R. 135
womanist scholarship 76
Woodson, C.G. 102
worthy witnesses 56–7
Wright, S. 185
writing from the heart 68–9, 81–2, 85

Yamamoto, A.Y. 184
Yamamoto, E.K. 47–8
Yancy, G. 71
Yanes, M. 115, 130, 159, 216, 219, 221
Yang, K.W. 153, 178
Yosso, T.J. 58

Zamudio, M. 110
Zepeda, O. 178
Zuberi, T. 100

For Product Safety Concerns and Information please contact our EU Authorised Representative:

Easy Access System Europe

Mustamäe tee 50

10621 Tallinn

Estonia

gpsr.requests@easproject.com

www.ingramcontent.com/pod-product-compliance
Lightning Source LLC
Jackson TN
JSHW070219191025
92739JS00010B/589

9781788928694